# Legacies and Mega Events

The use of sporting and other mega-events to bring about transformation of socially deprived areas of major cities is becoming an increasingly important part of the *raison d'être* for hosting such events, especially given the immense costs involved and the current economic climate. The tax-paying public increasingly has to be persuaded of the benefits, beyond the event itself, to spend the nation's resources in this way.

This edited book, written by international experts, critically explores these multiple facets of the Mega Event legacy looking at the various economic, environmental and social impacts and benefits in multiple continents. It considers topics such as volunteering, participation, economics, sponsorship, ethics and technology in relation to legacy.

This timely book provides a further understanding of the legacy discourse, as well as the potential pitfalls connected to legacy in relation to mega events. Filling a gap in the literature on legacy research, *Legacies and Mega Events* will be of interest to events, sports, tourism, urban development students, researchers and academics.

**Ian Brittain** is a Research Fellow in the Centre for Business in Society, Coventry University, UK. He is an internationally recognised expert in the study of disability and Paralympic sport. He is also the Heritage Advisor to the International Wheelchair and Amputee Sports Federation, who in a former guise founded the Paralympic Games, and he has attended every summer Paralympic Games since Sydney 2000. Dr Brittain has won and worked on research projects totalling over £1.3million.

**Jason Bocarro** is a university faculty scholar and Alumni Distinguished Undergraduate Professor at North Carolina State University. His research focuses on examining how recreation and sport programmes and organisations can impact the health of children and adolescents. Dr Bocarro has published over 50 peer-reviewed research journal publications and been awarded over US$5 million of research funding to support his research.

**Terri Byers** is an associate professor at University of New Brunswick, Canada. Her research focuses on community sport organisations, innovation and participation. She is widely published, active in consulting and teaching on sport and recreation management. Dr Byers has won and worked on research projects totalling over CA$2 million.

**Kamilla Swart** is a full professor in the College of Business Administration, American University in the Emirates. While at Cape Peninsula University of Technology, she served as the South African lead for Carnival. Her research interests include sport and event tourism, with a specific focus on mega-events and event policies, strategies and evaluations. She was instrumental in developing the 2010 FIFA World Cup Research Agenda and served as the City of Cape Town's Research Coordinator for 2010. Dr Swart has published on varied topics relating to the bidding and impacts of mega-events, especially in developing contexts, and has won and worked on research projects totaling over ZAR25 million.

# Routledge Advances in Event Research

Edited by Warwick Frost and Jennifer Laing
Department of Marketing, Tourism and Hospitality,
La Trobe University, Australia

For a full list of titles in this series, please visit www.routledge.com/tourism/series/RAERS

**Exploring Community Events and Festivals**
*Edited by Allan Jepson and Alan Clarke*

**Event Design: Social perspectives and practices**
*Edited by Greg Richards, Lénia Marques and Karen Mein*

**Rituals and Traditional Events in the Modern World**
*Edited by Warwick Frost and Jennifer Laing*

**Battlefield Events: Landscape, commemoration and heritage**
*Edited by Keir Reeves, Geoffrey Bird, Laura James, Birger Stichelbaut and Jean Bourgeois*

**Events in the City: Using public spaces as event venues**
*Andrew Smith*

**Event Mobilities: Politics, Place and Performance**
*Edited by Kevin Hannam, Mary Mostafanezhad and Jillian Rickly-Boyd*

**Approaches and Methods in Events Studies**
*Edited by Tomas Pernecky*

**Visitor Attractions and Events: Locations and linkages**
*Adi Weidenfeld, Richard Butler and Allan Williams*

**Critical Event Studies: A Guide for Critical Thinkers**
*Karl Spracklen and Ian R. Lamond*

**The Value of Events**
*John Armbrecht, Erik Lundberg, Tommy D. Andersson, Don Getz*

**Festival Encounters**
Theoretical Perspectives on Festival Events
*Michelle Duffy and Judith Mair*

**Legacies and Mega Events**
Fact or Fairy Tales?
*Edited by Ian Brittain, Jason Bocarro, Terri Byers, and Kamilla Swart*

# Legacies and Mega Events

Fact or Fairy Tales?

**Edited by Ian Brittain,
Jason Bocarro, Terri Byers,
and Kamilla Swart**

Routledge
Taylor & Francis Group

LONDON AND NEW YORK

First published 2018
by Routledge

2 Park Square, Milton Park, Abingdon, Oxfordshire OX14 4RN

52 Vanderbilt Avenue, New York, NY 10017

*Routledge is an imprint of the Taylor & Francis Group, an informa business*

First issued in paperback 2020

*British Library Cataloguing-in-Publication Data*
A catalogue record for this book is available from the British Library

*Library of Congress Cataloguing-in-Publication Data*
A catalog record for this book has been requested

ISBN: 978-1-138-67837-8 (hbk)
ISBN: 978-0-367-66763-4 (pbk)

Typeset in Times New Roman
by Apex CoVantage, LLC

# Contents

# Illustrations

# Contributors

**Hazel Barrett** is Professor of Development Geography at the Centre for Trust, Peace and Social Relations at Coventry University. Her research focusses on issues of social justice. She has a BA (Hons) in Geography from Sussex University and an MA and PhD in Geography and West African Studies from Birmingham University.

**Jason Bocarro** is a university faculty scholar and Alumni Distinguished Undergraduate Professor at North Carolina State University. His research focuses on examining how recreation and sport programmes and organisations can impact the health of children and adolescents. Dr Bocarro has published over 50 peer-reviewed research journal publications and been awarded over US$5 million of research funding to support his research.

**Ian Brittain** is a research fellow in the Centre for Business in Society, Coventry University, United Kingdom. He is an internationally recognised expert in the study of disability and Paralympic sport. He is also the Heritage Advisor to the International Wheelchair and Amputee Sports Federation, who in a former guise founded the Paralympic Games, and he has attended every summer Paralympic Games since Sydney 2000. Dr Brittain has won and worked on research projects totalling over £1.3 million.

**Terri Byers** is an associate professor at University of New Brunswick, Canada. Her research focuses on community sport organisations, innovation and participation. She is widely published, active in consulting and teaching on sport and recreation management. Dr Byers has won and worked on research projects totalling over CA$2 million.

**Libby Carter** is a PhD student in the School of Marketing and Management at Coventry University. As part of the Carnival research project, her research concentrates on how multiple consumption opportunities of a mega events opening ceremony can affect the social legacy of the overall mega event.

**Jonathan Casper** is an associate professor and Sport Management Program Coordinator in the Department of Parks, Recreation, and Tourism Management in the College of Natural Resources at North Carolina State University. His research seeks to help sport organisations integrate sustainability efforts into organisational operations, marketing and fan engagement.

**Laurence Chalip** is the Brightbill/Sapora Professor at the University of Illinois (Urbana-Champaign), where he serves as head of the Department of Recreation, Sport and Tourism. He has held positions and consulted to sport organisations throughout the United States, and also in Australia, Canada, Europe, Korea and New Zealand.

**Michael Edwards** is an associate professor in the Department of Parks, Recreation and Tourism Management (PRTM) at North Carolina State University. His research is guided by the idea that developing and managing socially responsible sport facilities, programs and events will encourage active lifestyles and community health.

**Jennifer Ferreira** is a researcher in the Centre for Business in Society, Coventry University. Her main research interests focus around the local and regional economic development, varieties of capitalism, labour markets, non-standard employment and retail industries. Specifically, she is interested in the role and activities of the temporary staffing industry and the coffee shop industry, and their impact in urban spaces and on their communities.

**Vassil Girginov** is a reader in sport management/development at Brunel University and a visiting professor at the Russian International Olympic University. His recent research interests and publications concern the governance of sports development legacy of the 2012 London Olympics and the leveraging of the Games for building the capacities of National Governing Bodies of sport.

**Chris Gratton** is Emeritus Professor of Sport Economics and Director of the Sport Industry Research Centre at Sheffield Hallam University. His main research interests are the economics of hosting major sports events, measuring the economic importance of sport and secondary analysis of large sport participation surveys.

**Débora Guerra** is a research associate of the Events and Mega Events Study Group in the School of Physical Education and Sports at the Federal University of Rio de Janeiro, Brazil. She has a bachelor's degree in Landscape Architecture from Algarve University, Portugal, and a master's degree in the same area from the University of Lisbon, Portugal.

**Andrew Jones** is a research assistant in the Centre for Business in Society, Coventry University, UK. His main research interest is in football, a sport which has undergone radical change in the last 25 years, which has left a lasting legacy on the way football clubs are owned and operated with investors from overseas using football clubs as a method of displaying wealth or status. His research has explored some of these changes and the resulting impacts, but with the football environment constantly changing this is an ongoing process.

**Gareth Jones** is an assistant professor at Temple University in the School of Sport, Tourism and Hospitality Management (STHM). Dr Jones's research focuses on the multifaceted impacts of sport organisations, events, and programs. His specific areas of interest include inter-organisational partnerships, organisational capacity building and non-profit management.

**Timothy Kellison** is an assistant professor in the Department of Kinesiology and Health and the director of the Sport and Urban Policy Initiative at Georgia State University. His primary areas of research focus on the politics of environmentally sustainable design, urban and regional planning and public policy.

**Eva Kipnis** is a senior lecturer in marketing at Coventry University. Her research intersects include culture studies in consumptionscapes and cultural meanings of brands. Her work has appeared in outlets such as the *Journal of Public Policy and Marketing*; the *Journal of Business Research*; *Marketing Theory*; *Consumption, Markets & Culture* and the *Journal of Marketing Management*.

**Brendon Knott** is an associate professor in the sport management department at the Cape Peninsula University of Technology in Cape Town, South Africa. Dr. Knott lectures and conducts research in applied areas of sport marketing, branding, sport tourism and sport mega-events, currently focusing on place branding through sport.

**Joerg Koenigstorfer** is Professor of Sport and Health Management at Technische Universität München. He received his doctorate from Saarland University and was a postdoc at Pennsylvania State University. His research focus is on consumer behaviour in sports and health and appeared in renowned journals, such as the Journal of Marketing Research.

**Wojciech Kulczycki** received his doctorate from Technische Universität München (2016), where he is currently employed as a postdoctoral researcher. In his research, he is interested in corporate social responsibility, business ethics, and sponsorship-linked marketing in sports.

**Michael Linley** is a senior research fellow at Victoria University and the director at BrandCapital International. His work and research is as strategist leading international engagements with clients in airlines, banks, tourism, sports and events, cities, energy and government. His doctoral thesis is on the impact of events on host cities.

**Gift Muresherwa** is a master's student at CPUT and serves as a research associate at the Centre for Tourism Research in Africa in the Tourism and Event Management Department. The focus of this dissertation is the media impact of the 2014 FIFA World Cup™ in Brazil.

**Olesya Nedvetskaya** is a lecturer in events management, Sheffield Hallam University (UK). Olesya received her PhD (2015) from the University of Glasgow. She previously worked at Sochi 2014 Winter Olympics and London 2012 Summer Olympics, which highly informs her teaching and research on mega sport events, their governance and legacy.

**Nicholas Passenger** is the division leader for Sport Business Management, Studies and the Outdoors at the University of Central Lancashire (UCLAN). Nick oversees the Physical Education component of Sport Studies at UCLAN, and has experience organising a variety of sport programs and events, including the prestigious Floodlit Cup.

**Girish Ramchandani** is Reader in the Sport Industry Research Centre at Sheffield Hallam University. His principal area of research is the evaluation of major sports events, and he has published widely on their economic, sport development, and elite performance outcomes.

**Harry Arne Solberg** is a professor of sport economics/sport management at the Norwegian University of Science and Technology. His research interests have focused on economic effects from various sport activities. He has more than 60 scientific publications, including the book *The Economics of Sport Broadcasting*, together with Professor Chris Gratton.

**Kamilla Swart** is a full professor in the College of Business Administration, American University in the Emirates. While at Cape Peninsula University of Technology (CPUT), she served as the lead for Carnival. Her research interests include sport and event tourism, with a specific focus on mega-events and event policies, strategies and evaluations. She was instrumental in developing the 2010 FIFA World Cup Research Agenda and served as the City of Cape Town's Research Coordinator for 2010. Dr Swart has published on varied topics relating to the bidding and impacts of mega-events, especially in developing contexts, and has won and worked on research projects totaling over ZAR25 million.

**Masayuki Takao** is a lecturer in the Department of Physical Education at Tokai University. His research interests include sport mega-events and their history in Japan. He is the joint author of *Orinpikku no Isan no Syakaigaku: Nagano Orinpikku to sonogo no Juunen* (*Sociology of 'Olym-pic Legacies': 10 years after the Nagano Olympic Games*; Seikyusha: Tokyo, 2014).

**Guy Thomas** is a PhD student at Coventry University investigating the factors that impacted upon the participation legacy of the London 2012 Olympic Games from the perspective of key informants within grassroots sports clubs from two Olympic (athletics and swimming) and two non-Olympic sports (cricket and netball).

**Mike Weed** is Professor of Applied Policy Sciences and Pro Vice-Chancellor (Research & Enterprise), Canterbury Christ Church University. He is the strategic director of the Centre for Sport, Physical Education & Activity Research (SPEAR), and editor of *Journal of Sport & Tourism* (Routledge) and the SAGE Library of Sport & Leisure Management.

# Foreword

## Legacy Research in the 21st Century

The populations of several bid cities in Europe and North America recently called for referendums that led to a number of cities withdrawing from Olympic bids. Some of these bids were stopped by politicians before referendums were even held. When Budapest withdrew their 2024 bid in March 2017, the International Olympic Committee (IOC) had to accept the 10th bid withdrawal in just 5 years. The most common reason behind each withdrawal was that the expected costs of hosting the Games outweighed any potential benefits.

The high number of withdrawals indicates that the stakeholder interests' change and the host city population and local politicians did not see the inherent value in hosting the Olympic Games. What happened? The gigantism of the Games reached a point that makes it difficult to balance the public costs and often intangible benefits for the host. However, it is important to state that the Olympic Games are not solely an event to maximise profits. Cities whose sole objective is to maximise profits should invest in industrial parks. No, the Olympic Games are different. The Olympic Games are one of the world's greatest events that accrue other benefits. They are a Mega Event, where many different cultures meet, compete peacefully against each other and interact. As with other Mega Events, they are a festival in which every culture shares the same understanding of rules and where everyone meets in venues, media centres, city centres or the Olympic Village. That, in itself, is a high value at a time, when nations are moving toward greater isolation, building walls and investing in their military. The World Sport Minister Conference in Berlin 2013 (MINEPS V) has explicitly noted in its "Declaration of Berlin" that major sport events should be used as "platforms to raise awareness on societal issues and for opportunities for cultural exchange" (§2.36).

However, the increasing financial burdens associated with many Mega Events to provide security, accommodate new sports and serve ever more visitors and media representatives makes it difficult to keep the costs and capacity demands at a level that can be utilised after the event. Additionally, political and economic-driven opportunism in the host nation adds to the costs. Politicians like to piggyback additional infrastructure investments by using the argument that those are needed for the event to avoid delays in the start of construction or enact policies that prevent corruption. The choice of suboptimal locations for a venue or the bloated construction increases the costs. Two prime examples, Beijing 2008 and Sochi 2014, are evidence of extreme Olympic Games overspend with a range around US$50 billion.

The withdrawal of bids, the financial burdens and other Mega Event contro-versies (e.g., doping, security, commercialisation, corruption) have resulted in organisers re-thinking the bidding process. For example, in December 2014, the IOC approved Agenda 2020, a strategic roadmap for the future of the Olympic Movement composed of 40 recommendations. One of the key areas of change is the bidding procedure, with a new philosophy to invite potential candidate cities to present a project that best fits their sporting, economic, social and environmental long-term needs. In other words, the IOC wants cities to prove that the investments they plan have a positive legacy. Thus, IOC president Thomas Bach created a new IOC commission for "Sustainability and Legacy" which has been working since 2015 to develop a legacy framework and legacy measurement.

At almost the same time, the European Commission incorporated "legacy" in its EU Work Plan 2014–2017 and established an "Expert Group on the Economic Dimension of Sport". One of the three subgroups presented "Recommendations on Major Sport Events, in Particular on Legacy Aspects" in January 2016. These are based on the "Declaration of Berlin" which was signed in 2013 by 121 sport ministers. The following main points touch the need for a better legacy inclusion when planning an event:

§2.13 Stressing the importance of increasing the positive effects of major sport events in terms of participation in and through sport, creating new sport programmes and providing new and/or improved sports facilities;

§2.15 Acknowledging the data which shows that many oversized stadia are not financially viable post-events (while generating maintenance costs);

§2.28 Commit, when hosting major sports events, to the sustainability of sport infrastructure for physical education, sport for all and high-performance sport and other community activities, in order to ensure that all concerned stakeholders can participate in and benefit from such events;

§2.39 Ensure that investment in infrastructure and facilities for major sport events complies with social, economic, cultural and environmental require-ments, notably through the reuse of existing facilities, the design of new ven-ues for ease of dismantling or downsizing, and the use of temporary facilities.

Therefore, this book addresses a very urgent, current and important issue, par-ticularly because legacy research is fairly new. The first paper published was on "tourism legacy" from cultural and sport events by Roche in 1992. However, for a long time, legacy was only seen as the value of sport facilities and public improvements turned over to communities or sports organisations after an event. Being aware of the importance of sustainable changes events such as the Olympic Games or the FIFA World Cup bring to a host city must be considered and has resulted in initiatives such as the IOC's Congress on "The Legacy of the Olympic Games: 1984–2000" in 2002. However, although many cases were presented, no satisfying definition of any type of legacy was available. One reason is that legacy was often assumed to be self-evident, so that there was no need to define precisely what it is. However, after 2006, the research about mega event legacy became more prominent and is now being fully acknowledged, as can be seen by the recommendations made by the European Commission, the UNECOs "Declaration of Berlin" and IOCs Agenda 2020.

An often-cited definition of legacy was provided by me in 2007. Legacy is

> irrespective of the time of production and space, legacy is all planned and unplanned, positive and negative, tangible and intangible structures created for and by a sport event that remain longer than the event itself.

However, after reconsideration and several papers that followed as well as discussions in the European Commission and the IOC, I came up with a little more manageable version in 2016:

> Legacy is any action (practice) in a given area (e.g., host city) and time driven from structural changes initiated by staging of the Olympic Games.

Therefore, one can say, that legacy derives from of all "structural changes" caused by staging the Olympic Games. The Games change a location (space) and people (humans). Legacies exist right after a change was made, which can be far before the Mega Event starts. The legacy exists as long as the "structural changes" exist which permanently offers opportunities for action. This makes measurement difficult because sometimes the change takes some time (sometimes years) to take effect. To me, it is important to not confuse legacy (actions driven from structural changes after) with the primary (direct) impacts of the mega event. These are the directly initiated activities due to the Mega Event, such as the economic impact from tourism derived from the event or advertising effects due to worldwide media interest during the event.

To not overlap the areas of changes, in detail, "structural changes" take place in space:

1. Urban development
2. Environment enhancement and in humans:
3. Policies, Governance
4. Human development (skills, knowledge and networks)
5. Intellectual Property
6. Social development (beliefs and behaviour)

These six fields are making up all possible legacies, which are mentioned in many of the chapters in this book. For example, the sport legacy is composed of new facilities (urban development), regulations to help high performance sports (policies) and more people practicing sports (social development). Furthermore, many people learn new sport skills (human development) and the national sport federations are better connected to other national federations or the world federation (networks in human resources). Another example is the economic legacy. It is achieved by higher productivity or new businesses based on better structures (better traffic systems, better labour policies, better-skilled workers, strengthened networks). Some industries, such as tourism are more profitable for the Olympic Games legacy than other producing industries).

I congratulate the authors Ian Brittain, Jason Bocarro, Terri Byers and Kamilla Swart on this book "Legacies and Mega-Events: Fact or Fairy Tales." The strategy of recruiting outstanding scholars from all over the world provides tremendous context and will help readers gain a deeper understanding of the ever-growing importance of this topic.

*Holger Preuss, Professor at Johannes Gutenberg University, Mainz; IOC*
*Commission member "Sustainability and Legacy"*

# Acknowledgements

We would like to acknowledge the fact that some of the research in this volume was supported by a Marie Curie International Research Staff Exchange Scheme Fellowship within the 7th European Community Framework Programme as part of the project titled 'Carnival'.

We would also like to thank all the staff at Routledge and, in particular, our Editorial Assistant, Carlotta Fanton, for helping to bring this book to fruition.

# Introduction

## One Upon a Time . . .

*Jason Bocarro, Ian Brittain, and Terri Byers*

This is an exciting time to publish a book focused on Mega Event legacy given the increased focus and interest by both the research community and those involved in the various stages of bidding and hosting these events. Although the *potential* impacts of mega-events are significant and well documented (e.g., Fourie and Spronk, 2011; Kaplanidou, Al Emadi, Sagas, Diop, and Fritz, 2016; Tien, Lo, and Lin, 2011), the *actual* impacts realised by host nations and regions often fall far short of expectations in terms of economic and non-economic impacts in both advanced and developing societies (Horne and Manzenreiter, 2006; Jago, Dwyer, Lipman, van Lill, and Vorster, 2010). For example, critics are already labeling the 2016 Rio Olympics as a legacy failure as expensive venues remain without owners and approximately 22,059 families were estimated to have been evicted from Rio's favelas because of the 2014 FIFA World Cup and 2016 Olympic games (Duignan and Ivanescu, 2017).

The use of sporting and other mega-events to bring about transformation of socially deprived areas of major cities, as well as a host of other legacy claims, are becoming an increasingly important part of the rationale behind hosting such events. The tax-paying public increasingly has to be persuaded of the benefits, beyond the event itself, to spend the nation's resources in this way. However, the facts suggest that previous widespread support for embracing these events has waned. For example, data suggest that potential hosts are becoming more reluctant to bid in that twelve different cities bid for the 2004 Olympics, whereas the 2020 Olympics elicited just five applicants (Zimbalist, 2015). After Oslo removed themselves from consideration, only two cities – Beijing and Almaty, Kazakhstan – remained as viable candidates to host the 2022 Winter Olympics. In looking at the hosts for upcoming Olympics and FIFA World Cups, it appears that the Dutch government's 2012 report that predicted in the future only non-democratic countries will pay up to host these events was correct (Zimbalist, 2015).

Hosting mega-events has also proved both costly and difficult to budget for with, for example, the Athens Olympic Games projected budget set at US $1.6 billion and the games eventually cost nearly $16 billion. For the Beijing Olympics projected costs for the organising committee alone were reported as $1.6 billion with a final budget including facilities and infrastructure being $40 billion (Sports Business Daily, 2009). Non-sporting mega-events do not often include a bidding process but also have the potential to produce considerable impacts for hosts. Cultural mega-events arguably produce less quantifiable economic impacts such as "trading opportunities for non-profit organisations and the contribution of the festival to local entrepreneurial culture" (Baker Associates, 2007). The fact is that mega-events are happening throughout the world and the costs associated with these appear to be increasing significantly. Another fact is that legacy has been promoted by organisations such as the International Olympic Committee (IOC) as well as national governments on the basis that long-term impacts can be gained from hosting mega events. Yet increasingly, questions arise as to whether legacy is a fact or a fairy tale.

The genesis of this book initially stemmed from research carried out as part of a European Union–funded, four-year Marie Curie International Research Staff Exchange Scheme (IRSES) project (Carnival). The project investigated what factors impact upon the planned and unplanned legacy outcomes of mega-events and their implications for stakeholders and included researchers from Brazil, Germany, South Africa, the United Kingdom and the United States. Research on mega events, and particularly mega sporting events, has grown considerably over the past 30 years. However, research and discussions specifically related to the legacy of these events is fairly new.

This edited volume is broken into two parts and provides a comprehensive summary of the issues related to many of the different facets of legacy of Mega Events. The first ten chapters were written by international experts covering a variety of facets of Mega Event legacy (e.g., economic, environmental, social, etc.). The book begins with a chapter by **Bocarro, Byers and Carter,** who report the findings from two systematic reviews of the Mega Event research literature (both sporting and non-sporting). The authors provide a summary of the work that has been conducted in this area and provide some recommendations for future research to advance this field of knowledge. **Laurence Chalip's** chapter provides a critique of the ways in which Mega Event frameworks have failed to capitalise on long-term impacts and positive legacies. Chalip proposes a framework that can be adopted to examine how events might be leveraged for a variety of long-term legacies. **Solberg's** chapter examines why cities continue to be enamored by mega events despite the questionable economic legacy. Solberg, through an intriguing examination of the stakeolders involved, shows how various stakeholders influence the bidding process. **Nedvetskaya and Girginov** examine the underpinning behind a volunteering legacy, a critical component of many Mega sporting events. Using the example of the London 2012 Games, they describe some of the shortcomings and successes of the 2012 volunteering strategy, describing how certain strategies can be highly beneficial for future bids and host cities. **Mike Weed's** chapter provides a summary of the sport participation legacies associated with many sport mega events. Despite many claims that mega events are successful in getting more people to participate in sport, Weed questions mega events' effectiveness at delivering a sport participation legacy. **Brittain's** chapter shows that the success of the 2012 London Paralympic Games had a surprisingly negative legacy for people with disabilities. Ordinary people with a disability felt little connection, if any, to Paralympians, in terms of the issues they face in their everyday lives. Furthermore, the perceived expectations by the non-disabled population that all people with disabilities can perform like Paralympians only accentuated this disconnection. **Gratton and Ramchandani** provide a useful framework for measuring economic legacy and demonstrate its application through the example of London 2012. They demonstrate how direct and indirect economic impacts should be considered and argue that whilst the immediate economic impacts of Sydney, Athens, Beijing and London Olympics seem minimal, there is some evidence that a London Olympic economic legacy is plausible.

As environmental issues have moved to the forefront of government policies and people's consciousness, there has been an increased interest in the role of mega events in ensuring an environmental legacy. **Kellison and Casper** describe how mega events, because of their sheer scale, provide unique sustainability challenges. Furthermore, "white elephant" stadia controversies in Brazil, Beijing and Athens have compounded the belief that many mega events are an environmental disaster. However, they also describe some successful strategies that mega event organisers have adopted to reduce a large environmental footprint from the event itself and educate and expose spectators to environmental practices that may influence sustainable behaviours within their everyday lives. Many developing countries have bid for mega events in order to change or enhance their international reputation. **Knott and Swart** describe how South Africa used branding opportunities created by hosting the 2010 FIFA World Cup to go beyond just "gaining attention". Finally, **Koenigstorfer and Kulczycki**, in light of some recent high-profile corruption cases that have affected mega events, examine the ramifications of what they call a corruption legacy. The chapter examines the levels at which corruption takes place when mega-sport events are hosted and the short-term and long-term consequences of corruption for one particular group of stakeholders – the sponsors.

The final chapters consist of five unique case studies written by both early career (including PhD students) and experienced researchers from each of the partner institutions and associates of the Carnival project investigating a wide variety of different types of legacy claims made by hosts of different mega-events held in each of the partner nations. These include case studies of the London Olympic Games (**Thomas, Brittain, and Jones**), Rio 2016 Olympic Games (**Guerra, Ferriera, and Kipnis**), the 2015 Rugby World Cup (**Jones, Edwards, and Passenger**), the 2010 FIFA World Cup (**Swart, Linley, and Muresherwa**) and Mardi Gras (**Barrett**). The sixth case study, not written by a Carnival partner, is an intriguing examination of the Nagano 1998 winter Olympic Games legacy nearly 20 years later (**Takao**).

This book is a substantial contribution to understanding legacy of mega events and we would like to acknowledge all 29 contributors for their efforts to challenge existing ways of thinking, to produce detailed and thought-provoking discussions of existing evidence and new cases/data. This process involved the shared commitment with our contributors to create a scholarly account of mega-event legacy, with their limitations and potential (facts and fairy tales). We would also like to acknowledge the institutional support we were provided – particularly by Coventry University and the Centre for Business in Society and North Carolina State University and the College of Natural Resources.

## References

Baker Associates. (2007). *Glastonbury festival 2007 economic impact assessment*. Shelton Mallet: Mendip District Council.

Duignan, M. B., and Ivanescu, Y. (2017). *Rio's Olympic legacy: Six months on, how has the city fared?* Retrieved from http://theconversation.com/rios-olympic-legacy-six-months-on-how-has-the-city-fared-72993

Fourie, J., and Spronk, K. (2011). South African mega-sport events and their impact on tourism. *Journal of Sport & Tourism, 16*(1), 75–97.

Horne, J., and Manzenreiter, W. (2006). Sports mega-events: Social scientific analyses of a global phenomenon. Oxford: Blackwell.

Jago, L., Dwyer, L., Lipman, G., van Lill, D., and Vorster, S. (2010). Optimising the potential of mega-events: An overview. *International Journal of Event and Festival Management, 1*(3), 220–237.

Kaplanidou, K. K., Al Emadi, A., Sagas, M., Diop, A., and Fritz, G. (2016). Business legacy planning for mega events: The case of the 2022 World Cup in Qatar. *Journal of Business Research, 69*(10), 4103–4111.

*Sports Business Daily*. (2009). Beijing eight months after 8/8/08. Retrieved from www.sportsbusinessdaily.com/Journal/Issues/2009/04/20090420/SBJ-In-Depth/Beijing-Eight-Months-After-8808.aspx

Tien, C., Lo, H. C., and Lin, H. W. (2011). The economic benefits of mega events: A myth or a reality? A longitudinal study on the Olympic Games. *Journal of Sport Management, 25*(1), 11–23.

Zimbalist, A. (2015). Circus maximus: The economic gamble behind hosting the Olympics and the World Cup. Washington, DC: Brookings Institution.

# Part I
# Main Chapters

# 1 Legacy of sporting and non-sporting mega event research

## What next?

*Jason Bocarro, Terri Byers and Libby Carter*

## Introduction

This chapter provides an overview of current research on legacy and mega-events, reporting and comparing the findings of two systematic reviews of the literature: one on Mega Sporting Events (MSE) and one on Non-Sporting Mega-Events (NSME). By examining the key trends in these two reviews, we identify key strengths and weaknesses of research on mega event legacy and develop recommendations for future research to advance this field of knowledge. To address the question of whether legacy of mega events is 'fact or fairy tale', the discussion section of this chapter applies a Critical Realist analysis of the concepts and themes presented in each of the systematic reviews. Our findings reveal that research on mega event legacy, both sporting and non-sporting, has been underpinned by a commercial ideology that perpetuates the justification of mega events through the measurement of legacy. We suggest that legacy in the context of mega events is both fact and fairy tale. On one hand, legacy is very real to governments, nations, and a variety of stakeholders involved in, either the planning or production of legacy or impacted positively and/or negatively through the mega event (e.g., new opportunity, skill development, homeowners who are displaced or business relocation). On the other hand, when we examine the concept of legacy and identify gaps in the literature at a deeper level, we see that legacy as a means to justify mega events, has been the predominant focus of the research, revealing that legacy is a fairy tale, socially constructed, deconstructed, and defined to appeal to a wide range of stakeholders.

The chapter begins with a brief background as to why systematic reviews of sporting and non-sporting mega events are needed. We then briefly explain the methods and research protocol behind the reviews. An overview of the results of each review is presented along with a comparative discussion of the similarities, differences, strengths, and weaknesses of the mega event literature. Finally, suggestions and implications for future research and practice are discussed.

## Background and rational for systematic reviews

The rising cost of hosting mega sporting events (MSEs) (Gibson et al., 2014; Madden and Giesecke, 2012), controversies over host government spending (Lundy,

2013; Newman, 2012), allegations of corruption (Broudehoux, 2007; Mason, Thibault, and Misener, 2006), and increased scrutiny by a variety of stakeholders (Hall, 2006), has led to concerns over the sustainability of MSEs (Coakley and Souza, 2013). This has resulted in a significant growth in MSE legacy research, which some have attributed to the International Olympic Committee (IOC) mandate in 2000 (Girginov and Hills, 2008) that stipulated hosts produce legacy plans.

Similarly, within mega-events more generally, researchers and policy makers point to these events as having the potential to provide significant economic, environmental, and social benefits (Raj and Musgrave, 2009). For example, mega events are expected to produce non-economic impacts in the form of "cultural legacies, variations to tourism culture and to the community's national and international perceptions." (Lamberti, Noci, Guo, and Zhu, 2011, p. 1477). As a more applicable example, legacy impacts of Expos include public museums, art galleries and new department stores for the host city (Roche, 2003). Although legacy has been examined and dissected theoretically and empirically, there has been little consideration of synthesising current knowledge to consider inherent strengths and weaknesses of current approaches as well as the contradictions that may prevent advancing knowledge on the legacy of MEs more generally. Thus, the purpose of this chapter is to report the findings of two systematic reviews of the legacy of MEs that examined ME articles with regard to (a) the conceptualisations of legacy, (b) the evidence for legacy, and (c) the evaluation tools used in legacy research.

## Methods

Systematic reviews are important in identifying trends, synthesising findings, and setting directions for future research agendas (Jackson, 2004). They are viable strategies for analysing literature focused on inferring generalisations about substantive issues from a set of studies that address these issues (Jackson, 1980). They can be used to provide an objective account and description of the state of a particular body of literature by assessing the quantity of articles published and identifying predominant themes or gaps in existing research and methodologies used in examining specific phenomenon (Floyd, Bocarro, and Thompson, 2008). Systematic reviews include three key activities: (1) identifying and describing the relevant literature, (2) critically appraising the literature in a systematic manner, and (3) bringing the findings together in a coherent synthesis (Gough, Oliver, and Thames, 2012). We conducted a narrative synthesis of the reviewed literature to identify determinants of mega sporting and non-sporting mega event legacies. A descriptive analysis identified the methodology employed, country of origin, and mega sporting event studied. Finally, a content analysis (Babbie, 2012) was used to understand how legacies of mega events were conceptualised, as well as the key findings. Overall, we sought to explore the approaches to studying mega events by identifying various thematic dimensions related to the process and mechanisms behind the legacy of mega events.

Using similar initial search queries to Preuss (2007), our multi-national research team searched ten academic databases (Academic Search Complete, Business

Source Complete, CAB Abstracts, ERIC, SciELLO, Science Direct, SCOPUS, SportDiscus, Sociological Abstracts, and Web of Science) using the guidelines developed by the Preferred Reporting Items for Systematic Reviews and Meta-analyses (PRISMA) group (Moher, Liberati, Tetzlaff, Altman, and The PRISMA Group, 2009). We searched using variants of the following search terms for the review on mega sporting events: "Mega Sporting Events," "Mega Sport Events" (with and without hyphen), "Legacy," and "Legacies." For the non-sporting review, terms searched included did 'mega event legacy', 'Mega-event legacy', 'Mega event legacy', 'Mega event legacies', 'Mega-event legacies', and 'Mega event legacies'. Initial searches for the Mega Sport review resulted in 372 articles. Articles were included if they were published in English or German and if they related to the legacy of mega sporting events (using the definitions of legacy and mega sporting events presented earlier). Filtering for articles based on whether the article was from a peer-reviewed journal or whether the article had relevance to the topic resulted in the elimination of 146 articles. This process resulted in 226 articles being included in our final analysis. Initial searches for the non-sporting review resulted in 171 journal articles. These journals were read to eliminate those with a sporting event focus, leaving only 23 journal articles in total with a sole focus on non-sporting mega events.

In order to synthesise how legacies of mega events have been conceptualised in the literature, we used content analysis methods informed by Hsieh and Shannon (2005) and based on previous studies (Edwards and Matarrita-Cascante, 2011; Floyd et al., 2008). Overall, we sought to explore the body of knowledge around legacy by identifying dimensions of legacy developed in the research. This is a necessary starting point to understanding how scholars have considered legacy and where more research is needed. Through a process of open coding, concepts related to the dimensions of legacy that were identified by each article, were determined by all authors of this paper based on keywords and content. Initial lists of themes were compared, discussed, consolidated, and refined by two authors. Themes were not designed to be mutually exclusive, and articles sometimes incorporated multiple dimensions of legacy.

## Trends in legacy research and major findings
## Sporting events

Narrative synthesis and content analysis of the MSE literature revealed five key findings as illustrated in Table 1.1. Each finding is explained, and the strengths and weakness discussed following the table.

*Table 1.1* Five key themes of mega event legacy research

1. Majority of events studied or referred to Olympics and World Cup sporting events.
2. Imbalance in methods with more conceptual articles than empirical research.
3. Research tends to narrowly focus on single contexts/types of legacy.
4. Timeframes used to capture legacy rarely exceeded 5 years.
5. Empirical studies of economic legacy offer little evidence to support the claim of mega sport events to create economic longevity.

First, research on legacy of mega events has been dominated by the World Cup and Summer Olympic games. This is unfortunate and a clear weakness of the literature as limited contextual comparisons can be made to understand the factors that affect legacy production. A greater variety and range of mega sporting events would enable some comparison of the effect of size, geographic location, social context, and historical development on legacy production. This is necessary as research strongly indicates that legacy is highly contextual (Preuss, 2015; Roche, 1992).

Our second finding shows there is an imbalance in methods used to investigate legacy. Over half of the research articles were qualitative/conceptual pieces with few data-driven or mixed-method articles. Many articles focus on categories of legacy but offer little empirical verification (except for those focused on measuring economic legacy). This is a significant weakness considering the consensus that legacy is a complex, multidimensional concept (e.g., Girginov and Hills, 2008; Griffiths and Armour, 2013; Horne, 2007), yet few have operationalised this argument and produced empirical data to support and explore the multidimensional nature of legacy and legacy production. For example, conceptual contributions of flexible frameworks and innovative approaches to legacy management exist but are not derived from data of actual legacy processes (e.g., Charlton, 2010; Dickson, Benson, and Blackman, 2011).

The third trend in the literature is that research has tended to examine single contexts and has yet to offer comparative research to explore how context influences legacy production or processes, similarities, and differences between contextual determinants. Many of the articles focused on whether a specific legacy was or was not realised (e.g., does a MSE increase economic returns; does a MSE promote more social capital) but do not reveal the factors that enabled and/or constrained the production of legacy, be these structural or agential. A focus on process is evident in a few articles. This means that research often acknowledges legacy as "all planned and unplanned, positive and negative, tangible and intangible structures created for and by a sport event that remain longer than the event itself" (Preuss, 2007, p. 211) but then only measures or focuses on a portion of that definition in an attempt to understand legacy.

The fourth finding suggests that, although scholars have debated what timeframe constitutes a legacy, the majority of the studies had a timeframe no more than five years after a MSE took place. For example, much of the research that emerged out of the 2010 World Cup in South Africa reported a positive legacy in relation to the nation branding (e.g., Allen, Knott, and Swart, 2013; Knott, Fyall, and Jones, 2015). However, it would be interesting to examine the legacy of the 2010 World Cup in light of the recent FIFA scandal.

Finally, the fifth trend identified that few empirical studies have offered evidence that mega sport events provided significant economic legacies to host cities (e.g., Du Plessis and Venter, 2010; Feddersen, Grotzinger, and Maennig, 2009; Porter and Fletcher, 2008). This has resulted in fewer cities bidding for Mega Sporting Events due to public scepticism on inconsistent economic returns on investment and concern over long-term debt. Even the Summer Olympic Games, arguably the most prestigious Mega Sporting Event, only received five formal bids for the 2020 games. With Budapest recently withdrawing as a host for the 2024 Summer Olympic Games, only Paris and Los Angeles are left, resulting in commentators suggesting that the Olympics are "in crisis mode" (e.g., Denver Post, 2017). As Hartman and Zandberg (2015) note, an event needs to be embedded in a larger pre- and post-development programme, articulating a need that goes beyond economic and infrastructure arguments in order to solicit more broad based community support. Our review showed a significant increase in security and surveillance legacies, a facet that Preuss (2015) recommended adding. This leads to some interesting questions. While organisers want a safe event, is this being justified to increase public expenditure on security and surveillance? In other words, is the MSE being used to permanently increase surveillance and security beyond the event itself?

## Trends in NSME research and major findings

Narrative synthesis and content analysis of the NSME literature revealed six key findings as illustrated in Table 1.2. Each finding is explained and the strengths and weakness discussed following the table. Although the review of the NSME literature indicates that the mega event non-sporting legacy literature is growing, it also highlights many gaps and limitations that need to be addressed. NSME legacy research is "nascent and incomplete" (Li and McCabe, 2013, p. 398) with a strong focus on impacts rather than the long-term legacy of the event, both positive and negative (Deng, 2012; Li and McCabe, 2013).

*Table 1.2* Key themes in non-sporting mega event research

1. NSME research focuses primarily on World Expositions and European Cities of Culture events.
2. There is a lack of conceptualisation of legacy for NSME contexts, and terms "impact" and "legacy" are used interchangeably and at times incorrectly.
3. The main type of legacy studied is urban renewal, referred to using a wide variety of terms including regeneration, reimaging, brandscaping and entrepreneurialism.
4. The majority of research focuses on positive legacy and fails to take a critical perspective to identify oppressive practices, disadvantaged communities, or power struggles between stakeholders.
5. Little empirical evidence of legacy with scant attention to the determinants of producing legacy.
6. Methods were primarily of a single-case design.

The most-researched NSME included World Expositions (Expos) and events that concentrated upon European Cities of Culture. Defined as "an event that enables buyers and sellers to meet together in a market situation" (Bowdin, 2011, p. 26), Expos are business events on a global scale. Similar to the characteristics of a MSE, Song, Ahn, and Lee (2014) define Expos as events that enhance "positive images of the destination, leverages business opportunities in export and new investment, increases citizen morale and pride, and promotes regional tourism development by attracting many domestic and international tourists" (p. 1267). In contrast, Cities of Culture place less emphasis on the business context in an attempt to position themselves as the "most prestigious European Cultural event" (Steiner et al, 2015, p. 374). Designed to promote history and heritage, each city hosts a variety of events that attract visitors to the area, in order to showcase the city to increase the tourism and economic spending. Both events require the host to participate in a vigorous pre-event bidding process that features elements of place and national branding within their rationale. By highlighting these character-istics within the literature, some NSME can be considered as a ME as they feature similar elements to SME (e.g., the bidding process and use of place for nation branding).

The non-sporting category of events included cultural events, business events, festivals, and celebrations. Within this review, no festival or celebratory one-off event, such as royal celebrations or anniversaries, was used as examples within the literature. When comparing these event types to the definitions of ME found within the literature, they do not meet the criteria set within the existing litera-ture. Current definitions highlight the need for international importance, costly investment, and sophisticated revitalisation strategies for urban re-imagining (Andranovich, Burbank, and Heying, 2001; Gotham, 2011). Although one off celebratory events can be internationally significant, they often do not have a long-term legacy (Harris, 2011). However, these events do have the potential to produce a legacy in the form of tourism, urban renewal, pride, community spirit, and destination promotion.

Most NSME studies adopted Preuss' (2007) conceptual framework developed for MSE's as a means to define and organise their analysis of legacy. Deng et al (2016) summarises and entwines examples to explain the definition offered by Preuss, "these structures can be planned (environmental improvement), unplanned (sporting ethos), positive (tourism boom), negative (financial deficit), tangible (upgraded infrastructure) or intangible (elevated global status)" (Deng, 2016, p. 163). However, most significant within this review is the definition created by Li and McCabe (2013) who build upon existing definitions to create their own defi-nition of tourism legacy for NSME. As they point out, legacy can be defined as "tangible and intangible elements of large scale events left to future generations of a host country where these elements influence the economic, physical and psy-chological well-being at both community and individual levels in the long-term" (p. 390). Although there has been some recent attempt at defining NSME legacy, the lack of explanation of what legacy is within the literature demonstrates that the term legacy still lacks a clear conceptualisation (Ferrari and Guala, 2017) that takes into consideration the contextual features of NSME and whether these are different from SME contexts.

Second, NSME articles that focused on legacy used the term *impact* interchange-ably with 'legacy' when attempting to document the legacy of the event. Sometimes mistakenly used as a replacement for the term legacy, 'impacts' are the effects left from a ME that can be used to provide examples of event legacy. However, as Tsaur et al (2017) point out, "events can have impact without creating a legacy" (p. 2). Put simply, Li and McCabe (2013) explain that the difference hangs on a specific period. For example, tourists at the time of the event are a short-term impact, whereas those pre, during and post are a legacy measure over the long term. Although the NSME literature is dominated by economic figures (Ferdinand, 2015), 17 of the 23 articles move to identify a wide range of impacts that are now expected from the hosting of a NSME. For example, MEs are expected to produce non-economic impacts in the form of "cultural legacies, variations to tourism culture and to the community's national and international perceptions." (Lamberti et al, 2011, p. 1477).

Legacy impacts of Expos include public museums, art galleries, and new department stores for the host city (Roche, 2003), as well as civic pride, increase in tourism and cultural understanding (Roche, 2002). However, there is limited theory or empirical evidence on legacy impacts (Li and McCabe, 2013) with those focusing on impacts over-emphasising "consumer motivation and economic impacts" which makes studies short-sighted (Ferdinand, 2015, p. 196). This could be because economic impacts are quite simply the easiest to identify and measure compared to some of the more intangible legacies such as satisfaction or pride. On the other hand, it could be argued that NSME organisers require economic figures as clear justification for the large-scale investment required to host a ME. Our literature review found that almost all papers used economic data alongside other legacy impacts, suggesting that measuring economic legacy is needed to support findings of other 'less-valued' legacies. To move away from the focus of economic legacy, many move to the triple bottom line as an all-encompassing impact assessment tool featuring categories of economic, social, and environmental themes (Getz, 2008). This form of evaluation, taken from the business sector, advocates a clear understanding of ME legacy components and provides a holistic framework for evaluating legacy effects (Tsaur, Yen, Tu, Wang, and Liang, 2017). Moreover, alongside the inclusion of 'broader impacts', legacy research has moved from "merely evaluating the impacts of events to understanding how host communities can strategically create positive outcomes and legacies from events" (Ziakas, 2015, p. 689). This stresses the importance of forward planning and strategic leveraging in order to utilise mega events to create desired legacy rather than unplanned or negative legacy outcomes.

Third, the majority of articles related to the NSME literature concentrate on urban renewal and development of the host city as the main focus for ME legacy, often juxtaposing events (Zeemering, 2013) with urban regeneration as a direct impact. Furthermore, there appeared to be a wide range of terms within the NSME literature used to describe urban renewal, including *urban entrepreneurialism*, *urban developments*, *urban reimaging*, and *urban regeneration*, all of which centre around the theme of a large economic investment into the development of infrastructure within host cities. Linked to this, many offer that urban renewal is a stepping-stone that is used as a branding tool to reposition the host city, termed "brandscaping" (Boland, 2013). Using the example of the UN World Summit in Johannesburg, Death (2010) offers that the benefits of improving the country's image by hosting the summit are significantly more than the benefits of spending money on marketing the city alone.

When using the term *urban development*, the non-sporting literature provides many examples to be included under its umbrella such as the design, reinvigorating and restructuring of facilities, infrastructure and urban spaces (Zeemering, 2013). The literature also highlighted that those involved within the event planning not only saw urban regeneration as a leveraging strategy, but as a catalyst for change (Deng, 2012; Deng, Poon, and Chan, 2016; Gotham, 2011). On the other hand,

Zeemering (2013) points out that events alone are not enough to revitalise cities. Instead events should enhance existing urban development strategies that are complimentary to the planning of the event. This way the development does not solely focus on the needs of the event, but on the need of the city's residents and spaces. By developing the infrastructure, landscape, and therefore the cities' global brand, host cities aim to increase tourism to the area not only at the time of the ME but also sustained many years after the event itself. Although Lamberti and colleagues (2011) add that this increase in tourism may not be the central goal of the event (culture or entertainment), public bodies have become more aware of their instrumental properties to develop tourism. This increase in tourism not only affects the event site but also generates lasting business opportunities for the host community; therefore, tourism legacy impacts are considered one of the most important reasons for hosting a ME (Li and McCabe, 2013). Yu, Wang, and Seo (2012) explain that by developing the landscape, the host city becomes more attractive, positively influencing the tourists both to attend the event but to also re-attend post event. Building from this the literature expands to include urban regeneration as a form of destination branding, often considering legacy as a key criterion.

Fourth, research on NSME legacy tends to focus on the positive elements of hosting mega events with little explanation as to the risks of creating a negative legacy. There was a heavy bias towards positive legacy, with only a small sample mentioning the negative side of ME legacy as a comparison. Those that did discuss the negative side of mega event legacy discussed large-scale economic impacts and smaller local disturbances such as traffic and anti-social behaviour at the time of the event (Death, 2010; Deng, 2012). Steiner, Frey, and Hotz (2015) explain that these smaller impacts, transport disruptions, overcrowding, or local inflation can affect the satisfaction of the host community, which, in turn, can contribute to the overall negative legacy of the event. This concept of negative legacy does not just fade away over time and can have a knock-on effect for future events in the same region. For example, the 'desolate legacy' of the Knoxville World Fair in 1982 effected the public opinion of the hosting of the Louisiana World Exposition in 1984 as the community struggled to forget their dashed expectations surrounded by reminders of empty buildings (Gotham, 2011).

'White elephant legacy' can become a problem if planning for legacy becomes a low priority for event organisers (Deng, Poon, and Chan, 2016). This is a very real possibility, as planning for legacy lacks urgency compared to the event deadline and can significantly increase the event's budget. However, without careful planning, impacts of MEs can be left underused in the future (Tsaur et al., 2017) appearing as constant reminders of wasted public investment and negative legacies of a once 'mega' event. Organising bodies such as the Bureau of International Expositions agree with the literature on the importance of planning for legacy in order to reduce risk, insisting that a feasible legacy plan is present within the bidding stage. In fact, "legacies have become key rationale underpinning the bidding process for hosting mega-events" (Li and McCabe, 2013, p. 388), reducing the risk of negative legacy and enhancing the sustainability of positive legacy.

Our fifth finding on NSME is that there is little empirical evidence of legacy with scant attention to the determinants of producing legacy. The literature reviewed in this research identified a range of intangible and tangible impacts of events that could serve as determinants of event legacy, but there was no strong empirical evidence to support that legacy is or can be created. However, in his review, Getz (2008), simply states that it is up to the host destination to identify what legacy they want for the event and how they will measure it. Thus, it is for this reason that most articles tended to focus on tangible legacies associated with economic values, visitor numbers to the host area and event attendance (Boland, 2013; Death, 2010). Only eight articles concentrate on understanding the parts of legacy that are difficult to quantify, choosing instead to consider visitor satisfaction (Song, Ahn, and Lee, 2014), cultural representation (Winter, 2015) and life satisfaction of the host population (Steiner et al., 2015). These outcomes are more difficult to forecast, estimate, and measure and have therefore been researched less (Ferrari and Guala, 2017; Li and McCabe, 2013).

Finally, our sixth finding from the NSME systematic literature review show that almost all of the articles relied upon a singular in-depth case study or a cross-comparison of case studies to demonstrate the impacts of legacy. Some articles used quantitative data to measure economic impacts (rather than legacy; e.g., Boland, 2013; Gotham, 2011; Lamberti et al., 2011; Steiner, Frey, and Hotz, 2015). Those that did not use quantitative data to examine economic legacy instead chose to look at a range of literature surrounding event legacy (Getz, 2008; Ziakas, 2015) to draw out common themes. Most commonly, the articles used a mixture of both primary and secondary research of a qualitative nature to explain the effects of event legacy. The review demonstrated a heavy bias towards the use of interviews to collect data. However, it should be noted that the articles were in disagreement as to who was best to interview – shown by the range of interview participants included. Some scholars chose to focus on participants directly related to the management of the event itself, such as sponsors and key stakeholders (Death, 2010; Edizel, 2013; Lamberti et al, 2011; Li and McCabe, 2013). Others focused on those who attended the event (Yu, Wang, and Seo, 2012) or those affected by the event in the host community (Tsaur et al., 2017).

## Discussion – sporting and non-sporting legacy of mega events

Research on mega event legacy suggests that legacy is a complex, multidimensional concept (Chappelet, 2012; Ziakas, 2015). Yet two streams of this research have developed, one focusing on sporting events and one focusing on non-sporting events. Using a Critical Realist (CR) ontological lens through which to examine the results presented on SME and NSME legacy, we identified similarities and differences that reveal shortcomings in the literature and serve to inform future research and practice related to legacy of mega events. CR advocates a multilevel ontology of the social world that serves to recognise different perspectives of reality and seeks to identify/resolve complimentary and contradictory assertions of a concept in an attempt to produce a more comprehensive, critical understanding of how and why phenomena occur (Edwards, O'Mahoney, and Vincent, 2014). CR considers the role of social structures and agents as important to understanding how and why concepts such as legacy are produced.

As illustrated in Table 1.3, the CR lens shows that the understanding of legacy evident in much of the literature barely scratches the surface of a multi-perspective reality. Research has predominantly addressed the material level of reality by focusing on what is legacy, whether it occurs or not and has relied on observable, tangible evidence of legacy through either qualitative or quantitative studies.

*Table 1.3* A Critical Realist lens for Examining Similarities and Differences in mega event research

| Level of reality | Similarities | Differences |
| --- | --- | --- |
| Material (tangible observable aspects) | Legacy conceptualised as complex, recognising many different types such as social, economic, cultural, etc. | Primary focus of SME research on economic legacy, then social forms and NSME on cultural economics, urban regeneration. |
| | Legacy defined a product, primarily produced through rational planning or a process such as leveraging. | SME research has extensive conceptual discussions of legacy concept and sees legacy as contextual, NSME literature has little discussion, adopts SME definitions. |
| | Insufficient length of time allowed post event to measure legacy, more focus on 'impacts'; resulting lack of empirical evidence that legacy was produced. | Variation in dominant methods used to study legacy. |
| Ideal (stakeholders' perspectives of reality) | Agreement that there are multiple stakeholders influencing the process of legacy and for whom legacy make exist. | SME larger in scope and expense/investment, therefore tend to have greater variety of stakeholders when considering if, how and for whom legacy produced. |
| Artifactual (stakeholders' interpretation of reality (legacy) as legitimate or oppressive) | Evidence of legacy potential as 'legitimate', positive legacies (for socially advantaged groups) and as oppressive, negative legacies (often minority or disadvantaged populations). | Greater recognition in the SME literature of negative stakeholder views of legacy, disadvantaged groups, and the potential for unplanned, undesirable legacy to emerge. |
| Social (taken for granted structures and ideologies that give rise to above realities) | Commercialisation and economic importance of mega events underpins academic and practitioner/ government interest in legacy. | Sport as a social institution capable of solving social problems and inequalities through mega events is promoted by governments and the IOC* as justification for high costs. |
| | Little examination of how social structures such as gender, race, class, government contribute to stakeholder perceptions/ assessments or what type of legacies are relevant at any one time. | SME offer a more focused context than the multiple types of NSME; challenge of understanding how and why legacy exists due to role of different social structures influence in these contexts. |

*International Olympic Committee

## Material reality

Much of the research on legacy of mega events focuses on the material level of reality, measuring observable, tangible evidence (Tsoukas, 1994) of legacy such as increases in tourists, spending and participation numbers. Our systematic reviews found that both SME and NSME research recognises that legacy is a complex concept, consisting of multiple forms/types of legacy. These included economic, social, and cultural forms among others, but they differed in what types of legacy they focused on, with SME research focusing more on economic and social legacies and NSME research focused on primarily cultural economic legacy (often referred to as urban regeneration) as a form of legacy. A wider variety of legacy types have featured in MSE legacy research, potentially reflecting the larger size, scope, and political and social climate surrounding these events. These include environmental and public health legacies as well as surveillance/security legacy. The considerably smaller NSME literature maintains a focus primarily on urban renewal and related types of legacy such as host branding, tourism, and marketing. Thus, our review found some common facets (economics, urban infrastructure and development, security and surveillance, and sport development) that reflect prior conceptualisations developed by either Cashman (2005), Chappelet (2012), or Preuss (2007, 2015). We also found that tourism, social development, host branding, and marketing were reflected in the studies, and so it appears that categories of legacy could be infinite.

Both SME and NSME research have failed to consider legacy over a longer time-period and often focused on measuring impacts as opposed to legacy (Deng, 2012; Li and McCabe, 2013). Coupled with this, NSME conceptualisations of legacy are often derived from the sport literature and do not take contextual features of their events into consideration when articulating what legacy is produced or how it is produced. Further concentration on identifying types of legacy seems futile and does little to understand the complexity of legacy beyond identification of types with little understanding of the legacy process. In response to this, researchers have suggested a focus on leveraging to illustrate the process of legacy production (Chappelet, 2012). The idea behind event leveraging is to use mega events to 'leverage' broader benefits (Getz and Page, 2016) both during and after the event. By using a leveraging strategy (see Chalip, Chapter 2), event stakeholders can identify in the planning stage what legacy the event could produce and use these benefits to justify the need for the event. Therefore, event legacy can provide a valuable leveraging resource, which can magnify and sustain the event benefits (Ziakas, 2015). Within our reviews both concepts of using mega events to leverage legacy benefits and using legacy benefits for justification of hosting mega events were widely identified.

The importance of using planning in conjunction with a leveraging strategy was described as 'necessary' in order to continue to receive benefits and continue the leveraging – hosting cycle (Ziakas, 2015). In their article, Ferrari and Guala (2017) go one step further in their examination of planning and leveraging in order to consider the importance of stakeholder involvement within this stage. They conclude that "events can only succeed if they are part of a scenario, a planning capacity that involves the legacy and a collective project, participated in by the social capital associations, public and private bodies" (p. 15). The inclusion of leveraging has been of significance to understanding legacy, yet it retains a characteristic weakness of the legacy concept in that it focuses on one level of reality, the planned, rational, and tangible mechanisms which may help to produce legacy. This is a significant shortcoming in that it prevents deeper knowledge of why we feel the need to produce legacy, why certain legacies may occur, and how different types of legacy relate to one another.

Despite using similar conceptualisations of legacy primarily in terms of product/outputs and as a process of strategic leveraging, the SME and NSME literature have adopted different methods to investigate legacy. SME literature contains many conceptual papers with few empirical research efforts to substantiate theoretical models. Of the empirical papers, many focus on economic legacy/impacts and therefore use quantitative data. Others are purely qualitative, reliant on interviews with key stakeholders of a particular event. In NSME research, methods tend to be of a single-case design, reliant on interview data of single stakeholder groups. Both SME and NSME research methods are limited and inconsistent with the conceptualisation of legacy as a complex concept.

A strength of this focus on the material reality is that legacy has been dissected and various dimensions of it (i.e. economic, social, etc.) have been studied. Also, the concept of leveraging begins to look at how to produce legacy rather than what types of legacy may be produced yet it is also limited in that it focuses on rational planning and tangible mechanisms as determinants of legacy. The predominant focus on economic legacy has led to few empirical studies able to confirm that mega sport events provide significant economic legacies to host cities (e.g., Du Plessis and Venter, 2010; Feddersen, Grotzinger, and Maennig, 2009; Porter and Fletcher, 2008). However, we have little understanding for how economic legacies may influence (positively or negatively) social or environmental legacies.

Our review showed increases in identification of different types of legacies, such as security and surveillance legacies for sporting events, a facet that Preuss (2015) recommended adding. This leads to some interesting questions for researchers and practitioners. While organisers want a safe event, is this being justified to increase public expenditure? In other words, is the MSE being used to permanently increase surveillance and security beyond the event?

## Ideal reality

Ideal reality refers to conceptual entities such as language and discursive entities such as ideas, beliefs and understandings that give rise to how to create the material world (Fleetwood, 2005). SME and NSME research is consistent in their agreement that there are a variety of stakeholders relevant to understanding what is legacy and how it is produced. However, the literature on SME reveals that these events are much larger in size, value, and economic significance and tend to have a greater variety of stakeholders to consider. Both literatures have identified how different groups of stakeholders' view legacy in relation to different mega events. However, it would appear that creating a legacy for sporting events might be more difficult because of the number of stakeholders. These include athletes, media, business, communities, sponsors, government, and disadvantaged groups who do not often have a voice in these matters. This level of reality – the stakeholder's perceptions, understandings and beliefs (Fleetwood, 2005) – is an important component of understanding legacy, yet it has not been examined/critiqued in relation to the material realm of reality. When considering how the ideal and material are related, we can begin to question how different stakeholder views, individually and collectively may enable or constrain legacy from production. For example, London 2012 had formal legacy plans related to disabled sport, and the event was meant to create a new appreciation for disabled persons in society. Yet the success of Britain's disabled athletes evoked some negative interpretations of disability, as revealed by Brittain (see Chapter 6).

The smaller number of stakeholders in NSME may also explain the tendency to advocate multiple stakeholder views in single case studies of NSME legacy/impacts, yet few include more than one view. Identifying larger numbers/groups of stakeholders may be a consequence of the rising costs of hosting MSE and the increased need to justify these expenses rather than a genuine consideration of stakeholders in legacy planning. Research is needed that measures legacy across multiple contexts to take account of how contextual features enable and constrain the process of legacy production. This also relates to the limited use of comparative perspectives in the literature. Therefore, we suggest models such as comparative case methods may encourage more in-depth understanding of the legacy process and its contextual imperatives. We also suggest that there is a need for more empirical research examining the processes behind mega events, specifically examining why certain legacies occur rather than if they occur. Many of the articles seem to focus on whether a specific outcome was or was not realised (e.g. does a mega event increase economic returns? or does it promote more social capital?) or how a specific stakeholder group perceives legacy. However very few articles examine factors that enabled and/or constrained the production of legacy, be they structural or agential.

Furthermore, few articles focused on the process. For example, to keep the event's memory alive, Chappelet (2012) suggests developing and adopting deliberate strategies, such as post community events and online spaces. How do event administrators know what the processes or strategies were that were successful, so that knowledge can be transferred? Furthermore, while the increased number of articles focused on the legacy of MSE's suggest a maturation, imbalance in methods suggests otherwise. For example, over half the research articles were qualitative/conceptual pieces with few data-driven or mixed-method articles. This indicates that most knowledge in the current literature is focused on one dimension of legacy such as stakeholders' perspectives, or one type of legacy such as economic or sport participation. This is a significant weakness as many authors have acknowledged that legacy is a complex, multidimensional concept (e.g., Girginov and Hills, 2008; Griffiths and Armour, 2013; Horne, 2007), yet few have operationalised this argument and produced empirical data to support and explore the multidimensional nature of legacy and legacy production. For example, conceptual contributions of flexible frameworks, innovative approaches to legacy management exist, but are not derived from data of actual legacy processes (e.g., Charlton, 2010; Dickson et al., 2011).

**Artifactual reality**

This reality speaks to stakeholders interpretations of legacy as legitimate or oppressive and is a synthesis of the physically, ideal and socially real in that these phenomenon are interpreted by agents (Fleetwood, 2005) in a socio-political context (Marsh, Johnston, Hay, and Buller, 1999). There is suggestion from NSME and SME literature that NSME are largely studied for the positive impacts/legacy they can create with limited consideration given to how negative or socially oppressive some events may be for different groups. The use of legacy is often thrown around as justification for the hosting of non-sporting mega events, often with no empirical evidence of their success (Li and McCabe, 2013). When explaining the success (triumph) of Europe's first global entrepreneurship congress, chief executive of Liverpool Vision claimed, "[W]e have created a real legacy for the city while raising the bar for future GEC host cities" (Boland, 2013, p. 257). When used in this context, legacy is seen to be an all positive concept used as a tool for event officials to favourably argue for significant public expenditure when hosting mega events (Steiner et al., 2015). SME research contains some recognition that legacies can be negative and oppressive to disadvantaged groups, while NSME literature focuses primarily on the positive impacts/legacies with very little attention to negative assessments.

Legacy, from a multitude of stakeholder assessments needs to be examined and compared over longer timeframes. Although scholars have debated what timeframe constitutes a legacy, our review showed that the majority of the studies had a timeframe no more than five years after a MSE took place. We propose more research examining events that occurred more than five years ago. For example, much of the research that emerged out of the 2010 World Cup in South Africa reported a positive legacy in relation to the nation branding (e.g., Allen et al., 2013; Knott, Fyall, and Jones, 2015). However, it would be interesting to examine the legacy of the 2010 World Cup in light of the recent FIFA scandal.

**Social reality**

The first three levels of reality focus on agents and what they do or think. The social layer of reality focuses more on structures (and the relationship between the structures and agents) to explain how structures can give rise to more observable phenomenon (Marsh et al, 1999) and how they influence agent behaviour (bearing in mind that agents create and recreate the structures in which they operate). There is little examination of how social structures such as gender, race, class, or government contribute to stakeholder perceptions/assessments of legacy or what type of legacy is deemed important at any one time, although some research (e.g., Ziakas, 2015) is beginning to suggest the importance of this in order to provide a more critical view of the legacy concept. The literature on mega event legacy is underpinned by commercial ideologies and powerful stakeholder's need to justify mega events and their considerable costs. The conceptualisation of sport event legacy has been emerging since the 1980s (Leopkey and Parent, 2012). Misener, Darcy, Legg, and Gilbert (2013) suggested there is no doubt the impetus to measure legacy emerged from the Olympic Movement and the desire to legitimise the movement, gain global recognition, increase power, and self-promote (Girginov and Hills, 2008). Increasingly, as local MSE advocates and governing bodies sought to justify considerable resource allocations for sport and supporting infrastructure required of MSEs to stakeholders, legacy has been promoted as providing tangible and intangible benefits to host states in return for their investments.

## Conclusion

Evidence suggests that legacy has become a taken-for-granted activity, a concept promoted to justify and legitimise the resources required to host mega events. Event managers should be aware that the process of legacy production is ill understood but that it is a complex process whereby many factors influence whether legacy occurs or not. Factors under the control of managers include legacy plans, training manuals and formal mechanisms that attempt to implement goals/plans of legacy. Given that the literature identifies a wide variety of stakeholders and divergent interpretations of the significance of legacy, event managers should be aware of bottom-up approaches whereby different voices (positive and negative) can be heard and considered in shaping legacy objectives and plans. Yet it is not possible to control all aspects of legacy. Thus, managers/event planners should focus on defining what legacy they (and stakeholders) wish to see develop and consider what leveraging strategies can be designed to complement those plans.

   Deeper understandings of legacy can be achieved through a more critical analysis of all layers of reality including the ideal, artifactual, and social realities that encourage understanding of how and why legacy exists, as well as why research has been preoccupied with dominant discourses of legacy promoted by powerful elites such as the IOC, national governments, and commercial business. Both sporting and nonsporting mega event legacy literatures include a growing body of studies that fail to capture this complexity and instead have produced conceptual and empirical papers that focus on narrow perspectives of the concept.

## References

Allen, D., Knott, B., and Swart, K. (2013). Africa's tournament'? The branding legacy of the 2010 FIFA World Cup™. *International Journal of the History of Sport*, *30*(16), 1994–2006.

Andranovich, G., Burbank, M., and Heying, C. (2001). Olympic cities: Lessons learned from mega-event politics. *Journal of Urban Affairs*, *23*(2), 113–131.

Babbie, E. (2012). *The practice of social research* (13th ed.). Belmont, CA: Wadsworth Publishing Company.

Boland, P. (2013). Sexing up the city in the international beauty contest: The performative nature of spatial planning and the fictive spectacle of place branding. *Town Planning Review*, *84*(2), 251–274.

Bowdin, G. (2011). *Events management*. Oxford: Elsevier.

Broudehoux, A. (2007). Spectacular Beijing: The conspicuous construction of an Olympic metropolis. *Journal of Urban Affairs*, *29*(4), 383–399.

Cashman, R. (2005). The bitter-sweet awakening: The legacy of the Sydney 2000 Olympic Games. Sydney: Walla Walla Press.

Chappelet, J. L. (2012). Mega sporting event legacies: A multifaceted concept. *Papeless de Europa, 25*, 76–86.

Charlton, T. (2010). 'Grow and sustain': The role of community sports provision in promoting a participation legacy for the 2013 Olympic Games. *International Journal of Sport Policy, 2*(3), 347–366.

Coakley, J., and Souza, D. L. (2013). Sport mega-events: Can legacies and development be equitable and sustainable? *Motriz: Revista de Educação Física, 19*, 580–589.

Death, C. (2010). Troubles at the top: South African protests and the 2002 Johannesburg summit. *African Affairs, 109*(437), 555–574.

Deng, Y. (2012). Shaping Mega-Event flagships: A case study of Expo Center of Expo 2010 Shanghai, China. *Facilities, 30*(13/14), 590–610.

Deng, Y., Poon, S. W., and Chan, E. H. W. (2016). Planning mega-event built legacies – a case of Expo 2010. *Habitat International, 53*, 163–177.

*Denver Post* (2017, February 23). Olympics in crisis mode as only 2 cities vie to host 2024 Summer Games. Retrieved from www.denverpost.com/2017/02/23/olympics-host-summer-games-2024/

Dickson, T., Benson, A. M., and Blackman, D. A. (2011). Developing a framework for evaluating Olympic and Paralympic legacies. *Journal of Sport & Tourism, 16*(4), 285–302.

Du Plessis, S., and Venter, C. (2010). The home team scores! A first assessment of the economic impact of World Cup 2010. In M-P. Büch, W. Maening, and H. Schulke (Eds.), *Sport und okonomie: Internationale sportevents im umbruch?* (pp. 31–50). Aachen: Meyer & Meyer Verlag.

Edizel, Ö. (2013). Mega-Events as a place marketing strategy in entrepreneurial cities: İzmir's EXPO 2015 Candidacy as a roadmap for hosting EXPO 2020. *Town Planning Review, 84*(5), 633–657.

Edwards, M. B., and Matarrita-Cascante, D. (2011). Rurality in leisure research: A review of four major journals. *Journal of Leisure Research, 43*(4), 447–474.

Edwards, P. K., O'Mahoney, J., & Vincent, S. (2014). *Studying organizations using critical realism: a practical guide* (Vol. 17). OUP: Oxford.

Feddersen, A., Grotzinger, A., and Maennig, W. (2009). Investment in stadia and regional economic development – evidence from FIFA World Cup 2006 stadia. *International Journal of Sport Finance, 4*(4), 221–239.

Ferdinand, N. (2015). Future of events and festivals. *Journal of Tourism Futures, 1*(2), 156–161.

Ferrari, S., and Guala, C. (2017). Mega-events and their legacy: Image and tourism in Genoa, Turin and Milan. *Leisure Studies, 36*(1), 119–137.

Fleetwood, S. (2005). Ontology in organization and management studies: A critical realist perspective. *Organization, 12*(2), 197–222.

Floyd, M., Bocarro, J. N., and Thompson, T. (2008). Research on race and ethnicity in leisure studies: A review of five major journals. *Journal of Leisure Research, 40*(1), 1–22.

Getz, D. (2008). Event tourism: Definition, evolution, and research. *Tourism Management, 29*(3), 403–428.

Getz, D., and Page, S. (2016). Progress and prospects for event tourism research. *Tourism Management, 52*, 593–631.

Gibson, H. J., Walker, M., Thapa, B., Kaplanidou, K., Geldenhuys, S., and Coetzee, W. (2014). Psychic income and social capital among host nation residents: A pre-post analysis of the 2010 FIFA World Cup in South Africa. *Tourism Management, 44*, 113–122.

Girginov, V., and Hills, L. (2008). A sustainable sports legacy: Creating a link between the London Olympics and sports participation. *The International Journal of the History of Sport, 25*(14), 2091–2116.

Gotham, K. (2010). Resisting urban spectacle: The 1984 Louisiana world exposition and the contradictions of Mega Events. *Urban Studies, 48*(1), 197–214.

Gough, D., Oliver, S., and Thames, J. (2012). *An introduction to systematic reviews*. London: Sage.

Griffiths, M., and Armour, K. (2013). Physical education and youth sport in England: Conceptual and practical foundations for an Olympic legacy? *International Journal of Sport Policy and Politics, 5*(2), 213–227.

Hall, C. M. (2006). Urban entrepreneurship, corporate interests and sports mega-events: The thin policies of competitiveness within the hard outcomes of neoliberalism. *The Sociological Review, 54*(s2), 59–70.

Harris, N. (2011, May 9). *Revealed: Royal Wedding TV audience closer to 300M than 2Bn (Because sport, not royalty, reigns)*. Retrieved from www.sportingintelligence. com/2011/05/08/revealed-royal-wedding%E2%80%99s-real-tv-audience-closer-to-300m-than-2bn-because-sport-not-royalty-reigns-080501/

Hartman, S., and Zandberg, T. (2015). The future of mega sport events: Examining the "Dutch approach" to legacy planning. *Journal of Tourism Futures, 1*(2), 108–116.

Horne, J. (2007). The four 'knowns' of sports mega events. *Leisure Studies, 26*(1), 81–96.

Hsieh, H., and Shannon, S. E. (2005). Three approaches to qualitative content analysis. *Qualitative Health Research, 15*(9), 1277–1288.

Jackson, E. L. (2004). Individual and institutional concentration of leisure research in North America. *Leisure Sciences, 26*(4), 323–348.

Jackson, G. (1980). Methods for integrative reviews. *Review of Educational Research, 50*(3), 438–460.

Knott, B., Fyall, A., and Jones, I. (2015). The nation branding opportunities provided by a sport mega-event: South Africa and the 2010 FIFA World Cup. *Journal of Destination Marketing & Management, 4*(1), 46–56.

Lamberti, L., Noci, G., Guo, J., and Zhu, S. (2011). Mega-events as drivers of community participation in developing countries: The case of Shanghai World Expo. *Tourism Management, 32*(6), 1474–1483.

Leopkey, B., and Parent, M. M. (2012). Olympic Games legacy: From general benefits to sustainable long-term legacy. *The International Journal of the History of Sport, 29*(6), 924–943.

Li, S., and McCabe, S. (2013). Measuring the socio-economic legacies of Mega-Events: Concepts, propositions and indicators. *International Journal of Tourism Research, 15*(4), 388–402.

Lundy, M. (2013, June 24). *Brazilians have reason to protest the costs of Olympics and World Cup*. Retrieved February 17, 2015, from www.theglobeandmail.com/ globe-debate/brazilians-have-reason-to-protest-the-cost-of-olympics-and-world-cup/ article12742114/

Madden, J., and Giesecke, J. (2012, July 26). *Olympic glory at any price?* Retrieved February 17, 2015, from www.businessspectator.com.au/article/2012/7/26/australian-news/ olympic-glory-any-price

Marsh, D., Johnston, J., Hay, C., and Buller, J. (1999). *Postwar British politics in perspective*. Cambridge: Polity Press.

Mason, D. S., Thibault, L., and Misener, L. (2006). An agency-theory perspective on corruption in sport: The case of the International Olympic Committee. *Journal of Sport Management, 20*, 52–73.

Misener, L., Darcy, S., Legg, D., and Gilbert, K. (2013). Beyond Olympic legacy: Understanding Paralympic legacy through a thematic analysis. *Journal of Sport Management*, *27*, 329–341.

Moher, D., Liberati, A., Tetzlaff, J., Altman, D. G., and The PRISMA Group (2009). Preferred reporting items for systematic reviews and meta-analyses: The PRISMA statement. *Annals of Internal Medicine*, *151*(4), 264–269.

Newman, R. (2012, March 22). *How the Olympics will cost London*. Retrieved February 17, 2015, from www.usnews.com/news/blogs/rick-newman/2012/03/22/how-the-olympics-will-cost-london

Porter, P. K., and Fletcher, D. (2008). The economic impact of the Olympic Games: Ex ante predictions and ex poste reality. *Journal of Sport Management*, *22*, 470–486.

Preuss, H. (2007). The conceptualisation and measurement of mega sport event legacies. *Journal of Sport & Tourism*, *12*(3–4), 207–227.

Preuss, H. (2015). A framework for identifying the legacies of a mega sport event. *Leisure Studies*, *34*(6), 643–664.

Raj, R., and Musgrave, J. (2009). *Event management and sustainability*. Oxford: CABI.

Roche, M. (1992). Mega-events and micro-modernization: On the sociology of the new urban tourism. *The British Journal of Sociology*, *43*(4), 563–600.

Roche, M. (2002). Mega-events and modernity: Olympics and expos in the growth of global culture. London: Routledge.

Roche, M. (2003). Mega-events, time and modernity on time structures in global society. *Time & Society*, *12*(1), 99–126.

Song, H., Ahn, Y., and Lee, C. (2014). Examining relationships among Expo experiences, service quality, satisfaction, and the effect of the Expo: The case of the Expo 2012 Yeosu Korea. *Asia Pacific Journal of Tourism Research*, *20*(11), 1266–1285.

Steiner, L., Frey, B., and Hotz, S. (2015). European capitals of culture and life satisfaction. *Urban Studies*, *52*(2), 374–394.

Tsaur, S-H., Yen, C-H., Tu, J-H., Wang, C-H., and Liang, Y-W. (2017). Evaluation of the 2010 Taipei International Flora Exposition from the perceptions of host-city residents: A new framework for mega-event legacies measurement. *Leisure Studies*, *36*(1), 65–88.

Tsoukas, H. (1994). Refining common sense: Types of knowledge in management studies. *Journal of Management Studies*, *31*(6), 761–780.

Winter, T. (2015). Cultural Diplomacy, Cosmopolitanism and Global Hierarchy at the Shanghai Expo. *Space and Culture*, *18*(1), 39–54.

Winter, T. (2013). Auto-exoticism: Cultural display at The Shanghai Expo. *Journal of Material Culture*, *18*(1), 69–90.

Yu, L., Wang, C., and Seo, J. (2012). Mega event and destination brand: 2010 Shanghai Expo. *International Journal Event and Festival Management*, *3*(1), 46–65.

Zeemering, E. (2013). Events and urban regeneration: The strategic use of events to revitalise cities by Andrew Smith. *Journal of Urban Affairs*, *35*(3), 390–392.

Ziakas, V. (2015). For the benefit of all? Developing a critical perspective in mega-event leverage. *Leisure Studies*, *34*(6), 689–702.

# 2  Trading legacy for leverage

*Laurence Chalip*

Legacy discourse abounds, as do legacy models. This chapter argues that the legacy framework fails to withstand conceptual and empirical scrutiny but that it persists because it serves the interests of event owners and some political elites. Strategic leveraging of events is a distinct alternative to legacy – one that is both practical and effective. Following a review of the purpose and problems of event legacy, the rationale and research supporting event leverage are reviewed. Leveraging is contrasted with legacy, including legacy planning. Implications for practice and for future research are described.

## The purpose and problems of legacy

The notion that large events with substantial public investment should leave a positive legacy has been with us since at least the 1980s (Leopkey and Parent, 2012). The reason that event owners, particularly the International Olympic Committee (IOC), have been concerned about what their events leave behind is that events have been widely criticized as poor investments. The claim that events may help to market cities has long been questioned because economic and tourism data simply do not support that claim (Whitson and Macintosh, 1996). The hope that events may nonetheless render a positive aggregate economic benefit has also been discredited. Indeed, the economic impact method most commonly used to ascertain the aggregate public value of an event (input-output analysis) is biased because it will render a positive estimate so long as the spending stimulated by the event is greater than the costs to run it (Mondello and Rishe, 2004). Crowding out effects and opportunity costs are not considered. When cost-benefit analysis is used to incorporate those effects and costs, initially positive estimates do not merely shrink; they can become negative (Taks, Késsene, Chalip, and Green, 2011). Worse still, construction to enable hosting an event can produce facilities that are too large or too specialized to be appropriate for use after the event (Bason, Cook, and Anagnostopoulos, 2015), which creates an ongoing economic burden.

These problems are exacerbated by the poor distribution of event benefits. Simply stated, although residents and businesses throughout the event's region may subsidize it through their taxes, only a few individuals and businesses actually reap benefits from it (Mules, 1998). For example, retailers close to an event can benefit temporarily from the added customers that an event might bring, but that will be at the expense of businesses that are more distally located (Putsis, 1998). Some hotels near an event may be able to raise prices temporarily, but the gains are not sustained, and business executives in the critical trading radius of events report that no aggregate positive effect is obtained (Lamla, Straub, and Girsberger, 2014).

Yet, event owners and event organizers rely on public support – both for their bid to host, and while organizing an event. So, positive outcomes (aka legacies) for the host community, region, and/or country are claimed. However, if large events do not render the positive gains that are professed, then public support will be eroded. In fact, that is precisely what is occurring. Research shows that there is increasing public skepticism about the investment required to bid and to host (Groothuis and Rotthoff, 2016), and about the distribution of whatever benefits are obtained (Tichaawa, Bama, and Swart, 2015). That skepticism seems to be justified not merely on economic grounds, but also because expectations for associated intangible benefits from an event may not be met. This is not merely because benefits have been overstated but also because the energy created by an event dissipates soon after the event is over (Cashman, 2006).

## From impact to legacy

The sustainability of the business model that has come to be associated with large events depends on creating sufficient positive expectations and outcomes to garner and retain public support. By so doing, event owners and the organizers they license to stage their events endeavor to build and retain public support. Therefore, owners increasingly require event organizers to incorporate legacy plans into their bids, and then to foster strategies and tactics to realize those legacies. The challenge has been that it is unclear what legacies might be possible, so there has been substantial work endeavoring to determine what events could achieve. There is scant agreement on the matter, as different models have been forthcoming. So, for example, Dickson, Benson, and Blackman (2011) present 11 categories of legacy; Swart and Bob (2012) suggest 33 possible positive event legacies but also identify 39 possible negative legacies, while Preuss (2015) identifies 18 possible legacies but notes that each can have both positive and negative aspects. Although these different models are cogently argued, they remain largely rhetorical. They provide the basis for rhetoric that legitimizes the expenditures necessary to host a large event, but they have not proved useful in practice. In fact, the complex but elusive nature of legacy has caused it to be a shifting target. So, when bidding for the Vancouver Olympic Games, proponents began with claims of economic benefits supported by infrastructure development, but as the event was being organized, they abandoned such claims and instead asserted that there would be intangible social benefits (Sant and Mason, 2015).

The shifting discourse about legacy is, in part, a consequence of its context dependence. Since the objective of legacy models has been to build a taxonomy of potential legacies, the models have been universalist in their design. The cultural, social, political, geographic, demographic, and economic differences among event hosts that might shape legacy objectives and processes are not engaged. Yet, such differences are known to be significant because what might work in one setting cannot simply be transferred to another (Beesley and Chalip, 2011) since the models cannot accommodate the many differences in event host contexts, the taxonomic approach to legacy modeling fails to provide a useful basis for formulating strategies to enable legacy.

As it turns out, the many categories of legacy identified in the models are themselves a source of the problem. If legacies are to be realized, then there must be investments of time and energy into them, the persons required to generate those legacies must have the skills to make them a reality, and there must be a sustained effort. Each of these requirements is problematic. It is simply impossible to invest wisely across the 11 or 18 or 33 categories of positive legacy the models identify or to invest to prevent between 18 and 39 negative legacies that the models also identify. Weed (2014) showed that the many legacy targets sought by organizers of the London Olympic Games diffused the effort to such a degree that demonstrably significant economic value, especially through tourism, became unobtainable. The same can be shown for declared social legacies, such as increased sport participation, for which insufficient energy or capital have been available (Bretherton, Piggin, and Bodet, 2016), with the result that local sport organizations do not develop the resources and skills to build sport events into their marketing mix (Taks, Misener, Chalip, and Green, 2013). The exaggerated ambitions for legacy also make it unsustainable, as the necessary alliances to obtain even simple legacies can simply unravel after the event is over (Bell and Gallimore, 2015), and the investments required to sustain legacy wane (Pentifallo and Van Wynsberghe, 2014).

## The persistence of legacy rhetoric

One might argue that the problem is not with legacy as a paradigm but, rather, the problem is that we do not yet fully comprehend how to pursue legacy. Perhaps our frameworks need to be honed so that we can do a better job of building legacy plans into event organizing. If we planned better, maybe legacies would be forthcoming. Perhaps if event organizers could focus on only a few legacies, or if further investments were made, or if there were a more sustained effort, things would be different. Or, perhaps, the paradigm is intrinsically flawed.

Among event owners, event organizers, and government bureaucrats, the conversation has focused primarily on ways to make legacy a workable framework for event planning and implementation. Thus, owners, organizers, and bureaucrats have worried about such matters as transparency, participation, accountability, and performance (Leopkey and Parent, 2015), as if those might solve the persistent problems of event legacy. Academics continue to ponder ways to refine legacy models to make them simultaneously more complex and more practical. Yet fundamental contradictions remain between the ways that event owners mandate that events be organized and what is required to enable legacy (Nichols and Ralston, 2015). In other words, what is required for legacy as it is currently envisioned is incompatible with the exigencies of event organizing.

Based on his participation in conversations that take place in Olympic circles, MacAloon (2008) observes that claims about Olympic legacies are routine despite the lack of persuasive supporting evidence. He likens legacy discourse to magical thinking, pointing out that the repetitive focus on legacy is akin to a superstitious incantation. He notes that the IOC's legacy mandates to event organizers (called "OCOGs" in Olympic parlance) serve the intended purpose of signifying that event organizers must ultimately work to support the IOC's interests. Thus, legacy is not deferred to public authorities or private enterprise. Rather, the legacy framework reserves power and authority to the IOC-and-OCOG relationship.

Governments have been complicit, as it has been useful for them to seek benefits from events while keeping an arm's length from the pitfalls and practical challenges of organizing them. Political elites benefit from events because their status is raised through hosting, particularly as they socialize with other political elites who attend the event or its associated functions (Whitson and Macintosh, 1996). Increasingly, political strategists have seen this not merely as an opportunity to build their networks and elevate their status, but also as a means to project influence in domestic and international affairs (Grix and Houlihan, 2014; Grix and Lee, 2013). In other words, hosting large events can be advantageous for political elites, even if it is not in the best interests of the economy or society for which they are responsible. Consequently, political elites have a vested interest in the legitimizing rhetoric of legacy. By adding their support, claims of legacy become more credible, and the public comes to overestimate the event's impact (Oshimi, Harada, and Fukuhara, 2016).

## The strategic leverage alternative

The fundamental flaw in the legacy framework is that it is focused on outcomes. For legacy schemes, what matters are the purported benefits to be obtained? Think about it. What is a legacy? It is what is left over after something is gone. So, legacy thinking focuses on what will be left behind from the event. It asks, "What can we get from the event?" One might also ask, "How?" or "When?" or "Why?" but the starting point remains the prophesized outcomes of the event.

Again, the interests of political elites and event owners coincide. Promises about event legacies legitimize the many millions of dollars it can cost to bid for and to host an event (Chalip, 2017). Projected legacies enable event owners to suggest that they are providing an investment opportunity; projected legacies enable politicians to claim that they are making wise use of public resources. In other words, legacy rhetoric is a vital public relations tool because it creates a vision for a better future to be enabled by an event. That is a core reason that the focus remains on outcomes rather than what might be required to obtain those outcomes. Consider the following analogy: It is akin to suggesting that having a hammer will enable new houses to be built; it fails to address the more fundamental questions having to do with what would need to be done with the hammer *along with the other necessary tools in the toolkit* to enable production of homes. Just as it is absurd to suggest that houses are simply a consequence of obtaining a hammer, it is comparably absurd to claim that legacies derive from events. In other words, legacy simply asserts that having an event will enable good things in the future; it cannot address how the event might be used in conjunction with the product and service mix in the host community, region, or nation in order to optimize strategic objectives that matter to those who live there. The integration of an opportunity – in this case, an event – into ongoing development strategies is essential, as the normal prescriptions for strategic planning demonstrate (Andrews, Boyne, Law, and Walker, 2012; Tjemkes, Pepijn, and Burgers, 2012).

For event owners, this is not an attractive insight because it would remove responsibility for event legacies from event organizers, who are beholden to event owners who grant their license, and shift it to the public and private sectors that are otherwise responsible for community development. That shift would disrupt the relationships of power that are otherwise inherent in the affiliation between event owners and event organizers (MacAloon, 2008). It would also shift responsibility to political elites, as they could no longer assert that any event is a good investment, but would instead have to demonstrate that they can and will use events effectively. The political stakes would rise.

The convergence of political and event owner interests has created conditions that give legacy rhetoric its dominion. Thus, legacy remains the dominant discourse despite conceptual and empirical analyses demonstrating the many flaws in its presuppositions (as reviewed earlier). Yet, the challenge of capitalizing on events remains. The fact that politicians and city marketers want events for their own reasons (Whitson and Macintosh, 1996) indicates that events will continue to take place. Thus, simply opposing events as bad investments seems less wise than seeking means to increase their value. Strategic leveraging is one way to do so.

The remainder of this chapter reviews the leveraging paradigm as a viable alternative to the current preoccupation with legacy. Leverage is distinct from legacy because it focuses on strategic processes, rather than categories of outcome, and can thereby be applied across disparate contexts. It treats events as potentially useful additions to the host community's product and service mix, rather than as isolated opportunities. Consequently, it places responsibility on those who otherwise manage development in the host community rather than on event organizers (who are thereby allowed to get on with the many challenges of staging the event for which they are responsible).

Work on event leverage has so far focused primarily on economic development and social development. Recent work has endeavored to extend the leveraging paradigm to other targets that host communities have identified as important. Leveraging for economic development and social development are each reviewed. Then other targets of leverage are considered. As leveraging research and theory are still embryonic, implications for future work are noted throughout.

## Economic leverage of events

The literature on economic impacts from events recognizes event visitors and trade to be a core source of an event's economic value (Dwyer, Mellor, Mistilis, N., and Mules, 2000). From a place-marketing perspective, the media that events can generate for the host community, region, or nation can be another source of value

(Chalip and Costa, 2005). In order to optimize the value of event visitors and trade, the tactical challenges are to lengthen visitor stays, entice visitor spending during their time at the host destination, retain expenditures in the host community, and use the event to build or strengthen the relationships local businesses have with suppliers, customers, or partners. The fundamental goal is to create and retain streams of revenue through the event and through relationships, the event enables. In order to capitalize on event media to enhance the host community's image, the tactical challenge is to use event images and/or mentions in destination advertising and promotions and to incorporate destination images and/or mentions into event advertising and promotions. It is fundamentally a task of event and destination co-branding. The model is shown in Figure 2.1. Procedures for formulating specific tactics pursuant to each challenge are described in the original presentation (Chalip, 2004).

An examination of Figure 2.1 shows another difference between leverage and legacy. Leverage recognizes that over time, there is likely to be more than a single event at the host destination. This is important because events in the host community's portfolio can be cross-leveraged to increase the reach and frequency of associated communications and to enable enhanced business development and trade (Ziakas, 2014). In the process, there is ample opportunity to test, develop, and implant event-leveraging skills (Jago, Chalip, Brown, Mules, and Ali, 2003). As each event in the portfolio is part of the product and service mix that enables leveraging, each can be built into an overall strategic framework.

The model was initially developed from empirical work on effective and ineffective uses of events for economic development, as well as the literature on economic impacts from events. Research into application of the model has focused primarily on only a few elements at a time, and is relatively recent. Findings reviewed below support the utility of the model.

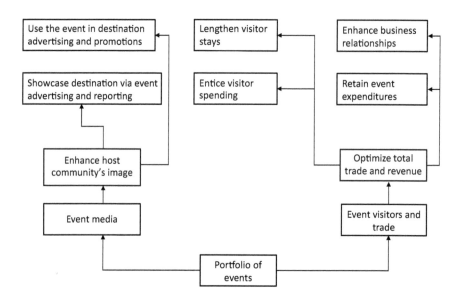

*Figure 2.1* A model for economic leverage of events

## Enticing visitor spending

The earliest demonstration of effective leverage to entice visitor spending comes from a comparative study of businesses surrounding the Gold Coast IndyCar race (Chalip and Leyns, 2002). That study demonstrated that most business managers hoped for an event legacy, failed to leverage, and thereby obtained scant benefit. Some businesses were harmed by the event as regular customers were deflected away by event crowds and activities. However, local businesses that formulated and implemented leveraging tactics benefited substantially. Further, the benefits were amplified when businesses in the same area formed alliances to initiate and implement coordinated leveraging tactics. Smith (2010) similarly showed that by working together and with the local council, businesses in Deptford were able to benefit from the Tour de France by using event-themed initiatives to capitalize on the event passing through their area.

Other research into economic leverage of events has focused primarily on tourism because tourism is a core driver of spending generated by events (Mondello and Rishe, 2004). Studies of tourism to events have demonstrated the value of thinking in terms of the host destination's product and service mix rather than about the event in isolation. By considering the overall product and service mix, marketing tactics that bundle the event with other attractions and activities can be applied to lengthen visitors' stays and increase visitors' overall spending (Chalip and McGuirty, 2004). The bundles can be made particularly attractive if they incorporate activities and experiences that are valued by the sport's subculture (Kim and Chalip, 2010) or that allow attendees to parade and celebrate their identification with the sport's subculture (Green and Chalip, 1998). Bundles that combine the event with other attractions may be particularly attractive to first-time visitors (Snelgrove and Wood, 2010), especially if they have engaged in long-haul travel to a novel destination (Kim and Chalip, 2004).

## Lengthening visitors' stays

Lengthening the term of an event by adding elements can also effectively increase visitors' stays and their consequent spending. The addition of adjunct activities can cause event attendees to come before the event or to stay after (Derom and Ramshaw, 2016; Derom and Van Wynsberghe, 2015; Green and Chalip, 1998). In order for those to be effective, however, they need to be consistent with the values and preferences of at least one segment of event attendees. Thus, the specific activities and experiences to be designed in any one case cannot be specified *a priori* but depend instead on the psychographics of the target market. Making it work is simply the application of marketing strategy (Green, 2001).

## Enhancing business relationships

Events are poor times to do business, but they can be useful occasions to create or strengthen business relationships. Using events, especially event-based hospitality, as a business-to-business relationship opportunity has a venerable place in sponsorship activation (Collett, 2008). Using events as relationship development opportunities is not limited to sponsors. The best documented application of leveraging an event to create and strengthen business relationships for sponsors and non-sponsors is the use of the Sydney Olympics by Australian economic developers to create venues and occasions for Australian business executives to meet and to host executives from overseas who attended the Games (O'Brien, 2006). Australian business development strategists found this tactic to be so effective that they have continued to use it at events hosted in Australia and have extended it to overseas events at which Australian athletes compete.

### *Retaining event expenditures*

If money is spent by event organizers or event attendees to purchase something from a vendor, and that vendor resides outside the local trading radius, then the money will leave the host area with the vendor, resulting in no economic gain to the host community or region (Dwyer et al., 2000). This has been termed "the booth effect" and is a challenge for event organizers who might prefer to hire expertise, purchase materials, or license merchandising from outside the event's local jurisdiction. It has been shown that the booth effect can be minimized by linking local labor and businesses to event organizers so that the use of local supplies of labor and material are optimized (Smith and Fox, 2007). This can require training and/or creation of alliances among local businesses (cf. Chalip, 2004).

### *Combining event media and destination promotions*

Integration of event media with destination media, as the model recommends, has also been shown to be of significant value. Australian tourism marketers were able to rebrand the country and promote tourist visits from overseas by creating a set of interlocking media tactics in key source markets throughout the lead-up to the Sydney Olympic Games (Chalip, 2000). Elsewhere, strategic integration of host destination images and icons into event media, particularly the event logo, has been shown to enhance the host destination's exposure through an event (Green, Fitzgerald, and Costa, 2003). Event communications featuring attractions that are consistent with event attendees' interests and values can attract them and encourage them to stay (Derom and Van Wynsberghe, 2015). Flow-on tourism beyond the event is fostered when prospective event attendees are encouraged and enabled to explore media that promotes destination features and opportunities (Taks, Chalip, Green, Késsene, and Martyn, 2009).

### *Lessons and challenges*

Taken together, these findings lend support to the model. However, the studies to date examine elements of the model in a piecemeal fashion. Evaluation of a comprehensive application has yet to be undertaken.

The need for such an evaluation is clear because applications remain haphazard and inconsistently applied. Pereira and her colleagues (2014) demonstrated that leveraging a portfolio of events can enhance economic development through tourism, and they subsequently showed (Pereira et al., 2015) that events in the portfolio can be cross-leveraged to enhance and strengthen the destination brand, particularly for brand associations that are featured among events in the portfolio. However, in both studies they found that leverage was incomplete and inconsistent because some vital alliances did not coalesce or were not sustained, and because the branding focus was not complemented by efforts to capitalize more fully on the visitors and trade that were generated by the portfolio. In a study of a small local event, O'Brien (2007) similarly found that leveraging could be effective but that its efficacy was compromised by haphazard and piecemeal formulation and implementation. These findings suggest that the efficacy of economic leverage of events could be strengthened through a more systematic application than has so far occurred. Further work is required to apply and test the model and to do so not merely with reference to single events but also with reference to a portfolio of events.

## Social leverage of events

Anthropologists have long recognized that events have social value and can even foster conditions that enable social change (Handelman, 1990). That insight and the associated requisites were built into the initial model for social leverage of events (Chalip, 2006). The model was subsequently modified to align more precisely with the model for economic leverage (O'Brien and Chalip, 2008). It is presented in Figure 2.2

Examination of the model shows that it recognizes liminality as the core leverageable resource. Liminality is a celebratory feeling associated with events that is accompanied by a sense that social rules and roles are relaxed or suspended altogether. When events render liminality, they enable exploration of social conditions that might be threatening if experienced outside a liminoid frame. This results in two opportunities: a social atmosphere of belonging (called "communitas" by anthropologists) and media attention that can explore social conditions in ways that might not otherwise be feasible. Together, these conditions bestow opportunities to align events with targeted social issues, to publicize target issues, to intensify engagement with those issues by lengthening visitor stays, and to showcase those issues in event advertising and reporting.

Although liminality has featured throughout anthropological studies of events (Chalip, 2006), it has rarely been invoked in studies of event leverage. A recent study of a soccer-for-the-homeless event (Welty Peachey, Borland, Lobpries, and Cohen, 2015) provides a salutary exception. Although the event is not a mega-event in the normal sense, it is relevant here because it illustrates that liminality is a potentially leverageable social resource. The study demonstrated that by aligning the event with the issue of homelessness, players' attachment to the event was cultivated, and they were thereby encouraged to make positive changes in their lives. Their engagement was furthered by the extension of the event through a four-day period. Throughout that time, social networking was encouraged, and empowering messages were layered through event communications. Ancillary events were incorporated, and theming was used to encourage celebrations that would intensify participants' and attendees' engagement with the issues of homelessness. The study concludes that the event "fostered liminality and associated

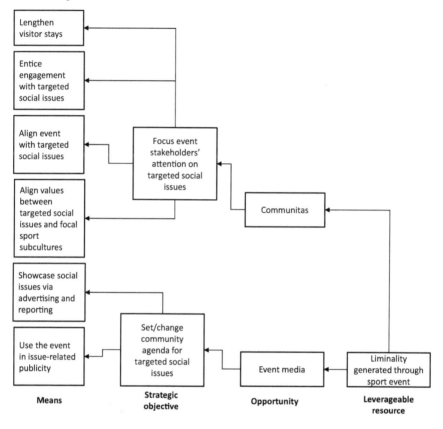

*Figure 2.2* A model for social leverage of events

*communitas*, which were then used to leverage bonding and bridging social capital and develop norms of trust and reciprocity" (Welty Peachey et al, 2015; p. 96).

The strategic use of communitas during an event was tested in the study of an annual event in a small Texas town (Ziakas and Costa, 2010). That study demonstrated that event organizers strategically combined arts with sport to foster communitas while celebrating local heritage. The result was a liminoid frame that enabled exploration of community discord, which was then resolved symbolically through the event and associated media. As a consequence, the community fabric was strengthened. The event became so meaningful to community residents that the vast majority attended each year, and former residents returned during the event to reestablish social ties.

Some studies have considered events that co-brand with social causes, but have done so without invoking liminality as a conceptual element. Rather, they have operationalized communitas as camaraderie. Yet the expected finding persists insomuch as the higher the sense of camaraderie, the greater the social impact, and the greater the sense of social responsibility that is engendered among participants (Inoue and Havard, 2014). Interestingly, the effect seems to be reciprocal insomuch as the association of an event with a social cause can enhance the quality of camaraderie (Filo, Funk, and O'Brien, 2009). Not only does the cause benefit, but so, too, do the sponsors – a finding that suggests a potential synergy between social leverage and economic leverage.

As with economic leverage, social leverage only seems to be effective if it is intentionally applied. It does not occur simply because an event takes place or because a legacy is invoked. For example, legacy planning around the parasport events at the Glasgow Commonwealth Games sought to broaden accessibility in order to enhance opportunities for persons with disabilities. However, since the effort was framed as legacy planning, it was focused on the event itself. Consequently, it was not strategically integrated into ongoing local, regional, or national initiatives. In other words, the parasport events were not strategically leveraged. As a result there was negligible impact (Misener, McGillivray, McPherson, and Legg, 2015). The difference that is made when legacy planning is supplanted by strategic leverage is illustrated in a study of social programming associated with the Melbourne Commonwealth Games (Kellett, Hede, and Chalip, 2008). Two communities that were enabled to form relationships with visiting teams were compared. One community developed an integrated set of tactics to deepen local knowledge and appreciation of the visiting team's national culture, and then to form sustainable networks reaching into the team's country. The other community chose only to welcome their visiting team ceremonially. The community that leveraged benefited tangibly; the one that did not leverage obtained no benefit.

The research reviewed earlier provides encouraging support for the social leveraging model. However, as with research into economic leverage, the studies remain piecemeal, and have considered only haphazard applications. A comprehensive evaluation of intentional efforts to apply the model needs to be undertaken. The potential for social and economic leverage to be made symbiotic should also be examined.

## Extending leverage

The idea that leverage can be beneficial is not new. It is inherent throughout the literature on strategic planning and management (Andrews et al., 2012; Tjemkes et al., 2012). Although the work to date has primarily considered economic and social leverage by host communities, other work has noted that the leveraging paradigm might be applied in unique ways to particular objectives of interest. The prominent four have been: environmental sustainability, sport participation, event leveraging by non-host communities, and leveraging event bids. Each of these is considered briefly in the following, and research needed to advance each is noted.

### Environmental sustainability

Events concentrate large numbers of people, their modes of transportation, and their equipment into a relatively small space for an intense time. Consequently, events can stress the environment. As a result, there has been substantial interest in how to predict and subsequently assess the environmental impact that events have

(Collins, Jones, and Munday, 2009), and some event owners and organizers, especially the IOC and its OCOGs, have endeavored to rebuff critics by claiming to be champions of environmental sustainability. Yet, event owners' and organizers' environmental policies and claims are often inconsistent and ephemeral (Paquette, Stevens, and Mallen, 2011; Casper & Kellison, Chapter 8). Given the significance of environmental challenges facing events, the initial effort to integrate economic and social models for event leverage (O'Brien and Chalip, 2008) endeavored to address environmental leverage by treating it as a special case of social leverage. It was suggested that events could be used to improve environmental attitudes and behaviors. Although that suggestion is consistent with the social leverage model, it has remained untested. The degree to which economic leverage or specifically targeted environmental interventions might also be brought to bear has not been considered. Further work is needed to develop, explore, and test leveraging to support environmental sustainability.

### *Sport participation*

Since physical activity is thought to support health, and sport is a form of physical activity, event bids typically claim (and some event owners require bids to claim) that hosting the event will stimulate sport participation in the host community, region, or nation. Sport participation is typically treated as an expected and valuable legacy from events. The problem with that expectation is that sport events do not normally render that outcome (Weed et al., 2015; Weed, Chapter 5). Since a participation legacy is anticipated, the necessary tactics for leverage are inadequately formulated, and poorly implemented, if at all (Bretherton, Piggin, and Bodet, 2016; Misener, Taks, Chalip, and Green, 2015), due in part to the complex array of sport organizations that need to be involved (Bloyce and Lovett, 2012). Yet, experts agree that tactics appropriate for building sport participation can be formulated, and the experience of building a lasting sport development infrastructure from the Los Angeles Olympic Games supports that view (Chalip, Green, Taks, and Misener, 2016). More work is needed to determine the parameters for effective leverage of sport events to build sport participation.

### *Leverage by non-host communities*

When an international sport event comes to a country, visiting teams must find places to do their acclimatization training, and event visitors may want to engage in some tourism. Thus, it could make sense for non-host communities in the region of an event to leverage it to attract visiting teams and event attendees. A comparative study of leveraging visiting teams' acclimatization training in three Australian communities prior to the Sydney Olympics demonstrated that the more intensively that a community formulated and implemented leveraging tactics, the more benefits it obtained (Gardiner and Chalip, 2006). A study of the ways that Cameroon and Nigeria leveraged South Africa's hosting of the FIFA World Cup also demonstrated some tourism and sport development gains (Tichaawa and Bob,

2015). Extending leverage to non-host communities has the potential to spread event benefits. It warrants more focused research attention.

### Event bids

More places bid for major events than actually win the right to host them. There is evidence that bidding can enable economic and social leverage even if the bid is not successful (Abebe, Bolton, Pavelka, and Pierstorff, 2014; Alberts, 2009; Beneworth and Dauncey, 2010). At the request of the Dutch NOC*NSF, Chalip and Heere (2014) formulated a model for leveraging an Olympic bid. However, when the government of the Netherlands decided not to bid to host the Olympic Games, the model was not applied. It needs to be tested.

## Concluding observation

Consider the magician. The magician's illusions work because the audience's attention is distracted. The audience is fooled because they do not see the trick. The legacy framework is illusory in precisely the same way. The hegemonic discourses of event owners (and, too often, event bidders and event organizers) focus attention on each event and its purported benefits. By the time we realize that we have been tricked, the event is over. Mega-events move on, and we are left with claims that fail to withstand conceptual or empirical scrutiny. By putting our faith and our attention on the event itself, we fail to develop a framework for integrating the event with the product and service mix at the host destination in ways that would enable us to use it strategically.

By so doing, we no longer focus on event legacy but think instead about leveraging each event as part of the host community's entire portfolio of events. Strategic leveraging has proved to be systematically coherent and empirically useful. What an event leaves behind is not a legacy of the event per se; rather, it is a result of how each event in the host community's portfolio has (and has not) been used as a tool. An event's utility as a tool depends on what the community seeks to achieve, and how it then pursues those ends by using the event in conjunction with the products and services it can also bring to bear. That is leverage.

Event owners, event advocates, and event organizers have a public relations interest in promoting legacy, but scholars and public officials have no obligation to play along. Leverage is not merely a generative framework for research; it is the more fulfilling framework for practice.

## References

Abebe, N., Bolton, M. T., Pavelka, M., and Pierstorff, M. (Eds.). (2014). *Bidding for development: How the Olympic bid process can accelerate transportation development.* New York: Springer.

Alberts, H. (2009). Berlin's failed bid to host the 2000 Summer Olympic Games: Urban development and the improvements of sport facilities. *International Journal of Urban and Regional Research*, *33*, 502–516.

Andrews, R., Boyne, G. A., Law, J., and Walker, R. M. (2012). *Strategic management and public service performance.* New York: Palgrave Macmillan.

Bason, T., Cook, D., and Anagnostopoulos, C. (2015). Legacy in major sport events: Empirical insights from the 2010 FIFA World Cup in South Africa. *Coregia*, *11*, 43–61.

Beesley, L. G., and Chalip, L. (2011). Seeking (and not seeking) to leverage mega-sport events in non-host destinations: The case of Shanghai and the Beijing Olympics. *Journal of Sport & Tourism*, *16*, 323–344.

Bell, B., and Gallimore, K. (2015). Embracing the Games? Leverage and legacy of London 2012 Olympics at the sub-regional level by means of strategic partnerships. *Leisure Studies*, *34*, 720–741.

Beneworth, P., and Dauncey, H. (2010). International urban festivals as a catalyst for governance capacity building. *Environment and Planning C*, *28*, 1093–1100.

Bloyce, D., and Lovett, E. (2012). Planning for the London 2012 Olympic and Paralympic legacy: A figurational analysis. *International Journal of Sport Policy and Politics*, *4, 361–377.*

Bretherton, P., Piggin, J., and Bodet, G. (2016). Olympic sport and physical activity promotion: The rise and fall of the London 2012 pre-event mass participation 'legacy.' *International Journal of Sport Policy & Politics*, *8*, 609–624.

Cashman, R. (2006). The bitter-sweet awakening: The legacy of the Sydney 2000 Olympic Games. Sydney: Walla Walla Press.

Chalip, L. (2000). An interview with Maggie White, Business Manager Olympic Games for the Australian Tourist Commission. *International Journal of Sports Marketing and Sponsorship*, *2*, 9–19.

Chalip, L. (2004). Beyond impact: A general model for sport event leverage. In B. W. Ritchie and D. Adair (Eds.), *Sport tourism interrelationships: Impacts and issues* (pp. 226–252). Clevedon: Channel View Publications.

Chalip, L. (2006). Towards social leverage of sport events. *Journal of Sport & Tourism*, *17*, 109–127.

Chalip, L. (2017). Event bidding, legacy, and leverage. In R. Hoye and M. M. Parent (Eds.), *Sage handbook of sport management* (pp. 401–421). Los Angeles, CA: Sage.

Chalip, L., and Costa, C. A. (2005). Sport event tourism and the destination brand: Towards a general theory. *Sport in Society*, *8*, 218–237.

Chalip, L., Green, B. C., Taks, M., and Misener, L. (2016). Creating sport participation from sport events: Making it happen. *International Journal of Sport Policy and Politics*. Retrieved February 13, 2017, from http://dx.doi.org/10.1080/19406940.2016.1257496

Chalip, L., and Heere, B. (2014). Leveraging sport events: Fundamentals and application to bids. In I. Henry and L-M. Ko (Eds.), *Routledge handbook of sport policy* (pp. 183–193). New York: Routledge.

Chalip, L., and Leyns, A. (2002). Local business leveraging of a sport event: Managing an event for economic benefit. *Journal of Sport Management*, *16*, 132–158.

Chalip, L., and McGuirty, J. (2004). Bundling sport events with the host destination. *Journal of Sport Tourism*, *9*, 267–282.

Collett, P. (2008). Sponsorship-related hospitality: Planning for measurable success. *Journal of Sponsorship*, *1*, 286–296.

Collins, A., Jones, C., and Munday, M. (2009). Assessing the environmental impacts of mega sporting events: Two options? *Tourism Management*, *30*, 828–837.

Derom, I., and Ramshaw, G. (2016). Leveraging sport heritage to promote tourism destinations: The case of the Tour of Flanders Cyclo event. *Journal of Sport & Tourism*, *20*, 263–283.

Derom, L., and Van Wynsberghe, R. (2015). Extending the benefits of leveraging cycling events: Evidence from the Tour of Flanders. *European Sport Management Quarterly*, *15*, 111–131.

Dickson, T. J., Benson, A. J., and Blackman, D. A. (2011). Developing a framework for evaluating Olympic and Paralympic legacies. *Journal of Sport & Tourism, 16*, 285–302.

Dwyer, L., Mellor, R., Mistilis, N., and Mules, T. (2000). A framework for assessing "tangible" and "intangible impacts of events and conventions. *Event Management, 6*, 175–189.

Filo, K., Funk, D. C., and O'Brien, D. (2009). The meaning behind attachment: Exploring camaraderie, cause, and competency at a charity event. *Journal of Sport Management, 23*, 361–397.

Gardiner, S., and Chalip, L. (2006). Leveraging a mega-event when not the host city: Lessons from pre-Olympic training. Gold Coast, QLD: Sustainable Tourism.

Green, B. C. (2001). Leveraging subculture and identity to promote sport events. *Sport Management Review, 4*, 1–19.

Green, B. C., and Chalip, L. (1998). Sport tourism as the celebration of subculture. *Annals of Tourism Research, 25*, 275–291.

Green, B. C., Fitzgerald, M., and Costa, C. (2003). Marketing the host city: Analyzing exposure generated by a sport event. *International Journal of Sports Marketing and Sponsorship, 4*, 48–66.

Grix, J., and Houlihan, B. (2014). Sports mega-events as part of a nation's soft power strategy: The cases of Germany (2006) and the UK (2012). *British Journal of Politics and International Relations, 16*, 572–596.

Grix, J., and Lee, D. (2013). Soft power, sports mega-events and emerging states: The lure of the politics of attraction. *Global Society: Journal of Interdisciplinary International Relations, 27*, 521–536.

Groothuis, P. A., and Rotthoff, K. W. (2016). The economic impact and civic pride effects of sports teams and mega-events: Do the public and the professionals agree? *Economic Affairs, 36*, 21–32.

Handelman, D. (1990). *Models and mirrors: Towards an anthropology of public events.* New York: Cambridge University Press.

Inoue, Y., and Havard, C. T. (2014). Determinants and consequences of the perceived social impact of a sport event. *Journal of Sport Management, 28*, 295–310.

Jago, L., Chalip, L., Brown, G., Mules, T., and Ali, S. (2003). Building events into destination branding: Insights from experts. *Event Management, 8*, 3–14.

Kellett, P., Hede, A-M., and Chalip, L. (2008). Social policy for sport events: Leveraging (relationships with) teams from other nations for community benefit. *European Sport Management Quarterly, 8*, 101–121.

Kim, H-I., and Chalip, L. (2010). Capitalizing on a sport's association with an international destination: The illustrative case of tae kwon do. *Journal of Sport & Tourism, 15*, 307–335.

Kim, N-S., and Chalip, L. (2004). Why travel to the FIFA World Cup? Effects of motives, background, interest, and constraints. *Tourism Management, 25*, 695–707.

Lamla, M. J., Straub, M., and Girsberger, E. M. (2014). On the economic impact of international sport events: Microevidence from survey data at the EURO 2008. *Applied Economics, 46*, 1693–1703.

Leopkey, B., and Parent, M. M. (2012). The (neo) institutionalization of legacy and its sustainable governance within the Olympic Movement. *European Sport Management Quarterly, 12*, 437–455.

Leopkey, B., and Parent, M. M. (2015). Stakeholder perspectives regarding governance of legacy at the Olympic Games. *Annals of Leisure Research, 18*, 528–548.

MacAloon, J. J. (2008). 'Legacy' as a managerial magical discourse in contemporary Olympic affairs. *International Journal of the History of Sport, 25*, 2060–2071.

Misener, L., Taks, M., Chalip, L., and Green, B. C. (2015). The elusive "trickle down effect" of sport events: Assumptions and missed opportunities. *Managing Sport and Leisure, 20*, 135–156.

Misener, L., McGillivray, D., McPherson, G., and Legg, D. (2015). Leveraging parasport events for sustainable community participation: The Glasgow 2014 Commonwealth Games. *Annals of Leisure Research, 18*, 450–469.

Mondello, M. J., and Rishe, P. (2004). Comparative economic impact analyses: Differences across cities, events, and demographics. *Economic Development Quarterly, 18*, 331–342.

Mules, T. (1998). Taxpayer subsidies for major sporting events. *Sport Management Review, 1*, 25–43.

Nichols, G., and Ralston, R. (2015). The legacy costs of delivering the 2012 Olympic and Paralympic Games through regulatory capitalism. *Leisure Studies, 34*, 389–404.

O'Brien, D. (2006). Event business leveraging: They Sydney 2000 Olympic Games. *Annals of Tourism Research, 33*, 240–261.

O'Brien, D. (2007). Points of leverage: Maximizing host community benefit from a regional surfing festival. *European Sport Management Quarterly, 7*, 141–165.

O'Brien, D., and Chalip, L. (2008). Sport events and strategic leveraging: Pushing towards the triple bottom line. In A. G. Woodside and D. Martin (Eds.), *Tourism management: Analysis, behaviour and strategy* (pp. 318–338). Oxford: CAB International.

Oshimi, D., Harada, M., and Fukuhara, T. (2016). Residents' perception on the social impacts of an international sport event: Applying panel data design and a moderating variable. *Journal of Convention and Event Tourism, 17*, 294–317.

Paquette, J., Stevens, J., and Mallen, C. (2011). The interpretation of environmental sustainability by the International Olympic Committee and Organizing Committees of the Olympic Games from 1994 to 2008. *Sport in Society, 14*, 355–369.

Pentifallo, C., and Van Wynsberghe, R. (2014). 'Leaving Las Megas' or can sustainability ever be social? Vancouver 2010 in post-political perspective. In J. Grix (Ed.), *Leveraging legacies from sports mega-events: Concepts and cases* (pp. 73–85). New York: Palgrave Macmillan.

Pereira, E. C. S., Mascarenhas, M. V. M., Flores, A. J. G., and Pires, G. M. V. S. (2014). Naurtical sports events portfolio as a driver to innovative dynamics. *Journal of Maritime Research, 11*, 17–23.

Pereira, E. C. S., Mascarenhas, M. V. M., Flores, A. J. G., and Pires, G. M. V. S. (2015). Nautical small-scale sports events portfolio: A strategic leveraging approach. *European Sport Management Quarterly, 15*, 27–47.

Preuss, H. (2015). A framework for identifying the legacies of a mega sport event. *Leisure Studies, 34*, 643–664.

Putsis, W. P. (1998). Winners and losers: Redistribution and the use of economic impact analysis in marketing. *Journal of Macromarketing, 18*, 24–33.

Sant, S-L., and Mason, D. S. (2015). Framing event legacy in a prospective host city: Managing Vancouver's Olympic bid. *Journal of Sport Management, 29*, 42–56.

Smith, A. (2010). Leveraging benefits from major events: Maximising opportunities for peripheral urban areas. *Managing Leisure, 15*, 161–180.

Smith, A., and Fox, T. (2007). From 'event-led' to 'event-themed' regeneration: The 2002 Commonwealth Games Legacy Scheme. *Urban Studies, 44*, 1125–1143.

Snelgrove, R., and Wood, L. (2010). Attracting and leveraging visitors at a charity cycling event. *Journal of Sport & Tourism, 15*, 269–285.

Swart, K., and Bob, U. (2012). Mega sport event legacies and the 2010 FIFA World Cup. *African Journal for Physical, Health Education, Recreation, and Dance*, (Supplement 1), 1–11.

Taks, M., Chalip, L., Green, B. C., Késsene, S., and Martyn, S. (2009). Factors affecting repeat visitation and flow-on tourism as sources of event strategy sustainability. *Journal of Sport & Tourism*, *14*, 121–142.

Taks, M., Késsene, S., Chalip, L., and Green, B. C. (2011). Economic impact analysis versus cost benefit analysis: The case of a medium sized sport event. *International Journal of Sport Finance*, *6*, 187–203.

Taks, M., Misener, L., Chalip, L., and Green, B. C. (2013). Leveraging sport events for participation. *Canadian Journal of Social Research*, *3*, 12–23.

Tichaawa, T. M., Bama, H. K. N., and Swart, K. (2015). Community perceptions of the socio-economic legacies of the 2010 FIFA World Cup in Nelson Mandela Bay, Port Elizabeth, South Africa: A four-year post-event analysis. *African Journal for Physical, Health Education, Recreation & Dance*, *21*, 1376–1388.

Tichaawa, T. M., and Bob, U. (2015). Leveraging mega-events beyond the host nation: A case study of the 2010 FIFA World Cup African Legacy Programme in Cameroon and Nigeria. *Leisure Studies*, *34*, 742–757.

Tjemkes, B., Pepijn, V., and Burgers, K. (2012). *Strategic alliance management*. London: Routledge.

Weed, M. (2014). Is tourism a legitimate legacy from the Olympic and Paralympic Games? An analysis of London 2012 legacy strategy using programme theory. *Journal of Sport & Tourism*, *19*, 101–126.

Weed, M., Coren, E., Fiore, J., Wellard, I., Chatziefstathiou, D., and Dowse, S. (2015). The Olympic Games and raising sport participation: A systematic review of evidence and an interrogation of policy for a demonstration effect. *European Sport Management Quarterly*, *15*, 195–226.

Welty Peachey, J., Borland, J., Lobpries, J., and Cohen, A. (2015). Managing impact: Leveraging sacred spaces and community celebration to maximize social capital at a sport-for-development event. *Sport Management Review*, *18*, 86–98.

Whitson, D., and Macintosh, D. (1996). The global circus: International sport, tourism, and the marketing of cities. *Journal of Sport & Social Issues*, *23*, 278–295.

Ziakas, V. (2014). Event portfolio planning and management: A holistic approach. London: Routledge.

Ziakas, V., and Costa, C. A. (2010). Between theatre and sport in a rural event: Evolving utility and community development from the inside-out. *Journal of Sport & Tourism*, *15*, 7–26.

# 3 Mega events

## Why cities are willing to host them, despite the lack of economic benefits

*Harry Arne Solberg*

Cities and nations bidding for mega sports events usually expect the events to leave behind a legacy. Although different definitions of legacy exist, the categorisation by Chappelet (2006), which distinguishes between (1) sporting legacy, (2) economic legacy, (3) infrastructural legacy, (4) urban legacy, and (5) social legacy may serve as an appropriate definition in this context. The expectations of potential host cities is best illustrated by Edinburgh's unsuccessful bid to host stages of the 2014 Tour de France race. In a report, the director of Corporate Governance in Edinburgh compiled a list of the following benefits they anticipated to achieve (City of Edinburgh Council, 2012):

- Health benefits for residents
- A boost for sport and leisure cycling and more active travel by residents
- Up to 10,000 bed-nights to accommodate the Tour riders, their entourage and the media
- An estimated economic impact of over £24 million for the city
- Global TV exposure worth over £4 million plus a significant proportion of the total media equivalent value of the Tour in Great Britain, valued at around £21 million
- Anticipated economic impact for Scotland as a whole, valued between £45 and £55 million

However, as pointed out by Preuss (2007), not all legacies are positive. The academic literature has questioned whether the benefits outweigh the investments. Empirical research has documented a number of cases where the benefits did not justify the investments. One example are the many cost overruns on venues, of which some have ended up as "White Elephants", where the capacity significantly exceeds the needs after the event, or cases where the tourism impacts have been more moderate than predicted (Alm, Solberg, Storm, and Jakobsen, 2014; Andreff, 2012; Flyvbjerg and Stewart, 2012; Solberg and Preuss, 2015; Spilling, 1998; Zimbalist, 2015).

Despite these experiences, the owners of these events have usually been able to recruit applicants. This is illustrated in Table 3.1, which shows the number of applicants for the Olympic Games for the period from 1980 to 2022. However, the table also shows two periods of exceptions. The first was in the 1980s when

*Table 3.1* Applicants of Olympic Games

|  | Applicants | Withdraws |
|---|---|---|
| 2022 Beijing Winter Olympics | 6 | 4 |
| 2020 Tokyo Olympics | 6 | 1 |
| 2018 PyenongChang Winter Olympics | 3 |  |
| 2016 Rio de Janeiro Olympics | 7 |  |
| 2014 Sochi Winter Olympics | 7 |  |
| 2012 London Olympics | 8 |  |
| 2010 Vancouver Winter Olympics | 8 |  |
| 2008 Beijing Olympics | 10 |  |
| 2006 Turin Winter Olympics | 4 |  |
| 2004 Athens Olympics | 11 |  |
| 2002 Salt Lake City Winter Olympics | 9 |  |
| 2000 Sydney Olympics | 8 |  |
| 1998 Nagano Winter Olympics | 5 |  |
| 1996 Atlanta Olympics | 6 |  |
| 1994 Lillehammer Winter Olympics | 4 |  |
| 1992 Barcelona Olympics | 6 |  |
| 1992 Albertville Winter Olympics | 7 |  |
| 1988 Seoul Olympics | 5 |  |
| 1988 Calgary Winter Olympics | 3 |  |
| 1984 Los Angeles Olympics | 1 |  |
| 1984 Sarajevo Winter Olympics | 3 |  |
| 1980 Moscow Olympics | 2 |  |
| 1980 Lake Placid Winter Olympics | 1 |  |

Source: http://gamesbids.com/eng/past-bid-results/

there were two occasions with only one applicant and on one occasion only two. The second period refers to the upcoming Olympic Games in the 2020s, where several cities have withdrawn their applications. For example, Oslo, Lviv, Krakow, and Stockholm all withdrew their application for the 2022 Winter Olympic Games. Additionally, Boston and Hamburg cancelled their plans of applying for the 2024 Olympic Games. Rome also withdrew their application for the 2020 Olympic Games because the national government was unwilling to financially support their bid.

Since 1986, the number of applicant nations for the FIFA World Cup has never been less than three, apart from 2014 when Brazil was the only applicant. The interest in hosting the UEFA Euro Cup has also been stable, as seen in Table 3.2 Since the tournament was extended to 16 teams in 1996, there has never been fewer than three bids.

In general, investors tend to pull out from industries where firms struggle with financial problems over some time. This, however, has not been the case in the business of major sports events, except from the two periods where the interest to host the Olympic Games was moderate. Table 3.2 and 3.3 shows that neither FIFA nor UEFA have lacked applicant to host the World Cup and the European Championship for national teams. Likewise, Amaury Sport Organisation (ASO), the owner of Tour de France has not struggled with finding cities willing to host races of the Tour de France. When London pulled out from the 2017 race, the city of Düsseldorf

*Table 3.2* Hosts and bidders of the FIFA World Cup

|  | Number of bidding nations |
| --- | --- |
| 2022 Qatar | 5 |
| 2018 Russia | 6 |
| 2014 Brazil | 1 |
| 2010 South-Africa | 5 |
| 2006 Germany | 5 |
| 2002 Japan/Korea | 3 |
| 1998 France | 3 |
| 1994 USA | 3 |
| 1990 Italy | 4 |
| 1986 Mexico | 4 |

Source: http://de.fifa.com/mm/document/fifafacts/mencompwc/51/97/81/fs-201_13a_fwc-host-announcement.pdf

*Table 3.3* Hosts and bidders of UEFA Euro

| Host | Number of bids | Joint bids |
| --- | --- | --- |
| 2016 France | 4 | 1 (withdrawn) |
| 2012 Poland/Ukraine | 8 | 2 |
| 2008 Austria/Switzerland | 7 | 4 |
| 2004 Portugal | 4 | 1 |
| 2000 Belgium/Netherlands | 3 | 1 |
| 1996 England | 5 | |

Source: UEFA.com

was willing to take over. Although some cities withdrawn the application to host the Olympics, it is too early to conclude that this tendency is permanent. When looking back the last 35 years, international sport governing bodies have not lacked applicants willing to host their events. After the successful hosting of the 1984 Olympics, cities were again lining up to host the Games. The International Olympic Committee's (IOC's) Agenda 2020, indicates that they are concerned that the many experiences with cost overruns can have a permanent effect (IOC, 2017). If it is successful, this can encourage more cities to apply for the Games.

The reason for this paradox is also the main research issue in this chapter. Why are cities and nations willing to expend so many resources on acquiring the events, despite negative previous experiences by other hosts? What are the dynamic forces behind this paradox? Theoretical perspectives based on auction theory and principal–agent theory are used to guide this analysis.

## Mega sports events – definition and ownership

The first definitions of mega events in the literature focused very much on the tourism dimension, that is, the ability to attract tourists (Jafari, 1988; Ritchie and Yangzhou, 1987). Since then, other dimensions such as media coverage and the cost perspective have become more prevalent. Müller (2015) proposes four constitutive dimensions of mega-events: visitor attractiveness, media reach, costs, and transformative impact. He developed a multidimensional, point based classification scheme of large events, which classifies events into three size classes: *major events*, *mega-events* and *giga-events*. It is important to have in mind the relative dimension, that is, size of the event relative to the city. In cities of a moderate size, events significantly smaller than the Olympic Games can have an impact that is comparable to what *giga-events* can have in large metropolitan areas. The geographical size of the region also affects the outcomes. For example, the impacts from team tournaments that are hosted in a number of cities, and cycling races that stretch out over large territories will be less concentrated compared with those that are hosted only in one city.

Most of the literature that has investigated the impacts has focused on one-off events, which refer to events that move from place to place (e.g., the Olympic Games and the FIFA World Cup). However, mega events can include recurring events (e.g., events that are held regularly within the same region). One such example is the Tour de France, the biggest mega sports event in the world in terms of spectators. The three-week cycling race attracts 10 to 15 million spectators along the roads each year (Andreff, 2016). In comparison, the Summer Olympic Games sold on average 5.7 million tickets in the period from 1984 to 2012, while the Winter Olympic Games had an average of 1.3 million in the period from 1988 to 2010 (IOC, 2014). The FIFA World Cup has attracted an average of 3.1 million spectators after the tournament was extended to 32 teams in 1998 (FIFA.com, 2017). In terms of TV viewers, however, the FIFA World Cup and the Olympic Games are the largest events.

Different ownership models exist, and the same applies to the objectives of the owners. The IOC, as the owner of the Olympic Games, and international sports federations (e.g., FIFA) as owners of the international football championships, operate as non-profit organisations. International non-profit sport federations earn most of their revenue from international championships and mega events such as the Olympic Games. A significant proportion of the revenue is distributed to national federations, which in turn, is used to finance sport activities.

## Mega events – what have they created?

This section presents an overview of experiences from mega events based on empirical research. The focus in this book is on legacy, a concept that usually relates to long-term impacts. However, for some of the stakeholders involved in the events (e.g., the tourism industry and local residents), the impacts during the event period are also of importance. These stakeholders can influence the application process, for example, by lobbying politicians to fund the event. Therefore, it is important to analyse the decision-making processes and factors that influence stakeholder behavior.

### *Cost overruns and white elephants*

Many previous hosts of the Olympic Games have invested heavily in upgrading communication and infrastructure, for example in new airports. This is in addition to investments in venues. Analyses of whether the investments are worth the money must be based on how much is being spent. Some events may be considered profitable for the host region if the initial cost budgets were sufficient. However, the history of such events includes many cases of cost overruns. Research by Flyvbjerg and Stewart (2012) showed that the Olympic Games from 1962 to 2010 had an average cost overrun of 179 per cent in real terms – and 324 per cent in nominal terms. Indeed, they concluded that significant cost overruns have been the rule, not the exceptions, and that Olympic cost overruns historically have been significantly larger than for other types of mega-projects.

The 2014 Winter Olympic Games in Sochi had the highest cost increase in history when investments in infrastructure were included. The total costs were measured at $55 billion, an increase of 4.5 times from the $12 billion forecast at the time of the bid. Of this, $16 billion were sports-related costs. This made Sochi the second-most expensive Olympic Games in terms of sports-related costs and the most expensive Olympic Games in terms of cost per event (Müller, 2015). However, Sochi is not the only host with such experiences. The 1976 Olympic Games in Montreal left local taxpayers with a debt of CAN$1.04 billion, which took 30 years to pay off. The 1992 Winter Olympic Games in Albertville, where the inhabitants were left with a debt of FF 11,000 on average (per capita), and which was financed by a 4% increase in local housing tax, and the 2004 Athens Olympic Games, where the Greek taxpayers will have to pay for the Games deficit until 2030, are other examples (Andreff, 2012).

The Olympic Games, however, are not the only events that have experienced cost overruns. In the bid book for the 2010 FIFA World Cup in South Africa, the estimated costs of stadia were $102 million, while the final costs amounted to $1.59 billion (Solberg and Preuss, 2015). Portugal, the host of the UEFA Euro Cup 2004, and Brazil, the host of the 2014 FIFA World Cup, also experienced significant cost overruns on the venues, which resulted in financial burdens for many cities in these countries (Alm, 2012; Matheson, 2014).

Many venues constructed for mega events have ended up as *white elephants*. One recent example is the 2014 World Cup in Brazil, where a total of $3.6 billion was spent on building five new stadiums and renovating seven existing ones, of which several have ended up as white elephants. One of the worst examples is the stadium in Brasilia, which hosted seven World Cup matches. The 72,000-capacity stadium cost $900 million, three times the estimated cost, making it the most expensive World Cup stadium. Brasilia does not have a professional team, and most of the matches staged here have involved local semi-professional sides. The stadium in Manaus, which hosted four World Cup matches cost $300 million, almost $50 million over budget. Matches in the Amazonian state championship have drawn attendances of fewer than 1,000, and like Brasilia, there is no local team playing in Brazil's top league. The stadium has a capacity of 44,000 and has been kept afloat using public money (Matheson, 2014). Similar problems also occurred after the FIFA World Cup in Japan/Korea (2002), South Africa (2010), and in Portugal after the UEFA Cup 2004, which were all left with several White Elephant stadia (Alm, 2012).

The major reason for the "white elephants" are the requirements by organization's governing bodies. For example, FIFA requires the venue hosting the opening game and the final to have a net capacity of at least 80,000, while the venues hosting the semi-finals must have a net capacity of at least 60,000. For the other group matches, the requirement is a capacity of at least 40,000 people. For the 2016 UEFA Euro Cup in France, UEFA required two stadiums with a net capacity of at least 50,000, preferably including one which held 60,000, three stadiums with a net capacity of at least 40,000 and four stadiums with a net capacity of at least 30,000 (Alm, 2012).

However, history also includes positive examples. Germany (2006), France (1998) and the US (1994) have all had satisfying utilisation of their stadia after the World Cup, both in terms of capacity utilisation and cost efficiency. Clubs in the German Bundesliga have attracted an average in excess of 40,000 people in recent years, which are the highest attendance figures in European club football (Statista, 2017). The 1994 World Cup in the US only used existing stadiums, and France only constructed one new stadium for the 1998 tournament. Therefore, the post event utilisation of venues used for these tournaments has been significantly more efficient than those used in 2002, 2010 and 2014 (see Preuss, Solberg, and Alm [2014] and Matheson [2014] for more details).

### Tourism legacy

The tourism industry often expects a growth in inbound tourism after the event is over. This can stimulate investments, (i.e. new hotels), but also other tourist related facilities. Whether this will occur depends on the ability of the events to promote the host city, both among the visitors during the event as well as in the media. Further, it cannot be taken for granted that the promotion will automatically create intentions for post-event visits. A survey from Norway by Ulvnes and Solberg (2016) investigated to what degree people remembered where previous sports events had been hosted, but also whether they were motivated to visit previous host cities as well as future events hosted elsewhere in the world. The research, which concentrated on sports and events that were popular among Norwegians, showed that peoples' explicit memory of previous host destinations was generally low and that the majority soon forgot where the events had been hosted. Not surprisingly, those that were most interested in sport scored better on explicit memory and remembered more about previous host cities and host nations than others. The results showed that the promotion created intentions among some respondents to visit previous host destinations, but also intentions to visit future hosts of similar events were stronger than the intentions to visit previous hosts. This indicates that the events are more efficient in stimulating people to visit similar events in the future, than causing post event tourism in previous host cities.

The lack of memory corresponds with the research by Oldenboom (2006), who investigated the promotion effects from the 2000 UEFA Euro Cup in Belgium and the Netherlands. The main conclusion was that an overwhelming majority soon forgot where the championships had been held. Ritchie and Smith (1991) documented a similar pattern for the 1988 Winter Olympic Games in Calgary, Canada. Some temporary improvements in the knowledge of Calgary were registered among Europeans, but also a quick "back to normal". Other literature has shown no or mixed results concerning changes in image (Chalip, Green, and Hill, 2003; Mossberg and Hallberg, 1999). Surveys in connection to the 2000 Sydney Olympic Games and the 2004 Winter Olympic Games in Turin show that the promotion effects can even have negative implications (Gripsrud, Nes, and Olsson, 2010; Rivenburgh, Louw, Loo, and Mersham, 2003).

For the tourism industry, the visitors during the event period may also be of importance. To precisely measure these impacts, it is necessary to adjust for crowding out impacts, which refer to visitors who otherwise would have come, but who stay away because of expectations of lack of accommodation and/or cost increases during the event period. Likewise, it is also necessary to not include casuals, that is, visitors who appear for other reasons than the event. If not, the event related impacts will be inflated. See Preuss (2005) for a profound discussion of these and related pitfalls. Empirical research has documented many incidents where consultants have overestimated the short-term tourism impacts (Zimbalist, 2015)

According to Baade and Matheson (2016), the number of international visitors to the UK fell to 6,174,000 visitors in July and August 2012, the months of the Olympic Games, from 6,568,000 the year before. Furthermore, some popular shows in London's theater district actually shut down during the Games. Similarly, Beijing reported a 30 per cent drop in international visitors and a 39 per cent drop in hotel occupancy during the month of the 2008 Games compared to the previous year. Utah ski resorts noted a 9.9 per cent fall in skier days in the 2001–02 season during the Salt Lake City Winter Games, compared to the previous year, along with a drop in taxable sales collections at these locations. Zimbalist (2015, pp. 39–40) presents an overview of studies from 19 events, where the findings show that net tourism effects were either not measured, or the impacts were moderate or significantly less than expected. This involves both short-term effects and long-term effects.

### Improvement of health conditions

Host cities often expect that the events will stimulate people to exercise more and in that way improve their health, as the document from Edinburgh showed (City of Edinburgh Council, 2012). It is well documented that acceleration in sports participation could improve people's health (Gratton and Taylor, 2000). However, whether the hosting of mega sports events causes a growth in sport participation is dubious. A systematic review of literature published between 1978 and 2008 by Mahtani et al. (2013, p. 1) concluded that "there is a paucity of evidence to support the notion that hosting the Olympic Games leads to an increased participation in physical or sporting activities for host countries". They also found little evidence to suggest other health benefits (See Chapter 5 for further details).

These findings correspond with research related to the Olympic Games, the FIFA World Cup and the Rugby World Cup, which concluded that

[i]t may be that the primary agenda of mass sporting events is not a serious public health opportunity, and that events are more in the arena of short term public entertainment, as "bread and circuses", rather than a missed public health opportunity. Although some civic infrastructure results, this has not been shown to relate to population physical activity levels. No examples from mass events, with shared interagency planning and a clear public health agenda can be identified to counter this.

(Murphy and Bauman, 2007, p. 18)

There have been some indications that the events create intentions to increase physical activity, particularly among men. However, evidence suggests that these intentions are not actually carried out after the events are over. The results from surveys related to 2000 Sydney Olympic Games and the 2012 London Olympic Games suggest that mega sporting events, by themselves, may be unlikely to have a sustained influence on population physical activity behaviour in the host cities and nations (Bauman, Bellew, and Craig, 2015; Downward, Dawson, and Mills, 2015).

### Intangibles – the "feel-good factor"

Despite the many examples of mega sports events failing to live up to the expectations in terms of tangible effects, the literature nevertheless indicates that people both welcome the events and do not regret hosting them. A survey by Preuss and Solberg (2006) based on empirical data from 117 polls of urban and national residents from 54 events, collected at 84 different locations, showed that three out of four residents supported hosting the event. The surveys came from both events that had been hosted, but also from cities that were never awarded any events. The data also showed growth in support during the period leading up to the events and that the peak level was reached shortly after they were finished. The support was strongest in low-income nations, while people in nations where the public sector had a high financial deficit per capita in the years before the poll tended to be sceptical. We can only speculate about the reasons for these findings. One explanation can be that people in low-income nations hope the events will stimulate activities and hence create jobs. Another reason can be that the events are welcome breaks from daily routines. While wealthy people can afford go away on holidays, this is something low-income groups may not afford.

Recent research has highlighted the "feel-good factor" as a major reason for this support. Kavetsos and Szymanski (2010) analysed the impacts of hosting the Olympic Games, the FIFA World Cup and the European Football Championships on happiness in European countries over a period of 30 years and found a significant and positive effect from the World Cup. Hosting major football championships improved life satisfaction. However, since the results derived from a sample of European nations where football is the dominant sport, the results could be different in regions of the world where football is not dominant. The findings showed a significant and positive short-term feel-good effect across all gender-age groups, but found little systematic evidence for long-term benefits, either before or after the event.

Surveys from previous hosts of the FIFA World Cup show positive, but also mixed effects. In Germany, the feel-good effect was so great that the 2006 World Cup turned into one of the most significant events in Germany (Maennig and Porsche, 2008). However, other surveys from Germany found that the increase in national pride in the period leading up to the event was followed by a significant reduction in the post-event period (Kersting, 2007).

In South Africa residents reported high levels of psychic income (e.g. excitement and happiness) in the lead up to the 2010 FIFA World Cup event, and they perceived the World Cup as encouraging a sense of community and celebration (Gibson et al., 2014; Thomson, Schlenker, Schulenkorf, and Brooking, 2016). Contrary to the pattern from Germany, the levels of psychic income increased after the event. On the other hand, findings relating to social capital (i.e. bonds felt amongst the community) and national pride showed that the benefits were mainly confined to the rich and big businesses and hence actually enhanced social inequality (Tichaawa, Bama, and Swart, 2015).

In South Korea, residents discovered that the benefits from co-hosting the 2002 FIFA World Cup together with Japan were lower than expected; in particular, the economic benefits were a big disappointment. Consequently, people considered the outcomes as losses because they were not good enough to justify the expense. Overall, the World Cup appeared to generate more societal and cultural benefits than economic gains for South Koreans (Kim, Gursoy, and Lee, 2006).

A survey among local residents in Beijing showed that support for the 2008 Olympic Games was still high two years after the Games. Entertainment opportunities and increased national pride were significant reasons why they continued to support the hosting of it. On the other hand, no direct relationship was determined between residents' improved quality of life and their continued support for the Games (Zhang, Chen, Lei, and Malone, 2013). Surveys in connection with the 2010 Vancouver Winter Olympic Games and the 2012 London Olympic Games showed that residents became more positive towards the Games when measured in terms of the "feel-good factor" (Hiller and Wanner, 2015).

The overall impression from the surveys is that although the events created some effects that directly or indirectly are measured in monetary term, these effects were not of a size that justified the costs. The conclusions from the research investigating the long-term effects from the 1994 Winter Olympic Games in Lillehammer, Norway probably summarise the findings in the academic research that have investigated economic impacts:

> Looking beyond the intermezzo, which is the main mechanism of an event, it turns out quite clearly that the long-term industrial impacts are very marginal and in no way justify the huge costs of hosting the events. If the main argument for hosting a mega-event like the Winter Olympics is the long-term, economic impacts it will generate, the Lillehammer experience quite clearly points to the conclusion that it is a waste of money. . . . However, this does not mean that there are no other arguments for hosting a mega-event. The Lillehammer Olympics was a great experience, although not in economic terms.
>
> (Spilling, 1998, p. 121)

The next section discusses why cities have continued bidding for the events, despite the many negative experiences with particular attention paid to the behaviour of the stakeholders involved in the application process.

## Dynamic forces in work during the application processes

The most popular events are distributed by auctions, with cities, often in collaboration with national sports federations being the bidders. Auction literature distinguishes between *private-value auctions* and *common-value auctions*, with the auctioning of major sports events falling into the latter category. In such auctions, the purpose is often to use the item in some kind of commercial activity, for instance to resell it or to use it as an input in some kind of production (Milgrom and Weber, 1982). The bidders often lack precise information regarding the value of the item, and thus have to estimate it based on the information that is available, a characteristic that is typical for major sports events.

As illustrated earlier, the benefits from the events include both tangibles and intangibles, with "feel-good" effects being an example of the latter. Different from ordinary auctions, the costs do not only include fees to the owners. Host cities often have to spend substantial resources upgrading venues, investing in infrastructure, transportation and accommodation, as well as associated operational costs. How much, depends on the size of the event relative to the size of the city. Large cities that have a tradition of hosting major events may have some existing venues and infrastructure, while others may have to invest heavily (see Preuss (2004) for more details). The need for investment also depends on the requests of the owners. The fiercer the competition, the easier it will be to add on requests, for example the numbers, size and quality of venues. When the competition has been fierce, the auctions have had characteristics of bidding wars. The results have often been investments in expensive stadia, of which many have had a capacity well beyond the post event demand.

Tables 3.1 through 3.3 showed that the IOC, FIFA and UEFA have not struggled with recruiting applicants, except in limited cases when the interest in hosting the Olympic Games was moderate.

Bidders who participate in auctions only on behalf of themselves or their organisation will be willing to increase their bid as long as the expected benefits that accrue to themselves or their organisation exceed their own costs. This is different for mega sports events since the benefits and costs are spread over a wide range of stakeholders. Those who expect to benefit will support the ideas of hosting them. This can involve stakeholders such as the local public sector, the tourism industry, sports clubs, entrepreneurs, national sports federations but also international sports federations, who are the owners of many events. Many of them can reap substantial benefits, but without financing the costs. In that way, they operate as free riders. The biggest financial contributor is usually the national government, particularly for the investments in venues and infrastructure.

A welfare economic rationale for governmental support exists if the events create positive externalities and merit goods. One relevant example is if new sport venues stimulate people to exercise more thus improving their health. Another rationale is if the impacts have characteristics of public goods, which means that there are no rivalling effects and that it is impossible to exclude people from consuming the benefits (Samuelson, 1954). For example, if the event promotes the host city, proponents argue that businesses and the local tourism industry will benefit. Another example is the feel-good factor. The non-exclusive criterion, however, can motivate those who benefit to operate as free riders and not participate in financing the events. The consequence can be a sub-optimal level of investment, and hence inefficiency. Preventing such outcomes represents a rationale for governmental intervention (Stiglitz, 2000).

### Principal–agent relations

If the government takes on the responsibility of financing the events, however, this creates a "principal–agent" relationship between the government as principal and the stakeholders benefiting from the impacts as the agents. Such situations can initiate behaviour that can lead to inefficiency. This has received substantial attention in the literature, and refers to situations characterised by asymmetric information, which in turn can cause opportunistic behaviour where informed agents take advantage of a less-informed principal. See for example Jensen and Meckling, (1976) and Eisenhardt (1989) for a profound discussion.

The objectives of the agents may not correspond with those of the respective governments. Those who benefit will prefer more inputs and/or outputs as long as their individual marginal benefits exceed their individual marginal costs. This has been common at mega events and is illustrated by Müller (2015), who investigated the reasons for the inefficiency and concluded that "since event-governing bodies set the requirements for infrastructure, but do not pay for its delivery, they have an incentive to demand excessively large stadia, airports, or hotel capacities" (p. 10). Efficient resource allocation, however, assumes the aggregated marginal benefits to equal the aggregated marginal costs.

Research on the 2011 FIS World Championship in Oslo, Norway, which investigated the cost overruns on the ski-jumps concluded in a similar way. The venues became 17.5 times more expensive than first planned. In an interview with the project director, Solberg and Preuss (2015) described the attitudes of stakeholders that influenced the process. This involved future tenants of the venues, the International Skiing Federation (FIS), representatives of the International Biathlon Union (IBU), the architects of the ski jumps, and the host broadcaster from the championship. None of these stakeholders participated in financing the costs:

> During the first stage, their requirements were not at all sober. Before the crisis, they showed absolutely no understanding of moderation. Their wishes were satisfied until the crisis appeared. After the crisis, this changed to some degree when it became clear how much the cost estimates had missed.
>
> (Solberg and Preuss, 2015, p. 357)

Entrepreneurs will, all things being equal, benefit the more that is spent on investments in venues and upgrading of infrastructure, and the same can apply to the suppliers of equipment. These motives can cause conflicts between individual and collective efficiency. Agents that only receive benefits, without financing any of the costs, will be interested in lobbying politicians to support the events financially. There can also be situations of asymmetric information, where some agents are in a position that allow them to deliberately underestimate the costs and exaggerate the benefits. The purpose can be to create an impression that the event is more beneficial for the host region and nation than it actually is. Since one-off events move from place to place (so-called footloose industries), applicants often hire consultants to forecast the economic outcome. Such forecasts often suffer from methodological weaknesses and shortcomings (Zimbalist, 2015)

The consultancy reports are often conducted on behalf of event organisers or other stakeholders who have strategic interests in motivating politicians to give the necessary financial guarantees. This explains why academic research and consultancy reports often give different results based upon analyses from the same event. One such example is the FIFA 2010 World Cup in South Africa, where the government hired consultants to prognosticate the economic impacts. In 2004, they predicted that South Africa would welcome 230,000 foreign tourists, who would stay for an average of 15 days. Four years later, they increased the number to 380,000 tourists. Post-event investigations, however, estimated the net number at somewhere between 40,000 and 90,000 visitors (Du Plessis and Maennig, 2010). Similar examples are presented by Zimbalist (2015). These examples illustrate how misleading the figures can be unless they are adjusted for crowding out impacts and other sources that can cause miscalculations.

International sports federations play a central role in the process. A large proportion of their revenues come from major events such as the Olympic Games and international championships. Their commercial value depends very much on the attention the events receive in the media. The most popular ones harvest substantial revenues from the sale of media rights, but also from sponsorship. The more TV viewers, the easier it is to recruit sponsors. The commercial value of the media products is best when the contests are surrounded by a lively audience in a large stadium. In some sports, for example ski jumping, the size of the venue can have similar effects. Other things being equal, the spectators find it more exciting to watch ski jumps at a 250-metre-ski jump venue rather than a 150-metre venue.

These forces can put pressure on event organisers to invest in upgrading the venues. It can also put them in unforeseen situations as the next quote illustrates. It is related to the 2011 FIS World Skiing Championship in Norway and is from an interview with the person who was the administrative leader of the municipality department that had the responsibility for the construction during the first stage of the process. After some time, the organiser realised that they had to construct new ski jumps, which they were not prepared for when the initiative to host the event first came up:

> The budget figures from 2005 were based on the arenas at that time, and we assumed that only some few renovations would be necessary. However, when FIS inspected the arena in autumn 2005, they presented the real requirements, with their consequences. Based on wisdom after the event, one can say that we should have spoken to FIS earlier. However, we had no reason to believe

that it would be necessary to substantially upgrade the arena. It was an FIS-approved arena, and we expected this to last in the future, at least to 2011.

(Solberg and Preuss, 2015, p. 357)

The underlying circumstances are often a competition between sports federations, but also between event organisers within the same sports. If some event organisers are willing to invest in upgrading venues and other facilities, this puts pressure on their rivals to do their same. Those that are unwilling to spend will risk being left behind. Therefore, they find themselves in situations that have the characteristics of a prisoner's dilemma (Dixit and Nalebuff, 1991). The consequences can be fewer spectators, which, in turn, can reduce the interest from the media and sponsors. Cities that are unwilling to demonstrate they have the required investments will find it difficult to be awarded events.

However, spending resources on events has other additional costs, which refer to the goods and services that alternatively could have been produced. This was the reason why London withdrew from hosting the opening races of the 2017 Tour de France, after being awarded the races. Boris Johnson, London's mayor at that time explained his decision:

I will not waste cycling money on something that would only deliver very brief benefits. . . . You've got to take some tough decisions in government and I think 35 million quid on a one-off event was just not worth it for London. . . . The money would be better spent on infrastructure.

(MacMichael, 2015)

Not everybody in London agreed with the decision to pull out. As Labour's London 2016 mayoral candidate, Sadiq Khan pointed out,

By not hosting the iconic Tour de France, the Mayor and the Government are wasting a huge opportunity to show London to the world. The Tour is one of the world's greatest sporting events. Londoners deserve to know why it's been cancelled at the last minute.

(The Week, 2015)

If local residents welcome the events, this can motivate politicians who seek reelection to support the events financially. Although the residents are taxpayers and hence participate in financing events, they will nevertheless be subsidised since residents from the rest of the nation also pay taxes but without receiving the same benefits themselves. Indeed, whether the financial support comes from the national government or from the local public sector can make a difference. This was illustrated in connection to New York's plans to host the 2012 Olympic Games. Polls showed that 69% of New Yorkers were supportive of the idea but also that the support declined to a mere 37 per cent if local taxpayer subsidies were required (Trumpbour, 2007, p. 233).

The agents can also become more powerful by collaborating against the principal, that is, the national government. If the local event organiser receives external funding, this makes it easier for international sports federations to require exten-sions and improvements, and to receive support, alleviating cost concerns. These circumstances can explain both the cost overruns and the white elephants.

After London pulled out from the Tour de France, the races were awarded to the city of Düsseldorf in Germany. However, not everybody in Germany was happy with the decision, and for the same reason as in London. Isabelle Klarenaar, a spokesperson for the German Cyclist Federation (ADFC) said that the high costs of up to €6 million for the city budget were not worth it (Barfield, 2015).

Recent incidents where several cities have followed London's example regard-ing the Tour de France and withdrawn their candidature for the Olympic Games indicate that both residents and politicians have become more aware of the alter-native costs of hosting the events. However, whether this pattern will continue remains to be seen. After the unsuccessful financial Games in the 1970s, it took only the success of the 1984 Los Angeles Olympic Games to change attitudes and again convince cities that it was worth applying for the Games. This indicates that people soon forget the negative experiences, but also that intangibles such as the "feel-good" effect is more important than the measureable effects.

## Conclusion

This chapter has investigated why cities continue to apply for mega sports events, despite academic research having documented that particularly the legacies mea-sured in monetary terms are usually not worth the investment.

When analysing the reasons for this paradox, it is important to bear in mind that the benefits and costs are spread over several stakeholders. The most popu-lar events are distributed by auctions. Many of the stakeholders who enjoy the benefits from the events operate as free riders who do not participate in fund-ing the events. However, they can nevertheless influence the bidding process, for example lobbying politicians to provide financial backing. This makes the circumstances different from ordinary auctions where the bidders base their strat-egies on the expected benefits and costs that fall upon themselves. The motivation to operate as a free rider also exists after the events have been awarded. This, in turn, can explain the many examples of cost overruns.

Additionally, mega events also create "feel-good" effects among local residents. Although such effects are difficult to measure in monetary terms, the literature provides several indications that they are highly emphasised. Whether they should be considered as a legacy or only a short-term effect should be explored further and in more detail. However, if the voters consider them important, this can make it easier for politicians who seek reelection to support the events financially.

## References

Akerlof, G. (1976). The economics of caste and of the rat race and other woeful tales. *Quarterly Journal of Economics, 90*(4), 599–617.

Alm, J. (2012). *World stadium index venues built for major sporting events – bright future or future burden?* Retrieved from www.playthegame.org/fileadmin/documents/ World_Stadium_Index_Final.pdf.

Alm, J., Solberg, H. A., Storm, R., and Jakobsen, T. G. (2014). Hosting major sports events: The challenge of taming white elephants. *Leisure Studies, 35*(5), 564–582.

Andreff, W. (2012). The winner's curse: Why is the cost of mega sports events so often underestimated. In Wolfgang Maennig and Andrew Zimbalist (Eds.), *International handbook on the economics of ega-sporting events*. Cheltenham/Northampton, MA: Edward Elgar.

Andreff, W. (2016). The tour de France: A success story in spite of competitive imbalance and doping. In D. Van Reeth and D. J. Larson (Eds.), *The economics of professional road cycling* (pp. 233–256). Switzerland: Springer International Publishing.

Baade, R. A., and Matheson, V. A. (2016). Going for the Gold: The Economics of the Olympics. *The Journal of Economic Perspectives, 30*(2), 201–218.

Barfield, T. (2015). *Cyclists slam Düsseldorf 2017 Tour de France bid*. Retrieved from www.thelocal.de/20151106/dsseldorf-will-bid-to-open-2017-tour-de-france

Bauman, A., Bellew, B., and Craig, C. L. (2015). Did the 2000 Sydney Olympics increase physical activity among adult Australians? *British Journal of Sports Medicine. 49*(4), 243–247.

Chalip, L., Green, B. C., and Hill, B. (2003). Effects of sport event media on destination image and intention to visit. *Journal of Sport Management, 17*(3), 214–234.

Chappelet, J-L. (2006). *The tale fo three Olympic Cities – forecast for Torino on basis of Grenoble and Innsbruck*. Torino 2006 – XX Winter Olympic Games Symposium, February 9, 2006, Turin.

City of Edinburgh Council. (2012). *British proposal to host parts of the Tour de France*. Retrieved from www.edinburgh.gov.uk/download/meetings/id/37529/item_no_87_british_proposal_to_host_parts_of_the_tour_de_france.

Dixit, A., and Nalebuff, B. (1991). Thinking strategically: A competitive edge in business, politics, and everyday life. New York: W. W. Norton.

Downward, P., Dawson, P., and Mills, T. C. (2015). Sports participation as an investment in (subjective) health: A time series analysis of the life course. *Journal of Public Health*, fdv164.

Du Plessis, S., and Maennig, W. (2010). *The World Cup high-frequency data economics: Effects on international awareness and (self-defeating) tourism*. Working paper, Hamburg contemporary economic discussions, No. 37, University of Hamburg. Retrieved from www.econstor.eu/dspace/bitstream/10419/42236/1/640051979.pdf.

Eisenhardt, K. (1989). Agency theory: An assessment and review. *Academy of Management Review, 14*(1), 57–74.

FIFA.com. (2017). *FIFA World Cup all time statistics*. Retrieved February 12, 2017, from www.fifa.com/fifa-tournaments/statistics-and-records/worldcup/

Flyvbjerg, B., and Stewart, A. (2012). *Olympic proportions: Cost and cost overruns at the Olympics 1960–2012*. Working paper, Said Business School, University of Oxford.

Gibson, H. J, Walker, M., Thapa, B., Kaplanidou, K., Geldenhuys, S., and Coetzee, W. (2014). Psychic income and social capital among host nation residents: A pre – post analysis of the 2010 FIFA World Cup in South Africa. *Tourism Management, 44*, 113–122.

Gratton, C., and Taylor, P. (2000). *Economics of sport and recreation*. London: Routledge.

Gripsrud, G., Nes, E. B., and Olsson, U. H. (2010). Effects of hosting a mega-sport event on country image. *Event Management, 14*(3), 93–204.

Hiller, H. H., and Wanner (2015). The psycho-social impact of the Olympics as urban festival: A leisure perspective. *Leisure Studies, 34*(6), 672–688.

IOC. (2014). *Olympic marketing fact file*. Retrieved February 21, 2017, from https://stillmed.olympic.org/Documents/IOC_Marketing/OLYMPIC_MARKETING_FACT_%20FILE_2014.pdf

IOC. (2017). *Olympic agenda 2020*. Retrieved February 21, 2017, from www.olympic.org/olympic-agenda-2020

Jafari, J. (1988). Tourism mega-events. *Annals of Tourism Research, 15*(2), 272–273.

Jensen, M. C., and Meckling, W. H. (1976). Theory of the firm: Managerial behavior, agency costs and ownership structure. *Journal of Financial Economics, 3*(4), 305–360.

Kavetsos, G., and Szymanski, S. (2010). National well-being and international sports events. *Journal of Economic Psychology, 31*(2), 158–171.

Kersting, N. (2007). Sport and national identity: A comparison of the 2006 and 2010 FIFA World Cups. *Politikon, 34*(3), 277–293.

Kim, H. J., Gursoy, D., and Lee, S-B. (2006). The impact of the 2002 World Cup on South Korea: Comparisons of pre- and post-games. *Tourism Management, 27*(1), 86–96.

MacMichael, S. (2015). *Boris Johnson says he pulled London's 2017 Tour de France Grand Depart*. Retrieved from http://road.cc/content/news/166305-boris-johnson-says-he-pulled-londons-2017-tour-de-france-grand-depart

Maennig, W., and Porsche, M. (2008). The feel-good effect at Mega Sports Events. Recommendations for public and private administration informed by the experience of the FIFA World Cup 2006. IASE/NAASE Working Paper Series, No. 08-17.

Mahtani, K. R., Protheroe J, Slight, S. P., Demarzo, M. M., Blakeman, T., Barton, C. A., Brijnath, B., and Roberts, N. (2013). Can the London 2012 Olympics 'inspire a generation' to do more physical or sporting activities? An overview of systematic reviews. *BMJ Open, 3*(1).

Matheson, V. (2014). *Were the billions Brazil spent on World Cup stadiums worth it?* Downloaded January 11, 2016, from http://fivethirtyeight.com/features/were-the-billions-brazil-spent-on-world-cup-stadiums-worth-it/

Milgrom, P., and Weber, R. (1982). A theory of auctions and competitive bidding. *Econometrica, 50*(5), 1089–1122.

Mossberg, L. L., and Hallberg, A. (1999). The presence of a mega-event: Effects on destination image and product-country images. *Pacific Tourism Review, 3*(3–4), 173–184.

Müller, M. (2015). The Mega-Event Syndrome: Why so much goes wrong in Mega-Event planning and what to do about it. *Journal of the American Planning Association, 81*(1), 5–17.

Murphy, N. M., and Bauman, A. J. (2007, April). Mass sporting and physical activity events – are they "bread and circuses" or public health interventions to increase population levels of physical activity? *Journal of Physical Activity. 4*(2), 93–102.

Oldenboom, E. R. (2006). Costs and benefits of major sports events: A case study of Euro 2000. Amsterdam: MeerWaarde Onderzoeksadvies.

Preuss, H. (2004). The economics of staging the Olympics: A comparison of the Games, 1972–2008. Cheltenham: Edward Elgar Publishing,

Preuss, H. (2005). The economic impact of visitors at major multi-sport-events. *European Sport Management Quarterly, 5*(3), 283–304.

Preuss, H. (2007). The conceptualization and measurement of mega sport event legacies. *Journal of Sport & Tourism, 12*(3–4), 207–227.

Preuss, H., and Solberg, H. A. (2006). Attracting major sporting events: The role of local residents. *European Sport Management Quarterly, 6*(4), 391–411.

Preuss, H., Solberg, H. A., and Alm, J. (2014). The challenge of utilizing World Cup venues. In D. Adair and S. Frawley (Eds.), *Managing the Football World Cup* (pp. 82–103). London: Palgrave McMillan.

Ritchie, J. R. B., and Smith, B. H. (1991). The impact of a mega-event on host region awareness: A longitudinal study. *Journal of Travel Research, 30*(1), 3–10.

Ritchie, J. R. B., and Yangzhou, J. (1987). *The role and impact of mega-events and attractions on national and regional tourism: A conceptual and methodological overview.*

AIEST Proceedings of the 37th Annual Congress of the International Association of Scientific Experts in Tourism (AIEST), Calgary (pp. 17–58). St. Gallen: AIEST.

Rivenburgh, N. K., Louw, P. E., Loo, E., and Mersham, G. (2003). *The Sydney Olympic Games and foreign attitudes towards Australia*. Gold Coast: CRCST Publishing.

Samuelson, P. A. (1954). The pure theory of public expenditure. *The Review of Economics and Statistics*, *36*(4), 387–389.

Solberg, H. A., and Preuss, H. (2015). Major sports events – the challenge of budgeting the venues. *Event Management*, *19*(3), 349–363.

Spilling, O. R. (1998). Beyond intermezzo. On the long-term industrial impacts of mega-events. The case of Lillehammer 1994. *Festival Management & Event Tourism*, *5*(3), 101–122.

Statista. (2017). *Average attendance "Big Five" European soccer leagues 1996/97– 2015/16*. Retrieved February 21, 2017, from www.statista.com/statistics/261213/ european-soccer-leagues-average-attendance/

Stiglitz, J. E. (2000). *Economics of the public sector* (3rd ed.). New York: Norton.

Thomson, A., Schlenker, K., Schulenkorf, N., and Brooking, E. (2016). The social and environmental consequences of hosting mega-sport events. In S. Frawley (Ed.), *Managing sport mega-events* (pp. 150–164). Abingdon: Routledge.

Tichaawa, T. M., Bama, H. K. N., and Swart, K. (2015). Community perceptions of the socio-economic legacies of the 2010 FIFA World Cup in Nelson Mandela Bay, Port Elizabeth: A four-year post-event analysis. *African Journal for Physical, Health Education, Recreation and Dance*, *21*(4:2), 1383–1395.

Trumpbour, R. C. (2007). *The new cathedrals*. Syracuse, New York: Syracuse University Press.

Ulvnes, A. M., and Solberg, H. A. (2016). Can major sport events attract tourists? A study of media information and explicit memory. *Scandinavian Journal of Hospitality and Tourism*, *16*(2), 143–157.

Walker, P. (2015). *Boris Johnson explains London's decision to turn down Tour de France*. Retrieved from www.theguardian.com/sport/2015/sep/29/boris-johnson-explains-londons-decision-to-turn-down-tour-de-france

*The Week* (2015). London turns down chance to host 2017 Tour de France start. Retrieved from www.theweek.co.uk/tour-de-france/65490/london-turns-down-chance-to-host-2017-tour-de-france-start

Zhang, M., Chen, L., Lei, O., and Malone, C. (2013). Residents perceived social-economic impact of the 2008 Beijing Olympic Games. *Journal of Research*, *8*(2), 19–25.

Zimbalist, A. (2015). Circus maximus: The economic gamble behind hosting the Olympics and the World Cup. Washington, DC: The Brooking Institution.

# 4 Volunteering legacy of the London 2012 Olympics

## Olesya Nedvetskaya and Vassil Girginov

When London hosted the 1948 Olympic Games, volunteering was the only way to deliver them, as there were no government subsidies, global commercial sponsorship or broadcasting fees (The Organising Committee for the XIV Olympiad, 1948). By the time London staged the Games in 2012, volunteering had become a strategically planned and professionally managed activity that was also integrated in the host country's social policy. The concept of the Olympic legacy has also gained popularity and has been framed as a rational process designed to ensure a range of individual and social benefits from hosting the Games. This chapter focuses specifically on the least researched area of Olympic volunteering – the processes through which the volunteering legacy can be achieved, for whom, in what circumstances, and over which duration. The overall purpose of the study was to explore the practices by which the London 2012 Volunteer Programme (the Games Maker Programme) was used to deliver a desired social legacy. This was carried out within the historical context of sport event volunteering in the UK, such as the XVII Commonwealth Games in Manchester and the volunteer programmes associated with them.

This chapter is divided into four sections. The first section offers a critical review of literature on Olympic volunteering in order to establish the key trends, processes and legacies from hosting the Games. The second section offers a critical realism-informed theoretical approach to understanding the legacy of Olympic volunteering. The third section presents the case of the volunteering legacy of London 2012, and finally, some conclusions are drawn.

### The Olympic legacy

The Olympic and Paralympic Games have the power to transform host cities and leave multiple legacies behind. However, these legacies are often complex, multidimensional, context-specific, and dependent on the socio-economic and political conditions of a country hosting the event (DCMS, 2013; Gold and Gold, 2011). Cumulatively, the magnitude, organisational complexity, high public expenditures and a variety of impacts affecting host destinations stipulate high expectations about the anticipated benefits. This triggered an increased academic interest in the study of Olympic legacies in comparison to smaller scale events (e.g., Chalip, 2014; Girginov, 2012, 2013, 2014; Gold and Gold, 2011; Leopkey and

Parent, 2012; Parent and Smith-Swan, 2013; Preuss, 2007, 2015; Vanwynsberghe, 2015). Yet, despite the origin of the modern Olympic Games in 1896, the concept of legacy did not gain appeal in the sport/event management discourse until the 1990s except for references to competition venues and their post-Games use (Leopkey and Parent, 2012). Gradually, scholars began to take a more complex view of legacy that went beyond sport, capital, tourism/commercial and economic elements to incorporate socio-cultural, psychological, environmental and political factors (e.g., Chappelet, 2012; Doherty, 2009; Minnaert, 2012; Silvestre, 2009). However, efforts to envision, frame and implement event legacies tend to be fragmented and lack a comprehensive approach due to incomplete selection of types of legacies, a confusion over what legacy means and how it should be evaluated (Chalip, Chapter 2, this volume; Preuss, 2015; VanWynsberghe, 2015).

In this sense, Preuss' (2015) legacy framework is arguably considered the most developed attempt so far for conceptualising multiple Olympic legacies. Based on the *Legacy cube* introduced by Preuss in 2007, this holistic perspective on legacy includes "planned and unplanned, positive and negative, tangible and intangible structures created for and by a sport event that remain longer than the event itself" (Preuss, 2007, p. 211) and can be evaluated over particular *time* and *space* and across various impacts. It follows that the nature and scale of an overall legacy is the result of structural changes in a host city caused by five 'event structures': infrastructure, knowledge, policy, networks and emotions (Preuss, 2015). These 'hard' (material) and 'soft' (non-material) structures are either created or affected by preparing for and staging a mega event. Each city differs in the structures available for and required by an event. Therefore, every city will have a unique legacy composition, which may have far-reaching effects that can extend beyond local communities. Moreover, some structures are short-lived while others are longer term, which means that legacies can be of a different duration.

Preuss (2015) argues that these five 'event structures' have the potential to change the quality of a location for living and doing business by attracting *new initiatives* in the form of social, economic or other kind of activity, thereby keeping those structures in use to generate value. This, however, usually happens long after the event itself and its directly initiated impacts. Moreover, too often legacies in all five 'event structures' remain latent, which can be costly. For example, the knowledge accumulated through bidding for the event is a 'latent legacy' and will not become a 'real legacy' unless needed for bidding for another event (Preuss, 2015). Skills and experiences gained through event volunteering can remain latent until and unless a person finds further opportunities to become involved in other events or community volunteering.

Legacies, therefore, can have different values that can change through time; positive legacies can turn into negative legacies, and "[a] positive legacy in one dimension can be a negative legacy in another dimension" (Preuss, 2007, p. 220). If not properly planned and managed, legacies can leave negative consequences, regardless of where the events are hosted (Preuss, 2015). Candidate and host cities, however, often overlook the negative effects of the Games. Our review of Olympic cities' strategies suggests that politics of events were often at odds with the needs and means of host destinations. The focal point was physical regeneration, image enhancement and profit making, which did not guarantee equal distribution of benefits among all stakeholders. Quite the opposite, the highest costs were experienced by those less able to protect their rights and interests, while the greater prizes accrued to corporate and political elites (Surborg, Van-Wynsberghe, and Wyly, 2008). To offset criticism and encourage the production of a lasting legacy, the IOC promoted principles of sustainable development and made 'positive legacy' a key component of the host selection process and Games governance. Legacy planning has shifted from post-Games to pre-Games, beginning from the time of the bid, which changed legacy from a retrospective to a prospective concept (Girginov, 2012).

The current approach to the governance of the Olympic legacy is associated with embedding planning for event-related legacies within existing structures and long-term host city developmental strategies. Political will combined with well-planned effort could replace the 'sport works' mentality of 'automatic' positive benefits and ensure that sustainable legacies are achieved, while negative legacies are minimised.

### Volunteering as social legacy

Volunteers represent one of many heterogeneous stakeholders in the Olympic and Paralympic Games, and are usually the largest group (Ferrand and Skirstad, 2015). Personal investment and the performance of many volunteers play a huge role in staging successful sport events (Chanavat and Ferrand, 2010; Kemp, 2002). Growing social demands, financial strains, and complexity of Olympic operations impact the scope of volunteer services and organisation, and pressure organising committees to mobilise volunteers in increasingly large numbers. Olympic volunteering began in 1896 when 900 volunteers provided their support for the Summer Olympic Games in Athens (Wei, 2010). The Los Angeles Olympic Organising Committee for the first time established the volunteer programme to officially recruit around 28,700 volunteers to perform various tasks during the Games (Chanavat and Ferrand, 2010). The London 2012 Olympic Games utilised 70,000 Games Makers, and additionally used Ceremony Volunteers and Olympic Ambassadors (LOCOG, 2013). As part of enormous human resource operations, volunteers fulfil back- and front-stage roles often in management and supervisory positions, and are required to have certain skills to perform a wide range of tasks (technologies, medicine, language services, etc.). They are called 'unsung heroes' (Baum, Deery, Hanlon, Lockstone, and Smith, 2009; Lockstone and Baum, 2009) who contribute invaluable resources to the Games. Solberg (2003) suggested that volunteers' assistance in executing the Games at all organisational levels makes the difference between financial loss and gain. London 2012 Games Makers contributed 8 million volunteer hours to the Games, which in monetary value equals £35 million (Nichols and Ralston, 2014). These numbers show the social value of unpaid work, implying the 'legitimacy' legacy, and serve as a rationale for respecting and further supporting volunteerism in society. The monetarisation of voluntary work is a deliberate attempt to legitimise it as an activity and to make a strong policy argument that governments should support it.

Volunteers' experiences represent an essential part of the social legacy of the Games, as they are reflective of both the status of volunteering in a society and the overall process of planning and delivering a volunteer programme. Volunteers personally benefit from their volunteering experiences, help organisations stage the Games and contribute to a greater sense of community and civic minded-ness. Volunteer training and experiences help boost personal skills, competen-cies, efficacy, self-confidence and give a sense of fulfilment and achievement that can enhance the quality of life of individuals and communities (Doherty, 2009; Hustinx, Cnaan, and Handy, 2010; Wilson, 2012). Furthermore, a significant posi-tive outcome from volunteering is a potentially broadened perspective and life opportunities that help volunteers transition to employment, education or further volunteering beyond the event (Dickson and Benson, 2013; Nichols and Ralston, 2014). Positive volunteering experiences may also have implications beyond the event itself, inspiring volunteers to revisit their experiences at other Games or get involved in community volunteering (Doherty, 2009; Parent and Smith-Swan, 2013). There are, of course, downsides to volunteering as well such as poor organ-isational practices leading to negative experiences and even volunteer attrition (Elstad, 1996; Kemp, 2002), lack of appreciation of voluntary work and demoti-vation through attempts to deliver essential services 'on the cheap' by substituting paid staff with under-funded and under-trained volunteers. This is at odds with the fact that many organisations are highly dependent on volunteers to attain their strategic and operational goals.

Yet, despite greater recognition of the time, effort and contributions made by volunteers, very little is known about mega sport event volunteering (Bang and Chelladurai, 2009; Khoo and Engelhorn, 2011), notably in the context of the Olympic Games (Chanavat and Ferrand, 2010; Giannoulakis, Wang, and Gray, 2008). A major gap in our knowledge concerns sport event volunteers' lived expe-riences (Green and Chalip, 2004) and the difference between sport event volun-teers and long-term volunteers in other settings (Baum and Lockstone, 2007). Olympic volunteering is quite different from the narrow image of helping those in need and traditional forms of long-term and membership-based commitments (Hustinx and Lammertyn, 2003). The sport events context provides a unique environment, determined by the events' episodic 'one-off' and 'fixed-term' nature and increasing commodification (Cuskelly, Hoye, and Auld, 2006; Hoye and Cuskelly, 2009). Due to the temporary nature of the Games Organising Commit-tees (OCOG), Games-time volunteers' commitment to the organisation is limited, which creates challenges for the volunteering legacy. Volunteers are 'hired' for a very short though intensive term, often determined by the length of the Games and role requirements. Therefore, sport event volunteering can be considered as a specific example of a project-based leisure opportunity (Stebbins and Graham, 2004) that is infrequent, short-term, yet of a complex nature. This has important implications for volunteer management, motivation, commitment, performance and retention.

Examples of successful volunteering legacies related to mega sport events are rare. The Manchester 2002 Games, however, serve as one such example, where the Games left both economic and social legacies, linking physical and social regeneration in one Legacy Programme (Smith and Fox, 2007). This unprecedented scheme marked a trend toward making the social dimension an important factor in hosting a mega sport event, demonstrating that ideas about what the Games can leave as legacy have changed (Doherty, 2009; Leopkey and Parent, 2012; Silvestre, 2009). For the first time, a mega sport event was used to target hard-to-reach groups to improve their life prospects and wellbeing (Jones and Stokes, 2003).

In particular, Manchester 2002 adopted specific plans to provide new transferable skills to unemployed local people using pre-Games and Games-time volunteer programmes. Silvestre (2009) called this type of social impacts 'employment, training and business development'. The Pre-Volunteer Programme (PVP) was used to empower socially excluded groups with enhanced skills and increase their employability (Smith, 2006). Upon completion of a free training course, graduates were given certificates as a tangible outcome of their participation, which they could leverage for future employment. Manchester 2002 also made a successful commitment to have 10% of the graduates from the PVP as part of the Games workforce, giving them a chance of a lifetime to be Games-time volunteers (Manchester, 2002, 2003). This is at odds with common practices where most volunteers tend to be well off with higher levels of education, knowledge of several languages and previous volunteering experience (Dickson and Benson, 2013; Lukka and Ellis, 2001; Smith, 1994). Thus, Manchester 2002 serves as a prime example where volunteering represents multiple structures and their various dimensions and becomes a strategically planned, transparent process of shared responsibility and accountability that encourages viable governance structures and enforcement mechanisms to ensure follow-through on promises.

Thus, based on Preuss' (2015) legacy approach, volunteering legacies are framed as a rational process designed to ensure a range of individual and social benefits from hosting the Games. Yet, this legacy framework remains rather vague, as it does not help us to understand how networks and accumulated knowledge can enhance different kinds of volunteering legacy. The *Legacy cube* alone cannot provide answers to fundamental questions such as how volunteering legacies occur, for whom and to what effect, which can be addressed by a critical realist perspective.

## Critical realism and volunteering legacy research

Since Olympic volunteering has become a rational policy, it is important to establish how such a policy and its legacy could be interpreted. A critical realist evaluation approach (Pawson, 2013; Pawson and Tilley, 1997) was used in this study to investigate three elements: the contexts, mechanisms and outcomes of the London 2012 Games Maker Programme.

Pawson and Tilley (1997) utilise contextual thinking and view programmes as sophisticated social interactions set amidst a complex social reality. They stressed 'Context + Mechanism = Outcome' pattern configurations (CMO) where the programme works (O) because of the action of underlying mechanisms (M), which only come into operation in particular circumstances or contexts (C) to bring about change. As argued by Pawson (2013), *"if the right processes operate in right conditions then the programme will prevail"* (p. 22). This 'if–then' framework reveals the causal and conditional nature of the relationship between CMOs. It helps address 'for whom' and 'in what circumstances' a programme will work. The argument is that certain contexts are supportive of the programme theory and some are not. The programme may work better for certain types of subjects but not for others, and certain institutional arrangements may be better at delivering certain outcomes.

Mechanisms, although often hidden, explicate the logic of intervention. These are various ideas and theories within the programme that create different resources, which trigger different reactions amongst participants. In realist view, *"it is not programmes that work but the resources they offer to enable their subjects to make them work"* (Pawson and Tilley, 2004, p. 6). Due to relevant variations in *contexts* and *mechanisms* thereby activated, programmes have mixed *outcomes*, which can take many forms and comprise intended and unintended consequences, with uneven patterns of successes and failures. This relates to the multidimensional nature of the *Legacy cube* and multiple aspects of the Games legacy outlined in Preuss (2007, 2015).

As volunteering literature suggests, sport event volunteering needs to be studied from a holistic yet interdisciplinary perspective, which is in line with the urge for critical realists to investigate the phenomenon in its complexity and multidimensionality (Byers, 2013; Byers and Thurston, 2011). Sport event volunteering is a synergistic phenomenon in that it is comprised of multiple units of analysis and relationships. To recognise the complexity of Olympic volunteering and maximise the explanatory potential, this study understood volunteering as a result of interactions between various structures, their causal powers, the contexts within which they operate and the outcomes produced.

The context of this study is the London 2012 Games; the case is the London 2012 Games Maker Programme, whereas units of analysis are different aspects of the Programme in order to understand how and to what extent volunteers benefited themselves, the Games and the community. Apart from methodological reasoning, the fact that the first author personally took part in the London Games as a Games Maker became the reason behind the choice of this particular case. The assumption was that this might open up avenues to access research participants and ease the process of data collection.

Learning about the structures, circumstances and experiences of research participants became possible through interpretations of meanings and perspectives of 16 volunteers and 6 managers attached to various events associated with London 2012. Information was gathered with the help of in-depth semi-structured interviews, participant observations, online survey (n 71) and documentary analysis. Interviews with volunteers took place several months prior to and one year after the Games, which is in line with a longitudinal case following Yin's (2014) 'before' and 'after' logic. This allowed for analysing the processes and consequences of the London 2012 volunteering in the context of its history and anticipated changes over time.

# The London 2012 volunteering legacy: context, mechanisms and outcomes

## Context

London 2012 claimed to be the first true 'legacy' Olympic Games that made a strategic use of the legacy concept in its bid document, and took a holistic sustainability approach to the legacy planning (DCMS, 2008, 2012). It is argued that among the main reasons London won its bid to host the Games was the attractive legacy plans in the area of sport, youth and the regeneration of East London (Horne and Houlihan, 2014). They had a vision of hosting "*an inspirational, safe and inclusive Olympic Games and Paralympic Games and leave a sustainable legacy for London and the UK*" (UEL/TGIfS, 2010, p. 17). Importantly, the London 2012 Games were heavily funded by taxpayer money. Therefore, justification of the long-term value of event-related structural changes was the first and foremost organisational priority. Apart from infrastructure, this shift was related to other structures, particularly concerning volunteering.

## Mechanisms

It was critical for London 2012 to have an outstanding volunteer programme that would be used to run both the successful Olympic Games and generate a sustainable volunteering legacy for local communities. For this to happen, the development of the London 2012 Volunteering Strategy (Volunteering Strategy Group, 2006) was initiated in 2006. The Volunteering Strategy Group was created and represented by over 100 stakeholders across voluntary, public and private sectors on national, regional and sub-regional levels. In a combined effort, they put their own reasoning (*causal powers*) into what they believed the Games-related volunteering legacy should be, capitalising on the experience gained from the organisation of the Manchester 2002 Games and their Pre-Volunteer initiative to trigger social change. The Volunteering Strategy (the Strategy) identified clear vision, aims, values and governance principles with regard to the pre-Games, Games-time and post-Games operations. The emphasis was placed on the values of *Excellence, Openness, Equality, Diversity, Inclusion* and *One Games*. One of the mechanisms through which the organisers aimed to exercise these principles was encouraging people from different ages, skills, abilities and backgrounds to apply to both Olympic and Paralympic Games (Volunteering Strategy Group, 2006).

LOCOG, the major stakeholder and the owner of the Games Maker Programme, took the aims directly related to delivery of the Games to the heart of their operations. The commitment was to have the best volunteer programme ever via the process of recruiting, deploying, training and managing the large volunteer force "*to deliver an unforgettable experience for athletes, officials and spectators alike*" (Volunteering Strategy Group, 2006, p. 4). Prior to recruitment, LOCOG established a baseline demand for Games-time volunteers (70,000) to perform 3,500 roles, which were split into three areas: technical (sport), technical (volunteer) and generalist roles (IOC, 2005). The results presented in this chapter focussed on generalist volunteers. Necessary planning was performed by LOCOG in relation to job titles, skills/qualification and training requirements, volunteer rosters, meals and uniform entitlements, retention and recognition practices as well as the contingency plan to have 20% of applicants on a reserve list. The official recruitment campaign aimed at attracting passionate volunteers able to commit at least ten days during the Games and act as ambassadors for the Games and the Olympic Movement. In exchange (the *Exchange* principle), organisers promised to meet the needs of the volunteers by providing first-class training, support and acknowledgement, including social events, pins, certificates and formal accreditation. These tangible and intangible rewards served as both a mechanism and a resource to encourage volunteers' high level of performance, loyalty and commitment.

However, the Volunteering Strategy was not exclusively bound to running a successful Games-time volunteer programme. As noted, it was designed as a deliberate approach to use the Games to leave a lasting volunteering legacy beyond 2012. The ambition was fourfold: to use the enthusiasm generated by the Games as a catalyst to inspire a new generation of volunteers; to mobilise a force of at least 25,000 community volunteers – would be Games-time volunteers – in the years leading up to the Games to work in a range of volunteering activities in local organisations in their communities; to transform and strengthen the culture and spirit of volunteering to build stronger, more-integrated volunteering infrastructure at national, regional and local levels; and to maximise the benefits of volunteering via skills development, training and qualifications to address the problems of long-term unemployment and low skill levels in the UK (Volunteering Strategy Group, 2006). Each of these four programme ambitions represents a different form of legacy.

This Strategy required LOCOG to work in partnership (the *Partnership* principle) with other relevant agencies in government, voluntary, education and employment sectors as well as to be consistent in their commitment in providing equal opportunities and truly diverse Games. The vision was to engage volunteers from the broadest possible range of backgrounds and communities. One of the mechanisms to achieve these ends, suggested in the Strategy, was to employ a fully devolved to nations and regions franchise recruitment model, which would give people a chance to volunteer from across the UK (the *UK-Wide* principle). Yet, in practice, LOCOG decided to utilise a centrally controlled recruitment scheme to meet their own targets and avoid additional organisational complexities. As a compromise, temporary selection centres were established in nine regions across the UK, which allowed tapping into regional and local volunteering resources and give a chance to out-of-London potential volunteers to be interviewed; although, this did not guarantee their ultimate participation (Nedvetskaya, Purcell, and Hastings, 2015). The adopted recruitment scheme along with the lack of a targeted approach and no policy on covering travelling and accommodation expenses of out-of-London volunteers violated initial promises to build on the existing volunteering infrastructure in the regions, deepen engagement and widen access to volunteering. This ultimately diminished the diversity and inclusivity of the Games-time workforce and the social legacy of the programme. This study revealed a limited engagement of Olympic volunteers in Paralympic volunteering, which further undermined the promise to have 'One Games'.

A Personal Best Programme (PB), developed from the PVP scheme in Manchester, was introduced as a mechanism to target marginalised groups who are under-represented in volunteering. Similar to Manchester 2002, the aim was to use the power of the Games to engage individuals from socially excluded backgrounds to raise their aspirations and achieve their potential through boosting employability skills, giving them their first qualification and a chance to volunteer at the Games. It was set to recruit 10% of 70,000 Games Makers from PB graduates to be part of the best qualified Games-time workforce. Out of projected 20,000 PB recruits (SQW, 2011), the target was to have at least 7,000 or more complete the course with Level 1 National Vocational Qualification in Event Volunteering to be eligible for an interview for Games-time roles. Inspired by London 2012, PB was viewed as its tangible legacy that would justify public funding. In order to attain this outcome, close collaboration was implied between the Games Maker Programme and the Personal Best Programme in the 'pre-Games' phase. Importantly, the PB graduates had to graduate in time to apply for the Games Maker roles.

### Outcomes

However, the scale of London 2012, operational demands and strict deadlines pressured LOCOG at the pre-Games phase to focus entirely on recruiting and training enough volunteers to deliver the Games. Therefore, despite the commitments, recruiting PB graduates was not among the organisational priorities. The aims of the PB and the Games Maker Programmes were not aligned, which shows rather poor coordination between major stakeholders, furthermore violating the partnership principle. No evidence was found that LOCOG had laid out the plan to prioritise PB graduates over the mainstream applicants, which further undermined the aspirations of having a diverse and inclusive Games-time workforce via encouraging participation of people from disadvantaged backgrounds. Given that the timing of the PB Programme was not fully adjusted to the time scale of the Games Maker Programme, and high costs of London 2012 volunteering almost pre-determined that those who were ultimately recruited and volunteered as Games Makers were predominantly a well-qualified, middle-class white British population. 63% of volunteers who took part in the online survey carried out for this research possessed a degree, were either employed or retired. They were predominantly white British women, over 45 years old, stable financially, with a third of the sample having an annual income of £30,000 or more. Notably, this highlights almost the opposite outcome from what was initially planned in the Strategy: further exclusion of people from lower socio-economic backgrounds, such as PB graduates, from volunteering and not valuing volunteering strongly enough as a way out of social exclusion.

Nonetheless, evidence from this and other published research (e.g., House of Lords, 2013; Nedvetskaya, Purcell, and Hastings, 2015; Nichols and Ralston, 2014) shows that LOCOG was successful in their initial target to recruit and manage 70,000 Games Makers, and was able to use the Games to generate interest among a new generation of volunteers. Since the early stages of implementation, the major focus was on training and integrating a large army of volunteers into one team of the Games-time workforce who can provide a high level of assistance to the Games. LOCOG created standard procedures to unify and simplify complex pre-Games and Games-time operations, where the requirements of functional areas were of upmost priority. They demanded from volunteers a high level of loyalty and commitment, although without placing volunteers' expectations, interests and needs foremost, such as giving them preferred tasks and level of responsibility, allowing them to choose with whom to work, use existing skills and learn new ones (Nedvetskaya, Purcell, and Hastings, 2015).

The argument, though, is that motivations and expectations play an important role in volunteer engagement as well as shape their ultimate performance and experiences. This research showed that a wide range of motivational factors pre-determined volunteers' involvement in London 2012, ranging from Olympic Games-related to altruistic, egoistic and solidarity or interpersonal contact motivations. The prestige and celebratory atmosphere of the Olympic Games were powerful motivators, 'a once-in-a-lifetime opportunity' not to be missed that inspired individuals of various ages, genders and backgrounds to volunteer for the first time or renew their previous volunteering experience. Some respondents volunteered to proudly represent their city and contribute toward community and society – a strong motivator for mature and regular volunteers. Unemployed people and students, in particular, were more motivated by the prospects of expanding their network and enhancing their employability skills. Retired and/or disabled people, in turn, viewed volunteering as a meaningful alternative to work and wanted to put their existing skills and knowledge to good use. Having fun, doing something different, socialising and making new friends were equally important for all volunteers. They were thrilled by the prospects of being 'insiders' and 'behind the scenes' and expected to be part of something unique and truly global in scale and significance. Younger and inexperienced volunteers did not have specific expectations related to their role assignments, the organisation of the Programme and volunteer management, whereas experienced volunteers had specific ideas of *the right* way they should be treated and supported.

As a result of not prioritising volunteers' motivations and expectations, LOCOG was not always successful in providing them with the best experience prior to and during the Games. This research indicated that positive experiences had those volunteers who were not bothered with lengthy recruitment and selection, had satisfactory interviews, and were properly matched to their roles. They were also able to learn something new during training and developed a personal connection with managers. In contrast, volunteers who thought they were not properly interviewed and matched to the roles, or not given details of their assignments and not able to learn a great deal had negative experiences. Other dissatisfactions included high costs, insufficient communication and inflexibility, all of which led to drop-outs. Older and experienced volunteers tended to hold such dissatisfied views. Although some volunteers noted that training sessions helped in boosting their self-confidence, communication, team building skills, Games and cultural awareness, knowledge about venues and safety procedures, they were not always successful in simulating the Games-time environment and equipping volunteers with job specifics necessary for their Games-time performance. Therefore, many learned about their role during their first shift at the Games. Still, the majority of volunteers persevered, as they did not want to miss the opportunity to be part of the Games (Nedvetskaya, Purcell, and Hastings, 2015).

Evidence from interviews and participant observations further showed that volunteering experiences, commitment, performance and satisfaction with the Games-time phase of the Programme varied greatly. These factors similarly depended on the personal attributes of participants and the management approach of immediate managers and team leaders, as well as placements and tasks performed. Whereas the pre-Games phase proved to be rather remote (volunteers were trained by people who were not necessarily their Games-time supervisors), during the Games the management style had the greatest effect on volunteers. Those who had helpful and supportive managers and team leaders reported high levels of motivation and satisfaction. Among management practices applied were allocating appropriate rosters and rotas that involved different types of job design and rotations, daily briefings and debriefings to evaluate performance, acknowledgement and rewards, although these varied across venues and teams. Those volunteers who utilised their skills and/or were given enough responsibility (especially in leadership positions) reported having fulfilling jobs, and were committed, despite the stress and intensity of the work. Volunteers with no previous volunteering experience, in particular, had notable learning experiences, were more pleased with the roles allocated and their volunteering experience. Others, who were able to develop various function-specific and job-specific competencies, increase their social skills and expand their knowledge about society or renew existing skills, were generally happy, too. Of particular value was the opportunity to build connections and friendships. However, those volunteers who felt underutilised (no new skills learned or existing ones not applied usefully) were largely dissatisfied. Again, these tended to be mature and experienced volunteers. Those who reported menial and 'back-of-house' jobs were often limited in opportunities for meaningful interactions. Negative experiences had also increased with unbalanced rosters and workload, poor rotation, mentoring and feedback. A lack of adequate rest and food on each shift further undermined the promise to provide volunteers with the best Games-time experience.

This finding comes as a surprise, since ultimately the success of the London 2012 Games depended on inspired, effective and happy volunteers. To keep volunteers motivated, the organisational challenge was to maintain the balance between the demands of the Games and the needs of volunteers, the responsibility for which was mainly with deputy venue managers and team leaders who were in direct daily contact with volunteers. Although roles and placements could not be changed, the personal support and feedback, as well as reward and recognition and the overall work environment, related to internal context, made a huge difference in how volunteers perceived their Games-time experience. This also impacted their efficacy and final commitment. However, LOCOG seemed to exploit the phenomenon of 'the Olympics' that not only furnished oversubscription at the outset but was also a strong incentive for volunteers to persevere despite difficulties and personal inconveniences. This external factor contributed to positive, memorable and transforming volunteering experiences. The distinctive atmosphere of the Games triggered emotional highs and adrenaline rushes, which seemed to offset negative feelings. Positive public perceptions and the acknowledgement of volunteers' exceptional contributions to the success of the Games at the closing ceremony boosted volunteers' pride and self-confidence. By the end of the Programme, volunteers were upset that the Games were finishing and expressed a desire to keep relationships via social media and off-line, where possible. The memory of the Games is kept alive via personal stories and memorabilia given to volunteers in the form of souvenirs, letters of appreciation, pins, badges and uniforms.

The extent to which volunteers translated their Games Makers experience beyond personal memories to something useful and productive, such as further volunteering, employment or education/training, depended on a number of factors. These included personal motives, the value volunteers attributed to volunteering activities as well as the existence and quality of follow-up support. Unlike full-time employed and retired volunteers, those who were young and unemployed aimed to boost their employability through volunteering, but were doubtful whether this might be a direct route into employment. Therefore, accrediting Games Makers training and receiving qualification, offered by LOCOG by the end of the Games, was not appealing to them. Similarly, the connection between London 2012 and further volunteering was not straightforward. As evidenced, the intensity of jobs negatively impacted the health and well-being of older and regular volunteers, which forced them to reconsider their further involvement. Dissatisfaction with poor volunteer management and a mismatch to roles resulted in some volunteers having no desire to continue volunteering in the context of mega events. This can be considered a negative legacy from London 2012, albeit not necessarily intended. On the other hand, positive experiences clearly encouraged volunteers to repeat their experiences in the future, particularly at other Olympic Games. Volunteers noted an increase in personal development, self-confidence and self-esteem, and having more volunteering opportunities as a result of being Games Makers, which was most evident in new volunteers. Yet, whether their enthusiasm continues and develops remains to be seen.

LOCOG, although able to attract first-time volunteers, neither prioritised nor had the capacity to make them regular volunteers who would volunteer outside the distinctive context of the Olympic Games and sport. Therefore, the creation of an organisation targeted directly at Games Makers to support them in continuing volunteering was critical. This relates to an element of *new initiatives* in Preuss' (2015) legacy framework where the 'structures' (in this case, volunteers' skills, expertise, and knowledge) remain latent until and unless they are used to generate *value*, which happens when new opportunities exist. The latter either proactively searched by volunteers themselves or provided with the help of existing or created organisations, such as Manchester Event Volunteers (MEV) considered as a true and lasting legacy of Manchester 2002. However, as evidenced, due to political and financial reasons, the momentum of capitalising on London 2012 euphoria to create a similar organisation was lost. Although *Join In* (a registered charity funded by the government through Big Lottery Fund and Official Partner BT) was launched in May 2012 (House of Lords, 2013) and is deemed an official legacy from London 2012, its effectiveness in sustaining the interest of Games Makers and generating a sustainable volunteering legacy attributable to London 2012 is not clear. As mentioned in the UK Government official report, "The work that the *Join In* programme is carrying out is commendable, but began too late to have maximum impact" (ibid., p. 85). Besides, its focus exclusively on sport is not comprehensive and inclusive, which limits its capacity, as "motivation for volunteering at a major event such as the Olympic and Paralympic Games [does] not necessarily extend to wishing to become involved with a sports club on a regular basis" (ibid., p. 84).

This outcome clearly illustrates that the nature of mega sport event volunteering is very different from ongoing community volunteering. Therefore, the concern is that many first-time volunteers can become one-time volunteers, and their volunteering journey would be limited to London 2012. In this sense, the community involvement of experienced volunteers, especially those who were already part of a strong cohort of regular, mature event volunteers continues more naturally. Thus, the unrealised commitment to mobilise 25,000 community volunteers in the years before London 2012 would greatly help new volunteers in transitioning smoothly to community volunteering after the Games.

## Conclusion

The title of this book *Legacies of mega-events: fact or fairy tale* implies a dyadic relationship. As this chapter has demonstrated, the social legacy of volunteering is a complex and multilayered phenomenon, which contains elements of both facts and fiction. The 'fact' delivered by London 2012 was 70,000 volunteers, which will go down in the history of the Games organisation as a success story. However, the social legacy of the fact remains highly contentious. As stated at the outset of this chapter, the Games Maker Programme was used to deliver the volunteering legacy associated with London 2012. Various elements of the Programme (strategic planning, identification, recruitment, selection, training, support, recognition and rewards) became underlying *mechanisms*, activated in a certain *context* (internal and external) at a certain *time* (before, during and after the Games) and *place* (e.g., trainings, Games-time venues), and triggered certain behavioural and psychological reactions (*positive* and *negative*) from volunteers and managers, which led to certain outcomes. Thus, at the pre-Games phase the Games stakeholders engaged in strategic planning as they set certain targets for the Games Maker Programme that were outlined in the Volunteering Strategy. Once these were specified, the programme was officially launched, triggered the involvement of volunteers through applications and initiated the process of corresponding activities associated with various stages of the programme, which lasted till the end of the Games.

Both internal and external factors highly influenced the processes and outcomes of the programme on individual, organisational and societal levels. The *external context* during the planning stage was related to a number of political, cultural, socio-economic and historical factors in the UK, and was highly influenced by the legacy rhetoric promoted by the IOC, which was reflected in the Volunteering

Strategy. The immediate internal context for volunteering was represented by organisational power and authority structures, organisational culture, working conditions and socio-emotional connections and relationships before and during the Games. Various resources (e.g., knowledge, networks) provided by LOCOG in the form of staff, training materials, volunteer uniforms and other artefacts, formal guidelines and procedures ultimately influenced who was eligible to volunteer, their experiences and outcomes of participation (both intended and unintended). As revealed by this research, the personal support and feedback, reward and recognition and the overall work environment made a huge impact on how volunteers perceived their involvements, efficacy and final commitment. During and immediately after London 2012, the Games time atmosphere and public perceptions of volunteers served as the external context, which also highly influenced volunteers' experiences and the outcomes of the Programme.

The post-Games phase, in particular, is critical in assessing the quantity and quality of volunteer services, volunteer satisfaction with the Games experiences as well as the overall achievement of operational and strategic goals. From the point of view of individuals, it is the stage when volunteers can reflect retrospectively on what they gained from their participation and how they can use this experience beyond the Games. From organisational and societal points of view, this stage allows to identify successes and failures of the programme as well as legacy outcomes. Although the Strategy, drafted many years prior to the Games, implied good quality volunteer management as essential for positive and worthwhile volunteer experiences to ensure the success of the Volunteer Programme, in reality volunteers were approached as a replaceable resource mainly used to achieve a greater organisational goal – delivering the Games effectively and efficiently. Mismanagement and inefficiencies, especially at the start, led to volunteer dissatisfaction and in some cases attrition. This, in turn, resulted in negative volunteering legacy outcomes, as those volunteers with negative experiences did not wish to continue volunteering. The rest of the volunteers – those with positive experiences and willing to continue volunteering or just one-off volunteers – were not provided with adequate and well-organised support, although it is argued that volunteers must be nurtured after the event to ensure their skills, experiences and expertise can be of good use in the future. LOCOG seemed to have lost the momentum to build on the enthusiasm of 70,000 volunteers who could potentially be available for local events beyond 2012. Despite the fact that the success of the London 2012 Games depended on inspired, loyal and committed volunteers, this result could be foreseen and treated as inevitable, given the scale, complexity of operations and fast-approaching deadlines.

In conclusion, the case of London 2012 clearly showed that the major focus of LOCOG was delivering an excellent Games Maker Programme, albeit with mixed outcomes. Therefore, the central principle of the Volunteering Strategy to leave a sustainable volunteering legacy for local communities was severely violated, and became a legacy declared rather than a legacy delivered. Although the political will was in place and resulted in explicit commitments developed by multiple event stakeholders prior to the Games, this was not enough to deliver on those promises. Various factors prevented achieving a sustainable volunteering legacy attributable to the Games, which would have at least in part justified the £9.3 billion in public sector investments. On top of a changed political environment and worsened socio-economic conditions, a lack of detailed, well-planned, coordinated and effectively managed effort, tied in with too many expectations on LOCOG to deliver on legacy promises, became the major weakness that contributed to a London 2012 volunteering legacy not being realised to the extent it was hoped. These involved poor coordination between major stakeholders, the confusion over who is responsible for what outcomes, and the lack of specific plans on *how* to achieve these outcomes, such as how to encourage Games volunteers to continue volunteering in their own communities beyond the Games. Although London 2012 organisers successfully established valuable relationships and networks, they were not able to foster and cultivate them in order to facilitate the process of legacy creation. In fact, they could not do this as the organisation ceased to exist six months after the Games were over. This inevitably poses a question about the effectiveness of the current rhetoric on legacy planning and delivery, an issue that can inform potential and current host cities. It also confirms the main tenet of critical realism that it is not the programmes that produce results but their interpretations by the subjects and their actions.

## References

Bang, H., and Chelladurai, P. (2009). Development and validation of the volunteer motivations scale for international sporting events (VMS-ISE). *International Journal of Sport Management and Marketing, 6*(4), 332–350.

Baum, T., Deery, M., Hanlon, C., Lockstone, L., and Smith, K. (2009). *People and work in events and conventions.* Oxfordshire: CABI Publishing.

Baum, T., and Lockstone, L. (2007). Volunteers and mega sporting events: Developing a research framework. *International Journal of Event Management Research, 3*(1), 29–41.

Byers, T. (2013). Using critical realism: A new perspective on control of volunteers in sport clubs. *European Sport Management Quarterly, 13*(1), 5–31.

Byers, T., and Thurston, A. (2011). Using critical realism in research on the management of sport: A new perspective of volunteers and voluntary sport organizations. 19th Conference of the European Association for Sport Management, Madrid, Spain.

Chalip, L. (2014). From legacy to leverage. In J. Grix (Ed.), *Leveraging legacies from sports mega-events: Concepts and cases* (pp. 2–12). London: Palgrave Macmillan.

Chanavat, N., and Ferrand, A. (2010). Volunteer programme in mega sport events: The case of the Olympic Winter Games, Torino 2006. *International Journal of Sport Management and Marketing, 7*(3/4), 241–266.

Chappelet, J. L. (2012). Mega sporting event legacies: A multifaceted concept. *Papeless de Europa, 25*, 76–86.

Cuskelly, G., Hoye, R., and Auld, C. (2006). *Working with volunteers in sport: Theory and practice.* Oxon: Routledge.

DCMS (Department of Culture, Media and Sport). (2008). *Before, during and after: Making the most of the London 2012 Games.* London: Department of Culture, Media and Sport.

DCMS (Department of Culture, Media and Sport). (2012). *Beyond 2012: The London 2012 legacy story.* London: Department of Culture, Media and Sport. Retrieved October 23,

2014, from www.gov.uk/government/uploads/system/uploads/attachment_data/file /77993/DCMS_Beyond_2012_Legacy_Story.pdf

Department of Culture, Media and Sport (DCMS). (2013). *2012 Games meta evaluation: Report 5 post-Games evaluation summary report.* Retrieved December 1, 2016, from www.gov.uk/government/uploads/system/uploads/attachment_data/file/224181/1188-B_Meta_Evaluation.pdf

Dickson, T., and Benson, M. (2013). *London 2012 Games makers: Towards redefining legacy.* London: Department for Culture, Media and Sport (DCMS).

Doherty, A. (2009). The volunteer legacy of a major sport event. *Journal of Policy Research in Tourism, Leisure and Events, 1*(3), 185–207.

Elstad, B. (1996). Volunteer perception of learning and satisfaction in a mega-event: The case of the XVII Olympic Winter Games in Lillehammer. *Festival Management and Event Tourism, 4,* 75–83.

Ferrand, A., and Skirstad, B. (2015). The volunteers' perspective. In M. M. Parent and J-L. Chappelet (Eds.), *Routledge handbook of sports event management* (pp. 65–88). New York: Routledge.

Giannoulakis, C., Wang, C. H., and Gray, D. (2008). Measuring volunteer motivation in mega-sporting events. *Event Management, 11,* 191–200.

Girginov, V. (2012). Governance of the London 2012 Olympic Games legacy. *International Review for the Sociology of Sport, 47*(5), 543–558.

Girginov, V. (2013). Handbook of the London 2012 Olympic and Paralympic Games. Volume One: Making the games. London: Routledge.

Girginov, V. (2014). Handbook of the London 2012 Olympic and Paralympic Games. Volume Two: Celebrating the games. London: Routledge.

Gold, J. R., and Gold, M. M. (2011). Olympic cities: City agendas, planning and the world's games, 1896–2016. London: Routledge.

Green, C., and Chalip, L. (2004). Paths to volunteer commitment: Lessons from the Sydney Olympic Games. In R. A. Stebbins and M. Graham (Eds.), *Volunteering as leisure/ leisure as volunteering: An international assessment* (pp. 49–70). Cambridge, MA: CABI Publishing.

Horne, J., and Houlihan, B. (2014). London 2012. In J. Grix (Ed.), *Leveraging legacies from sports Mega-events: Concepts and cases* (pp. 107–117). London: Palgrave Macmillan.

House of Lords (2013). *Keeping the flame alive: The Olympic and Paralympic legacy. Report of session 2013–14.* London: Select Committee on Olympic and Paralympic Legacy. Retrieved October 23, 2014, from www.publications.parliament.uk/pa/ld201314/ ldselect/ldolympic/78/78.pdf

Hoye, R., and Cuskelly, G. (2009). The psychology of sport event volunteerism: A review of volunteer motives, involvement and behaviour. In T. Baum, M. Deery, C. Hanlon, L. Lockstone and K. Smith (Eds.), *People and work in events and conventions: A research perspective* (pp. 171–180). Oxfordshire: CABI.

Hustinx, L., Cnaan, R. A., and Handy, F. (2010). Navigating theories of volunteering: A hybrid map for a complex phenomenon. *Journal for the Theory of Social Behaviour, 40*(4), 410–434.

Hustinx, L., and Lammertyn, F. (2003). Collective and reflexive styles of volunteering: A sociological modernization perspective. *Voluntas: International Journal of Voluntary and Nonprofit Organizations, 14*(2), 167–187.

IOC. (2005). *Technical manual on workforce.* Lausanne: International Olympic Committee. Retrieved November 5, 2014, from www.gamesmonitor.org.uk/files/Technical_ Manual_on_Workforce.pdf

Jones, M., and Stokes, T. (2003). The Commonwealth Games and urban regeneration: An investigation into training initiatives and partnerships and their effects on disadvantaged groups in East Manchester. *Managing Leisure, 8*(4), 198–211.

Kemp, S. (2002). The hidden workforce: Volunteers' learning in the Olympics. *Journal of European Industrial Training, 26*(2–4), 109–116.

Khoo, S., and Engelhorn, R. (2011). Volunteer motivations at a national Special Olympics event. *Adapted Physical Activity Quarterly, 28*, 27–39.

Leopkey, B., and Parent, M. M. (2012). Olympic Games legacy: From general benefits to sustainable long-term legacy. *The International Journal of the History of Sport, 29*(6), 924–943.

Lockstone, L., and Baum, T. (2009). The public face of event volunteering at the 2006 Commonwealth Games: The media perspective. *Managing Leisure, 14*(1), 38–56.

London Organising Committee for the Olympic Games (LOCOG). (2013). *London 2012 report and accounts*. London: Organising Committee of the Olympic and Paralympic Games Ltd. Retrieved May 17, 2013, from www.olympic.org/Documents/Games_London_2012/London_Reports/LOCOG_18month_Report_Sept2012.pdf

Lukka, P., and Ellis, A. (2001). An exclusive construct? Exploring different cultural concepts of volunteering. *Voluntary Action, 3*(3), 87–109.

Manchester 2002. (2002). The XVII Commonwealth Games pre volunteer programme: Executive summary. Manchester.

Manchester 2002. (2003). The XVIIth Commonwealth Games Manchester 2002 pre volunteer programme: Final report. Manchester.

Minnaert, L. (2012). An Olympic legacy for all? The non-infrastructural outcomes of the Olympic Games for socially excluded groups (Atlanta 1996 – Beijing 2008). *Tourism Management, 33*, 361–370.

Nedvetskaya, O., Purcell, R., and Hastings, A. (2015). Looking back at London 2012: Recruitment, selection and training of games makers. In G. Poynter, V. Viehoff, and Y. Li (Eds.), *The London Olympics and urban development: The mega-event city (regions and cities)* (pp. 293–306). London: Routledge.

Nichols, G., and Ralston, R. (2014). Volunteering for the games. In V. Girginov (Ed.), *Handbook of the London 2012 Olympic and Paralympic Games. Volume two: Celebrating the games* (pp. 53–70). London: Routledge.

The Organising Committee for the XIV Olympiad. (1948). *The official report of the organizing committee for the XIV Olympiad*. London: Mc Corquodale & Co. Ltd. Retrieved December 4, 2016, from http://library.la84.org/6oic/OfficialReports/1948/OR1948.pdf.

Parent, M. M., and Smith-Swan, S. (2013). *Managing major sports events: Theory and practice*. London: Routledge.

Pawson, R. (2013). *The science of evaluation: A realist manifesto*. London: Sage Publications.

Pawson, R., and Tilley, N. (1997). *Realistic evaluation*. London: Sage Publications.

Pawson, R., and Tilley, N. (2004). *Realist evaluation* [Online]. Retrieved February 2012, from www.communitymatters.com.au/RE_chapter.pdf

Preuss, H. (2007). The conceptualisation and measurement of mega sport event legacies. *Journal of Sport & Tourism, 12*(3–4), 207–227.

Preuss, H. (2015). A framework for identifying the legacies of a mega sport event. *Leisure Studies, 34*(6), 643–664.

Silvestre, G. (2009). The social impacts of mega events: Towards a framework. *Esporte e Sociedade, 4*(10), 1–26.

Smith, A. (2006). After the circus leaves town: The relationship between sports events, tourism and urban regeneration. In M. K. Smith (Ed.), *Tourism, culture and regeneration* (pp. 85–100). Oxfordshire: CABI Publishing.

Smith, A., and Fox, T. (2007). From 'Event-led' to 'Event-themed' Regeneration: The 2002 Commonwealth Games legacy programme. *Urban Studies, 44*(5–6), 1125–1143.

Smith, D. H. (1994). Determinants of voluntary association participation and volunteering: A literature review. *Non-Profit and Voluntary Sector Quarterly, 23*(3), 243–263.

Solberg, H. A. (2003). Major sporting events: Assessing the value of volunteers' work. *Managing Leisure, 8*(1), 17–27.

SQW. (2011). *LDA ESF programme evaluation 2007–2010. Final report.* London. Retrieved March 9, 2014, from www.london.gov.uk/sites/default/files/Final%20 LDA%20ESF%20Evaluation%20Report%20Personal%20Best%2013-03-2012_0.pdf

Stebbins, R. A., and Graham, M. (2004). Volunteering as leisure/leisure as volunteering: An international assessment. Cambridge, MA: CABI Publishing.

Surborg, B., VanWynsberghe, R., and Wyly, E. (2008). Mapping the Olympic growth machine: Transnational urbanism and the growth machine diaspora. *City, 12*(3), 341–355.

University of East London/Thames Gateway Institute for Sustainability (UEL/TGIfS). (2010, October). *Olympic Games impact study OGI study – London 2012 pre-Games report.* Economic and Social Research Council. Retrieved March 5, 2013, from www. uel.ac.uk/geo-information/documents/UEL_TGIfS_PreGames_OGI_Release.pdf

VanWynsberghe, R. (2015). The Olympic Games Impact (OGI) study for the 2010 Winter Olympic Games: Strategies for evaluating sport mega-events' contribution to sustainability. *International Journal of Sport Policy and Politics, 7*(1), 1–18.

Volunteering Strategy Group. (2006). The London 2012 Olympic Games and Paralympic Games volunteering strategy. London: London 2012.

Wei, N. (2010). Experience. Value. Influence. A research report on the volunteer work legacy transformation of the Beijing 2008 Olympic Games and Paralympic Games. Beijing: China Renmin University Press.

Wilson, J. (2012). Volunteerism research: A review essay. *Nonprofit and Voluntary Sector Quarterly, 41*(2), 176–212.

Yin, R. K. (2014). *Case study research: Design and methods* (5th ed.). Thousand Oaks, CA: Sage Publications.

# 5 Sport participation legacies of mega sporting events

*Mike Weed*

There has been much discussion about the extent to which mega sport events, such as the Olympic and Paralympic Games, can lead to increases in sport participation in host communities (e.g., Vigor, Mean, and Tims, 2004). However, evidence to either confirm or refute such legacies as fact or fairytale is mixed, and it is not just the outcome evidence that is important, but also how far policies and processes have been put in place to attempt to deliver sport participation legacies.

It is a long-held belief among governments, event organisers and sport professionals that mega sport events can lead to increases in sport participation among those who watch them. The assumption has been that mega sport events inherently and automatically inspire people and stimulate an increase in demand to participate in sport (Coalter, 2004). Consequently, it has been assumed that all that is required to increase participation is to ensure that there is an adequate supply of sport participation opportunities and facilities to provide for what is assumed to be an inevitable increase in demand associated with mega sport events. Four years before the 2012 Olympic and Paralympic Games in London, Lord Sebastian Coe, former double Olympic gold medalist and the chair of the London Organising Committee for the Olympic Games (LOCOG), stated that

> in the run-up to the 2012 Olympics there will be no better opportunity in my lifetime to drive sport legacy. In terms of boosting participation in sport in this country the red carpet has been rolled out with a gilt edge attached.
>
> (Coe, 2008, p. 3)

Coe's belief was shared by Tessa Jowell, at the time the UK government minister responsible for the Olympic Games (DCMS, 2008), Boris Johnson, the mayor of London (The Guardian, 2008), and innumerable other politicians and public servants seeking to demonstrate that the investment that UK taxpayers were making in the 2012 Olympic and Paralympic Games could be justified across a number of policy sectors. However, some critiques (e.g., Coalter, 2007; Murphy and Bauman, 2007) suggested that this "belief" might more accurately be described as a 'political position' derived from a political need to demonstrate positive outcomes from the Games.

Despite a widely quoted assertion at this time that no previous Games had increased participation in sport (Conn, 2008; House of Commons Select Committee,

2007), there was an "illusion" of a research base that appeared to support the belief that mega sport events could raise sport participation. Two Health Impact Assessments, in London (London Health Commission and London Development Agency, 2004) and the North East of England (North East Public Health Observatory, 2006), of the health-related potential of the 2012 Games were presented in such a way as to suggest that there was some relevant evidence. However, each of these reports was largely based on the opinions of health experts at round tables and workshops rather than any empirical evidence. Consequently, their conclusions were prefaced by statements such as, "hosting the Games is thought to. . . . " (London Health Commission and London Development Agency, 2004, p. 103) or the Games "could result in increased interest in sports" (p. 8) and "could have a health benefit for the North East" (North East Public Health Observatory, 2006, p. ii). Similarly, Coalter's (2004) contribution to the Joint Institute for Public Policy Research and Demos publication, "After the Gold Rush" was a discussion of intents, potential models and possibilities as, again, there was no evidence base. In fairness, Coalter (2004) recognised this and concluded that potential positive outcomes for sport participation are likely to be the result of "complex and not well understood interactions" (p. 108). This reinforced Murphy and Bauman's (2007) conclusions that the "health potential of major sporting and physical activity events is often cited, but evidence for public health benefit is lacking" (p. 193).

The adoption of supposed potential processes and possibilities as evidence has characterized the debate around whether mega sport events can lead to increases in sport participation, and this is one factor that contributes to confusion about the evidence. In addition, there are also problems regarding attribution and precision, particularly when looking for effects in national statistics (Henry, 2016; Veal, Toohey, and Frawley, 2012). Preuss (2007), in his review of the way in which event legacies are measured, and Crompton (2006), in his critique of the conduct of economic impact studies, both discuss the problems with using structural or macro-data such as national sport participation statistics. These data are often collected for far more general purposes than assessing the impact of a particular sport event, to examine the impacts of such events. The first problem with such data is that any changes in sport participation rates are impossible to isolate to the effect of an event, even one as large as the Olympic and Paralympic Games. This leads to a second related problem. That is, even if it was possible to isolate changes to an event, macro-data is rarely sensitive enough to pick up changes because within the context of the range of social, economic, and cultural forces that might affect sport participation, mega sport events are likely to produce relatively small variations in the data.

A further source of confusion about the evidence is the conflation of both effects and impacts. In respect of the former, this may relate to a failure to differentiate between an increase in the number of sports participants and an increase in the frequency of participation among existing participants. Similarly, commentaries have also often not accounted for activity switching, in which participants drop out of one sport to take up another (Weed et al., 2015), or have assumed that investments in new programmes represent an impact on participation itself (Weed, 2014). More broadly, impacts that are assumed to include participation outcomes are often presented in an aggregated way that can obscure specific effects (Barget and Gouget, 2007; Faulkner et al., 2003). This has often also involved the use of inappropriate proxies as measures of participation, such as increased facilities, or increased availability of opportunities, presented together as an overall effect on "sport development".

The aim of this chapter, therefore, is to distinguish evidence from opinion, and to interrogate interpretations of evidence to explore how far claimed effects of mega sport events on sport participation are attributable and precise. Key to informing this discussion are two systematic reviews that collated, quality assessed and analysed the worldwide English-language evidence for the deliverability of sport participation legacies from mega sport events (McCartney et al., 2010; Weed et al., 2009). These reviews provide much of the substantive evidence to inform the first two substantive parts of this chapter, which comprise a discussion of evidence that supports the possibility of participation legacies from mega sport events followed by a discussion of evidence that refutes the possibility of such legacies. However, evidence is rarely unequivocal, and the discussion here is more nuanced than a simple accumulation of evidence towards a conclusion that participation legacies are fact or fairy tale. This is because the possibility of delivering a sport participation legacy from a mega sport event depends on a supportive context for the event and on the extent to which policies and practices have been put in place that are derived from the evidence. In addressing this issue, a third substantive section discusses the extent to which the evidence base has not been significantly advanced. Since the McCartney et al. (2010) and Weed et al. (2009) reviews because mega sport events since 2010 have either pursued policies that were not evidence-informed (e.g., London, 2012) or have not pursued policies towards delivering a sport participation legacy at all (e.g., Rio, 2016). In both cases, sport participation legacies have not been delivered, but this appears to be a failing of policy rather than of possibility.

## Evidence supporting participation legacies: towards tentative facts?

There is a range of evidence that supports the existence of processes by which a mega sport event can deliver increases in sport participation. However, for such processes to be effective there must be a supportive context for the event. As such, if a population holds negative perceptions of, or attitudes towards, a mega sport event, the potential to use such an event to increase sport participation is likely to be considerably reduced, if not negated.

### *The importance of a supportive context*

Brown and Massey (2001) reviewed previous social impact studies prior to the Manchester 2002 Commonwealth Games and, in drawing together lessons for the Manchester 2002 Research Programme, concluded that

> the perception of the local population and local communities are important in how people respond to a major event – if their experience and perception

is a negative one, they are less likely to be enthusiastic about taking up the sports involved. As such, understanding how the Manchester Games are perceived and why, and understanding the reactions of the Manchester public (in particular near the main Games site) are vital elements of understanding its social and sporting impact.

(p. 18)

Similarly, a discursive review of the Arctic Winter Games (Lankford, Neal, and Szabo, 2000), following a field questionnaire of participants' attitudes, claimed (although not deriving from the empirical work) that the building of healthy lifestyles was enabled through the "*spirit of play, competition, inclusion, development and understanding*" (p. 52) that the Games engendered.

Cragg Ross Dawson, reporting on empirical qualitative research into public attitudes about the London 2012 Games (CRD, 2007), suggested that a lack of awareness of legacy goals or plans leads to cynicism about the likely legacy:

many wondered why they should believe that the aims and targets will be met. This scepticism was partly due to an underlying cynicism borne of experience or perceptions of government or public projects and promises and, to a lesser extent, recent media coverage of the budget and knowledge of shortcomings in previous Games legacies. . . . But it was also a result of an almost complete lack of awareness on the part of many of any concrete plans or initiatives currently in place which might give confidence in aims and targets for the future." (pp. 17–18) . . ." [This] led to a range of initial 'positions' regarding the Games legacy from 'wait and see' to outright cynicism.

(pp. 5–6)

However, this cynicism was tempered by the fact that many respondents wanted to believe that the Games would bring positive benefits:

There was a widespread desire to believe in the Games and their legacy, but most were 'held back' in their views by questions which remained unanswered; few could be more positive than the initial 'wait and see' position.

(p. 6)

The initial views of respondents in this research, expressed before legacy details were explained in more detail, after which responses were much more positive, were derived from a range of public sources, beliefs, and memories:

Prior expectations of what legacy would include seemed to have been influenced by what respondents had heard in the media or on the grapevine, their beliefs about what it should include, and (for some) their knowledge of legacies of previous Games.

(p. 16)

As such, it appears that the delivery of a sport participation legacy needs to align to wider strategies of public engagement and the development of positive attitudes towards the wider impacts of the mega sport events. Crompton (2004), in relation to US Major League sports teams, and Ohmann, Jones, and Wilkes (2006), in relation to the 2006 Football World Cup in Germany, each note that a local community's positive perceptions of the impact of a sports team or event on that community is an important factor in generating engagement with the team or event. In addition, Waitt (2003) describes 'altruistic surplus', whereby the perceived benefits of the Sydney 2000 Olympic Games were not necessarily direct to the individual, but to other groups that the individual would like to see receive such benefits. Similarly, Cragg Ross Dawson (CRD, 2007) found that many respondents wished to see the impacts of the London 2012 Games directed at young people. Importantly, communities weigh up the costs and benefits of mega sport events, and if communities *"perceive the costs to outweigh the benefits, they will hold negative attitudes . . . and may . . . withdraw from the relationship"* (Fredline, 2005, p. 271), following which they will be beyond the reach of any legacy initiatives (Weed et al., 2009).

Cragg Ross Dawson noted that respondents wanted to believe in the benefits of the 2012 Games, but were cynical because of previous experience of other events or projects, or because of information in the media (CRD, 2007). They also reported that when the legacy plans for the 2012 Games were explained to respondents, they became much more positive about the potential legacy. This seems to reinforce Deccio and Baloglu's (2002), conclusion that there is a need to direct attention and effort towards the communication of benefits, particularly those that local communities will feel are relevant to them. This may explain Brown and Massey's (2001, p. 18) summary recommendation prior to the 2002 Manchester Commonwealth Games that

> a broad notion of participation is needed. . . [A]ssessing the benefit gained from a major sporting event in terms of sports participation can only be fully accounted for and fully explained if a broader understanding of the social impacts of the Games are understood.

Beyond the mega sport event, it appears that a positive attitude and engagement with sport itself among the target population is an important factor in raising sport participation. This is something that has long been reported in the wider exercise and sport psychology literature, in which a meta-analytical review of evidence from 72 previous studies of sport and physical activity participation (Hagger, Chatzisarantis, and Biddle, 2002) shows that the effect of past behaviour on current behaviour is twice that of any other variable studied. In addition, there is also some limited evidence that past behaviour predicts engagement with sport in a sport event context.

A range of sources relating to sport events in general (Green and Chalip, 1998), to the Manchester 2002 Commonwealth Games (ICRC, 2003; Ralston, Downward, and Lumsdon, 2004) and to swimming (Burgham and Downward, 2005) all indicate that previous interest in, experience of, or participation in sport is a general predictor of current and future sport engagement. Such previous interest or experience may have been as a participant, as a live spectator, as a mediated spectator (i.e. watching on television), as a previous volunteer, or as a result of the involvement of family or friends. Downward and Ralston (2006) found, through factor analysis of questionnaire responses among sport volunteers, that both previous sport volunteering and previous live attendance at sport events appeared to be factors in raising interest and participation but that this did not extend to those who watched sport on television. Similarly, Kim and Chalip (2004) found that previous interest in the Football World Cup as an event was the variable with the largest impact on desire to travel to the World Cup in Korea and Japan. This evidence supports the wider evidence base related to physical activity and sport mentioned in the previous paragraph that previous participation makes current or future participation more likely.

Therefore, the supportive context required for the processes by which a mega sport event can deliver increases in sport participation to be effective comprises a positive engagement with the event and its potential to impact positively on the community, and a positive previous engagement with, and attitude towards, sport itself. Within this context, evidence suggests that a process called a *demonstration effect* can take place, in which those positively disposed towards elite sports, sports people, and sports events may be inspired by those sports, people, or events to change their own sport participation.

### The potential of a demonstration effect

Several authors (EdComs, 2007; LERI, 2007, Murphy and Bauman, 2007; Weed et al., 2015) have argued that reported increases in sport participation surrounding mega sport events are, in fact, increases in sport participation frequency. Thus, this is the first impact that a demonstration effect has shown to have the potential to deliver given a supportive context and the enactment of policies to lever this effect. Sport and Recreation Victoria (2006) reported, for example, that 59% of the participants in 'Warming up for the Games', a programme designed to increase participation in the run up to the 2006 Melbourne Commonwealth Games, were sport club members, thus strongly suggesting that the programme was encouraging those already participating to participate more. Similarly, EdComs (2007) noted that quantitative data showed increases in participation frequency (i.e. a positive response to the question: "[D]o you play *more* sport?") among schoolchildren and young people in Manchester following the 2002 Commonwealth Games.

Both Hamlyn and Hudson (2005) and LERI (2007) cited market research commissioned by Sport England (2004), carried out one month after the end of the Athens 2004 Olympic Games, that suggested that "[m]ore than a quarter of the population in England (26%) have been inspired by British medal-winning performances at the Olympic Games in Athens" (p. 66). While this appears to suggest a demonstration effect in inspiring people to take up sport and physical activity, the figure of 26% refers to those "who are now involved in *more* sport" (11%) and those "interested in doing *more* sport" (15%), "as a result of Team GB's success." Also in 2004, 6% of respondents to the Sporting Motivations Survey (TNS, 2004) claimed that UK sporting success had resulted in them doing *more* sport.

More recently, Weed's (2010) re-analysis of Sport England's Satisfaction with the Quality of the Sport Experience (SQSE) survey showed that existing low level but regular sport participants (those participating between twice a month and twice a week) were highly responsive to a demonstration effect, with 32% of this group claiming that the success of the national team in major events positively affected (i.e. increased) their personal participation in sport.

Brown and Massey (2001) and Newby (2003) also cited wider evidence from the social policy arena that those who gain most from new facility provision, are the groups identified by Ravenscroft (1993) as "leisure gainers" (predominantly professional white middle-class males) who are already engaged with recreation (Coalter, 1993; Collins, Henry, Houlihan, and Buller, 1999). Again, this suggests an increase in participation among those who are already participating.

The evidence that a demonstration effect can inspire those that are already participating to participate a little more accords with the evidence that those whose participation is most likely to be affected by mega sport events are those who are already positively engaged with sport, and who are positive about the event. However, such positive engagement with sport is also likely to exist among those who may have previously participated in sport but whose participation has lapsed. Systematic reviews of the assumptions of an approach called the transtheoretical model as applied to sport and exercise participation (Marshall and Biddle, 2001; Spencer, Adams, Malone, Roy, and Yost, 2006) suggest that when participation in sport lapses, positive attitudes towards sport are unlikely to change. In fact, Spencer et al. (2006) found that there was "some evidence" to support the conclusion that those whose participation had lapsed at some point behaved differently to those whose participation had never lapsed. Specifically, that lapsed participants were likely to have a very low level sporadic participation pattern, with such a pattern including a number of abortive attempts at getting restarted. This implies continued engagement despite actual participation being very low and irregular. This previous participation and continued engagement suggests that, although they may often be listed in statistics as non-participants, there is some potential to re-engage lapsed participants through similar demonstration effect processes to those by which participation frequency is increased among current participants.

However, there is little evidence available to assess the potential of mega sport events to re-engage lapsed sport participants. This is because information on sport participation history is rarely collected in sport participation surveys – information is most often limited to current participation or non-participation. One exception to this is Weed's (2010) analysis of the SQSE survey, in which data were available about those participants who had not participated in the previous month, but had done so at some point in the previous year. This profile aligns with that described by Spencer et al. (2006) of the sporadic participation pattern of the lapsed participant. Importantly, Weed (2010) found that these lapsed participants were even more responsive to a demonstration effect than low level but regular sport participants, with 35% claiming that the success of the national team in major events would positively affect their personal participation in sport.

A final group that evidence suggests may be affected by a demonstration effect are those who are current regular participants in sport, who are positively engaged with the event and with sport, but for whom their enthusiasm for their current sport may be waning. Brown and Massey (2001), EdComs (2007), Hindson, Gidlow, and Peebles (1994), LERI (2007), and VANOC (2007) all suggest that where there have been reported increases in participation in particular sports, thought to be associated with a mega sport event, these increases are likely, at least in part, to be among those who are already participating in other sports and are "switching" their participation.

Reported increases in participation in curling following the success of the Scottish women's team in the 2002 Olympic Winter Games are suggested by EdComs (2007, p. 43) to result from activity switching:

> those who say they have been influenced by success may have been physically active in other sports. This does seem to have been the case in the curling example and, if true on a wider scale, means that success simply encourages interchange between sports rather than increased participation in sport overall.

Following the Sydney Olympic Games in 2000 Veal's (2003) quantitative analysis of sports participation data across Australia as a whole showed increases in participation in seven Olympic sports but declines in nine others, which further supports a switching effect. Brown and Massey (2001) and Schmid (1996) suggest that activity switching is perhaps particularly likely if the influence of the demonstration effect is linked to the presence of new or unusual sports in a forthcoming event programme which may lead to the sport being more widely available to be played.

Two comments must be made about an activity switching effect. First, while it is consistent with the evidence that the most likely impacts of a demonstration effect are on those who are already engaged with sport, like the impact on lapsed participants, it is often difficult to detect. This is because participation data for individual sports do not show the sport participation history of any "new" participants, and therefore whether they are switching or not cannot be captured, whilst overall participation data for all sports would show no net effect from activity switching. Second, although the impact of activity switching on sport participation as a whole may appear to be neutral, it is not clear whether those switching sports would have dropped out of sport altogether if they had not been inspired to participate in their new sport.

While the evidence in this section is not definitive, it does suggest that there is the possibility that, given a supportive context, a demonstration effect from a mega sport event can (1) encourage those who already participate to participate more, (2) encourage those who have participated previously to participate again, and (3) reduce drop-out by re-invigorating enthusiasm through encouraging participation in new activities. The extent to which recent mega sport events provide a further test of this evidence is discussed later in the chapter. However, the next section explores the evidence that refutes the possibility of delivering sport participation legacies from mega sport events.

## Evidence refuting sport participation legacies: exposing fairytales?

In 2010, a systematic review published in the *British Medical Journal* (McCartney et al., 2010) concluded that, "the available evidence is not sufficient to confirm or refute expectations about the health or socio-economic benefits for the host population of previous major multi-sport events". Possible impacts on sport participation or physical activity were among the aspects considered as a health benefit of mega sport events by McCartney et al. (2010).

McCartney et al's (2010) conclusions would normally invite two possible interpretations: either that no effect on physical activity or sport participation should be expected from mega sport events or that there has been no robust evidence collected that proves or disproves that there is such an effect. However, in the case of mega sport events a third interpretation is suggested. It is certainly true that at the time of McCartney et al.'s (2010) review there was no evidence that mega sport events had resulted in sustained increases in mass participation in sport or in population level increases in physical activity. However, it was also true that no previous mega sport event had pro-actively and systematically attempted to use the event to raise population levels of physical activity and sport participation. Participation data had merely been examined ex poste to explore whether simply hosting a mega sport event had affected participation levels. Consequently, McCartney et al.'s (2010) review might be most usefully interpreted to mean that there is no evidence for an inherent effect on sport participation, in which benefits occur automatically.

The year before McCartney et al.'s (2010) review was published, another systematic review, conducted for the UK Department of Health, also showed that there was no evidence for an inherent effect on physical activity or sport participation from mega sport events (Weed et al., 2009). In fact, this review went further in suggesting that there is evidence that inherent effects do not occur. However, Weed et al. (2009) also suggested that there is evidence that mechanisms associated with mega sport events – the demonstration effects discussed in the previous section – have had a positive effect on participation frequency and on re-engaging past participants where specific initiatives have been put in place to harness such mechanisms to stimulate demand.

Evidence presented by Weed et al. (2009) and McCartney et al. (2010), suggests that the perception among governments, event organisers and sport professionals that mega sport events can lead to increases in sport participation among those who watch them is flawed. This is because, first, there is evidence that there is no inherent effect. As such, it is not the mega sport event itself that should be considered to be the intervention to increase sport participation, rather the event presents the context in which linked interventions can be developed and delivered alongside the event to increase sport participation. Second, there is no evidence that a demonstration effect can be harnessed among those who do not participate, and never have participated, in sport. Consequently, there is no evidence that mega sport events can bring new people into sport. In fact, there is some evidence that attempting to use a demonstration effect among long-term non-participants may be off-putting and thus have a detrimental effect on potential participation.

London East Research Institute (LERI, 2007, p. 47) summarised the potential to increase participation as follows:

> Sports participation increases are often assumed very readily by host cities. Both Barcelona and Sydney provide evidence for some positive short term impacts. However there is doubt about the sustainability of Olympic effects and Sydney evidence is ambiguous.

LERI (2007) also cited Cashman (2006) in support of the view that there has been a paucity of studies on post-Games participation in sport and, in particular, to question whether an Olympic 'bounce' is short or long term. Such studies, where they do exist, mostly retrospectively utilise quantitative secondary data (largely population-level surveys) that measure sport participation but do not ask more qualitative questions about the factors that have influenced such participation. In Barcelona, host city of the 1992 Games, Truno's (1995) analysis compares two "similar" quantitative studies published by the municipality in 1985 and 1995. These studies showed that attitudes towards sport had grown more positive, and that the proportion of the population participating in sport at least once a week had grown from 36% in 1983 to 47% in 1989 to 51% in 1995. This suggests some evidence for an effect, but the strength of the evidence is ameliorated by the "similarity" rather than the direct comparability of the studies, and the fact that the vast majority of the participation change had taken place more than three years before the Games commenced. In addition, across this 12-year period there were many other influences on sporting life in Barcelona which may have an impact on sport participation and attitudes, not least the highly successful FC Barcelona football team.

There is mixed evidence from the Sydney Games in 2000. Haynes (2001) suggested anecdotal reports from the media of large post-Games increases in interest and participation in Olympic sports, but Cashman (2006) showed that, in relation to recreational swimming at least, attendances in Sydney were static or slightly falling in the two to three years following the Games. Murphy and Bauman (2007), in their systematic review of public health initiatives, suggested that there was no evidence from Sydney that the euphoria of the Games turned into increased activity afterwards, despite a great deal of "rhetoric".

In the run-up to the Sydney 2000 Olympic Games, Hogan and Norton (2000) examined quantitative evidence for a demonstration effect linked to elite success at both home and abroad in Australia in the 20 years between 1976 and 1996. This study is particularly significant because it compares investment in elite sport in Australia, which targeted investment towards elite sport over a more sustained period than any other social democracy in the world, with elite performance at the Olympic Games and the level of the Australian sedentary population. Over a 20-year period expenditure on elite sport rose from virtually zero in 1976 to AUS$150million in 1995. This was matched by a steady increase in Australia's position in the Olympic medal table from 32nd in 1976 to 7th in 1996 (fifth if population size is accounted for). However, over a similar period, the number of Australians reporting they were completely sedentary rose from an average of 29.1% of the population in 1984, to 40.6% in 1999. Hogan and Norton (2000, p. 216) concluded that these data suggest that

> [t]he expectation that successful sporting heroes as role models inspire others to participate in sport and physical activity may have run its race. Perhaps it was never a legitimate starter. . . . Directing approximately one billion dollars to the elite apex of the sports pyramid in expectation that mass participation will result is irresponsible. . . we should not accept as a matter of fact that our elite sports success translates into motivation to become active among the rest of the population.

Because Hogan and Norton (2000) were comparing elite success with sedentariness (i.e., non-participation in sport, exercise or physical activity), their findings suggest that a demonstration effect does not entice new participants into sport. Furthermore, the comparison with data for non-participation means that such figures cannot be confused by a potential increased frequency or activity switching effect. Therefore, Hogan and Norton's (2000) findings suggest that over a considerable time in Australia there has been no demonstration effect in increasing the number of new participants in sport.

Following the Manchester Commonwealth Games of 2002, Faber Maunsell (2004) collated quantitative data that showed increased participation of 7% in adults in the UK and 19% among 6- to 15-year-olds in the North West. However, EdComs (2007) questioned the extent to which this is was inherent demonstration effect, or is attributable to media coverage, Games attendance, facility development, schools initiatives or other factors (which may or may not be part of a strategic leveraging programme). Faber Maunsell (2004) recognised this, noting that

> [s]ome stakeholders. . . argued that the Games themselves only resulted in a small and short-term increase in participation in sport and that more proactive methods to encourage participation are required to have greater and longer term impact.

Therefore, although there is some weak evidence that suggests a short-term "spike" in participation, or at least interest, around the times of mega sport events (Perks, 2015; VANOC, 2007), evidence for an inherent (or unleveraged) effect is, at best, equivocal. Consequently, there is wide agreement (Coalter, 2007; EdComs, 2007; Hindson et al., 1994; LERI, 2007) that a demonstration effect is a potential effect that must be leveraged. Collectively, these sources suggest that, as noted earlier, mega sport events themselves do not represent interventions to increase sport participation, rather such events offer a context in which linked interventions can be developed and delivered alongside the event, to increase sport participation. However, care needs to be taken with targeting such interventions, as Weed et al. (2015) note that there is the potential for aversion effects.

Hindson et al. (1994) suggested that seeking a demonstration effect through elite participants may result in the role models being too remote to influence behaviour directly. More significant, EdComs (2007) noted that the use of elite role models and elite success to try to develop sport participation may deter others who may fear that sport as represented by elite athletes is beyond them. Hindson et al. (1994) recognised potentially dual processes at play here. On the one hand, elite sports people can be inspirational as role models, but on the other, they may deter participation among non-participants because of the perceived competence gap and remoteness from their experience. In fact, that elite sport may not be the best way to encourage mass participation is a point made across a range of studies and contexts (e.g., Coalter, 2007; EdComs, 2007; Hindson et al., 1994; Murphy and Bauman, 2007; RAND Europe, 2007). Coalter (2007) noted that patterns of engagement are complex and that the relationship of these processes to role models is ill defined. It may partly depend on a range of factors including how role models are seen, how accessible or "normal" their profile is, and also on individual or community self-efficacy. Qualitative empirical evidence (e.g., Hindson et al., 1994) also suggested that for elite sporting role models to be effective, target groups must already be psychologically engaged with sport and the idea of sport participation, a notion supported by the evidence in the previous section. Thus, RAND Europe (2007) notes that campaigns with a focus on sport participation inspired by an Olympic Games require careful targeting to avoid potential aversion effects.

The evidence in this section, despite being presented as refuting sport participation legacies, is entirely consistent with the evidence in the previous section supporting sport participation legacies. Like evidence in the previous section, it is not definitive, but it does expose two fairy tales: (1) there is no inherent effect of mega sport events on sport participation; (2) mega sport events do not bring new people into sport participation. But, this does not undermine the conclusion from the previous section that if mega sport events are effectively leveraged, there is the potential to encourage those who participate a little to participate a little more, to entice previous participants to participate again, and to re-enthuse current participants by introducing them to new sports.

### Sport participation legacy delivery since 2010: a test of facts and fairy tales?

At a population level, McCartney et al.'s (2010) systematic review shows that there is no evidence that any major multi-sport event prior to the London 2012 Olympic and Paralympic Games had impacted upon sport participation. But, importantly, no major multi-sport event prior to 2010 had put in place explicit population-wide strategies to deliver a sport participation legacy. As such, it is to be expected that there would be no evidence of a population-level outcome as events had not set out to achieve this.

However, the evidence set out above suggests that if effective leveraging investments are put in place there may be the *potential* to achieve specific sport participation outcomes through a demonstration effect among specific target groups, namely those who are already participating a little, or those who have participated in the past. It also suggests that there is no inherent effect without leveraging investments and that regardless of leveraging investments a sport mega event cannot attract new people into sport. This evidence is largely, although not exclusively, derived from more local interventions that were not on a large-enough scale to affect population-level sport participation demand. Consequently, the key question is whether the potential identified is scalable to whole populations given appropriate leveraging investments, and whether conclusions about the lack of inherent effects and the inability to attract new people into sport hold if attempts are made to deliver sport participation legacies at a population level.

It is useful, therefore, to consider the evidence as set out above as a set of hypotheses to be tested rather than a definitive conclusion that sport participation legacies are fact or fairy tale, and the purpose of this section is to explore how far mega sport events since 2010 represent a test of such hypotheses. Specifically, in varying levels of detail, the Rio 2016 and London 2012 Olympic and Paralympic Games, and the Glasgow 2014 Commonwealth Games, are discussed.

The most recent Olympic and Paralympic Games in Rio in 2016 took place in a context of major political protest, which included a considerable backlash against the hosting of the Games. The political protests surrounded alleged corruption by both the suspended and the acting presidents of Brazil, in the context of a considerable economic downturn. Part of this, however, included *Jogos da Exclusao* (Exclusion Games) and *Calamidadea Ollimpica* (Olympic Calamity) protests that in terms of both scale and longevity went some way beyond the protests that are routinely associated with mega sport events. In the week before the Games it was reported that nearly two out of three Brazilians believed the Games would bring more harm than good and that half disapproved of hosting the Games (Barbassa, 2016). One of the key suggestions of the available evidence is that for a mega-sport event to deliver increases in sport participation it must take place in a supportive context in which there is a positive engagement with the event and its potential to impact positively on the community, and this was certainly not the case in Rio in 2016. Furthermore, in their analysis of Rio 2016's potential to deliver a sport participation legacy, Reis, de Sousa-Mast, and Gurgel (2014) note that the Rio 2016 bid book (Rio, 2016, 2009) highlights a legacy for sport that refers only to developing elite sport participation and that

> [t]he health and educational benefits of mass sport/physical activity participation so promoted by the IOC (2008, 2011), particularly through its 'Sport for All' programme, seem to be disregarded.
>
> (Reis et al., 2014, p. 440)

As such, with an unsupportive context and a lack of leveraging investments for a sport participation legacy, the only test of the evidence that Rio 2016 can provide is for the hypothesis that there are no inherent effects from hosting a mega sport event. Unfortunately, sport participation data is not yet available for the time around the Rio 2016 Games, but if the evidence holds, a sport participation legacy should not be expected.

The London 2012 Olympic and Paralympic Games was the first sport mega event to explicitly set out to increase mass participation in sport, committing to "getting one million more people playing sport by 2012" (Slater, 2009). The specific detail of this commitment was to get an additional 1 million people participating in sport three times a week or more over the four years from 2008 to 2012. Thus, the goal was to target the very groups of people – those already participating between once a year and twice a week – that some of the evidence presented in this chapter by Weed (2010) had shown to be most responsive to a demonstration effect. As such, it had the potential to be an excellent test of the hypothesis that mega sport events have the potential to get those already playing to play a little more or those who had played in the past to play again.

Unfortunately, however, London 2012 did not invest in measures to stimulate sport participation increases but instead relied on inherent effects. Sport England's strategy (Sport England, 2008) for the four years during which the 1million sport participation target would need to be achieved (2008–2012), made little mention of the Olympic and Paralympic Games and set out no initiatives to harness the London 2012 Games to stimulate participation. Similarly, the London 2012 Mass Participation Plan, "Places People Play" (Sport England, 2010b) contained a £135 million investment that was almost entirely focused on supply; two-thirds for the supply of facilities and the rest for the supply of "provision capacity", leaders, and opportunities. Places People Play contained no strategies to stimulate sport participation increases, only investments to increase supply to cater for the inherent effect on sport participation that it was assumed the Games would bring

The result, as evidenced by the Active People survey in England, which provides official national statistics, was that despite an encouraging increase of 115,000 people doing sport three times a week in 2008/9, the following year (2009/10) the increase was only 8,000 (Sport England, 2009, 2010a). The following year, six months after the launch of Places People Play, sport participation figures showed a fall of 4,000 in those doing sport three times a week (Sport England, 2011). Furthermore, post-Games data for England showed that the number of people doing sport at least once a month had increased by an average of 1% per year in the four years since 2007/8, whilst those doing sport at least three times a week had increased by an average of 2.2% per year in the four years since 2007/8 (Sport England, 2012). However, the context for this latter figure is that achieving the participation target of 1 million people doing more sport would have required an average year on year increase of 3% and that the average increases in the two years prior to the period for which the target had been set (2006/7 and 2007/8) were 4% per year (Sport England, 2009). Furthermore, in the year following the Games those participating at least once a month actually fell by 1% (Sport England, 2013). By any measure, this is not a successful outcome for population-level sport participation and appears to reinforce the evidence discussed in this chapter that there is no inherent impact without effective investment targeting sport participation.

Therefore, despite a clear goal and a clear target to develop a sport participation legacy, London 2012 failed to put in place any initiatives or strategies to harness a demonstration effect to stimulate increases in sport participation. Consequently, while London 2012 had the potential to be an excellent test of the hypothesis that mega sport events can be used to increase participation among those who are already participating a little, or those who have participated in the past, its reliance on inherent effects meant that the only hypothesis it provides evidence for is that there are no inherent effects.

Finally, the Glasgow 2014 Commonwealth Games sought to use the Games to develop health outcomes in the Scottish population, with Games auditors finding that there were clear legacy plans in place, including plans to regenerate rundown areas of the city, and to increase levels of physical activity and sport (Audit Scotland, 2015). Unfortunately, however, Glasgow 2014 appears to have used sport initiatives to target those that did not participate, and had never participated in sport. This resulted in static levels of physical activity in the Scottish population following the Games in both 2015 and 2016 (Scottish Government, 2015, 2016), whilst the first stage of a study examining exercise levels in the most-affected communities found residents did less sport after the event than before (Clark and Kearns, 2015). Consequently, Glasgow 2014 appears to provide evidence to support the hypothesis that mega sport events cannot attract new people into sport.

In summary, mega sport events since 2010 collectively provide evidence to reinforce as fact the hypotheses that mega sport events cannot attract new people into sport and that such events do not have inherent effects on sport participation. However, the existing evidence that sport mega events appear to have the potential to encourage those who participate a little in sport to participate a little more, to entice previous participants to participate again, and to re-enthuse current participants by introducing them to new sports is limited (Weed et al., 2012, 2015).

## Conclusion – neither fact nor fairy tale

Following the closing ceremony of the Rio 2016 Olympic and Paralympic Games, evidence points to the case that no mega sport event has yet managed to deliver population-level increases in sport participation. However, this does not mean that this chapter can conclude that sport participation legacies from mega sport events are a fairy tale, despite some facts that show what mega sport events cannot achieve. Evidence from systematic reviews related to health legacies of mega events (McCartney et al., 2010; Weed et al., 2009, 2012, 2015), suggests that (1) there are no inherent effects on sport participation from mega sport events and (2) sport mega events cannot attract new people into sport. However, there is evidence that suggests that, in a supportive context, and with appropriate investments to leverage a demonstration effect, a mega sport event may have the potential to (1) encourage those who already participate to participate more, (2) encourage those who have participated previously to participate again, and (3) reduce drop-out by re-invigorating enthusiasm through encouraging participation in new activities. This evidence should be regarded as an evidence-informed hypothesis that has yet to be tested for scalability at a population level. That it has not been tested is a clear failure of policy and strategy for recent mega sport events, particularly those such as the London 2012 Olympic and Paralympic Games and the Glasgow 2014

Commonwealth Games that have explicitly set out to raise sport participation. It is this policy failing that leads to the conclusion that sport participation legacies from mega sport events are neither fact nor fairy tale.

## References

Audit Scotland. (2015). *Commonwealth Games 2014*. Third Report. Edinburgh: Audit Scotland.

Barbassa, J. (2016). *Behind the Olympic curtain, Rio at a crossroads*. Retrieved November 10, 2016, from www.espn.co.uk/olympics/story/_/id/17224414/2016-rio-olympics-olympic-curtain-rio-crossroads

Barget, E. G., and Gouget, J. (2007). The total economic value of sporting events theory and practice. *Journal of Sports Economics, 8*(2), 165–182.

Brown, A., and Massey, J. (2001). *Literature review: The impact of major sporting events*. Manchester: MMU/UK Sport.

Burgham, M., and Downward, P. (2005). Why volunteer, time to volunteer? A case study from swimming. *Managing Leisure, 10*(2), 79–93.

Cashman, R. (2006). The bitter sweet awakening: The legacy of the Sydney 2006 Olympic Games. Sydney: Walla Walla Press.

Clark, J., and Kearns, A. (2015). *The Glasgow 2014 Games: Regeneration and physical activity legacy*. Glasgow: University of Glasgow.

Coalter, F. (1993). Sports participation: Price or priorities? *Leisure Studies, 12*(3), 171–182.

Coalter, F. (2004). Stuck in the blocks? A sustainable sporting legacy. In A. Vigor, M. Mean, and C. Tims (Eds.), *After the gold rush* (pp. 91–108). London: IPPR/DEMOS.

Coalter, F. (2007). London Olympics 2012: 'The catalyst that inspires people to lead more active lives'? *Journal of the Royal Society of Health, 127*(3), 109–110.

Coe, S. (2008, September 1). We must not fail the capital's young athletes again. *London Evening Standard*.

Collins, M. F., Henry, I. P., Houlihan, B., and Buller, J. (1999). *Research report: Sport and social exclusion*. London: DCMS.

Conn, D. (2008, July 23). Games promise to generate only ripples when Britain needs to splash out. *The Guardian*.

Cragg Ross Dawson. (2007). Before, during and after: Making the most of the London 2012 Games. London: DCMS.

Crompton, J. L. (2004). Beyond economic impact: An alternative rationale for the public subsidy of major league sports facilities. *Journal of Sport Management, 18*(1), 40–58.

Crompton, J. L. (2006). Economic impact studies: Instruments for political Shenanigans? *Journal of Travel Research, 45*(1), 67–82.

DCMS (Department for Culture, Media and Sport). (2008). *Before, during and after: Making the most of the London 2012 Games*. London: Department of Culture, Media and Sport.

Deccio, C., and Baloglu, S. (2002). Nonhost community resident reactions to the 2002 Winter Olympics: The spillover impacts. *Journal of Travel Research, 41*, 46–56.

Downward, P. M., and Ralston, R. (2006). The sports development potential of sports event volunteering: Insights from the XVII Manchester Commonwealth Games. *European Sport Management Quarterly, 6*(4), 333–351.

EdComs (2007). London 2012 legacy research: Final report. London: COI/DCMS.

Faber Maunsell. (2004). *Commonwealth Games benefits study*. Manchester: North West Development Agency.

Faulkner, B., Chalip, L., Brown, G., Jago, L., March, R., and Woodside, A. (2001). Monitoring the tourism impacts of the Sydney 2000 Olympics. *Event Management*, *6*(4), 231–246.

Fredline, E. (2005). Host and guest relations and sport tourism. *Sport in Society*, *8*(2), 263–279.

Green, B. C., and Chalip, L. (1998). Sport volunteers: Research agenda and application. *Sport Marketing Quarterly*, *7*(2), 14–23.

The Guardian. (2008). *London 2012 Olympics: Boris Johnson vows to create 'massive sporting legacy*. Retrieved August 29, from www.theguardian.com/politics/2008/aug/26/boris.olympics2012

Hagger, M., Chatzisarantis, N., and Biddle, S. J. H. (2002). A meta-analytic review of the theories of reasoned action and planned behavior in physical activity: Predictive validity and the contribution of additional variables. *Journal of Sport and Exercise Psychology*, *24*(1), 3–32.

Hamlyn, P. J., and Hudson, Z. L. (2005). 2012 Olympics: Who will survive? *British Journal of Sports Medicine*, *39*(12), 882–883.

Haynes, J. (2001). *Socio-economic impact of the Sydney Olympic Games*. Barcelona: Centre d'Estudis Olimpics l de l'Esport (UAB).

Henry, I. (2016). The meta-evaluation of the sports participation impact and legacy of the London 2012 Games: Methodological implications. *Journal of Global Sport Management*, *1*(1–2), 19–33.

Hindson, A., Gidlow, B., and Peebles, C., (1994). The 'trickle-down' effect of top level sport: Myth or reality? A case study of the Olympics. *Australian Leisure and Recreation*, *4*(1), 16–24.

Hogan, K., and Norton, K. (2000). The 'price' of Olympic gold. *Journal of Science & Medicine in Sport*, *3*(2), 203–218.

House of Commons Select Committee. (2007). London 2012 Olympic Games and Paralympic Games: Funding and legacy – second report (cms070122a). London: HMSO.

ICRC (International Centre for Research and Consultancy for the Tourism and Hospitality Industries) (2003). *Sports development impact of the Commonwealth Games: Study of volunteers*. Manchester: ICRC/UK Sport.

Kim, N. S., and Chalip, L. (2004). Why travel to the FIFA world cup? Effects of motives, background, interest, and constraints. *Tourism Management*, *25*(6), 695–707.

Lankford, S., Neal, L. L., and Szabo, C. (2000). Arctic Winter Games: A study of benefits of participation. *Journal of the International Council for Health, Physical Education, Recreation, Sport & Dance*, *36*(4), 50–54.

Lenskyj, H. (2014). Sexual diversity and the Sochi 2014 Olympics: No more rainbows. London: Palgrave Macmillan.

London Health Commission and London Development Agency. (2004). Rapid HealthImpact assessment of the proposed London Olympic Games and their legacy. London: LDA.

London East Research Institute (LERI) and University of East London. (2007). *Lasting legacy for London? Assessing the legacy of the Olympic Games and Paralympic Games*. London: LERI.

Marshall, S. J., and Biddle, S. J. H. (2001). The transtheoretical model of behaviour change: A meta-analysis of applications to physical activity and exercise. *Annals of Behavioural Medicine*, *23*(4), 229–246.

McCartney, G., Thomas, S., Thomson, H., Scott, J., Hamilton, V., Hanlon, P., et al. (2010). The health and socioeconomic impacts of major multi-sport events: A systematic review. *British Medical Journal*, *340*, c2369.

Muller, M. (2015). After Sochi 2014: Costs and impacts of Russia's Olympic Games. *Eurasian Geography and Economics*, *55*(6), 628–655.

Murphy, N., and Bauman. A. (2007). Mass sporting and physical activity events – are they "Bread and Circuses" or public health interventions to increase population levels of physical activity. *Journal of Physical Activity and Health*, *4*(2), 193–202.

Newby, L. (2003). The extent to which the Commonwealth Games accelerated the social, physical and economic regeneration of East Manchester. Manchester: DTZ Pieda Consulting.

North East Public Health Observatory. (2006). The health impact of the 2012 Games. A screening health impact assessment of the North East's draft vision for the London Olympic Games and Paralympic Games 2012. Newcastle: NEPHO.

Ohmann, S., Jones, I., and Wilkes, K. (2006). The perceived social impacts of the 2006 Football World Cup on Munich residents. *Journal of Sport & Tourism*, *11*(2), 129–152.

Perks, T. (2015). Exploring an Olympic "Legacy": Sport participation in Canada before and after the 2010 Vancouver Winter Olympics. *Canadian Review of Sociology/Revue Canadienne de Sociologie*, *52*(4), 462–474.

Preuss, H. (2007). The conceptualisation and measurement of mega sport event legacies. *Journal of Sport and Tourism*, *12*(3–4), 207–227.

Putin, V. (2007, July 4). *Speech at the 119th International Olympic Committee session, Guatemala*. Retrieved March 12, 2009, from http://archive.kremlin.ru/eng/text/speeches/2007/07/04/2103_type82912 type84779type127286_136956.shtml

Ralston, R., Downward, P., and Lumsdon, L. (2004). The expectations of volunteers prior to the XVII Commonwealth Games, 2002: A qualitative study. *Event Management*, *9*(1–2), 13–26.

RAND Europe. (2007). Setting the agenda for an evidence-based Olympics. Cambridge: RAND.

Ravenscroft, N. (1993). Public leisure provision and the good citizen. *Leisure Studies*, *12*(1), 33–44.

Reis, A. C., de Sousa-Mast, F. R., and Gurgel, L. A. (2014). Rio 2016 and the sport participation legacies. *Leisure Studies*, *33*(5), 437–453.

Rio 2016. (2009). Candidature file for Rio de Janeiro to host the 2006 Olympic and Paralympic Games (Vol. 1). Rio de Janeiro: Rio 2016.

Schmid, S. (1996). Capitalization: Olympic involvement is benefitting several parks and recreation departments. *Athletic Business*, *20*(7), 22–24.

Scottish Government. (2015). *Scottish health survey 2014: Main report*. Edinburgh: Scottish Government.

Scottish Government. (2016). *Scottish health survey 2015: Main report*. Edinburgh: Scottish Government.

Slater, M. (2009). *Burnham issues grass-roots plea*. Retrieved January 10, 2013, from http://news.bbc.co.uk/sport1/hi/front_page/7936129.stm

Spencer, L., Adams, T. B., Malone, S., Roy, L., and Yost, E. (2006). Applying the transtheoretical model to exercise: A systematic and comprehensive review of the literature. *Health Promotion Practice*, *7*(4), 428–443.

Sport England. (2004). *Press release: Athens success inspires one in four to take up sport*. Retrieved August 3, 2008, from www.sportengland.org/news/press_releases/athens_success_inspires.htm

Sport England. (2008). *Sport England strategy 2008–2011*. London: Sport England.

Sport England. (2009b). *Active people survey 3*. Retrieved January 10, 2013, from www.sportengland.org/research/active_people_survey/active_people_survey_3.aspx

Sport England. (2010a). *Active people 4*. Retrieved January 10, 2013, www.sportengland.org/research/active_people_survey/active_people_survey_4.aspx

Sport England. (2010b). *Places people play – delivering a mass participation sporting legacy from the 2012 Olympic and Paralympic Games*. Retrieved January 1, 2013, from www.sportengland.org/about_us/places_people_play_ – _deliverin.aspx

Sport England. (2011). *Active people 5, quarter 2 results*. Retrieved January 10, 2013, from www.sportengland.org/research/active_people_survey/aps5/aps5_quarter_2.aspx

Sport England. (2012). *Active people 6*. Retrieved January 10, 2013, from www.sporteng land.org/research/active_people_survey/active_people_survey_6.aspx

Sport England. (2013). *Active people 7*. Retrieved December 22, 2013, from www.sport-england.org/research/active_people_survey/active_people_survey_7.aspx

Sport and Recreation Victoria. (2006). *Warming up for the Games: Program report. 17*. Victoria: SRV.

TNS. (2004). Sporting motivations: Why the public watches, plays and wants to see UK success in sport. London: UK Sport.

Truno, E. (1995). Barcelona: City of sport. In M. de Moragas, and M. Botella (Eds.), *The keys to success: The social, sporting, economic and communications impact of Barcelona'92* (pp. 43–56). Barcelona: UAB.

Van Rheenan, D. (2014). A skunk at the garden party: The Sochi Olympics, state-sponsored homophobia and prospects for human rights through mega sporting events. *Journal of Sport & Tourism*, *19*(2), 127–144.

VANOC (Vancouver Organising Committee for the 2010 Olympic and Paralympic Winter Games). (2007). *Legacies of North American Olympic Winter Games*. Vancouver: VANOC.

Veal, A. J. (2003). Tracking change: Leisure participation and policy in Australia 1985–2002. *Annals of Leisure Research*, *6*(3), 245–277.

Veal, A. J., Toohey, K., and Frawley, S. (2012). The sport participation legacy of the Sydney 2000 Olympic Games and other international sporting events hosted in Australia. *Journal of Policy Research in Tourism, Leisure and Events*, *4*(2), 155–184.

Vigor, A., Mean, M., and Tims, C. (2004). *After the gold rush*. London: IPPR/DEMOS.

Waitt, G. (2003). Social impacts of the Sydney Olympics. *Annals of Tourism Research*, *30*(1), 194–215.

Wang, W., and Theodoraki, E. (2007). Mass sport policy development in the Olympic city: The case of Qingdao – host to the 2008 Sailing Regatta. *Journal of the Royal Society of Health*, *127*(3), 125–132.

Weed, M. (2010). The potential of the demonstration effect to grow and sustain participation in sport. London: Sport England.

Weed, M. (2014). London 2012 legacy strategy: Did it deliver? In V. Girginov (Ed.), *Routledge handbook of the London 2012 Olympic Games volume two* (pp. 281–294). London: Routledge.

Weed, M., Coren, E., Fiore, J., Mansfield, L., Wellard, I., Chatziefstathiou, D., and Dowse, S. (2009). A systematic review of the evidence base for developing a physical activity and health legacy from the London 2012 Olympic and Paralympic Games. London: Department of Health.

Weed, M., Coren, E., Fiore, J., Mansfield, L., Wellard, I., Chatziefstathiou, D., and Dowse, S. (2012). Developing a physical activity legacy from the London 2012 Olympic and Paralympic Games: A policy-led systematic review. *Perspectives in Public Health*, *132*(2), 75–80.

Weed, M., Coren, E., Fiore, J., Wellard, I., Chatziefstathiou, D., Mansfield, L., and Dowse, S. (2015). The Olympic Games and raising sport participation: A systematic review of evidence and an interrogation of policy for a demonstration effect. *European Sport Management Quarterly*, *15*(2), 195–226.

# 6 Legacy of sporting mega events for people with disabilities

## The Paralympic Games

*Ian Brittain*

Over the last decade, a large body of work has been published examining major sporting event legacies, particularly with reference to the Olympic Games. However, very little of this published work has investigated event legacies in terms of the Paralympic Games (Misener, Darcy, Legg, and Gilbert, 2013). This lack of research in the area makes deciding whether claims made by the Paralympic movement for the potential legacies of the Paralympic Games are fact, fairy tale or somewhere in between difficult to assess. This is despite the fact that, in many ways, the Paralympic Games, and their forerunners the Stoke Mandeville Games, were founded with the aim of providing a positive legacy for people with disabilities, an aim which still forms a key underpinning in the aims and objectives for the International Paralympic Committee today.

Prior to World War II there is little evidence of attempts to organise sport for people with disabilities, particularly those with spinal injuries who were considered to have no hope of surviving their injuries. However, after the end of World War II, the medical community were forced to re-evaluate the rehabilitation methods used at the time as they were not adequately responding to the medical and psychological needs of the large number of soldiers disabled in combat (Steadward, 1992). According to McCann (1996), Dr Ludwig Guttmann (founder of the International Stoke Mandeville Games that went on to become the Paralympic Games) recognised the physiological and psychological values of sport in the rehabilitation of paraplegic hospital inpatients. Guttmann introduced sport as part of their rehabilitation with the aim of not only giving patients hope and a sense of self-worth but also to change the attitudes of society towards the spinally injured. The overarching goal was to show them that they could not only continue to be useful members of society but could take part in activities and complete tasks that most of the non-disabled society would struggle with (Anderson, 2003).

## Ableism

To assist with the discussion in this chapter ableism forms the underlying theoretical foundation in order to try to explain the need for some of the social legacies that are often claimed for the Paralympic Games and the reasons why these legacies are often so difficult to fulfil. According to Wolbring (2012) "ableism describes prejudicial attitudes and discriminatory behaviours toward persons with a disability. Definitions of ableism hinge on one's understanding of normal ability and the rights and benefits afforded to persons deemed 'normal'" (p. 78). Siebers (2008) calls ableism the 'ideology of ability', which at its most extreme "defines the baseline by which humanness is determined, setting a measure of body and mind that gives or denies human status to individual persons" (p. 8). Ableism, therefore, devalues people with disabilities and results in segregation, social isolation and social policies that limit opportunities for full societal participation. In the context of sport for people with disabilities, the prioritisation of non-disabled sport (and bodies) within society devalues sport for athletes with disabilities and potentially undermines much of the hard work done by disability activists to gain acceptance for people with disabilities in all walks of life.

## The founding philosophy of the paralympic movement

From its inception in the late 1940s, the founder of the international Paralympic sport movement, Sir Ludwig Guttmann, described the aims of his use of sport in the rehabilitation process of persons with spinal cord injuries to be social re-integration and to change the perceptions of the non-disabled within society regarding what people with disabilities were capable of. Guttmann (1976) highlighted three main areas in which participation in sport could benefit people with disabilities and these may be seen as the original founding fundamental principles of the Paralympic movement.

### *1. Sport as a curative factor*

According to Guttmann, sport represented the most natural form of remedial exercise and could be used to successfully complement other forms of remedial exercise. Sport could be invaluable in restoring the overall fitness, including strength, speed, co-ordination and endurance, of someone receiving a disabling injury. Tasiemski, Bergstrom, Savic, and Gardner (1998) pointed out how sport could be of particular benefit to individuals with certain disabilities. Following a pilot study on individuals recovering from a spinal cord lesion, they stated:

> Systematically practised [*sic*] physical activity and sports allows the disabled person to keep the high level of physical fitness that was obtained during rehabilitation. It also helps to maintain compensatory processes and prevent complications caused by inactivity. Physical activity and sports are amongst the most important factors that determine the effectiveness and final outcomes of physical rehabilitation.
>
> (Tasiemski et al., 1998)

Tasiemski et al. (1998) also found that the annual frequency of hospital readmissions following discharge was three times less in athletes than non-athletes, adding weight to their claim that those involved in activities away from the home, especially physical ones such as sport, were physically fitter, more independent and had fewer avoidable complications. Similar claims have been made by Groff, Lundberg, and Zabriskie (2009), who state,

> Several studies have suggested that participation in sport may impact elements of quality of life such as one's overall enjoyment with life, sense of well-being, and ability to complete daily life activities. Researchers have concluded that athletes with disabilities exhibit higher levels of positive mood, increased wheelchair mobility skills, lower levels of tension and depression and have better perceived health and well-being.
>
> (Groff et al., 2009, p. 319)

### 2. The recreational and psychological value of sport

Guttmann (1976) claimed that the biggest advantage of sport for the disabled over other remedial exercises lay within its recreational value in that it restored "that passion for playful activity and the desire to experience joy and pleasure in life, so deeply inherent in any human being" (p. 12). Guttmann also pointed out that much of the restorative power of sport was lost if the person with the disability did not enjoy their participation. As long as enjoyment was derived from the activity, then sport could help develop an active mind, self-confidence, self-dignity, self-discipline, competitive spirit and camaraderie, all of which were essential in helping overcome what he perceived as the all-consuming depression that could occur with sudden traumatic disability.

### 3. Sport as a means of social re-integration

There are certain sports where people with disabilities are capable of competing alongside their non-disabled peers, for example archery, bowls, and table tennis, as Neroli Fairhall of New Zealand proved when she competed from a wheelchair in archery at the 1984 Olympic Games in Los Angeles (Associated Press, 2006), but this wasn't by accident. Guttmann (1952) claims that archery was "of immense value in strengthening, in a very natural way, just those muscles of the upper limbs, shoulders and trunk, on which the paraplegic's well-balanced, upright position depends" (1952, p. 8). However, it was far more than that. Archery was one of very few sports that, once proficient, paraplegics could compete on equal terms with their non-disabled counterparts. This led to visits of teams from Stoke Mandeville to a number of non-disabled archery clubs. This provided an opportunity to break down some of the perceived barriers between the public and people with a disability by giving them the chance to socialise whilst taking part in an activity of mutual interest. In addition it provided an opportunity for the people with disabilities to demonstrate their capabilities to an audience who rarely had the opportunity to mix with people with disabilities and had often been socialised into very negative perceptions regarding disability. It also meant that once discharged from hospital, the person with paraplegia had access to society through their local archery club. Guttmann (1976) claims this helped create a better understanding between people with disabilities and their non-disabled peers and aided in their social re-integration through the medium of sport.

## The international Paralympic committee and legacy

The three areas highlighted by Guttmann above still provide the underlining driving force for much of the International Paralympic Committee's (IPC's) Vision and Mission Statement as well as the Paralympic legacy plans put forward by recent Olympic and Paralympic Games Organising Committees with regard to the Paralympic Games. However, there has been virtually no academic investigation of whether the Paralympic Games actually helps achieve these aims or not. According to the IPC Strategic Plan (2015–2018) the ultimate aspiration of the Paralympic movement is "to make for a more inclusive society for people with an impairment through para-sport" (IPC website, 2016). They follow this up with the claim that

> [t]he Paralympic Games are the world's number one sporting event for transforming society's attitudes towards impairment. By broadening the reach of the Paralympics, growing para-sport events and furthering brand awareness, the Paralympic Movement's transformational legacy will be amplified.
>
> (IPC website, 2016)

It is clear then from these claims that the IPC believe in the potential for a transformational legacy from the Paralympic Games, especially in changing non-disabled attitudes towards people with disabilities and thereby helping to overcome the pervasive and negative impacts of ableism within society.

## Previous legacy claims from Paralympic Games

In this section I will briefly highlight some of the legacy claims made by various academics and practitioners for a selection of previous Paralympic Games.

*Tokyo 1964*: It is claimed that the Games and the media coverage of them within Japan had quite a profound impact upon the way people with disabilities were viewed within Japan. At the International Stoke Mandeville Games Committee (ISMGC) meeting, held in conjunction with the annual Stoke Mandeville Games of 1965, Mr Kasai, chairman of the Tokyo Organising Committee confirmed that since the Games there had been an increasing interest in the welfare of the disabled within Japan and that the Ministry of Labour were building a factory to provide jobs for paraplegics by the side of Lake Shigain in Nagano (ISMGC, 1965). This factory eventually spread into a chain of factories all over Japan under the banner of Sun Industries, which is still in existence today called Japan Sun Industries and located in Oita.

*Toronto 1976*: Despite the fact that the Games in Toronto possibly came to the world's attention for all the wrong reason's due to the political rows that erupted over the participation of a racially integrated team from Apartheid South Africa (Brittain, 2011), Robert Jackson, Chairman of the Canadian Organising Committee, claims the Canadian public learnt valuable lessons from the wide-spread media coverage such as "physically disabled are human individuals with emotions, ambitions, fears, likes, similar to anyone else" and "are capable of exceptional achievements if given the opportunity" (Jackson, 1977, p. 69). In addition, a number of the volunteers at the Games (administrators, officials, coaches), who all received specialist training prior to the Games, still continue to work in Canadian disability sport to this day. Finally nearly half a million dollars of government money originally meant for the Games, but withdrawn due to the political row, was eventually donated towards Canadian disability sport. This led to a far more coherent and professionally run sports structure that eventually led to the inception of the Canadian Paralympic Committee (Brittain, 2011).

*Seoul 1988*: The 1988 Paralympic Games in Seoul, South Korea, returning as they did to the same host city and venues as the Olympic Games for the first time since Tokyo 1964, are considered by many to be the beginning of the modern Paralympic Games and movement (Jeon and Legg, 2011). The legacy and impact of this return to being hosted in the same city and venues as the Olympic Games a couple of weeks after the Olympic Games have concluded can be clearly seen in Figure 6.1. Since Seoul, the growth in the number of nations participating at the Paralympic Games has been almost exponential (e.g., Rome 1964–21 nations; Seoul, 1988–60 nations; London 2012–164 nations). The dip in participation that occurred for Rio 2016 is largely down to the economic and political issues that blighted the Games, and particularly the Paralympic Games, in Rio. For further details see Brittain and Mataruna (2017).

*Atlanta 1996*: The Atlanta Paralympic Games are possibly best known for the horrendous way they were treated by the Atlanta Olympic Organising Committee. This was possibly driven by an ableist perspective of the value of sport for people with disabilities within the Olympic Organizing Committee that caused numerous additional problems for the Paralympic organisers. However, even this was deemed a positive in the long-term as the IOC Director of the Olympic Games at the time, Gilbert Felli, claimed it was the 'fiasco' caused by this situation in Atlanta that eventually led to the signing of the first IOC/IPC Co-operative Agreement in Sydney four years later (Mushett and Cody, 2011). According to Mushett and Cody, Atlanta was also the first Paralympic Organising Committee to successfully raise major sponsorship for a Paralympic Games from the private sector. In fact they were apparently so successful that they were left with a 'multi-million dollar surplus' most of which was invested into a legacy organisation called BlazeSports America that is still in operation today and which works with children and adults with physical disabilities to advance their lives through sport (Mushett and Cody, 2011, p. 68).

*Sydney 2000*: As a sporting event the Sydney 2000 Paralympics Games were heralded as a huge success. They are also possibly the first Paralympic Games to have their 'legacy' critically and systematically appraised (Cashman and Darcy, 2008). Simon Darcy, an Australian Professor of Business and Lois Appleby, the chief executive of the Sydney 2000 Paralympic Games critically analysed the legacy of the Sydney Paralympic Games a decade after they had ended and concluded that ultimately the Sydney 2000 Paralympic Games lacked a well-thought-out legacy strategy. Specifically, they concluded there was no ownership of implementation and that the sustainability of the legacy process was never clearly articulated. As a result, they claimed that "a great deal of what is regarded as the event/ social/ community legacy is without a research base and remains largely

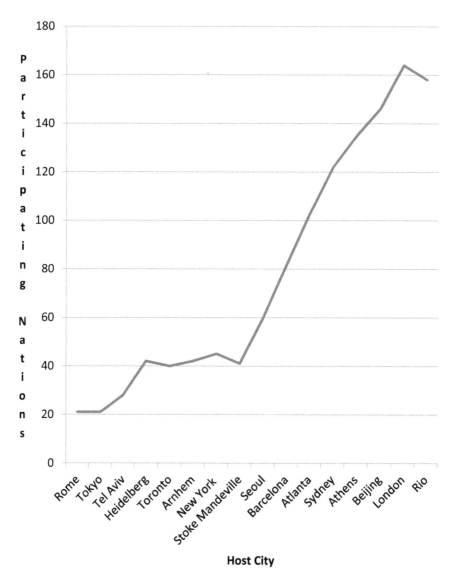

*Figure 6.1* Nations participating at the summer Paralympic Games.

anecdotal" (Darcy and Appleby, 2011, p. 92). Unfortunately, this is claim regarding the reliance on anecdotal evidence is one that is still being raised regarding mega event legacy claims today (Weed et al., 2015).

*Athens 2004*: According to Hums (2011), the major impact of the Paralympic Games in Athens was one that has become a regular target for recent organising committee legacy plans over the last decade or so – that of increased accessibility of the transport system and major tourist spots within the city. In Athens this included accessible buses and trains, the addition of elevators and escalators to the Metro system and the addition of a lift at the Akropolis, a World Heritage site. However, despite these modifications, Hums claims that even though she has visited Athens every year since the Games she has not noticed a "significant change in accessibility in the main areas of downtown Athens" and that "it is still quite unusual to see people with (visible) disabilities out and about on a daily basis" (Hums, 2011, p. 104).

*Beijing 2008*: Sun and Le Clair (2011) highlight both improvements in the accessibility of the transport system as a result of the 2008 Paralympic Games and a shift in national disability policies, with China being one of the first countries to ratify the UN Declaration on the Rights of Persons with Disabilities. However, Sun and Le Clair (2011) also point out that there is "a gap between stated goals and what takes place on the ground" (p. 123), which is highlighted further in the differing outcomes reported following the London 2012 Paralympic Games by governmental and Disabled People's Organisations' sources that follow. This issue was also highlighted prior to the 2008 Games by Brittain (2006) and something that is relevant to many other countries making high-profile legacy claims in connection to the Olympic or the Paralympic Games.

## Legacy and the London 2012 and Rio 2016 Paralympic Games

### London 2012

The London 2012 bid was prepared with a major legacy element that incorporated both Olympic and Paralympic legacies. However, an analysis on the impact of the London 2012 Paralympic Games on British society identified one prominent factor – there is a marked difference in opinion between the findings and focus of the British government and the Organising Committee, on one hand, and those of Disabled People's Organisations and the experiences of disabled individuals, on the other. A joint UK Government and Mayor of London report published in July 2013, nearly a year after the London Paralympic Games had ended, cited the following two headline achievements under the chapter titled 'The Legacy of the Paralympics':

- 81% of people surveyed thought that the Games had a positive effect on how disabled people are viewed by the British public.
- And Disabled people's participation in sport is increasing.

(UK Government/ Mayor of London Office, 2013)

In contrast, however, the results of research by some Disabled People's Organisations and the experiences of individual disabled people differed markedly from the upbeat findings of government claims such as those highlighted earlier.

A report by the charity Scope published at around the same time reported the following findings after interviewing around 1,000 disabled people:

- 81% of disabled people said that attitudes towards them hadn't improved in the last 12 months and 22% said that things had actually got worse
- One in five (17%) of disabled people report they have either experienced hostile or threatening behaviour or even been attacked.

(Scope website, 2013)

It could be argued that it is in the best interests of disability organisations to not have too much positive data as this may place their funding in jeopardy. However, Brittain and Beacom (2016) compare and contrast the claims of both sides against a backdrop of public policies that are targeting large-scale benefits cuts. Recent media coverage appears to have hardened attitudes towards anyone on benefits and potentially negated any positive impacts the Games in London may have had. They argue that the continued predominance of 'ableist' perspectives on disability underpins many of the challenges faced by disabled people concluding that sports mega-events do not take place in a vacuum. They are subject to wider social, economic and political dynamics, and as such, it is extremely challenging to effectively plan for legacy. Such dynamics can work for or against the legacy process in many unexpected ways. By way of highlighting this issue they point to three factors that they believe may have had an impact on the legacy plans made for the London 2012 Paralympic Games, particularly around changing attitudes towards disability.

*Austerity budgets*

Despite the UK Government apparently backing the legacy plans for the London 2012 Paralympic Games, the austerity budgets they implemented around the same period, and particularly those relating to benefit cuts, appear to be entirely at odds with the legacy plans. The neo-liberal policies they implemented around benefit cuts appear to be underpinned by a 'survival of the fittest' mentality which actually make the lives of people with disabilities even harder, rather than improving them.

*Media reporting*

The media reporting of these cuts, and the 'benefit scrounger' rhetoric associated with it has had a negative impact upon attitudes towards disability manifesting in a hardening of attitudes towards anyone who requires state-aided financial assistance to survive. The reporting of a minority of non-disabled individuals pretending to be disabled in order to claim benefits, at a time of austerity when everyone was suffering financially, had the effect of all people with genuine disabilities being labelled as benefit cheats or scroungers in the eyes of the public. Indeed, even where ministers have presented arguments in favour of protecting disability payments, the language of dependency which permeates their statements, has the potential to reinforce the 'otherness' which predicates ableist thinking.

*IPC and the elite sports model*

The IPC has steadily been moving towards an elite 'Olympic' sporting model for the Paralympic Games in order to better fit non-disabled conceptions of what elite sport looks like and thus bring in the media coverage and sponsors they need to survive and develop. However, this has the potential to cause a partial fracture with the community they are supposed to represent as those with the highest levels of impairment are overlooked in favour of those that better fit this conception of 'elite' sport.

*It's not all doom and gloom!*

It may appear so far that nothing positive came out of the London Paralympic Games, particularly for people with disabilities. On a positive note, however, Brittain and Beacom (2016) conclude that the worldwide media coverage of recent (up to London 2012) Paralympic Games presents a strong platform from which to start a debate around disability issues. There is no other current platform that provides such an opportunity to reach so many non-disabled people. In general, the non-disabled populations are oblivious to disability issues other than the little, frequently politically charged information they receive through the newspapers, as mentioned earlier, or the often ableist views they are socialised into whilst growing up. While there are indications that the Paralympic Games do have agency in the sense that they provide a platform from which to engage in debate about disability issues, one important lesson for future hosts is that heightened expectations can create as many problems as they solve. Legacy aims can be viewed as facilitators for discreet areas of public policy. However, by themselves they cannot hope to challenge long-term systemic difficulties associated with the political and economic direction of travel. In a very real sense, each Games is a child of its time.

However, overall what happened as a result of the London 2012 Paralympic Games isn't all negative, particularly from a sporting perspective. Since London 2012, in the UK at least, there has been a significant increase in athletes with disabilities appearing on TV and in the media, including on Game shows and other non-sports-related programming (e.g., Dame Sarah Storey on *A Question of Sport* 2016).

To coincide with the Games, the host broadcaster, Channel 4, introduced a new programme called the *The Last Leg* presented by three comedians, two of whom (Adam Hills and Alex Brooker) have disabilities. They raise topical issues around disability in a humorous, but enlightening way in order to overcome many of the negative stereotypes around disability. They also introduced a way people could tweet using the hashtag #isitokay where the public could ask any question they wanted about disability but had possibly been too afraid to ask. *The Last Leg* is still running today nearly five years after the London Games ended and had regular nightly shows from the Rio 2016 Paralympic Games.

Social media also played a significant role in spreading interest in Paralympic sport. A report published by Twitter revealed that the hashtag #Paralympics topped the table for the most trending UK sport event of 2012 beating off stiff competition from the Olympic Games and many leading Premiership football clubs. Although this result is potentially very interesting, so far no research has been carried out as to why this was the case. However, it is clearly something that might be of great interest to branding experts and marketeers as to how this came about. In addition, around 50 leading athletes also took part in the Samsung Bloggers project which saw them record and post video blogs from behind the scenes before, during and after the London 2012 Games, and over 600 video blogs were uploaded and were viewed by over 300,000 people (Brittain, 2014).

The structure of elite disability sport in the UK was transformed in the lead up to London 2012 with the inclusion of many disability sports into their non-disabled national governing body. This has led to a professionalisation of disability sport at the elite level in the UK to bring it into line with the same standards expected from the non-disabled sports. This has had a positive impact on the results of British teams, post-2012, such as the men's wheelchair basketball team who won the European Men's Wheelchair Basketball Championships for the third time in a row in 2015 (Euro2015 website, 2015).

The higher education sector in the UK has also seen big changes with regard to disability and Para-sport post-2012 with competitive sport for students with disabilities being added to the university sports structure (British Universities and Colleges Sport website, 2016) From a personal perspective as someone who has been researching in the field of disability and Paralympic sport for nearly 20 years I have also witnessed a significant increase in interest in academic enquiry in the field from students, lecturers and researchers alike. This can only bode well for the future of disability sport by having graduates who understand the needs of people with disabilities working within the UK sporting structure at all levels.

In 2012, there were records for the number of competing nations (164), number of athletes (4,237), number of tickets sold (2.7 million) with most events and sessions selling out and, perhaps most important, the London 2012 Paralympic Games were televised in more countries than ever before, attracting their biggest ever international audience. According to the figures released by the IPC, the London Paralympic 2012 Games were watched by a cumulative international audience of 3.4 billion (excluding the host nation), which is an increase of around 37 per cent on the last summer Games in Beijing. The London 2012 Games were broadcast in over 115 countries and the number of hours broadcast outside the host market grew by 82 per cent on 2008 to over 2,500 hours of content (Brittain, 2014).

Finally, London was left with an increased supply of physically accessible housing due to the organising committee and the Government working together to ensure that all the accommodation for the Village was built with Paralympians and future potential owners with disabilities in mind. For example, all doorways in the village were made wider than the standard usually used in order to cater for wheelchair users (Brittain, 2016).

### Rio 2016

The following excerpt from the Rio 2016 bid documents clearly highlights an intention to positively change attitudes towards people with disabilities in Brazil as it is highlighted in three out of the seven concepts that underpinned their philosophy and concept for the Games. These three concepts are as follows:

- Fresh inspiration: New and diverse heroes and leaders with disabilities will emerge, to educate and inspire.
- Inclusive culture: Children and young people will have a positive regard for people with disabilities, improving inclusiveness throughout society.
- Tangible legacy: Both physical and social, with new infrastructure and venues such as the Olympic Training Center facilities which will integrate Olympic and Paralympic athletes, an extensive workforce trained and ready as a resource for future events in Brazil and South America, and **changes in the perception of people with disabilities**.

(Rio, 2016 website, 2016)

*Is a Paralympic legacy needed in Brazil?*

The answer may seem obvious, but the question should still be asked – is there really a need to change attitudes towards people with disabilities in Brazil? The following small example would appear to quite clearly show that there is. A campaign run in November 2015 by Movimento pela Reforma de Direitos (Movement for Rights Reform; MRD) appears to clearly demonstrate some of the issues faced by people with disabilities in Brazil. MRD placed large billboard advertisements demanding an end to 'privileges' for disabled people. This was backed up with text on its website that stated,

> They have privileges for everything. Half-price discounts, exemptions, special queues, reserved seats on the bus, their own bathrooms, VIP treatment for all! They have a quota law that guarantees them a place at University and in the job market/ public service exams. And those of us who have to compete and battle for everything, what do we get that is special?

(Mundoconectado website, 2015)

However, everything is not quite as it might seem. This was actually a campaign by the Municipal Council for the Rights of Persons with Disabilities from the city of Curitiba in the south of Brazil, and it got just the response it was hoping for –almost-universal condemnation that went viral around the world within hours of the first pictures of the billboard being posted on the Internet. Within a few days an addition was made to the billboards with a very clear and important message that read "if so many of you were outraged by this, why do so many of you still disrespect them?

What this highlights is that there is a big difference in the way people think and the way they may actually act. The key aim of the Paralympic Games should be to change the way non-disabled people act, but in order to do this it is necessary to help them make the important link between the way they may think and the way they actually act and to clearly understand the implications of their actions.

## Apparently it's not just Brazil that needed a positive legacy from the Rio 2016 Paralympic Games

Sir Philip Craven, president of the IPC, in his New Year's message for 2016, claimed that the year ahead was going to be one of the most important years yet for the Paralympic Movement and that it was "vital" that the Paralympic Games in Rio de Janeiro were a "triumph". He went on to say,

> As we work together towards making for a more inclusive society for people with an impairment through Para-sport, it is vital that South America's first Paralympic Games are a real triumph. . . . We must show to the world that Beijing 2008 and London 2012 were not exceptions, but the norm.
> (Insidethegames, January 2016)

As the quotes from Sir Philip clearly show it was not just the Rio 2016 Organising Committee and possibly people with disabilities in Brazil that were relying on a successful Paralympic Games in Rio. The IPC and the Paralympic movement were relying on a successful Games in order to maintain the massive upward trajectory of the Paralympic movement. Peers (2012), a Paralympian and academic, might well argue that this is simply the IPC continuing to try and reproduce itself in order to continue its existence. Peers (2012) is critical of those involved in the running and promotion of the Paralympic Movement, painting them as self-serving and claiming that the IPC, "continually reproduces the figure of the tragic disabled in order to reproduce itself" (p. 9). She claims that, historically, the IPC and its predecessors have used the image of the 'tragic disabled' in order to justify its aims and existence and that the IPC continues this practice today. However, it could also be argued that the stronger the Paralympic Games get, and the more attention they receive, the stronger the platform becomes from which to advocate for disability rights.

## Some of the potential legacies of the Rio 2016 Paralympic games so far

So what are some of the potential legacies of the Rio 2016 Paralympic Games so far? The Inclusion of People with Disabilities Act (2015) was passed into law last year covering issues such as Accessibility, Education, Health and Social Inclusion (IPC website, 2015a). However, it should be noted that a law is only as effective as its enforcement.

In September 2015, Rio de Janeiro's municipal government announced an initiative to improve accessibility to major tourist points across the city for people with a disability, ahead of the Games (IPC website, 2015b). This will of course not only assist tourists, but people with disabilities, the elderly and parents with young children living in Rio.

Funding for Para-sport in Brazil has increased with a greater slice of the lottery funds being allocated to it and a National Para-sport training centre in Sao Paulo is nearing completion that will be open for use by other South American Paralympic Committees, as well as activities for the wider society (IPC, 2015a)

## Some possible barriers to a Paralympic legacy from Rio 2016

Given the sheer size of Brazil it has to be asked whether an event in Rio de Janeiro can really impact the whole of the country. To achieve this would require an expensive and comprehensive communication and sustainability strategy that would appear next to impossible given the current economic and political situation in Brazil, which is nothing like as strong as it was when Brazil won the right to host the Games in 2009. Given the decision to cut 30 per cent from the Games budget last year (InsidetheGames, 2015) it seems unlikely that the cost of planning and sustaining any gains made during the Games could be met, meaning that these gains are likely to die quite quickly as was the case after London 2012.

Finally, as already mentioned, if the new Inclusion of People with Disabilities Act and laws are not effectively applied and enforced, then any potential gains for the general population of people with disabilities from the Rio Paralympic Games are likely to be negligible.

In the end, as the work of Brittain and Mataruna (2017) highlights, it may well be that the political economy in Brazil in the build up to and during the Games may well have put paid to any real opportunity for a legacy for people with disabilities in Brazil. The Paralympic Games (as well as the Olympic Games) were severely hit by an ever-worsening financial situation for the Games organisers (Parker, 2016) that almost led to the complete cancellation of the Paralympic Games.

## An alternative perspective on legacy and the Paralympic games

Braye, Dixon, and Gibbons (2013a) interviewed 32 members of the United Kingdom Disabled People's Council (UKDPC) in order to elicit their views on the Paralympic Games of London 2012 and concluded that "the portrayal of equality in the Paralympics is an apparent misnomer when compared with the lives of ordinary disabled people" (p. 20). By way of highlighting this viewpoint they cited the following comment from one of their participants:

> I'm afraid that the focus on elite Paralympians promotes an image of disabled people which is so far from the typical experiences of a disabled person that it is damaging to the public understanding of disability
>
> (Colin in Braye et al., 2013a, p. 9)

Hodges, Jackson, Scullion, Thompson, and Molesworth (2012) found similar results in research that they carried out for Channel 4 claiming that for some disabled people the Paralympic Games "was a source of deep frustration because the Paralympics represented something distant from their everyday reality" (p. 4). With regard to London 2012, Braye, Gibbons, and Dixon (2013b) concluded that "the IPC's positive rhetoric on improving equality can also be regarded as having a limited effect on the negative daily reality faced by disabled people living in the UK today" (p. 3). It should also be noted that this is not a new finding with

Purdue and Howe (2012) citing Cashman and Thomson (2008) regarding the Sydney 2000 Paralympic Games, who found that disabled people in Australia "had reservations about the Paralympians and did not regard them as relevant to their situation" (Purdue and Howe, 2012, p. 195). By making Paralympians the yardstick by which all disabled people are measured and expectations of them within non-disabled society are set, thus making Paralympians the 'norm' by which all other disabled people are measured, further isolates those that are unable or simply do not wish to take part in sport and reinforces ableist perspectives of their capabilities.

## The Paralympic games and legacy: only for athletes with a disability?

Certainly, some Paralympians in the UK have become celebrities as a result of the media coverage they received from London 2012 (combined, of course, with their sporting successes). However, the apparent inability of some people to differentiate between Paralympians and the average everyday disabled person appears to cause problems. The following quote from Bush, Silk, Porter, and Howe (2013) is indicative of this:

> He'd already sensed the disappointment lurking behind people's eyes when he told them he was not training for a future Paralympics. People would now expect this, yet he was more worried about the day-to-day struggles of being disabled.
>
> (Bush et al., 2013, p. 635)

Research carried out by the Australian Paralympic Committee (APC) interviewing spectators at disability sports events in Australia appear to confirm this as according to Tony Naar, the former knowledge services manager at APC, the results appear to indicate that it is only spectators attitudes towards the actual athletes and not the disabled population as a whole that are changed (Naar, 2014; personal communication).

## Conclusion

What this chapter really highlights is that sports mega events do not take place in a vacuum. They are just as subject to outside pressures and (mis)uses as any other happening within society and, as such, it is extremely difficult to accurately and effectively plan for any legacy to occur. Political, economic, and cultural specificities can all work either for or against the legacy process in many complicated and often unexpected ways. It is clear that the austere economic situation, combined with UK government plans for benefit cuts and the media reporting of these cuts had a negative impact upon attitudes towards disability, manifesting in a hardening of attitudes towards anyone who requires state-aided financial assistance to survive. It is also clear that the ordinary everyday person with a disability feels little connection, if any, to Paralympians, in terms of the issues they face in their everyday lives and the perceived expectation by the non-disabled population that all people with disabilities can perform like Paralympians only makes this sense of disconnection greater.

On a positive note Paralympians and the Paralympic Games may act as a positive influence on some disabled people to try to do more with their lives than society may have socialised or conditioned them to believe possible. The worldwide media coverage the Paralympic Games are now receiving make them an amazing platform from which to start a debate around disability issues. There is no other current platform that provides an opportunity to reach so many non-disabled people who are otherwise generally oblivious to disability issues other than the little, often politically charged, information they receive through the media or the often ableist views they are socialised into whilst growing up. As Richard Hawkes, chief executive of UK disability charity Scope, points out we shouldn't write off the Paralympic Games effect because disabled people tell Scope that the greater visibility and public discussion of their lives does make a difference (Scope website, 2013).

Overall then, whilst there are indications that the Paralympic Games does have agency in the sense that it provides a platform from which to engage in debate about disability issues, one important lesson for future hosts is that heightened expectations can create as many problems as they solve. This chapter has highlighted deep societal/structural and ideological impediments to a more enlightened view of disability. No Paralympic Games can in itself, hope to counter such forces. As highlighted earlier, with regard to the contrasting fortunes of the London 2012 and Rio 2016 Paralympic Games, each Paralympic Games is a child of its time and location.

## Bibliography

Anderson, J. (2003). Turned in tax payers': Paraplegia, rehabilitation and sport at stoke Mandeville, 1944–56. *Journal of Contemporary History*, *38*(3), 461–475.

Associated Press. (2006). Neroli fairhall, champion archer, dies at 61. *The New York Times Online*. Retrieved from www.nytimes.com/2006/06/13/sports/13fairhall.html

Braye, S., Dixon, K., and Gibbons, T. (2013a). "A mockery of equality": An exploratory investigation into disabled activists' views of the Paralympic Games. *Disability and Society*, *28*(7), 984–996.

Braye, S., Gibbons, T., and Dixon, K. (2013b). 'Disability 'Rights' and 'Wrongs'? The claims of the International Paralympic Committee, the London 2012 Paralympics and disability rights in the UK. *Sociological Research Online*, *18*(3).

British Universities and Colleges Sport website. (2016). *Disability sport*. Retrieved from www.bucs.org.uk/athlete.asp?section=18387&sectionTitle=Disability+Sport

Brittain, I. (2006). Paralympic success as a measure of national social and economic development. *International Journal of Eastern Sport and Physical Education*, *4*(1), 38–47.

Brittain, I. (2011). The Toronto Olympiad for the physically disabled: 'Aka' the fifth summer Paralympic Games held in 1976. In D. Legg and K. Gilbert (Eds.), *Paralympic legacies* (pp. 35–44). Champaign, IL: Common Ground Publishing.

Brittain, I. (2014). From stoke Mandeville to Sochi: A history of the summer and winter Paralympic Games. Champaign, IL: Common Ground Publishing.

Brittain, I. (2016). *The Paralympic Games explained* (2nd ed.). Abingdon: Routledge.

Brittain, I., and Beacom, A. (2016). Leveraging the London 2012 Paralympic Games: What legacy for people with disabilities? *Journal of Sport and Social Issues, 40*(6), 491–521.

Brittain, I., and Mataruna, L. (2017). The Rio 2016 Paralympic Games. In I. Brittain and A. Beacom (Eds.), *The Palgrave handbook of paralympic studies*. Hampshire: Palgrave MacMillan.

Bush, A., Silk, M., Porter, J., and Howe, P. D. (2013). Disability [sport] and discourse: Stories within the Paralympic legacy. *Reflective Practice, 14*(5), 632–647.

Cashman, R., and Darcy, S. (2008). *Benchmark Games: The Sydney 2000 Paralympic Games*. Petersham, Australia: Walla Walla Press.

Cashman, R., and Thomson, A. (2008). The community. In R. Cashman and S. Darcy (Eds.), *Benchmark Games: The Sydney 2000 Paralympic Games* (pp. 124–141). Petersham, Australia: Walla Walla Press.

Darcy, S., and Appleby, L. (2011). Sydney 2000: The Oceania Games. In D. Legg and K. Gilbert (Eds.), *Paralympic legacies* (pp. 73–96). Champaign, IL: Common Ground Publishing.

Euro2015 website. (2015). *Great Britain men's wheelchair basketball team crowned European champions for third time in a row*. Retrieved from www.euro2015.uk/euros/index. cfm/news1/great-britain-mene28099s-wheelchair-basketball-team-crowned-european-champions-for-third-time-in-a-row/

Groff, G., D., Lundberg, N., R., and Zabriskie, R. B. (2009). Influence of adapted sport on quality of life: Perceptions of athletes with cerebral palsy. *Journal of Disability and Rehabilitation, 31*(4), 318–326.

Guttmann, L. (1952). On the way to an international sports movement for the paralysed. *The Cord, 5*(3), 7–23.

Guttmann, L. (1976). *Textbook of sport for the disabled*. Aylesbury: HM & M Publishers.

Hodges, C. E. M., Jackson, D., Scullion, R., Thompson, S., and Molesworth, M. (2012). *Tracking changes in everyday experiences of disability and disability sport within the context of the 2012 London Paralympics*. Bournemouth University: CMC Publishing.

Hums, M. A. (2011). Athens 2004: Personal reflections. In D. Legg and K. Gilbert (Eds.), *Paralympic legacies* (pp. 97–108).Champaign, IL: Common Ground Publishing.

Insidethegames website. (2015). *Rio 2016 announce series of savings to appease Brazilian public amid financial crisis*. Retrieved from www.insidethegames.biz/articles/1030731/ rio-2016-announce-series-of-savings-to-appease-brazilian-public-amid-financial-crisis

Insidethegames website. (2016). *Craven says Rio Paralympics success is "vital"*. Retrieved from www.insidethegames.biz/articles/1032911/craven-says-rio-paralympics-success-is-vital

International Paralympic Committee. (2015a). *New law hailed as a landmark in Brazil*. Retrieved from www.paralympic.org/news/new-law-hailed-landmark-brazil

International Paralympic Committee. (2015b). *City of Rio's accessibility improvement plans praised by IPC President*. Retrieved from www.paralympic.org/news/ city-rio-s-accessibility-improvement-plans-praised-ipc-president

International Paralympic Committee. (2016). *Strategic plan 2015–2018*. Retrieved from www.paralympic.org/sites/default/files/document/150619133600866_2015_06+IPC+St rategic+Plan+2015-2018_Digital.pdf

ISMGC. (1965). Minutes of the meeting of the International Stoke Mandeville Games Committee held at Stoke Mandeville Hospital on Wednesday 21st July 1965. IWAS Archives.

Jackson, R. (1977). What did we learn from the Torontolympiad? *The Canadian Family Physician, 23*, 586–589.

Jeon, J., and Legg, D. (2011). Seoul 1988: The first modern Paralympic Games. In D. Legg and K. Gilbert (Eds.), *Paralympic legacies* (pp. 45–50). Champaign, IL: Common Ground Publishing.

McCann, C. (1996). Sports for the disabled: The evolution from rehabilitation to competitive sport. *British Journal of Sports Medicine*, *30*(4), 279–280.

Misener, L., Darcy, S., Legg, D., and Gilbert, K. (2013). Beyond Olympic legacy: Understanding Paralympic legacy through a thematic analysis. *Journal of Sport Management*, *27*, 329–341.

Mundoconectado website. (2015). *Movimento pede fim de "privilégios" para deficientes e causa revolta na web.* Retrieved from http://mundoconectado.net/noticias/movimento-pede-fim-de-privilegios-para-deficientes-e-causa-revolta-na-web/

Mushett, T., and Cody, A. (2011). Atlanta 1996: Trials and triumphs of the human spirit. In D. Legg and K. Gilbert (Eds.), *Paralympic legacies* (pp. 63–72). Champaign, IL: Common Ground Publishing.

Naar, T. (2014). Personal communication with author – e-mail dated February 21, 2014.

Parker, N. (2016). *Olympics under threat Rio 2016 faces economic meltdown, building delays, ticket sale slumps, pollution and a Zika epidemic.* Retrieved from www.thesun.co.uk/news/1202664/rio-2016-faces-economic-meltdown-building-delays-ticket-sale-slumps-pollution-and-a-zika-epidemic/

Peers, D. (2012). Patients, athletes, freaks: Paralympism and the reproduction of disability. *Journal of Sport and Social Issues*, *36*(3), 295–316.

Purdue, D. E. J., and Howe, P. D. (2012). See the sport, not the disability: Exploring the Paralympic paradox. *Qualitative Research in Sport, Exercise and Health*, *4*(2), 189–205.

A Question of Sport. (2016). *Series 46 Episode 2, Friday 2nd September.* Retrieved from www.bbc.co.uk/programmes/b07tj694

Rio 2016 website. (2016). *Rio 2016 Candidature file*, Vol. 2, p. 169. Retrieved from www.rio2016.com/en/organising-committee/transparency/documents

Scope Website. (2013). *Paralympics legacy in balance as attitudes fail to improve.* Retrieved from www.scope.org.uk/About-Us/Media/Press-releases/August-2013/Paralympics-legacy-in-balance-as-attitudes-fail-to.

Siebers, T. (2008). *Disability theory.* Ann Arbor, MI: University of Michigan Press.

Steadward, R. D. (1992). Excellence – the future of sports for athletes with disabilities. In T. Williams, L. Almond, and A. Sparkes (Eds.), *Sport and physical activity: Moving towards excellence* (pp. 293–299). London: E & FN Spon.

Sun, S., and Le Clair, J. M. (2011). Beijing 2008: Legacies and tensions after the 2008 Beijing Paralympic Games. In D. Legg and K. Gilbert (Eds.), *Paralympic legacies* (pp. 109–130). Champaign, IL: Common Ground Publishing.

Tasiemski, T., Bergstrom, E., Savic, G., and Gardner, B. P. (1998). *Sports, recreation and employment following spinal cord injury – a pilot study.* Unpublished.

UK Government/ Mayor of London Office. (2013). *Inspired by 2012: The legacy from the London 2012 Olympic and Paralympic Games* (pp. 67–72). Retrieved from www.gov.uk/government/uploads/system/uploads/attachment_data/file/224148/2901179_OlympicLegacy_acc.pdf.

Weed, M., Coren, E., Fiore, J., Ian Wellard, I., Chatziefstathiou, D., Mansfield, L., and Dowse, S. (2015). The Olympic Games and raising sport participation: A systematic review of evidence and an interrogation of policy for a demonstration effect. *European Sports Management Quarterly*, *15*(2), 195–226.

Wolbring, G. (2012). Expanding ableism: Taking down the ghettoization of impact of disability studies scholars. *Societies*, *2*(3), 75–83.

# 7 Economic legacy to cities of hosting major sports events

## A case study of London 2012

*Chris Gratton and Girish Ramchandani*

Many governments around the world have adopted national sports policies that specify that hosting major sports events is a major objective. A broad range of benefits have been suggested for both the country and the host city from staging major sports events including economic impact, urban regeneration legacy benefits, sporting legacy benefits, tourism and image benefits, and social and cultural benefits.

This chapter provides a framework to identify the key elements that make up economic legacy and then uses that framework to measure the direct economic benefits to London and the UK from hosting the summer Olympics in 2012. The final section addresses the indirect economic benefits (caused by an increase in sport participation) that are generated as a result of hosting the Olympics.

### Economic impact and economic legacy

A broad range of benefits have been suggested for both the country and the host city from staging mega sports events. The direct economic impact benefit, however, is the reason most cities have suggested as the main reason for their wanting to host events. Economic impact is the increase in economic activity generated during the event by the hosting of the event. It is dominated by the additional spending of visitors to the event. It also includes the economic value of all the investment generated by the event mainly occurring prior to it happening.

Kasimati (2003) summarised the potential benefits to a city of hosting the summer Olympics: newly constructed event facilities and infrastructure, urban revival, enhanced international reputation, increased tourism, improved public welfare, additional employment and increased inward investment. In practice, however, there is also a possible downside to hosting the event including high construction costs of sporting venues and other related investments, in particular in transport infrastructure, temporary congestion problems, displacement of other tourists because of the event, and underutilised elite sporting facilities after the event which are of little use to the local population.

Kasimati (2003) analysed all impact studies of the summer Olympics from 1984 to 2004 and found, in each case, that the studies were done prior to the Games, were not based on primary data, and were, in general, commissioned by proponents of the Games. She found that the economic impacts were likely to be inflated since the studies did not take into account supply side constraints such as investment crowding out, price increases due to resource scarcity, and the displacement of tourists who would have been to the host city had the Olympics not been held there. Although no proper economic impact study using primary data has ever been carried out for the summer Olympics, Preuss (2004) has produced a comprehensive analysis of the economics of the summer Olympics for every summer Games from Munich 1972 using secondary data and employing a novel data transformation methodology which allows comparisons across the different Olympics. Despite collecting a massive amount of secondary data, Preuss's conclusion on the estimation of the true economic impact of the summer Olympics is the same as Kasimati's:

> The economic benefit of the Games . . . is often overestimated in both publications and economic analyses produced by or for the OCOG [Organising Committee of the Olympic Games] . . . multipliers tend to be too high and the number of tourists is estimated too optimistically.
>
> (p. 290)

Preuss (2004), however, does make some strong conclusions from his analysis. He shows, for instance, that every summer Olympics since 1972 made an operational surplus that the OCOG can spend to benefit both national and international sport. Stories relating to massive losses from hosting the Olympics have nothing to do with the Games' operational costs and revenues. Rather it is to do with the capital infrastructure investments made by host cities on venues, transport, accommodation and telecommunications. These are investments on capital infrastructure that have a life of 50 years or more and yet many commentators count the full capital cost against the two to three weeks of the Games themselves. Preuss (2004) points out that this is economic nonsense:

> it is impossible and even wrong to state the overall effect of different Olympics with a single surplus or deficit. The true outcome is measured in the infrastructural, social, political, ecological and sporting impacts a city and country receive from the Games.
>
> (p. 288)

It is often argued, however, that such events generate a longer-term legacy of economic benefits. One example that is often quoted to support this argument is the case of the Barcelona Olympics in 1992. Sanahuja (2002) provided evidence on the longer-term economic benefits of hosting the Olympics in Barcelona in 1992. The paper analysed the benefits to Barcelona in 2002, ten years after hosting the Games. Sanahuja shows almost a 100 per cent increase in hotel capacity, number of tourists, and number of overnight stays in 2001 compared to the pre-Games position in 1990. By 2002, Barcelona was the number one short-break tourist destination in Europe.

Barcelona became not only a major European tourist destination it also became Spain's main business city. This is evidenced by Barcelona's rise in Cushman and Wakefield's European Cities Monitor of the best European cities in which to locate a business. Cushman and Wakefield have conducted this survey on Europe's major business cities each year since 1990. Senior executives from 500 European companies give their views on Europe's leading business cities: Barcelona was eleventh in 1990 and sixth in 2002 higher than Madrid. By 2007 it had risen even higher to replace Brussels in fourth place. Barcelona is generally regarded as the most successful Olympics ever in terms of the long-term legacy effects on the city. As far as the Olympics are concerned the success of Barcelona switched the emphasis from economic impact to economic legacy.

## A framework for defining and measuring economic legacy

Preuss (2007), Gratton and Preuss (2008), and Gratton, Preuss, and Liu (2015) review the literature on the nature of economic legacy. Preuss (2007) argued that previous approaches to measuring the legacy of an event were flawed and that there was a need for a new bottom-up approach. Such an approach would measure all 'soft' and 'hard' structural changes (which he referred to as 'event structures' generated by an event). 'Soft' structures include knowledge, networks and culture. 'Hard' structures include primary structure (e.g. sport infrastructure), secondary structure (villages for athletes), and tertiary structure (security, power plants, telecommunications, and cultural attractions).

Preuss (2007) proposed the following definition of legacy:

> legacy is all planned and unplanned, positive and negative, tangible and intangible structures created for and by a sport event that remain longer than the event itself.
>
> (p. 211)

He identified five main 'event structures' usually preserved after an event: infrastructure; knowledge (including skill development and education); image; networks; and emotion. Below we look at each of these structures in relation to the economic legacy of London 2012 based on the best evidence that is available currently.

## Economic legacy of London 2012

### Infrastructure

Infrastructure obviously means not only sport infrastructure for competition and training, but also the general infrastructure of a city such as airports, roads, telecommunication, hotels, housing (athletes, media and officials), entertainment facilities, parks, and so on (Gratton and Preuss, 2008). Responsibility for the Queen Elizabeth Olympic Park after the Olympics fell to the London Legacy Development Corporation which was set up in April 2012. Its website sets out its objectives:

> The Legacy Corporation is responsible for delivering one of the most important Olympic Legacy promises made in the original London 2012 Games bid. This pledge concerns the physical legacy of the Games-the long-term

planning, development, management and maintenance of the Park and its impact on the surrounding area after the 2012 Games.

It is our task to transform and integrate one of the most challenged areas in the UK into word-class, sustainable and thriving neighbourhoods.

This will create a new part of the city in east London – an inclusive community, a thriving business zone and a must-see destination where people will choose to live, work and play, and return time and time again.

(London Legacy Development Corporation, 2016)

In terms of sporting infrastructure only five facilities were planned as permanent facilities on the Olympic Park: the Copper Box Arena, Lee Valley Hockey and Tennis Centre, Lee Valley Velopark, London Aquatics Centre, and the Stadium. By August 2016 all five have a secure legacy:

- The Copper Box Arena opened on July 27th, 2013 with over 10,000 visitors in the first weekend alone. It is the third-largest indoor arena in London.
- Lee Valley Hockey and Tennis Centre opened in June 2014. It consists of four indoor tennis courts, six outdoor tennis courts and two top-class hockey pitches made of water based artificial turf.
- Lee Valley Velopark opened in March 2014. It consists of the Olympic velodrome and the Olympic BMX track plus two new facilities constructed since the Olympics: a one-mile road circuit and five miles of mountain bike trails.
- London Aquatics Centre opened in March 2014 after substantial modification after the Olympics involving mainly the removal of 15,000 spectator seats.
- The Olympic Stadium became the new home of West Ham United in August 2016 when they played their first home match there. The capacity has been reduced to 54,000 seats. It will also host major athletics championships including the World Athletics Championships in 2017.

The other three permanent facilities on the Olympic Park are not sport facilities. They consist of

- Here East, which is the new name for what was the Press and Broadcast Centre during the Olympics. Currently there are three tenants: BT Sport (from August 2013), Hackney Community College (from September 2015), and Loughborough University (from September 2015).
- East Village, which is the new name for what was the Athletes Village accommodation during the Olympics. The village has been transformed into 2,818 new homes, of which 1,379 are affordable homes and houses for sale or rent and 1,439 are privately rented by Get Living London. In September 2016, East Village was given the prize of Development of the Decade at the RESI (Redefining Early Stage Investments) Conference.
- The ArcelorMittal Orbit is the tallest sculpture in the UK at 114.5 metres high which was designed by artist Sir Anish Kapoor and structural engineer Cecil Balmond. People can go up to the upper observation deck at 80 metres to see right across London. This has not proved as popular as expected, and a giant slide was added in 2016 to hopefully attract more visitors.

In addition to the permanent physical facilities on the Olympic Park other infra-structure investment in transport was made for the Olympics. Investments that were planned prior to London winning the Olympics were brought forward to be completed before the 2012 Games. The Olympic Delivery Authority invested over £500 million towards the following improvements:

- a second new Docklands Light Railway line;
- a new branch of the East London Line;
- new and improved piers for river services on the Thames;
- enhancements to more than 100 walking and cycling routes.

These improvements remain in place to make a lasting improvement to transport links for those living and working in East London.

### Knowledge, skill development, and education

The host population gains knowledge and skills from staging a mega sport event. Employees and volunteers develop skills and knowledge in event organization, human resource management, security, hospitality, service, and so on (Gratton and Preuss, 2008).

There were a large number of employment and skills initiatives connected to the 2012 Games. The employment and skills legacy is being delivered through a partnership approach involving the Department for Business, Innovation and Skills (BIS), Skills Funding Agency (SFA), Job Centre Plus, and other regional bodies (DCMS, 2013a). The main focus of London's attempt to use the Games to promote employability and skills development was the London Employment and Skill Taskforce (LEST) 2012 programme. As DCMS (2013a) pointed out,

> LEST 2012 had an aspirational target to reduce worklessness in London by 70,000 by the end of 2012, of which 20,000 would be from the host boroughs. The programme delivered three 'pillars' of activity across London: employer leadership; linking people, work, and training more effectively; and engage-ment and communications. The LDA and the GLA supported a range of employment and job brokerage projects focussed on supporting workless people into Games time jobs and other jobs.

GLA (2013) evaluated the success of these initiatives and found that between 61,749 and 76,050 unemployed workers in London secured Games-related jobs through the LEST 2012 programme, and 20,000 of these were previously unem-ployed Londoners that were employed by LOCOG. LOCOG recruited and trained 70,000 volunteers, and this provides a trained group of people available for future events in London and throughout the UK (National Audit Office, 2012). Over 240,000 people applied to be volunteers. The volunteers were called 'Games Makers' and most worked at both the Olympics and the Paralympics.

DCMS (2013b) commissioned a survey of all 70,000 volunteers. The survey was an online survey and was distributed two days after the end of the Paralym-pic Games. Five days later the response was 11,451 completed questionnaires.

The respondents were asked out of 22 skill areas which were the five main skills they considered had developed most as a result of their London 2012 experience. These were customer service skills (31%), teamwork skills (29%), communication skills (25%), interpersonal skills (25%), and the ability to work under pressure (21%). Of respondents, 82% considered they would be able to apply their new set of skills in other volunteering situations and 57% in their paid employment. Furthermore, 92% were either satisfied of very satisfied with their London 2012 volunteer experience, and nearly 50% said that they expected to increase their volunteering levels over their pre-Games levels.

It was generally recognised in the media that the Games Makers had made a significant contribution to the London 2012 visitor experience and so much so that the British Olympic Association's chairman Colin Moynihan said that they should be nominated for the BBC's Sports Personality Team of the Year award.

### *Image*

Mega sport events have tremendous symbolic significance and form, and contribute to the repositioning or solidifying the image of a city, region and country. Usually events create a positive imagery and the city and politicians can 'bask in [its] reflected glory' (Snyder, Lassegard, and Ford, 1986). On the other hand, the worldwide exposure of the event, the host city and its culture depends on the media representatives and cannot be entirely controlled by the organisers (Gratton and Preuss, 2008; Preuss and Alfs, 2011; Preuss and Messing, 2002).

The legacy of image is one of the intangible or soft legacies in contrast to the tangible or hard legacy such as infrastructure. Intangible legacies are more difficult to measure and quantify, but certain agencies have made significant attempts to do so. In the case of the image legacy of London 2012, VisitBritain, the national tourism agency tasked with attracting foreign tourists to visit Britain, invested in this initiative.

As soon as London was awarded the Olympics in 2005, VisitBritain started to develop an Olympic and Paralympic strategy. The aim of the strategy was 'to ensure the maximum tourism legacy for the whole of the UK in cooperation with both tourism and non-tourism partners at home and overseas – recognising that our greatest return would come from the visitors motivated as a result of the Games' exposure rather than from visitors to the Games themselves' (VisitBritain, 2013).

The objective of the strategy was to improve economic benefit, image and welcome. VisitBritain (2013) indicated how the strategy was implemented:

> The global exposure that Britain enjoyed in 2012 provided an unprecedented opportunity for VisitBritain to ensure that the whole of the UK visitor economy benefitted from the 2012 Games. It gave us a platform to promote the wider messages and interests of destination Britain, to deliver and showcase a world class welcome in 2012 and beyond, and to maximise the economic benefits of tourism across the UK.
>
> Our mission was not to promote the few weeks of the 2012 Olympic and Paralympic Games. It was to make full use of the opportunities to promote

Britain before, during, and after those few weeks to reach new customers in emerging markets and to refresh our appeal in core markets.

In terms of brand building or perceptions of Britain we wished to capitalise on the global platform offered by the 2012 Games to accelerate the development of Britain's image.

VisitBritain continuously tracks perceptions of Britain using the Nations Brand Index, which is a national study looking at the views of people in 20 countries around the world. This survey showed that on the three main indicators, nation brand, welcome, and culture, all were higher following the Games than before them. Nation brand moved from fifth to fourth, welcome moved from twelfth to ninth, and culture moved from fifth to fourth.

Further research commissioned by VisitBritain showed that London 2012 had been a public relations success for Britain:

Among over 100 communications experts from 24 countries

• 79% judged their 'local' media coverage of the London Olympics as largely positive;
• 73% to have changed the image of the British for the better;
• 99% that the Olympics will encourage more people from their country to visit Britain

(VisitBritain, 2013)

This evidence seems to be supported by what happened to international visitors to Britain following the Olympics. In 2012, there was only a 1% increase in visitor numbers although the expenditure generated by these visitors was 4% higher than in 2011. In 2013, visitor numbers rose 5%, but expenditure rose 14%, the largest increase in expenditure since 1995. In 2014 visitor numbers grew 5% and spending by 3%. In 2015 visits grew a further 5%, and spending grew by 1%. Thus by 2015 visitor numbers were more than 16% higher than in 2012, and expenditure was more than 18% higher.

*Networks*

Major sports events require close cooperation between the international sport federation, the national sport federation, the local organising committee, politicians, the media, and a multitude of other organisations. The networks created through these interactions can provide a lasting legacy from the event (Gratton and Preuss, 2008). The largest networking event during the 2012 Games was the UK Trade and Investment British Business Embassy. This was attended by over 4,000 business leaders from 63 countries and was held at Lancaster House in London. The event began with the Global Investment Conference and continued over 18 days with sector summits for advanced engineering, life sciences, the creative industries, infrastructure, retail, and other sectors. UKTI (2013) indicated that this was followed up by a series of 50 other events throughout the country: 'For example, UKTI South West and the Dorset Local Enterprise Partnership ran a British Business Club over five days to coincide with sailing in Weymouth, attracting 500 attendees' (UKTI, 2013). Within one year of London 2012 UKTI (2013) estimated that these initiatives had generated £5.9 billion of additional sales for British companies and attracted £2.5 billion of additional inward investment into the UK, 58% of it invested outside London.

### *Emotion*

Major sports events can generate huge national pride for the citizens of the host city and host nation. For Beijing 2008, the Olympics were deliberately used to increase the confidence and self-esteem of the Chinese people. Part of this was related to the staging of the Games: the pride that comes from the association of this global event with your own country. This was reinforced by the demonstration of Chinese culture at the opening ceremony. The euphoria generated in China by their topping the medal table added further to China's sense of national pride, self-esteem and confidence (Jing, 2012).

Immediately prior to the Olympics in 2012 British media were highly sceptical about whether the Games would be a success. There was a lot of criticism of the cost of the Games rising to £9.3 billion. It was questioned whether such a budget could be justified following the 2008 global economic crisis followed by the largest recession in the UK since the 1930s. Just before the Olympics the company handling security for the Games, G4S, announced that around half of the workforce they had recruited earlier failed to turn up for duty in July 2012. The army plugged the gap in security personnel. There was genuine fear that the Games could prove a disaster.

However, despite these fears expressed in the media the mood in the country was much more positive. The Olympic torch relay went across the whole of the UK from May 19 to July 27, attracting over 15 million people to Olympic torch events. It created huge enthusiasm for the Olympic Games and was particularly successful in attracting children and young people. The mood generated in the country was in sharp contrast to the scepticism in the media.

However, this media scepticism quickly disappeared the day after the opening ceremony. This was widely acclaimed across all media. Once the medals for Team GB started to roll in the whole country was in a state of high emotion and euphoria. On August 12, 2012, the final day of the Olympics, the editorial in the *Sunday Times*, which had prior to the Games been critical of the cost, suggested that if we find something else next year on which we could spend £9.3 billion and make us feel this good as a nation, then let's do it.

This emotional impact of the Olympics has until recently received little attention. However, it is now a focus in the literature on the economic legacy of an event.

The argument on why cities bid to host major events has over recent years been based on the economic development paradigm set out below. That is, events will influence people living *outside* the host city and country to visit or invest in the city or country either during the event itself or in subsequent years because the place marketing effects of seeing the event on television will generate more tourism in the longer term.

## Economic development paradigm

The American sport economics literature, however, has argued consistently that no evidence exists to suggest such economic benefits from hosting events ever actually materialise. As Crompton (2004) states,

> the prevailing evidence is that substantial measurable economic impact has rarely been demonstrated. This is causing the focus of the argument for public subsidy to be redefined, away from economic impacts and economic development towards the psychic income benefits. This is the new frontier.
>
> (p55)

This literature is mainly concerned with the economic impact of teams in the four major American team sports, American football, ice hockey, baseball, and basketball. Other economists have shown that major events do generate substantial economic impact. The soccer World Cup in Germany in 2006 generated an economic impact of 2.56 billion euros, an average of 40 million euros from each match (Preuss, Kurscheidt, and Schütte, 2009).

There is little evidence to suggest that the Olympics, summer or winter, generate a significant economic impact. During the period July to September 2012 there were 4% fewer visits to the UK by overseas residents than in the same period in 2011. A similar pattern was observed in Beijing in 2008, Athens in 2004, and Sydney in 2000.

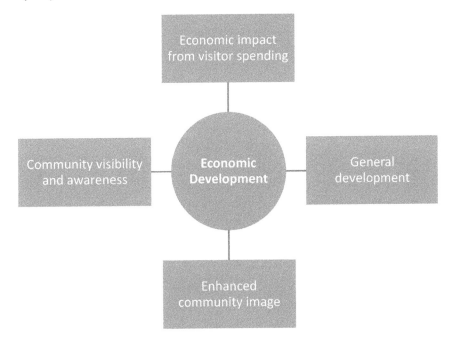

*Figure 7.1* Economic development paradigm

Source: Adapted from Crompton (2004).

In contrast to the economic argument, which focuses on audiences external to the host city or country, psychic income focuses *internally* on the host city or host country residents, and refers to the emotional and psychological benefit residents receive from hosting as indicated below.

Such emotional benefits have also been identified by Gratton and Preuss (2008) as an important part of the economic legacy of major events. In addition in the last few years sport economists have adopted the methodology developed in the economics of happiness literature to analyse the effect of hosting major events on national pride and social wellbeing. Some studies have examined the willingness to pay (WTP) for both hosting sports events and success at sporting events. Atkinson, Mourato, Symanski, and Oxdemiroglu (2008) explored the willingness of citizens of London, Manchester, and Glasgow to host the 2012 London Olympic Games. They found the average WTP was highest among Londoners (£22), about twice as much as in Glasgow and Manchester, and was £2 billion for the UK population as a whole. Sussmuth, Heyne, and Maennig (2010) found similar levels of WTP for German citizens for the 2006 World Cup. Wicker, Hallman, Breuer, and Feiler (2012a) and Wicker, Hallman, Breuer, and Feiler (2012b) found significant levels of willingness to pay for both Olympic success and World Cup success amongst German citizens.

## Psychic income paradigm

Kavetsos and Szymanski (2010), using Eurobarometer data, for twelve European countries showed that hosting major events had a significant impact on

*Figure 7.2* Psychic income paradigm

Source: Adapted from Crompton (2004).

national pride. Kavetsos (2012), using Eurobarometer data for sixteen countries, also found significant effects on national pride from hosting major events. De Nooij, Van den Berg, and Koopmans (2013), using a social cost-benefit analysis of the recent Netherlands World Cup bid, found that a greater sense of happiness, national pride, harmony, and national identity were the main economic benefits to the hosts from staging a World Cup rather than economic impact.

Jing (2012) carried out an exploratory study of Chinese young people to estimate the impact of Beijing 2008 on national pride and self-esteem. The study was carried out in 2012, just before the London Olympics and four years after the staging of Beijing 2008. A sample of 184 university students aged 18 to 24 were asked whether they agreed or disagreed with the statement '*China's hosting of the Beijing 2008 Olympic Games created a strong sense of national identity*'; 86.4 percent either agreed or strongly agreed. Another question was whether they agreed or disagreed with the statement '*I am proud that China topped the medal table in Beijing 2008*'; 90.8 percent either agreed or strongly agreed. The study supports the argument that staging a summer Olympic Games can generate substantial psychic income and that this can be a true legacy of the Games as it can remain in the hosting city and country a long time after the Games have finished.

The evidence cited earlier suggests that the 'old' economic paradigm is no longer the main benefit of hosting major events. The 'new' psychic income paradigm is increasingly more important. However, it is difficult to quantify the economic magnitude of these emotional benefits from hosting events and particularly the legacy benefits. Prior to the London Olympics the UK was going through a double-dip recession. In the third quarter of 2012 it emerged from that recession and has been one of the strongest economies in Europe in the years that immediately followed, which tends to suggest that the Olympics had some impact on national economic confidence. However, further research in this relatively new area of economics needs to be done to establish stronger evidence on the value of psychic income benefits from hosting major sports events.

## Indirect economic legacy: the economic benefits of increased sport participation

One of the arguments put forward to the International Olympic Committee by those presenting London's bid to host the 2012 Games was that London would inspire people, and young people in particular, to take part in sport. If this happened further economic benefits would flow from the increase in sports participation. The impact of hosting mega sports events on sport participation in the host city and country is considered in detail by Mike Weed in Chapter 5, and he concluded that the hypothesised positive effect on sport participation is neither fact nor fiction on the weight of the existing evidence. However, we would like to look briefly at the London evidence both before and after the 2012 Olympics.

Sport England's Active People Survey has been measuring sport participation in England since October 2005, which is since the Olympics were awarded to London. Figure 7.3 shows the trend in participation in London for those taking part in sport at least once a week for a minimum of 30 minutes (1 × 30 measure) and those taking part for at least three times per week (3 × 30 measure). The data do not relate to a calendar year but October to October; thus, the 2005/6 data are for October 2005 to October 2006 and the same for the other years. Thus, data related to when the Olympics took place is the 2011/2012 data, and all years after this are a legacy period in that they represent participation after the Olympics finished.

Figure 7.3 (below) shows that on the 1 × 30 measure, participation rose strongly between 2005/6 and 2007/8, rising from 35.3% to 38%. It then dropped back in each of the next two years to reach a low of 36.6% in 2011/12, the year immediately before Olympic year. This reduction could be due to the economic crisis because there was a sharp drop in participation in the most expensive sports following the global financial crisis in 2008. Participation then rose in the next two years reaching a peak of 38.5% in 2012/13, the year following the Olympics. It then dropped back to 38% in the next two years but was still substantially higher than the 2010/11 low. So there is evidence of an Olympic participation legacy in London. On the 3 × 30 measure, there was a similar pattern except the difference between the low in 2010/11 (16.9%) and the high in 2012/13 (19%) was greater. Again in all years following 2012/13 it remained above the 2010/11 low.

Figure 7.4 presents the same picture for the 1 × 30 measure using 2005/6 as a baseline year with an index value of 100. All the other data are then directly comparable to this baseline. Thus, the index figure for 2012/13 is 109.1 (i.e. 38.5%/35.3% × 100), indicating that participation in that year was 9.1% higher than in 2005/6.

Figure 7.5 shows the trend in participation for those taking part at least three times a week for at least 30 minutes (3 × 30 measure) using 2005/6 as a baseline

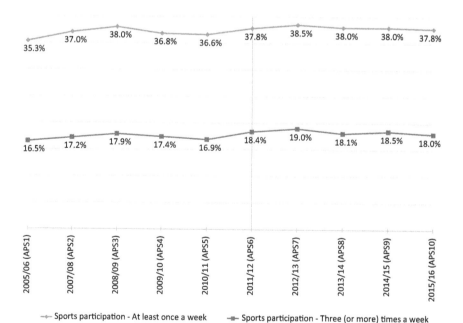

*Figure 7.3* London 1 × 30 and 3 × 30 sports participation rates 2005–2016

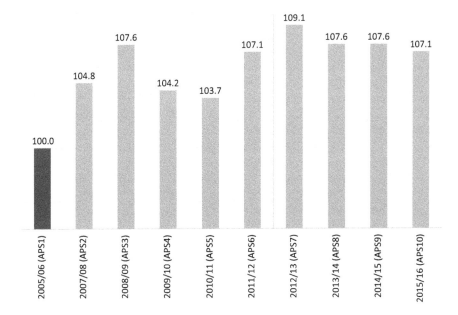

*Figure 7.4* London 1 × 30 sports participation 2005–2016 (APS1 = 100)

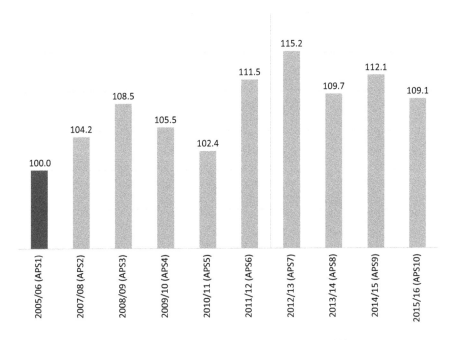

*Figure 7.5* London 3 × 30 sports participation 2005–2016 (APS1=100)

year with an index value of 100. Again it shows clearly all years following 2005/6 have a higher participation rate and all years following 2010/11 have higher rates.

If we compare London to England on the 1 × 30 measure, London has a higher participation rate than England as a whole in every year but the gap is greatest in 2012/13 and 2013/14. Thus, in 2005/6 London's sport participation was 2.3% above England, in 2012/13 it was 5.5% above, and in 2013/14 it was 5.3% above. This is to be expected for a capital city that is likely to attract a younger, better-educated, and overall higher income population than the average for the country as a whole, and all these variables are positively correlated with sport participation.

The peak in participation rates on this measure is greater in 2012/13 with London rates 6.7% higher in that year than in England. The pattern of changes over time in London is similar to England but the peak in 2012/13 is much sharper for London. There is still a participation legacy for England as a whole in that every year following 2010/11 has a higher participation rate but the effect is smaller than for London. The same is true for the 3 × 30 measure.

London clearly comes top of the league table for participation rates when we compare London with the other English regions and this is true for both measures of participation. Thus, London's sports participation did seem to increase significantly as a direct result of hosting the Games. This is the first time such clear evidence of this effect for a city hosting the summer Games has emerged.

An increase in sport participation has its own long term economic benefits so if the increase in London's sport participation between 2010/11 and 2012/13 is a direct result of London hosting the Games these benefits contribute to the economic legacy of the Games. The most direct economic benefit is on consumers' expenditure on sport and the resulting effects on output and employment. Sports participation is the main driver of the sports market. When participation in sport increases so does expenditure on sports clothing, equipment, shoes, and on sports facilities. Consumer sport-related spending increased from £26.4 billion in 2010 to £29.2 billion in 2012: a 10.6% increase in current prices (or 4.5% in constant prices). Consumer spending on sport was 2.9% of all UK consumer spending in 2012, up from 2.8% in 2010 and 2011 (DCMS, 2015a).

There are other economic benefits of increased sport participation, however, that are not evident in the sport market. The most accepted of these is the health benefits of increased sport participation.

DCMS (2015b) indicated that

> [s]ports participants are 14.1% more likely to report good health than non-participants. . . . In turn, people in good health are 25.4% less likely to frequently visit GPs (defined as 6+ GP visits or more per year) and 8.4% less likely to have used psychotherapy services in the last year than those who are not in good health. . . . The estimated per person annual NHS cost savings due to predicted reductions in GP visits are: £13.25 for people who participate in sport. . . . The estimated per person annual NHS cost savings due to predicted reductions in psychotherapy usage are: £17.86 for people who participate in sport.

(p 15)

Using these estimates suggests the annual cost saving to the NHS in England on these services alone for those taking part in sport would be £903.7 million (DCMS, 2015b). The increase in sport participation at least once a week in England of 1.3% between 2010/11 and 2012/13 (36.6%/35.6%) therefore represents an additional saving in one year alone of around £11.7 million, and since participation continues to remain above its 2010/11 level, similar savings are realised in subsequent years.

These savings, however, are only part of the health benefits of increased sport participation. Participation in sport leads to significant reductions in the risk of developing certain diseases. In particular it reduces the risk of developing cardiovascular disease, stroke, colon cancer, breast cancer and Type 2 diabetes. DCMS (2016) estimated that the savings to the NHS from a reduced number of cases in sports participants amounted to £1.5 billion in England. The increase in participation of 1.3% between 2010/11 and 2012/13 therefore represents an additional saving in one year alone of £195 million with further savings in subsequent years.

These health savings of increased participation, however, are dwarfed by another benefit of increased sport participation, the value to subjective well-being. We have seen earlier that hosting a major sport event can generate psychic income to the residents of a host city and country. Taking part in sport has a similar effect by increasing the participant's subjective well-being. Over the last decade sport economists have started to put an economic value on this sport-related increase in subjective well-being (SWB). DCMS (2016) estimated this economic value to be £30.4 billion for all sport participants in England. The increase in participation of 1.3% between 2010/11 and 2012/13 therefore represents an increase in the value of sport-related SWB in one year alone of £395 million with further savings in subsequent years.

## Conclusion

The literature on the economics of hosting major sports events has concentrated on whether or not these events generate a significant economic impact for the host city and country. On the evidence collected at the Sydney, Athens and Beijing Olympic Games it seems the additional economic impact is very limited. In all three cases the additional tourism generated by the Games was matched by a decline in the tourism that these cities generate on a regular basis. The non-sport tourists seem to avoid going to Olympic cities while the Games are taking place, not least because hotel prices are at a premium for these weeks. A similar effect happened in London: the number of tourists in the third quarter of 2012, when the Games were taking place, was less than for the same quarter in 2011. Thus, the initial economic impact generated by the summer Olympic Games seems to be more fiction than fact. What we have seen in this chapter, however, is that the benefits of hosting major sports events go beyond the immediate economic impact and are quite wide ranging. By using data and sources that are currently available in relation to London 2012, this chapter has provided some evidence that the economic legacy benefits are positive. Whether the value of these benefits justifies the large investment required to host the Olympic Games is not so clear, and it is therefore somewhat premature to conclude that the economic legacy benefits are either fact or fiction. However, we have seen that most of the investment is on general infrastructure such as airports, rail and road transport infrastructure and all of this continues to yield a rate of return on the investment well after the Games are finished. It will always be difficult to answer the question of whether the benefits outweigh the cost. To evaluate the true economic legacy of London 2012 we will have to wait a further ten to fifteen years. What is evident, though, is that it is the economic legacy benefits that now determine the economics of the Olympics not the direct economic impacts during the event itself.

## References

Atkinson, G., Mourato, S., Symanski, S., and Oxdemiroglu, E. (2008). Are we willing to pat to 'Back the Bid'? Valuing the intangible impacts of London's bid to host the 2012 summer Olympic Games. *Urban Studies, 45*(2), 419–444.

Crompton, J. (2004). Beyond economic impact: An alternative rationale for the public subsidy of major league sports facilities. *Journal of Sport Management, 18*, 40–58.

de Nooij, M., Van den Berg, M., and Koopmans, C. (2013). Bread or games? A social cost-benefit analysis of the World Cup bid of the Netherlands and the winning Russian bid. *Journal of Sports Economics*.

Department of Culture, Media and Sport (DCMS). (2013a). Meta-evaluation of the impacts and legacy of the London 2012 Olympic Games and Paralympic Games: Report 5: Post-games evaluation. London: DCMS.

Department of Culture, Media and Sport (DCMS). (2013b). *London 2012 games maker survey*. London: DCMS.

Department of Culture, Media and Sport (DCMS). (2015a). *UK sport satellite account, 2011 and 2012*. London: DCMS.

Department of Culture, Media and Sport (DCMS). (2015b). *Further analysis to value the health and educational benefits of sport and culture*. London: DCMS.

Department of Culture, Media and Sport (DCMS). (2016). *Social return on investment in sport*. London: DCMS.

Gratton, C., and Preuss, H. (2008). Maximising Olympic impacts by building up legacies. *International Journal of the History of Sport, 25*(14), 1922–1938.

Gratton, C., Preuss, H., and Liu, D. (2015). Economic legacy to cities from hosting major sports events: A case-study of Beijing 2008. In R. Holt and D. Ruta (Eds.), *Routledge handbook of sport and legacy*. London: Routledge.

Greater London Authority (GLA). (2013). *Olympic jobs evaluation*. London: GLA.

Jing, Z. (2012). *An evaluation of Chinese young people's perceptions of the 2008 Beijing Olympic Games*. Unpublished MSc Sport Business Management Thesis, Sheffield Hallam University, Sheffield, UK.

Kasimati, E. (2003). Economic aspects and the Summer Olympics: A review of related research. *International Journal of Tourism Research, 5*(6), 433–444.

Kavetsos, G. (2012). National pride: War minus the shooting. *Social Indicators Research, 106*, 173–185.

Kavetsos, G., and Szymanski, S. (2010). National well-being and international sports events. *Journal of Economic Psychology, 31*, 158–171.

London Legacy Development Corporation. (2016). Retrieved September 30, 2016, from http://queenelizabetholympicpark.co.uk/our-story/the-legacy-corporation

National Audit Office. (2012). The London 2012 Olympic Games and Paralympic Games: Post-games review. London: NAO.

Preuss, H. (2007). The conceptualization and measurement of mega sport event legacies. *Journal of Sport & Tourism*, *12*(3–4), 207–227.

Preuss, H., and Alfs, C. (2011). Signalling through the 2008 Beijing Olympics: Using mega sport events to change the perception and image of the host. *European Sports Management Quarterly*, *11*(1), 55–71.

Preuss, H., Kurscheidt, M., and Schütte, N. (2009). Ökonomie des Tourismus durch Sportgroßveranstaltungen: Eine empirische Analyse zur Fußball-Weltmeisterschaft 2006. Wiesbaden: Gabler Verlag.

Preuss, H. (2004). Calculating the regional economic impact of the Olympic Games. *European Sport Management Quarterly*, *4*(4), 234–253.

Preuss, H., and Messing, M. (2002). Auslandstouristen bei den Olympischen Spielen in Sydney 2000. In A. Dreyer (Ed.), *Tourismus im sport* (pp. 223–41). Wiesbaden: Deutscher Universitäts-Verlag.

Sanahuja, R. (2002). *Olympic city-the city strategy 10 years after the Olympic Games in 1992*. Paper delivered to the Conference, Sports Events and Economic Impact, Copenhagen, April 2002.

Snyder, C. R., Lassegard, M., and Ford, C. E. (1986). Distancing after group success and failure: Basking in reflected glory and cutting off reflected failure. *Journal of Personality and Social Psychology*, *51*(2), 382–388.

Sussmuth, B., Heyne, M., and Maennig, W. (2010). Induced civic pride and integration. *Oxford Bulleting of Economics and Statistics*, *72*(2), 202–220.

UK Trade and Industry (UKTI). (2013). *London 2012: Delivering the economic legacy*. London: UKTI.

VisitBritain (2013, January). *Foresight, Issue 111*.

Wicker, P., Hallman, K., Breuer, C., and Feiler, S. (2012a). The value of Olympic success and the intangible effects of sports events – A contingent valuation approach in Germany. *European Sport Management Quarterly*, *12*(4), 337–355.

Wicker, P., Prinz, J., and von Hanau, T. (2012b). Estimating the value of national sporting success. *Sport Management Review*, *15*(2), 200–210.

# 8 Environmental legacy of mega sport events

*Timothy B. Kellison and Jonathan M. Casper*

This chapter covers mega sporting events in relation to environmental protection. We first introduce why sport and associated mega-events serve as important platforms for environmental protection and actions. Next, we explain the basic processes related to environmental planning and implementation. The history of environmental legacy at mega-events is covered before introducing case studies which show how mega-events provide an environmental legacy while also addressing challenges. Finally, the barriers and issues related to environmental legacy are discussed.

Fact: Mega-events provide unique sustainability challenges, and they require long-term strategic planning to ensure environmental legacies will remain intact in the years and decades following the event.

Fairy tale: The positive environmental legacies proposed by mega-event organisers during the bid process are typically realised without challenges or alternations.

## Introduction

Mega events must leave enduring legacies that benefit societies long after games are over. All hosts of mega events should integrate sustainability at their core. Let us work together so that the motto of all mega events in the future is cleaner, greener and more sustainable.

—UN Secretary General Ban Ki-Moon (FIFA, 2016)

Sport presents broad opportunities to promote environmental awareness, capacity building and far-reaching actions for environmental, social, and economic development across society (International Olympic Committee: IOC, 2012). Sustainable development has become increasingly integrated into the objectives of hosting mega-events (Hall, 2012). Therefore, a vast majority of mega sport event organisations (e.g., International Olympic Committee [IOC], Fédération Internationale de Football Association [FIFA]) have sustainability management plans designed to integrate the principles, actions, and projects related to sustainability when hosting events. The goal is to integrate sustainability in all aspects of the organisational processes, thus reducing the impact of the event, and setting an example of good practice for society as a whole (IOC, 2013).

## Why sport?

Sport is part of global cultural fibre (Klein, 2014). Sport is interwoven in culture and society, and the sport industry can use its unique influence to provide much-needed business leadership in ecology and sustainable practices (Barth, 2016). The reason for using sport to enhance environmental protection stems from both the environmental impact of the events themselves (the focus of this chapter) and, even more important, how they serve as a platform to enhance environmental behaviour to the significant number of fans that attend mega-events. There are few cultural or social phenomenon in the world that can leverage such numbers. Some examples include

- we follow sports: 16% of Americans follow science, but 70% follow sports (Barth, 2016).
- we are loyal to sport at a young age: According to ESPN's 2013 Sports Poll, 88% of Americans age 12 or older state they are fans of and follow at least one sport (Luker, 2014).
- we attend and watch sport: FIFA reported about 3.3 million people attended the 64 games and nearly half the planet (3.2 billion people) tuned in to at least one match of the 2014 World Cup (FIFA, 2015).

Sport events provide a visible platform for environmental corporate social responsibility efforts that, in turn, influence spectator behaviour. Consequently, sporting organisations and events can not only reduce a large environmental footprint from the event itself but also educate and expose spectators to environmental practices that may influence sustainable behaviours within their everyday lives (Casper and Pfahl, 2015).

## What is event greening?

Event-greening is the process of incorporating socially and environmentally responsible decision-making into the planning, organisation and implementation of, and participation in, an event. It involves including sustainable development principles and practices in all levels of event organisation, and aims to ensure that an event is hosted responsibly. It represents the total package of interventions at an event, and needs to be done in an integrated manner. Event-greening should start at the inception of the project and should involve all the key role players, such as clients, organisers, venues, subcontractors, and suppliers. It aims to achieve the following (Ackermann, 2011, p. 25):

- To improve the resource efficiency of the entire event and supply chain management;
- To reduce negative environmental impacts, such as carbon emissions, waste ending up on landfill sites, and the effect on biodiversity;
- To increase economic, social and environmental benefits (triple-bottom line);

- To enhance the economic impact, such as local investment and long-term viability;
- To strengthen the social impact, such as community involvement and fair employment;
- To improve sustainable performance within an available budget;
- To present opportunities for more efficient planning and use of equipment and infrastructure;
- To reduce the negative impact on local inhabitants;
- To protect the local biodiversity, water and soil resources;
- To apply the principles of eco-procurement of goods and services; and
- To raise awareness of sustainability.

## Basic planning and implementation

There are three major phases for integrating sustainability within a mega-event (Rio, 2013):

> *Preparation phase:* includes the conceiving and designing of permanent infrastructure, venues and facilities; detailed operational planning; construction of new permanent facilities and renovation of existing venues; construction of temporary venues and facilities; human resources development; legacy planning
>
> *Operational phase:* starts a few months before the mega-event. Along with the competitions themselves, includes cultural and educational activities, test events, the opening and closing ceremonies and the disassembly of the venues and facilities
>
> *Legacy phase:* after the mega-event, the work continues to ensure lasting positive transformations that maximise the social, economic, environmental, and sporting benefits of hosting

While most sustainability mega-event plans focus on three major categories (people, planet, and prosperity), this chapter will focus on environmental planning and implementation, or *planet*. Major elements within the environmental focus include transportation and logistics, sustainable design and construction, environmental conservation and clean-up, and waste management (Table 8.1).

*Table 8.1* Major themes and objectives for a reduced environmental footprint for the 2016 Rio Olympic and Paralympic Games

| Themes | Specific objectives |
| --- | --- |
| Transport and logistics | Provide public transport for spectators and the labour force |
| | Implement actions to reduce pollution, including greenhouse gas (GHG) emissions in public transport systems |
| | Operate the Olympic and Paralympic fleet using cleaner fuels |
| | Rationalise and optimise logistics operations in the transportation of materials and equipment |

*(Continued)*

*Table 8.1* (Continued)

| Themes | Specific objectives |
| --- | --- |
| Sustainable construction and urban improvement | Implement criteria for the rational use of resources, efficiency and minimisation of environmental impacts in the design and construction of all facilities |
| | Meet international and national environmental planning standards for development and construction of the entire Games infrastructure |
| | Encourage the growth of economic activity and improvements in the quality of life in the various Olympic Zones |
| Environmental conservation and clean-up | Minimise the impact on the existing ecosystems at the Olympic and Paralympic facilities and their immediate surroundings |
| | Promote the environmental clean-up of bodies of water in the regions of the Games |
| | Strengthen and accelerate environmental protection, conservation, restoration and rehabilitation programs |
| | Expand monitoring of air and water quality in the Games regions |
| Waste management | Decommission and commence environmental clean-up of landfills and implement integrated solid waste treatment |
| | Align and implement management plans for all construction waste, ensuring appropriate management and final treatment |
| | Management and responsible treatment of the solid waste operations of the Games |
| | Management and responsible treatment of corporate solid waste |

Source: Rio 2016 Organising Committee (2013, p. 12).

## Environmental legacy

While there is tremendous planning and efforts toward environmental sustainability with mega-events, there is still controversy about the sincerity of the efforts as well as follow through once the event is over, and ultimately the event's environmental legacy. Mega-events are still often considered as "footloose industries" in that their organisations mobilise considerable resources in the short term but then disappear, leaving long-term consequences (Preuss, 2013). They come to a place with a need for resources and then disappear. Have past mega-events been environmentally friendly, genuinely "green" games or only a "green washing" exercise? The next section explores this controversy, both the positive and the negatives, through an overview of the history of environmental legacy at mega-events and subsequent case studies.

## Reconciling rhetoric and reality: a collective case study of sustainability claims

The formalisation of environmental legacy in mega-event planning is a relatively recent development resulting from rising awareness of environmental issues from sport organisations and key international organisations like the United Nations and the IOC (Kellison, Trendafilova, and McCullough, 2015; McCullough, Pfahl, and Nguyen, 2015). Calls for ecological stewardship from activists, policymakers, and sport leaders have undoubtedly affected the increasing attention on environmental legacy planning among mega-event organisers and hosts. While it is highly likely that any mega sporting event today will pledge to minimise its impact on the natural environment, such planning can be derailed by any number of reasons, including reduced funding for pro-environmental initiatives (e.g., because of cost overruns on infrastructure; Flyvbjerg and Stewart, 2012) or pressure from governing bodies (e.g., Bob and Swart, 2009). Thus, pre-event claims predicting that a major sporting event will be "the greenest" or "most sustainable" can only be realised after months and years of post-event analysis.

This section discusses the history of environmental issues related to mega sporting events, which traces back to the 1930s and became an Olympic mainstay in the 1990s. Additionally, there is an exploration of several recent examples of sport's largest international events – the Olympic and Paralympic Games, FIFA World Cup – through a comparison of pre-event legacy development with post-event environmental impact analyses. The chapter concludes by outlining the challenges that come with planning and operating a mega sporting event, many of which come in the weeks, months, and years after the event has ended.

## Early environmental protection initiatives

No other major sport governing body has been tied to environmental issues longer than the IOC. After all, the wide range and scale of events between the Summer and Winter Olympic and Paralympic Games require significant infrastructural developments to accommodate the competitions, athletes, spectators, press, and officials. According to Chappelet (2008), "[t]he Olympic Winter Games are partly held in mountain resorts and are thus closer to nature, a fact that has frequently led them to encounter strong opposition from environmental organizations" (p. 1884). The construction of stadiums and other competition venues, housing for athletes and visitors, and roads are a few examples of Games-related projects that could impact the surrounding environment, particularly when events are held in isolated locations (e.g., Mbombela Stadium in South Africa, Arena da Amazônia in Brazil; Manfred, 2015; Young, 2015). Less than a decade after the first Winter Olympic Games were held in Chamonix, France, in 1924, environmental activists began pushing back at Olympics organisers. For instance, when organisers of the 1932 Winter Olympics in Lake Placid, New York, considered removing 2,500 trees to make room for a bobsled run, a local activist group called the Association for the Protection of the Adirondacks successfully blocked the run's construction (Chappelet, 2008).

Chappelet (2008) recounted the first mega sporting event that took "the environment in a serious way" (p. 1889), the 1972 Winter Olympic Games in Sapporo, Japan. The IOC's selection of Sapporo as the host city came as a surprise to many, especially the delegation from Banff, Alberta, who were considered frontrunners to host the 1972 Games after being narrowly beaten in their bid for the previous Games. A number of factors contributed to the selection of Sapporo over Banff, but the influence of environmental activists was unmistakable: while the Japanese delegation was unified in its commitment to protect the natural environment, the Canadian bid committee faced threats of protests from the Canadian Wildlife Association and other environmental groups. In subsequent Winter Games, the environment played prominent roles (e.g., as a consideration during the bidding process, as subjects of protests) for aspirant (e.g., Denver and Interlaken in 1976) and host cities (e.g., Lake Placid in 1980).

In the 1990s, the growing commercialisation of the Olympic Games led to fears that the event was becoming unsustainable – a concern that still persists today. The IOC, recognising the need to temper criticisms of the increasing spectacle of the Olympic Games and bolstered by the momentum of several high-profile environmental meetings (including the release of the historic Brundtland Report that defined sustainability and then Norwegian prime minister Gro Harlem Brundtland's subsequent address to the IOC in Seoul in 1988; Cantelon and Letters, 2000; Mallen, Stevens, and Adams, 2011), sponsored several key environmental initiatives. As recounted by Gold and Gold (2013), these initiatives included

- an amendment to the Olympic Charter in 1991 compelling host cities to hold the Games under "conditions which demonstrate a responsible concern for environmental issues" (International Olympic Committee, 1991, p. 9);
- the adoption of the environment as the third pillar of Olympism in 1994 (IOC, 1996); and
- an additional modification to the Olympic Charter in 1996 that symbolised the IOC's commitment to "sustainable development" (IOC, 1996).

In addition to the aforementioned drivers of the IOC's environmental focus, the 1992 Winter Games in Albertville, France, were highly influential. These Games were deemed "an environmental disaster" that could have been avoided had "the IOC had in place a carefully considered policy for environmental protection" (Cantelon and Letters, 2000, pp. 300–301). In its official report following the Games, the local organising committee (Comité d'Organisation des Jeux Olympiques; COJO) said as much, though in admittedly more charitable tones: "Albertville and Savoie proved that this event could activate and sustain essential projects which will have a long-term effect on this region" (p. 124). In its review of the Games, the COJO offered a buoyant view of the Games' poor environmental performance:

> Even if everything was not perfect, at least the Winter Olympic Games of 1992 will have brought to light one imperative point: in September 1991, [COJO co-president] Michel Barnier presented a proposition to the IOC that henceforth, every town or region applying to host the Games should present an impact study to show the effects of their project on the environment.
>
> (COJO, 1992, p. 124)

The 1994 Olympic Winter Games in Lillehammer, Norway, were a reversal to the Albertville Games and marked a major shift in the way in which the Olympics would be managed. In 1990, the Lillehammer Olympic Organising Committee (LOOC) clashed with environmental groups on the location of Hamer Olympic Hall (*Vikingskipet*, or "The Viking Ship) in Åkersvika (LOOC, 1994). As a result of this conflict, the LOOC developed five primary environmental goals: (1)

increase environmental awareness, (2) maintain regional social considerations, (3) promote sustainable development and growth, (4) ensure environmentally friendly arenas, and (5) demand environmental quality at every stage of the event. By the start of the Games, more than 21 projects had been included in the LOOC's environmental agenda, including management and training, food services and accommodation, sponsors and suppliers, and transportation and waste. In their post-Olympics evaluation, the LOOC identified four conditions deemed "essential" to the success of the Games' environmental-related initiatives:

1   Environmental responsibility must be anchored in the organisation from the top leaders and throughout the entire organisation.
2   Environmental goals and requirements must be defined and followed up.
3   Cooperation with environmental organisations and public authorities is important.
4   Careful selection of environmentally inclined sponsors. (LOOC, 1994, p. 86).

The Lillehammer Games were largely celebrated for their comprehensive environmental design and led the IOC and subsequent host cities to consider more carefully what would be left behind once the Olympics had concluded (Andranovich and Burbank, 2013).

Although previous cities had considered the long-term impact of hosting an international mega-event, the explicit association between mega sporting events and the term *legacy* first surfaced in the early planning stages of the 1956 Melbourne Candidature File (Leopkey, 2009). From that point on, references to legacy appeared sporadically until the 1996 Centennial Olympic Games in Atlanta (ACOG, 1997; Andranovich and Burbank, 2013). In sum, eight primary legacies were cited by the IOC in its analysis of the Atlanta Games: economic, reputation, urban regeneration, accommodation, tourism, environment, telecommunications, and venues (IOC, 2012).

More generally, the IOC and its local organising committees categorise the long-term effects of the Games into five categories of legacy: sporting, social, environmental, urban, and economic (IOC, 2013). But these legacies are aspirational, and they are not always realised by a host city. Furthermore, legacies are difficult to measure, can develop slowly, and are not exclusively benefits. For example, shortly after the Centennial Olympic Games had concluded, an analysis of its impact on Atlanta reported some negative consequences: "While Atlanta has made progress on redeveloping some of its poorest communities, the extensive redevelopment generated by the Olympics damaged several communities" (Research Atlanta, 1996, p. 16). Nearly two decades after the Atlanta Games, local news headlines still reflect the challenges of defining the city's Olympic legacy: "The eroding legacy of the 1996 Olympics in Atlanta" (Browne, 2014); "Nearly 20 years later, the legacy of Atlanta's Olympic venues is still being written" (Nickisch, 2015); and "Atlanta's Olympic legacy in the eye of the beholder" (Chapman, 2016).

Although mega-event organisers are demonstrating a commitment to legacy planning with increasing frequency, there may still be large contrasts between the legacy aspirations and the actual impact of an international sporting event.

These contrasts may be particularly pronounced when it comes to environmental legacy, as sustainability initiatives may be pushed aside in favour of new priorities or because of budget shortfalls. Every case is different, and examples can be extended beyond the Olympic and Paralympic Games to include mega-events such as the FIFA World Cup, which is discussed in further detail below.

## Environmental legacy planning in select mega-events

Unsurprisingly, international governing bodies like the IOC and FIFA often tout the positive environmental impact of their events. Yet, an event's legacy encompasses both its positive *and* negative effects (Kaplanidou, 2012). As Sant and Mason (2015) note, it is often the case that the negative aspects of an event are obscured: "[One] point of contention is that legacy is most often employed when expressing positive outcomes of hosting a mega-event, whereas negative legacies, such as overcrowding and environmental damage, are ignored by bid and event proponents" (p. 43). In addition to the possibility that an official environmental assessment authored by a governing body may contain incomplete information, the uniqueness of each event and host city necessitates that researchers exercise caution when evaluating an event's environmental legacy. In this section, differences are examined by highlighting the sustainability claims of some of the largest and most celebrated sporting events globally.

### *The Olympic and Paralympic Games*

As illustrated previously, the IOC has stressed its commitment to environmental stewardship by selecting the environment as one of its three Olympic pillars and mandating that prospective host cities include comprehensive environmental legacy plans in their Bid Books. While the 1994 Olympic Winter Games in Lillehammer are usually credited with setting the pro-environment precedent, momentum for sustainability really escalated in the 2000s. After Salt Lake City hosted the first carbon-neutral Olympic Games in 2002, every Olympic city that followed has proclaimed itself to be the most sustainable Games, beginning with Athens, then Torino, then Beijing, then Vancouver, then London, and so on (Westerman, 2010).

For its part, the Torino Organising Committee (TOROC) made environmental sustainability a central component of its Candidature Files to host the 2006 Olympic Winter Games. As noted by Minnaert (2012), TOROC's commitment to the environment was prioritised over other legacy programming such as social inclusion: "The consensus clearly indicates that the social aspect of sustainability was relatively neglected, particularly compared to the environmental aspect" (p. 367). After the Games, TOROC disseminated a 213-page report highlighting its sustainability policies, initiatives, and environmental performance. Although the report was produced shortly after the Games, TOROC was already defining the long-term impact of the Torino Games:

> The Torino Games have left a twofold legacy. The Games were a driving force for the development of sport and mass events in general, but they also

were a stimulus to improving sustainability policies both for the territory and for the world of sport.

(TOROC, 2006, p. 95)

This statement highlights an important theme of legacy planning: an environmental legacy encompasses not only the impact on the host city but also the influence on future Olympic programming.

Few Olympic events have drawn more attention to the environment than the 2008 Summer Games in Beijing, a city with a history of environmental problems. After losing its bid to host the 2000 Olympics to Sydney, which heavily promoted environmental initiatives, Beijing planners refocused their 2008 effort accordingly (Beyer, 2006). More than $17 billion was allocated to projects related to improving environmental performance (Ramzy, 2008). Additionally, in light of concerns that atmospheric pollutants could adversely affect air quality, the Chinese Government responded by "shutting down factories, restricting car usage and slowing down construction" (Ramzy, 2008, para. 3). The Games produced clear environmental benefits, particularly when it came to educating citizens (Chen and Tian, 2015; Jin, Zhang, Ma, and Connaughton, 2011). Despite these advances and proclamations from the UN Environmental Programme that the "Beijing Olympics met or exceeded green goals" (Gronewold, 2009), analysis by Wang et al. (2011) suggested the Beijing Olympics were "the most polluted games ever" (Jamieson, 2009). This dramatic contrast illustrates the importance of context when evaluating the legacy of mega-events: though the Beijing Olympics provided some relief to a taxed natural environment, the size and scale of the Games meant the environmental impact was still substantial.

Similar to other legacies, environmental legacies can range in scope, and may be planned or unplanned. For example, the Vancouver Organising Committee for the 2010 Olympic and Paralympic Winter Games (VANOC) made a concerted effort to comprehensively evaluate the environmental impact of the Winter Olympics, as measured by a number of criteria. These included the location and size of land used within protected areas of high biodiversity value, the number of infractions for non-compliance with environmental laws and regulations, the number and volume of significant spills, the number of newly constructed venues applying for green building certification, and the weight of solid waste diverted (VANOC, 2010, p. 16). VANOC's focus on sustainably designed facilities was particularly important to projecting Vancouver as a world-class, pro-environmental destination (Kaplanidou and Karadakis, 2010). Ten years earlier, the Sydney Organising Committee for the Olympic Games (SOCOG) predicted a similarly positive effect from building green stadiums, but this expectation has not been fully realised:

It was forecast that world-class, environmentally friendly sports facilities would attract international sporting competitions for decades. . . Ironically, then, one of the strongest subjects of criticism of Sydney's Olympic legacy has been the use of, or lack thereof, of the facilities that were constructed for the games, especially those at Sydney Olympic Park.

(Toohey, 2008, p. 1960)

*Plate 8.1* National Stadium, or the "Bird's Nest," under construction in Beijing in 2008. ("Bird's Nest Workers" by Micah Sittig is licensed under CC BY-SA 2.0).

Interestingly, one unplanned legacy of the Sydney Games was the creation of a conservation plan to protect the endangered green and golden bell frog, which was found during the development of the Olympic Park site (Darcovich and O'Meara, 2008).

The development (and post-Games redevelopment) of the Queen Elizabeth Olympic Park site for the 2012 Summer Games represented one of three primary foci of the London Organising Committee of the Olympic and Paralympic Games' (LOCOG) sustainability agenda (Gold and Gold, 2013). The site on which the Olympic complex was constructed was a mix of green- and brownfields, which required builders to remediate contaminated soil before construction could begin (Raco, 2015). The competition facilities, many of which were temporary and made from sustainably sourced or recycled materials, received acclaim for their pro-environmental designs. The transformation and post-Games transition of the Olympic Park was an ambitious undertaking; accordingly, it represented the crown jewel of the London Olympic legacy plan. Despite the pronounced effort on the part of LOCOG, a study by Konstantaki and Wickens (2010) indicated Londoners were less aware, and in some cases, sceptical, of the Games' positive environmental impact.

Most recently, the 2016 Olympics in Rio represented an opportunity for Brazil to use "sport as a catalyst for social integration and the Games for 'celebration and inclusion' of the city, the region and the country" (IOC, 2009, p. 84). For the IOC, it "could help the country develop faster and could bring an entire continent of people close to the Olympic movement" (Macur, 2009, p. A1). Given our temporal proximity to the Games, the environmental legacy of the Games will take time to fully evaluate. Still, based on the significant number of negative news reports leading up to and during the Games, it is likely the Rio Games did not live up to expectations. For example,

> [i]n 2009, when Rio de Janeiro was named the Olympic host city for the 2016 games, Governor Sergio Cabral was full of promises. The residents of Rio, he told *The Guardian*, will "gain more metro lines, more trains, more sewage treatment, more in terms of the environment, social services, in terms of sport and culture." Pretty much none of those promises were kept; at least, they weren't kept for everyone equally.
>
> (Delgadillo, 2016, paras. 1–2)

For Allen Hershkowitz, a former scientist with the Natural Resources Defense Council and co-founder of the Green Sports Alliance, the challenges faced by Rio underscore the significant planning and capital required to minimise the environmental effects of mega-events: "I very much understand the IOC's desire to be more equitable in delivering the Olympics to the developing world. But the Sochi and Rio Olympics indicate that there are such huge environmental, transportation, water and air-quality questions" (as quoted in Powell, 2016, para. 21). These challenges may be even more pronounced for mega-events with larger geographical footprints, as discussed further below.

### The FIFA World Cup

FIFA formalised its first environmental programme in 2006 and established comprehensive "Green Goal" initiatives to coincide with the 2006 and 2011 World Cups in Germany and 2010 World Cup in South Africa. In 2009, it instituted a requirement that all applicant nations include environmental protections as well as plans for avoiding, minimising, or offsetting any negative effects of hosting the World Cup in their Bid Books (FIFA, 2013). The current iteration of FIFA's environmental programme, called "Football for the Planet," centres on waste, water, energy, transportation, procurement, and climate change.

Called "one of the biggest infrastructure investment projects in South Africa" by the national government, the 2010 FIFA World Cup cost nearly $4 billion, including $1.3 billion to construct or renovate 10 stadiums across the country (Egan, 2014; Molloy and Chetty, 2015). In preparation for the event, FIFA invested in several environmental initiatives, including a carbon offsetting project that used sewage gas to generate electricity and the installation of solar arrays at 20 "Football for Hope" community centres in South Africa (FIFA, 2013). In addition to the direct benefits of the solar panels, they also served to educate citizens about alternative forms of clean energy. Although South Africa reported a lower carbon footprint the year it hosted the World Cup (Melo et al., 2014), it was still double the carbon footprint of the Beijing Olympics (Cornelissen, Bob, and Swart, 2011). As Cornelissen et al. (2011) observed, despite efforts to raise awareness of environmental issues, the World Cup suffered from logistical problems including South Africa's reliance on coal and the need for air travel to reach competition venues.

These logistical challenges were also present in Brazil during the 2014 World Cup. World Cup organisers elected to place competition venues in 12 cities rather than the recommended eight, a decision Rio mayor Eduardo Paes later called "a mistake" (Baxter, 2014). Because of the distance between venues, the U.S. team reportedly travelled close to 9,000 miles to compete in three games across 10 days. These long travel distances had a clear impact on teams, but they also placed more stress on the environment because of the demand for long-haul flights. Furthermore, the Brazilian government had to confront a number of issues in the time leading up to the World Cup (which continued into the 2016 Olympics), with the environment representing just one of many concerns:

> The economy is sputtering, Brazilians are furious at the bill for the costliest World Cup ever, corruption allegations are flying and public services like health, education, housing and transportation are in decline. Environmental impacts are near the bottom of a long list of grievances
>
> (Spanne, 2014, para. 5).

On a positive note, more than half of the World Cup stadiums received Leadership in Energy and Environmental Design (LEED) certification (Sport and Urban Policy Initiative, 2017), though a facility's sustainable design does little good for facilities that are not actively occupied and operated.

Looking forward, FIFA's selection of Qatar to host the 2022 World Cup has presented new challenges because of the country's arid climate and desert landscape. On the other hand, organisers are already considering how they can improve upon past World Cups (Henderson, 2016). For example, in contrast to the large distances between Brazil's football stadiums, the Qatari Bid Book indicated most events would take place within a 60-kilometre radius. Furthermore, they have committed to several pro-environmental initiatives, including "zero carbon emissions through strategies such as the adoption of sophisticated air-conditioning technologies" (p. 87). Henderson (2016) continues: "Stadia [will be] designed in a modular fashion to enable several to be dismantled and reconstructed at 22 venues in needy developing countries after the World Cup" (p. 87).

Like similar policies created by the IOC, FIFA's mandate ensures that any state seeking to host the World Cup has a plan in place for producing a positive environmental legacy. However, as discussed throughout this section, the mere presence of a plan does not guarantee that a positive environmental legacy will be realised. Competing or misguided priorities; unforeseen obstacles arising before, during, or after an event; and difficulties measuring environmental performance can each play a role in the development and execution of an environmental legacy plan. We discuss these barriers in turn below.

## Barriers to effective environmental legacy planning

By definition, an environmental legacy is meant to be sustainable, or long-lasting. To be effective, it must be able to withstand the natural changes that occur over time.

Furthermore, it must be comprehensive and cannot be hastily implemented. As Allen Hershkowitz noted, "You can't just do this for a one-month event; it's got to be a decades-long planning. Otherwise, you're left with empty stadiums and a wrecked environment" (as quoted in Powell, 2016, para. 27). So, why do the pro-environmental plans of so many mega-events seem to unravel so quickly? Certainly, unforeseen events like poor economic conditions or new legislative directives can alter the course of a legacy plan – though ideally, a legacy plan would weather these shocks. Other obstacles to effective environmental planning, however, are more predictable.

## Greenwashing

Looking to gain a competitive advantage over their rivals, businesses may promote charitable or community-centred programmes to demonstrate their corporate social responsibility. On occasion, these programmes may be accompanied with hollow promises or exaggerated claims about their benefits. When applied to environmental programming, this embellishment is known as greenwashing. Examples of greenwashing include claiming oneself to be a "green" organisation despite implementing minimal pro-environmental controls, promoting environmental initiatives that are considered industry standards or regulatory requirements, or simply lying about one's positive environmental impact.

Both the IOC and FIFA have been accused of greenwashing because their continued pursuit of seemingly contradictory goals: to advance their events (and brands) to new markets – many of which lack the infrastructure to host an international mega-event – while promoting a pro-environmental agenda. Additionally, while both the IOC and FIFA include some form of environmental programme mandates in their bid specifications, it is unclear how enforceable – or even meaningful – these requirements are. For example, given the evidence that FIFA officials accepted bribes from the Russian and Qatari delegations (both nations were later selected as future World Cup hosts), how serious can FIFA's policies be taken ("Black Marks on the Beautiful Game," 2015)?

On the subject of FIFA's selection of Qatar as 2022 World Cup host, Klotz (2015) contended that FIFA's desire to hold the mega-event there (regardless of motive) raised serious environmental questions:

> Qatar's winning bid included the construction of 12 new stadiums, including the one where the finals will be played – in a city that doesn't even exist yet. While the number of stadiums may be lowered to 10, the event may move to the winter (conflicting, however, with the European club season), and the stadiums may not be air-conditioned, it is a sure bet that the 2022 World Cup will be an environmental disaster.
>
> At a time when the world is increasingly troubled by global warming and arguing over how to reduce environmental impacts, the ability of FIFA to escape serious and sustained criticism in this field is amazing.
>
> (Klotz, 2015, paras. 5–6)

As of early 2017, the total number of stadiums had still not been finalised, though FIFA had approved the tournament's move to Qatar's winter season. Similar critiques of the IOC and FIFA's separate endorsements of Rio and Brazil have focused on the unfulfilled promises made in that nation's Bid Books. In his reproach of Rio's Olympics preparation, Jules Boykoff, a professor and former professional soccer player, accused FIFA and Brazilian organisers of overstating their sustainability claims: "These days, Olympic bids come chock full of so-called legacy projects that gleam green. But Rio 2016 is in the running for the most greenwashed Games ever" (as quoted in Young, 2016, para. 21).

In response to negative perceptions about its selection process, FIFA recently considered new reforms to be instituted for 2026 World Cup bidding. Included in these proposed reforms were more specific environmental and sustainability requirements (Das, 2016). For critics, however, these reforms offer little promise; instead, they argue, the governing bodies must enact more comprehensive rules related to environmental legacy planning. For instance, Preuss (2013) provided four suggestions for ensuring that environmental legacy plans are legitimate and sustainable, including publishing the promises made in Bid Books and exerting "political pressure on the organizers to fulfil them" (p. 3595). Stuart and Scassa (2011) took these suggestions one step further, arguing that "if the IOC were serious in their professed intent that Games' legacies be beneficial for residents of host cities, regions and countries over time, they could require the enactment of straightforward legislation guaranteeing planned and sustainable outcomes" (para. 1). After all, they argue, the IOC has successfully implemented strict policies in order to protect the Olympic brand and its official sponsors.

## Reprioritisation

Implicit in the argument that international governing bodies should enact and enforce laws that require pro-environmental legacy planning *and* implementation is the assumption that they have good incentive to do so. Previous research has shown that the public often shows little awareness about a mega-event's environmentally friendly initiatives (Konstantaki and Wickens, 2010). Additionally, according to Agha, Fairley, and Gibson (2012), local Olympic organising committees have little motivation to think critically about post-Games legacy because their primary responsibility is the production of the Games themselves. Once the Games conclude, the organising committee typically dissolves, unofficially delegating the local community – the group affected most by Olympic legacy – to see the legacy plan through. Because of this lack of incentive, organising groups typically propose broad, but ambitious, legacy plans "with no accountability leading to a slew of broken promises" (p. 126). In light of this potential issue, several recent host cities have created post-Games legacy organisations to actively monitor and deliver on post-event promises (e.g., London Organising Committee of the Olympic Games and Paralympic Games Ltd., 2012).

As noted in previous sections, mega-event organisers may face conflicting priorities after the initial planning stages of an international event. Pressure from governing bodies, local governments, sponsors, the media, activists, and local citizens may force organising committees to reprioritise projects. With the possibility that environmental initiatives could be sacrificed in favour of other projects,

Agha et al. (2012) pointed to the IOC's Olympic Games Global Impact (OGCI) study as an encouraging model for making host cities more accountable for legacy planning and monitoring. While still not forcing sanctions on cities with failed legacies, the OGCI study – currently underway in Beijing, Vancouver, and London – may help temper the tendency of bidding cities to make unrealistic promises in their Bid Books. Of course, until groups like the IOC and FIFA no longer incentivise bold (and overambitious) promises in Olympic and World Cup Bid Books, the practice of offering hollow assurances is unlikely to subside.

## Stadiums

Competition venues are important aspects of a mega-event's legacy plan, as they mark the culmination of years of planning, negotiation, and labour. Often, the extent to which these facilities are utilised after a mega-event provides an unscientific evaluation of the organisers' legacy plan. Projects like John Pack and Gary Hustwit's (2013) *The Olympic City* showcase what happens to mega-event facilities after the event has ended. Images of abandoned and crumbling stadiums surface biennially, illustrating what can happen when organisers do not have a post-event plan for a facility constructed for specialised use (be it an 80,000-seat athletics stadium, 10,000-seat arena, or 5,000-seat velodrome). As discussed in the previous section, those entrusted to see an environmental legacy plan through must prepare for shifting priorities before, during, and after a mega-event (Smith, 2015).

On the plus side, Olympic and World Cup stadiums are frequently featured during coverage of the events, and they can serve as physical symbols of a city or nation's pro-environmental agenda (Kellison and Mondello, 2012). Furthermore, planners, architects, and builders can leverage pro-environmental stadiums to showcase their own skills: "Global construction and development firms are now using the Games as a showcase for their own skills and ways of working 'with' sustainability regulations" (Raco, 2015, p. 129). Given the high visibility of large sport stadiums, a well-executed plan can attract positive attention many years after the conclusion of a major international sporting exhibition.

From an environmental perspective, stadiums built for mega-events are not ideal. They may be used infrequently, and when they are used, they create significant strains on local resources by drawing thousands of individuals to a single site (Kellison, 2015). Recent advances to building systems and sustainable technologies have allowed stadium designers to moderate a facility's environmental impact. Still, when selecting stadium sites and considering tournament logistics, governing bodies and local organising committees may place other priorities (like aesthetics and surrounding neighbourhoods) before the environment (e.g., Bob and Swart, 2009). The potential incompatibility between site selection and sustainable design can be illustrated by several stadiums constructed for the Brazil World Cup, as reported by Dave Zirin (2014):

> There's no question the World Cup will put greater stress on Brazil's critical ecosystem. This can be seen most clearly in the efforts to build a

*Plate 8.2* Hellinikon Olympic Canoe/Kayak Slalom Centre, a competition venue for the 2004 Olympic and Paralympic Games in Athens, in 2014(credit: Ioanna Sakellaraki, republished with permission)

*Plate 8.3* Seating at the Hellinikon Olympic Canoe/Kayak Slalom Centre in 2014 (credit: Ioanna Sakellaraki, republished with permission)

"FIFA-quality stadium" in the middle of the Amazon rainforest. Brazil will be spending $325 million, almost $40 million more than the original estimates, while uprooting acres of the most ecologically delicate region on the planet. The project has been a disaster since the first plant life was destroyed, before the cement was even poured. Building a new stadium doesn't just ignore environmental concerns, it defies logic – the Amazon is already home to a stadium that draws far less than its capacity. And all of this to house a mere four World Cup matches.

(para. 6)

As further illustration of the way in which competing motives in mega-events can create juxtapositions, Arena da Amazônia, the subject of Zirin's contempt, is LEED Silver certified.

## Measurement

Even when a mega-event is well organised, its sustainability initiatives are intact, and a defined legacy plan is in place, organisers may face difficulties when trying to measure the effectiveness of the event's environmental management initiatives. The initiatives themselves may be complex and difficult to measure. Additionally, because an environmental legacy takes place over a long period of time (i.e., years and decades), most assessments are incomplete (Collins, Jones, and Munday, 2009). In light of the challenges with accurately measuring mega-event legacies, Dickson, Benson, and Blackman (2011) suggested a framework that included both positive and negative outcomes, that could be utilised across multiple events, and was robust to changes made by planners. Pitts and Liao (2013) expanded on the need for a comprehensive list of metrics in their own proposed evaluation framework. First, they identified nine assessment issues, or typical "problems associated with the large-scale development and operation" (p. 726) of mega-events before outlining nine evaluation issues: strategic development goals, master plan and site selection, energy consumption, water conservation, materials and structures, transport, post-Olympic usage, functionality, and environmental impacts. In his proposed analytical framework, Preuss (2013) suggests looking not just at infrastructural markers of sustainability (like those proposed by Pitts and Liao) but also other dimensions like knowledge, networks, culture, policy, and emotions.

For their part, both the IOC and FIFA have published their own sustainability reports following recent mega-events (e.g., Stahl, Hochfeld, and Schmied, 2006; TOROC, 2006; VANOC, 2010; Wolter and Schulte, 2011). However, these reports are typically produced within 12 months of the closing of an event, so while they provide important information about waste, consumption, and other environmental impacts occurring during the event itself, they are inadequate evaluations of a host's long-term environmental legacy. Furthermore, based on Agha et al.'s (2012) point that most organising committees suspend operations within two years of the end of an event, it is unlikely that either governing body will produce a comprehensive legacy evaluation 10 to 20 years after an event, when it perhaps would be most appropriate. Thus, the responsibility remains with the local community, independent researchers, and anyone else with an honest commitment to minimising the environmental impact of mega sporting events.

## Conclusion

From the planning phase to the legacy phase, mega-events provide unique sustainability challenges. Based on the sheer scale of environmental impact, in addition to social and political pressures, environmental sustainability has become a point of parity for all mega-events. Much of the attention on the environmental impact of mega-events – particularly from governing bodies like the IOC and FIFA – is relatively recent, although there is a much longer history of sporadic environmental stewardship employed by local organisers. The case studies in this chapter highlight the positive legacy implementation can have for the events as well as sustainability policies that affect the host city/region. On the other hand, despite the earnest intentions of event organisers, pro-environmental legacy planning can be derailed by overstated claims, the reprioritisation of public funds, complications related to stadium design and operation, or inadequate measurement tools. Therefore, in many cases, the environmental goals and claims are aspirational and not always realised without challenges or alterations. Recent reforms by governing bodies and event organisers have been implemented to address some concerns related to environmental legacy, but given the complexity and long-term nature of effective legacy planning, it remains unclear whether these strategies will lead to any profound change in the degree to which mega sporting events impact the natural environment.

## Further Reading

International Olympic Committee: www.olympic.org/sustainability
FIFA: www.fifa.com/sustainability/
United Nations Environment Programme: www.unep.org/sport_env/
Database of major LEED-certified sports facilities: www.stadiatrack.org/green

## References

Ackermann, K. (2011). *Sustainable mega-events in developing countries*. Konrad-Adenauer-Stiftung. Retrieved from www.kas.de/wf/doc/kas_29583-1522-2-30.pdf?111209095502
ACOG. (1997). *The official report of the Centennial Olympic Games* (Vol. 1). Atlanta, GA: Atlanta Committee for the Olympic Games.
Agha, N., Fairley, S., and Gibson, H. (2012). Considering legacy as a multi-dimensional construct: The legacy of the Olympic Games. *Sport Management Review, 15*(1), 125–139.
Andranovich, G., and Burbank, M. J. (2013). Contextualizing Olympic legacies. *Urban Geography, 32*(6), 823–844.
Barth, B. J. (2016, March 8). *Can sports environmentalists aid in the fight against climate change?* Pacific Standard. Retrieved from https://psmag.com/can-sports-environmentalists-aid-in-the-fight-against-climate-change-85a7b2cd65d2#.vrzmctfhb

Baxter, K. (2014, June 7). Travel distances, hot weather will affect teams in World Cup. *Los Angeles Times*. Retrieved from www.latimes.com/sports/soccer/la-sp-world-cup-geography-20140608-story.html

Beyer, S. (2006). The green Olympic movement: Beijing 2008. *Chinese Journal of International Law, 5*(2), 423–440.

Black marks on the beautiful game. [Editorial]. (2015, May 28). *The New York Times*, p. A24.

Bob, U., and Swart, K. (2009). Resident perceptions of the 2010 FIFA Soccer World Cup stadia development in Cape Town. *Urban Forum, 20*(1), 47–59.

Browne, R. (2014, January 31). The eroding legacy of the 1996 Olympics in Atlanta. *Grantland*. Retrieved from http://grantland.com/the-triangle/the-eroding-legacy-of-the-1996-olympics-in-atlanta/

Cantelon, H., and Letters, M. (2000). The making of the IOC environmental policy as the third dimension of the Olympic movement. *International Review for the Sociology of Sport, 35*(3), 294–308.

Casper, J. M., and Pfahl. M. E. (2015). Environmental sustainability practices in U.S. NCAA Division III athletic departments. *Journal of Event Management Research, 10*(1), 12–36.

Chapman, D. (2016, July 26). Atlanta's Olympic legacy in the eye of the beholder. *Atlanta Journal-Constitution*. Retrieved from www.myajc.com/news/news/atlantas-olympic-legacy-in-the-eye-of-beholder/nrxPT/

Chappelet, J-L. (2008). Olympic environmental concerns as a legacy of the Winter Games. *The International Journal of the History of Sport, 25*(14), 1884–1902.

Chen, F., and Tian, L. (2015). Comparative study on residents' perceptions of follow-up impacts of the 2008 Olympics. *Tourism Management, 51*, 263–281.

COJO. (1992). *Official report of the XVI Olympic Winter Games of Albertville and Savoie* (C. Blanc and J-M. Eysseric, Eds.). Albertville, France: Organizing Committee of the XVI Olympic Winter Games of Albertville and Savoie.

Collins, A., Jones, C., and Munday, M. (2009). Assessing the environmental impacts of mega sporting events: Two options? *Tourism Management, 30*(6), 828–837.

Cornelissen, S., Bob, U., and Swart, K. (2011). Towards redefining the concept of legacy in relation to sport mega-events: Insights from the 2010 FIFA World Cup. *Development Southern Africa, 28*(3), 307–318.

Darcovich, K., and O'Meara, J. (2008). An Olympic legacy: Green and Golden Bell Frog conservation at Sydney Olympic Park 1993–2006. *Australian Zoologist, 34*(3), 236–248.

Das, A. (2016). FIFA announces timeline for '26 World Cup bidding. *The New York Times*, p. B9.

Delgadillo, N. (2016, August 22). Olympic development in Rio leaves a tarnished legacy. *CityLab*. Retrieved from www.citylab.com/design/2016/08/olympic-development-in-rio-leaves-a-tarnished-legacy/496754/

Dickson, T. J., Benson, A. M., and Blackman, D. A. (2011). Developing a framework for evaluating Olympic and Paralympic legacies. *Journal of Sport & Tourism, 16*(4), 285–302.

Egan, M. (2014, June 10). South Africa's World Cup warning to Brazil. *CNN*. Retrieved from http://money.cnn.com/2014/06/09/investing/world-cup-south-africa-brazil/

FIFA. (2013). *Football for the planet*. Zürich, Switzerland: Fédération Internationale de Football Association.

FIFA. (2015). *2014 FIFA World Cup™ reached 3.2 billion viewers, one billion watched final*. Retrieved from www.fifa.com/worldcup/news/y=2015/m=12/news=2014-fifa-world-cuptm-reached-3-2-billion-viewers-one-billion-watched – 2745519.html

FIFA. (2016, March 11). *Value of mega sports events for sustainable development discussed at UN*. Retrieved July 18, 2016, from www.fifa.com/sustainability/news/y=2016/m=3/news=value-of-mega-sports-events-for-sustainable-development-discussed-at-u-2768070.html.

Flyvbjerg, B., and Stewart, A. (2012). *Olympic proportions: Cost and cost overruns at the Olympics 1960–2012*. Saïd Business School Working Papers.

Gold, J., and Gold, M. (2013). "Bring it under the legacy umbrella": Olympic host cities and the changing fortunes of the sustainability agenda. *Sustainability, 5*(8), 3526–3542.

Gronewold, N. (2009, February 18). Beijing Olympics met or exceeded green goals. *Scientific American*. Retrieved from www.scientificamerican.com/article/beijing-olympics-met-or-e/

Hall, C. M. (2012). Sustainable mega-events: Beyond the myth of balances approaches to mega-events sustainability. *Event Management, 16*, 119–131.

Henderson, J. C. (2016). Hosting the 2022 FIFA World Cup: Opportunities and challenges for Qatar. *Journal of Sport & Tourism, 19*(3–4), 281–298. doi:10.1080/14775085.2015.1133316

International Olympic Committee. (1991). *The Olympic charter*. Lausanne, Switzerland: International Olympic Committee.

International Olympic Committee. (1996). *The Olympic charter*. Lausanne, Switzerland: International Olympic Committee.

International Olympic Committee. (2009). *Report of the 2016 IOC evaluation commission*. Lausanne, Switzerland: International Olympic Committee.

International Olympic Committee. (2012). *Factsheet: Legacies of the games*. Lausanne, Switzerland: International Olympic Committee.

International Olympic Committee. (2013). *Olympic legacy*. Lausanne, Switzerland: International Olympic Committee.

Jamieson, A. (2009, June 22). Beijing Olympics were the most polluted games ever, researchers say. *Telegraph*. Retrieved from www.telegraph.co.uk/sport/olympics/london-2012/5597277/Beijing-Olympics-were-the-most-polluted-games-ever-researchers-say.html

Jin, L., Zhang, J. J., Ma, X., and Connaughton, D. P. (2011). Residents' perceptions of environmental impacts of the 2008 Beijing Green Olympic Games. *European Sport Management Quarterly, 11*(3), 275–300.

Kaplanidou, K. (2012). The importance of legacy outcomes for Olympic Games four summer host cities residents' quality of life: 1996–2008. *European Sport Management Quarterly, 12*(4), 397–433.

Kaplanidou, K., and Karadakis, K. (2010). Understanding the legacies of a host Olympic city: The case of the 2010 Vancouver Olympic Games. *Sport Marketing Quarterly, 19*, 110–117.

Kellison, T. B. (2015). Building sport's green houses: Issues in sustainable facility management. In J. Casper and M. E. Pfahl (Eds.), *Sport management and the natural environment: Theory and practice* (pp. 218–237). New York: Routledge.

Kellison, T. B., and Mondello, M. J. (2012). Organisational perception management in sport: The use of corporate pro-environmental behaviour for desired facility referenda outcomes. *Sport Management Review, 15*, 500–512.

Kellison, T. B., Trendafilova, S., and McCullough, B. P. (2015). Considering the social impact of sustainable stadium design. *International Journal of Event Management Research, 10*(1), 63–83.

Klein, K. (2014). *Can sports make sustainability mainstream?* Ensia. Retrieved from http://ensia.com/voices/can-sports-make-sustainability-mainstream/

Klotz, D. (2015, June 9). Will reform at FIFA shrink the World Cup's environmental footprint? *National Geographic*. Retrieved from http://voices.nationalgeographic.com/2015/06/09/fifa-footprint/

Konstantaki, M., and Wickens, E. (2010). Residents' perceptions of environmental and security issues at the 2012 London Olympic Games. *Journal of Sport & Tourism*, *15*(4), 337–357. doi:10.1080/14775085.2010.533921

Leopkey, B. (2009). *2008 post graduate grant final report: The historical evolution of Olympic Games legacy*. Unpublished manuscript, IOC Olympic Studies Centre, Lausanne, Switzerland.

London Organising Committee of the Olympic Games and Paralympic Games Ltd. (2012). *London 2012 post-Games sustainability report*. London: London 2012.

LOOC. (1994). *Official report* (Vol. 1). Norway: Lillehammer Olympic Organizing Committee.

Luker, R. (2014, January 6). Survey says: Twenty insights from poll's 20 years. *SportsBusiness Journal*, 12–13.

Macur, J. (2009, October 3). Rio de Janeiro picked to hold 2016 Olympics. *The New York Times*, p. A1.

Mallen, C., Stevens, J., and Adams, L. J. (2011). A content analysis of environmental sustainability research in a sport-related journal sample. *Journal of Sport Management*, *25*(3), 240–256.

Manfred, T. (2015, January 23). Brazil's $3 billion World Cup stadiums are turning into white elephants 6 months later. *Business Insider*. Retrieved from www.businessinsider.com/brazil-world-cup-stadium-white-elephants-2015-1

McCullough, B. P., Pfahl, M. E., and Nguyen, S. N. (2015). The green waves of environmental sustainability in sport. *Sport in Society*, *19*(7), 1040–1065.

Melo, F. P., Siqueira, J. A., Santos, B. A., Álvares-da-Silva, O., Ceballos, G., and Bernard, E. (2014). Football and biodiversity conservation: FIFA and Brazil can still hit a green goal. *Biotropica*, *46*(3), 257–259.

Minnaert, L. (2012). An Olympic legacy for all? The non-infrastructural outcomes of the Olympic Games for socially excluded groups (Atlanta 1996 – Beijing 2008). *Tourism Management*, *33*(2), 361–370.

Molloy, E., and Chetty, T. (2015). The rocky road to legacy: Lessons from the 2010 FIFA World Cup South Africa stadium program. *Project Management Journal*, *46*(3), 88–107.

Nickisch, C. (2015, June 5). Nearly 20 years later, the legacy of Atlanta's Olympic venues is still being written. *WBUR*. Retrieved from www.wbur.org/news/2015/06/05/atlanta-olympic-venue-lessons-for-boston

Pack, J., and Hustwit, G. (2013). *The Olympic city*. (n.p.): Jon Pack and Gary Hustwit.

Pitts, A., and Liao, H. (2013). An assessment technique for the evaluation and promotion of sustainable Olympic design and urban development. *Building Research & Information*, *41*(6), 722–734.

Powell, M. (2016, August 24). Olympic model is riddled with flaws. *The New York Times*, p. B9.

Preuss, H. (2013). The contribution of the FIFA World Cup and the Olympic Games to green economy. *Sustainability*, *5*(8), 3581–3600.

Raco, M. (2015). Sustainable city-building and the new politics of the possible: Reflections on the governance of the London Olympics 2012. *Area*, *47*(2), 124–131.

Ramzy, A. (2008, July 14). Beijing orders pollution to vanish. *TIME Magazine*. Retrieved from http://content.time.com/time/world/article/0,8599,1822476,00.html

Research Atlanta, I. (1996). *The Olympic legacy: Building on what was achieved*. Atlanta, GA: Research Atlanta, Inc.

Rio 2016 Organizing Committee for the Olympic and Paralympic Games. (2013). *Sustainability management plan: Rio 2016 Olympic and Paralympic Games*. Retrieved from www.rio2016.com/sites/default/files/parceiros/sustainability_management_plan_aug2013.pdf

Sant, S-L., and Mason, D. S. (2015). Framing event legacy in a prospective host city: Managing Vancouver's Olympic bid. *Journal of Sport Management, 29*(1), 42–56.

Smith, A. (2015). From green park to theme park? Evolving legacy visions for London's Olympic Park. *Architectural Research Quarterly, 18*(4), 315–323.

Spanne, A. (2014, June 19). Brazil World Cup fails to score environmental goals. *Scientific American*. Retrieved from www.scientificamerican.com/article/brazil-world-cup-fails-to-score-environmental-goals/

Sport and Urban Policy Initiative. (2017). *Greentrack*. Retrieved from www.stadiatrack.org/green

Stahl, H., Hochfeld, C., and Schmied, M. (2006). *Green goal legacy report*. Frankfurt, Germany: Organizing Committee of the 2016 FIFA World Cup.

Stuart, S. A., and Scassa, T. (2011). Legal guarantees for Olympic legacy. *Entertainment & Sports Law Journal, 9*(1), 1.

Toohey, K. (2008). The Sydney Olympics: Striving for legacies – Overcoming short-term disappointments and long-term deficiencies. *The International Journal of the History of Sport, 25*(14), 1953–1971.

TOROC. (2006). *Sustainability report*. Italy: Organising Committee for the XX Olympic Winter Games Torino 2006.

VANOC. (2010). *Sustainability report 2009–10*. Vancouver, BC: Vancouver Organizing Committee for the 2010 Olympic and Paralympic Winter Games.

Wang, W., Jariyasopit, N., Schrlau, J., Jia, Y., Tao, S., Yu, T-W., . . . Simonich, S. L. M. (2011). Concentration and photochemistry of PAHs, NPAHs, and OPAHs and toxicity of PM2.5 during the Beijing Olympic Games. *Environmental Science & Technology, 45*(16), 6887–6895.

Westerman, M. (2010). Are the games really green? *E: The Environmental Magazine, 21*(1), 14–16.

Wolter, U., and Schulte, S. (2011). Football's footprint legacy report: Final report on the environment initiative of the FIFA Women's World Cup 2011. Frankfurt, Germany: FIFA Women's World Cup 2011 Organising Committee.

Young, J. A. (2015, February 2). South Africa, Brazil World Cup stadia largely remain national burdens. *Sports Illustrated*. Retrieved from www.si.com/planet-futbol/2015/02/02/world-cup-stadiums-brazil-south-africa-fifa-white-elephants

Young, J. A. (2016, August 1). Rio has broken its promises of an environment-friendly Olympics. *VICE*. Retrieved from https://news.vice.com/article/rio-has-broken-its-promise-of-an-environment-friendly-olympics

Zirin, D. (2014, April 22). Brazil's World Cup will kick the environment in the teeth. *The Nation*. Retrieved from www.thenation.com/article/brazils-world-cup-will-kick-environment-teeth/

# Part II
# Short Case Studies

# 9 Mega-events and place branding legacy for emerging economies

*Brendon Knott and Kamilla Swart*

Countries and cities are increasingly looking to sport mega-events to change or enhance their international reputation or image. The scale of these events, the passionate support they elicit and the prestige associated with hosting them has led to a recognition of the marketing potential they carry for their hosts (Heslop et al., 2012). While few would argue with the global attention these events command, assessing a definitive longer-term legacy for the place brand of the host is a more complex exercise. Important, from a branding perspective, is whether these events carry opportunities beyond merely international attention for the period of the event.

This chapter focuses on an in-depth analysis of South Africa and the 2010 FIFA World Cup, based on empirical investigations conducted by the authors. This case is then supplemented and expanded to include reflections from the changing environment of mega-events and other mega-event host contexts. From a theoretical perspective, the chapter highlights the contribution of intangible legacies, such as place branding, particularly among emerging economy nations. It also extends the place branding theory by identifying specific place branding opportunities created by sport mega-events beyond merely "gaining attention". The chapter supports the emerging discussion of "leveraging", as it reflects the stakeholder understanding of legacy, as well as describing a number of practical recommendations for place brand and event stakeholders to sustain these legacies. While highlighting the value of mega-events from a branding perspective, it also states potential pitfalls and challenges for place brand and event stakeholders.

## Background

*Place branding legacies through mega-events*: While branding theory has developed as a means of differentiation and competitive advantage for products and services in an increasingly competitive and cluttered global marketplace, the brand concept has more recently been extended and applied beyond consumer marketing to a number of different environments, including places, such as cities, destinations, and countries. Globalisation has led to countries competing in a number of markets, for the attention, respect and trust of investors, tourists, consumers, donors, immigrants, media, and governments (Anholt, 2007). Although there was initial uncertainty over whether a country could be considered a brand (Olins, 2002), many today would agree with Kapferer (2012, p. 2), who stated that "whether they like it or not, (countries) act de facto as a brand – a summary of unique values and benefits". Place branding theory contends that a place's brand needs to be skillfully created and carefully managed in order to realise its competitive potential. Creating a powerful and positive place brand is viewed as a means of creating a strong competitive advantage for a country, city, or destination.

The opportunity presented by place branding is of particular interest to countries that either do not have a strong brand identity and reputation or that have an image that is either misplaced or unhelpful to its broader developmental aims. Freire (2014) explained how nation branding has become increasingly important to African nations in particular. Recent years have seen greater periods of relative peace and stability rather than warfare, which plagued the continent in much of the post-colonial period. This, combined with a more prevalent process of democratisation in many nations, has made Africa a more attractive investment opportunity. For many African nations, an increased flow of investment and the development of improved business and tourism infrastructure, combined with the emergence of a stronger middle class, led to greater competition between the nations. Place branding has been viewed as a means of assisting African nations to overcome what Anholt (2007) refers to as the "Brand Africa" dilemma, where all African nations are viewed as a collective by outside nations, usually associated with the many negative aspects of the continent that are continually in the media, such as violence, corruption and disease (with the recent Ebola outbreak a pertinent example of this). This context has left very little opportunity for differentiation, although, as Freire (2014, p. 32) suggested, place branding is viewed as a means to achieve this: "Countries all over Africa have been making an effort to build their brands and to differentiate their offerings in order to attract tourists, investment and people".

Sport can be a powerful agent in the imaging, re-imaging and branding of places, especially through the hosting of sport mega-events (Getz, 2003; Higham and Hinch, 2009). There has been a growing awareness of the potentially significant brand-related impacts that hosting sport mega-events can have for a country. Some authors have linked this with political ambitions of nations, describing sport mega-events as objects of political policy or global diplomacy (often termed "soft power" (Grix, 2012; Nauright, 2013) for an increasing number of states in the world, especially "as a means to gain international visibility in some ways" (Cornelissen, 2007, p. 242), or as a means of achieving international prominence and national prestige (Essex and Chalkley, 1998).

Indeed, the perceived brand-related opportunities that a mega-event provides for a host nation have been mentioned among the primary reasons for a nation bidding to host such an event, particularly so among the recent number of emerging or "middle-income" mega-event host nations such as China (Beijing 2008 Olympic Games), South Africa (2010 FIFA World Cup), Brazil (2014 FIFA World Cup and Rio 2016 Olympic Games) (Tomlinson, Bass, and Bassett, 2011, p. 38), and India (Delhi 2010 Commonwealth Games). Increasingly, emerging economy nations and cities have been bidding for and hosting mega-events. This has even become "an object of policy" for many of these nations (Cornelissen, 2007). The Brazil, Russia, India, China, South Africa (BRICS) emerging economy group in particular have embraced the hosting of these events, most commonly as a means for gaining international attention and enhancing or changing global reputation (see Table 9.1).

Further to these nations, the Emirates of Dubai and Qatar in particular have also chosen mega-events as a strategic means of signaling their global ambitions, investing heavily in event infrastructure and bidding, with Dubai set to host the 2020 World Expo and Qatar the 2022 FIFA World Cup. Heslop, Nadeau, O'Reilly, and Armenakyan (2013, p. 13) noted the perceived nation brand benefits for emerging nations from hosting sport mega-events, stating that

> [m]any emerging nations have risked a great deal in betting that hosting of a mega-event can be a fast-track to world recognition and reputation enhancement, and there is considerable evidence that this bet has payoffs in positive impacts on country images and reputations as producers of products and as tourism destinations.

While few would argue with the global attention these events command, assessing a definitive longer-term legacy for the place brand of the host is a more complex exercise.

*Intangible legacies*: Beyond event impacts, the focus more recently has turned to creating legacies from sport mega-events. As Cornelissen (2007, p. 248) explained, "Leaving appropriate long-term legacies has become a discourse which has left an indelible mark on the way in which planning for today's sport mega-events takes shape". Legacy has therefore become a crucial aspect of sport mega-event planning, although Cornelissen et al. (2011) noted that there was still

*Table 9.1* BRICS emerging economies and sport mega-events

| Country | Sport mega-events hosted (post-1994) | Nation Brand Index Ranking (FutureBrand 2014) |
| --- | --- | --- |
| Brazil | • 2007 Pan-American Games<br>• 2014 FIFA World Cup<br>• Rio 2016 Olympic Games | 43 |
| Russia | • Sochi 2014 Winter Olympic Games<br>• 2018 FIFA World Cup | 31 |
| India | • Delhi 2010 Commonwealth Games<br>• 2011 Cricket World Cup | 50 |
| China | • Beijing 2008 Olympic Games<br>• Beijing 2015 IAAF World Athletics Championships<br>• Beijing 2022 Winter Olympic Games | 28 |
| South Africa | • 1995 Rugby World Cup<br>• 2003 Cricket World Cup<br>• 2010 FIFA World Cup<br>• Durban 2022 Commonwealth Games | 40 |

little consensus on the definition of legacy, what it entails and how it should be measured.

Beyond the tangible legacy aspects, intangible aspects, such as city, nation or destination branding, are just as valuable yet are often overlooked because of their measurement complexity. Moreover, they are often associated with longer term impacts for the host destination, yet, as is commonplace within the legacy literature, most brand-related legacy studies have been conducted in the short-term. Cornelissen et al. (2011) therefore recommend that the legacy of the 2010 FIFA World Cup should be continuously examined. This chapter contributes to the legacy body of knowledge by providing empirical evidence of the intangible legacy of place branding associated with a mega-event by drawing on a range of different studies undertaken using multiple methods over different time periods.

## South Africa and the 2010 FIFA World Cup

The case of South Africa and the 2010 FIFA World Cup presented an example of a nation particularly interested in the hosting of sport mega-events for strategic nation branding benefits. Cornelissen (2008, p. 486) suggested that the hosting of the mega-event was part of a larger national agenda for nation building as well as showcasing the state as a "global middle power". The importance of sport mega-events to the nation is manifested in its hosting of a series of major and mega sport events, such as the 1995 Rugby World Cup, the 1996 African Nations Cup (football), and the 2003 Cricket World Cup. However, the 2010 FIFA World Cup represented by far the largest sport event to be hosted by the nation.

The first ever FIFA World Cup on African soil was awarded to South Africa and took place from 11 June to 11 July 2010. From the outside, South Africa appeared to be a good choice as it represented Africa's most developed economy, boasted the wealthiest football league system in Africa and was host to the continent's largest sports' media and television companies (Knott and Swart, 2011). The success by South Africa in attracting the FIFA World Cup to its shores was particularly remarkable in that it was only re-admitted to FIFA twelve years prior to the decision being made, after decades of sporting isolation as a result of its apartheid political policies. With Nelson Mandela, the new democracy's first president, in attendance at the final announcement, the hosting of the World Cup appeared to confirm the transformation of the nation from political outcast to the hub of a new breed of developing countries. Although South Africa had also had its share of publicised problems, such as rising crime rates, high unemployment, a lack of access to basic services such as housing and education, and a high HIV infection rate (Donaldson and Ferreira, 2009), the hosting of the World Cup symbolised hope for the country and a chance to prove that this emerging nation could host an event of this magnitude as efficiently as the developed economies who had hosted the previous editions of the event, namely Germany (2006) and South Korea and Japan (2002), as well as other emerging nations that had hosted or bid to host mega-events, such as China, Russia, and Brazil (Tomlinson et al., 2011).

Proclaimed as "Africa's World Cup" due to FIFA's newly-instated rotational hosting policy, the following quotation by the CEO of the 2010 Local Organising Committee (LOC) made it clear that the vision for the event, and one of its main objectives, was to improve and reposition the image of the country:

> [The World Cup] is about nation-building, it's about infrastructure improvement, it's about country branding, it's about repositioning, it's about improving the image of our country, and it's about tourism promotion. It's also about return on investment, job creation and legacy. These are the things that drive not only our nation but the nations of the world"
>
> (Allmers and Maennig, 2009, p. 500).

The 2010 FIFA World Cup was therefore promoted as a platform for the nation to be showcased through one of the largest global media platforms, creating an opportunity to destabilise common stereotypes about Africa and dispel Afro-pessimism (Donaldson and Ferreira, 2009) as well as positioning the nation alongside its emerging-nation economic trade partners (Tomlinson et al., 2011).

## Assessing place branding legacies

While the sentiment within South Africa was that the event was a resounding success (Cape Town Tourism, 2010) and a government report concluded that the event resulted in many important intangible legacies for the nation (SRSA, 2011), there was little empirical evidence that the event successfully elevated the nation brand. In the immediate post-event period of the tournament there was a proliferation of evaluative literature (for example, special journal issues of *Soccer & Society*, 2010; *Development Southern Africa*, 2011; and *African Journal for the Physical, Health Education, Recreation and Dance [AJPHERD]*, 2012). The majority of these papers reviewed the historical, social, and political context of the event, emphasising the importance of the event in national identity formation and political symbolism for the host nation. Residents' perceptions, expectations, and fears, particularly of crime and safety, were also topics frequently covered. According to Tomlinson et al. (2011, p. 38), a central issue of much of the post-event literature reflected the change in image and identity of South Africa (and by association Africa), both domestically and internationally. However, these short-term impacts are limited in terms of their ability to assess legacy. As a result, these papers further raised the question of whether these impacts were sustainable, especially in the light of post-event domestic political, social and economic struggles.

Among the many diverse stakeholder groups involved in the delivery of the event, there did not appear to be any critical assessment of the place branding impact, nor did there appear to be any communications regarding plans to leverage and sustain the branding benefits post event. Would this be just another transient moment for the nation, or would it result in a longer-lasting brand legacy, as was promised?

The authors were directly involved in and coordinated a number of different studies in the pre-, during- and post-event period that aimed to elucidate different aspects of the branding legacy for host cities and the nation as a whole from the 2010 FIFA World Cup. While most of these were once again short-term in scope (up to two years post the event), there are also studies that were expanded to assess the longer-term post-event period, between three and five years post the event. Nonetheless, the authors acknowledge the need for even longer-term legacy assessments that should still be implemented. Table 9.2 sets out a summary of the types of studies that were undertaken, with a brief explanation of the methods given, along with the timeframe. The following sections discuss an overview of these findings, highlighting key aspects that either support or refute place branding legacy.

*Table 9.2* Overview of brand-related studies conducted by the authors linked to the 2010 FIFA World Cup

| Study focus | Method | Time period |
|---|---|---|
| Residents* (Tichaawa and Bama, 2012), informal residents* (Hendricks, Bob, and Nadasen, 2012; & host city business (formal & informal) (Swart and Jurd, 2012) perceptions of the internal nation brand changes; | Quantitative; survey interviews; Host cities of Cape Town & Durban; stadium precinct areas | 3 months pre- and post-event |
| International visitor perceptions of nation brand (Knott et al., 2013; Turco et al., 2012) | Quantitative; survey interviews conducted in stadium precinct & fan park areas of various host cities | During event |
| Media analysis of the event on views of South Africa and Cape Town internationally in key and emerging tourism markets (Swart, Linley, and Hardenberg, 2012) | Qualitative; analysis of major online media sources (key markets – UK, Germany, Netherlands and USA) | Pre- (24 months), lead-up (12 months), during and post-event (12 months) |
| Impact of event on destination and city brand of host city (Knott, Allen, and Swart, 2012) | Qualitative; in-depth interviews; brand & event stakeholders | 18–20 months post-event |
| Nation brand & event stakeholder perceptions of legacy, leveraging activities & lessons learned (Knott, Fyall, and Jones, 2015) | Qualitative; in-depth interviews; brand & event stakeholders & experts | 22–40 months post-event |
| Strategic contribution of the 2010 mega-event to city branding (Knott and Hemmonsbey, 2015) | Qualitative; in-depth interviews; city brand and sport stakeholders; Cape Town | 4 years post event |

* This excludes a range of other resident perceptions studies conducted in the stadium precinct area prior (one to two years) to 2010, as well as perceptions of African immigrants and residents of non-host cities.

# Discussion

## *Evidence supporting place branding legacy*

The overwhelming overall sense from all of the variety of studies undertaken point to a large impact of the 2010 mega-event on both city and nation brands in the host country. In the short-term, immediate post-event period, local residents and businesses showed significant improvements in their perceptions of aspects of the nation brand that pointed to an improved overall perception of the host nation's capability, as well as a more favourably perceived internal brand image and identity. These perceptions particularly related to the sense of unity among local residents, better-than-expected event hosting, and fewer negative event outcomes than anticipated.

Results from the international visitor survey during the event period also exhibited significant positive changes for the nation brand. Most notably, the aspects of the brand that showed high degrees of change were related to: the local population (e.g., friendly, welcoming, diverse) and to urban images of the nation (e.g., modern, developed, technologically advanced, good tourism infrastructure). This was somewhat mirrored in the international media analysis findings that the desired exposure of the nation and city (Cape Town) brand image was mostly positive with the coastline, culture, natural attractions, and information about visiting all receiving stronger coverage; however, there was a difference in emphasis across the various markets as elaborated in the media legacy chapter by Swart et al. (Chapter 16). While these positive sentiments are largely to be expected in the immediate aftermath of an extremely positive event that exceeded local and global expectations in terms of its operational success, it was of great importance to discover the longer-term legacy assessments.

Although two to four years post an event is still relatively a short period in which to assess legacy, it at least allowed sufficient time for the euphoria of the event period to subside and allow a more critical assessment to be reflected. The focus of these studies was more qualitative in nature as they focused on the key event and place brand stakeholders and experts (comprising event and brand consultants and academic researchers) rather than the local population or visitors. The in-depth interview format allowed for these participants to reflect on their activities, expectations, post-event leveraging in order to assess the degree to which place branding legacies had been achieved. Once again, there were a variety of very positive assessments of the legacy for the nation and host city brands.

Overall, the 2010 mega-event was regarded by the respondents as leaving a positive legacy for the place brand, most notably in terms of a change in brand image for the host nation (Knott, 2014). This was identified as the foremost legacy of the event for the nation. A number of stakeholders interviewed echoed similar responses, such as (Knott, 2014, p. 230): "The biggest benefit (for the host country) has been the change of image and perception of South Africa internationally", and "The world started to see South Africa in a different way". This new positive overall view of the nation brand was mostly the result of positive changes to a few specific brand attributes. In particular, redressing the negative media focus and

international perceptions of safety, security and crime, was a notable factor mentioned by many of the stakeholders. Another key perception change was affected
by the changed perceptions of citizens of the host nation, as explained in these
responses by stakeholders (Knott, 2014, p. 231): "The event changed perceptions
on the hospitality of the nation", and "People didn't know that we have very
friendly people". The third-most notable change in perception of the host nation
related to technology and advancement or development, with South Africa being
viewed post the event as (Knott, 2014, p. 221): "[A] more, let's say, first-world,
technologically advanced nation". A further important dimension of the legacy
was the internal confidence in the nation and its capabilities, manifested in a sense
of self-belief and capability among residents.

Despite the largely positive expressions of place brand legacy in the case of
South Africa, it is also of great interest to note more critical comments that many
respondents made.

### Evidence refuting place branding legacy

Notwithstanding the very positive legacies mentioned above, there was a concern
that the negative events in the years following the 2010 mega-event may detract
from these branding gains. It was mentioned that after the event there were a
series of negative occurrences and news stories coming from the nation relating to things such as political tensions and labour strikes. These were viewed
as detracting from the euphoria surrounding the event, although not viewed as
significant enough to completely eradicate the place branding legacy from the
event. However, a place brand stakeholder explained how in her view there was
still a 'net gain' for the nation brand as a legacy two years post the event (Knott,
2014, p. 209):

> We got knocks here and there – the strikes and the [South African President]
> Zuma antics, the Secrecy Bill, nationalisation of mines. But it depends on
> what markets you talk about. A lot of people won't hear about that. We prob-
> ably went five steps forward and two back. We haven't maintained as high
> as we got to, but we certainly haven't gone back to where we were. We have
> a net gain.

Once again, this highlights the imperative of long-term legacy assessments. The
preceding quotation implies that in the absence of further positive brand stimuli,
the positive impacts of the FIFA World Cup could be eroded by a continual stream
of negative sentiments emanating in the years following the event.

Furthermore, the concern mentioned earlier appears to stem from that fact that
despite some good planning for legacy, there was a lack of implementation of
legacy plans post event, as revealed in this sentiment expressed by a key event
stakeholder (Knott, 2014, p. 219): "We had a whole legacy planned that we never
got to. We could have had a better legacy than we ended up with". This highlights the importance of not only legacy planning, but the imperative of implementing this legacy. There were reasons given for this, including a lack of time,

budget, energy or the fact that many event stakeholder jobs only existed up until the event concluded. Some suggestions to address this were to create a separate legacy implementation team, with a mandate and budget to implement and leverage legacy post the event.

The post-event period appeared to be a critical part of the perceived legacy outcomes. As good as the event period was for the place brand, there was a strong criticism of the lack of efforts in this period, as revealed in these quotations from stakeholders and experts (Knott, 2014, p. 216): "As a nation brand, I think we had an outburst of brand silence after the World Cup", and "There were a lot of things that hype and momentum built up, which really could have taken the brand to the next level, but then there was a bit of a lull". The post-event period was characterised by a lack of policy and strategic leveraging of the benefits gained, as the following quotation reveals (Knott, 2014, p. 240:

> I think in terms of policy, there didn't seem to be a structured policy that said this is how we are going to leverage off it. There was no master plan to say that we've hosted the World Cup, let's leverage off it in these ways to make it clear.

Furthermore, another criticism was that beyond the place brand legacy for the nation and major host cities, it is not clear if there was a significant brand legacy for smaller cities, towns, and destinations. Some respondents noted this as missed opportunities for the smaller cities.

## Critical questions and issues for the future

This section draws key elements from the discussion to set out key critical questions and issues related to place branding legacies from mega-events.

### *Leveraging place brand legacy for emerging place brands*

The critical assessment of stakeholders of the post-event period highlights the imperative of planning and implementing strategic leveraging activities in order to realise longer-term legacy gains for the place brands. This may need to result in a separate "team" being mandated with this task. All stakeholders need to be made aware of the vital importance of the post-event period in terms of sustaining the momentum of the positive brand impacts and possibly even extending these gains to other cities, towns, and destinations that did not immediately appear to benefit from the event hosting period. Notwithstanding the significant impact of the 2010 mega-event, these studies certainly highlighted the need for on-going, positive place brand exposure. It is further underscored that there does not appear to be many examples of how mega-events, especially first-order mega-events, have been used as a platform to leverage long-term gains for a destination. Perhaps destinations have been able to achieve more through the use of lower order mega-events as in the case of Singapore hosting the Youth Olympics Games in 2010 as part of its positioning as a sport city.

*The role of stakeholders in creating and sustaining legacy*

Implicit in the imperative of leveraging legacy gains in the post-event period is the involvement of brand stakeholders. These statements make it clear that positive brand legacy is not an expected outcome from hosting a mega-event without the strategic planning for legacy and the implementation of leveraging activities by a multitude of different brand and event stakeholders. For these stakeholders, legacy is by definition a positive outcome that is sought and planned for. For brand stakeholders, the concept of legacy has much in common with "sustainability", in relation to longer-term impacts as a result of continued strategic efforts. While it is clear that legacy is assessed in the longer-term post-event period, it is clear that the strategic leveraging efforts of brand stakeholders can assist to sustain the duration and impact of these legacies.

*Place branding legacies beyond mega-events*

Although the legacy from the 2010 FIFA World Cup was largely a very positive one for South Africa, many of the place brand stakeholders questioned the need to prioritise mega-events over other event types. Some stakeholders warned about the costs involved in such a bid and the implicit risk involved, especially for an emerging economy nation, while some prefer the opportunities created by smaller, recurring, and home-grown events. In particular, one place brand stakeholder explained, "You know, you don't have to choose the mega-events. If you have a good portfolio of small to medium range events you can be as profitable and as successful as you could be with a big event" (Knott, 2014, p. 225). In terms of the context and timing of the post-event studies, it should be noted that there is far more awareness of the pitfalls of mega-events and especially the host federations due to the recent global scandals involving FIFA and the excessive spending by some nations in order to host an Olympic Games. The current global climate is far more sceptical of or even opposed to these mega-events and this has caused many event bids to suffer as a result or for event hosts to receive public backlash from their bidding or hosting. The reputation of these events and federations should especially be considered in the interests of aligning a place brand image with it. Building homegrown events including arts, cultural and lifestyle events contributes to developing a portfolio of events and can build on the brand image communicated through 2010 to maximise the legacy benefits.

This chapter has revealed that there are significant opportunities that can be created for place brands through the hosting of mega-events, particularly so for an emerging place brand such as South Africa, that suffered from a poorly understood identity and global positioning. The chapter acknowledges that legacy is difficult to measure and should be assessed in longer-term studies rather than the shorter-term studies that abound. Nonetheless, the chapter has given examples of a variety of methodologies that can be used to assess a place brand legacy from different perspectives. Despite the overall rather positive brand legacy in the case of South Africa in the short to medium term, it is also clear that positive impacts need to be sustained and leveraged long after an event has concluded in order for a positive brand legacy to result. In the absence of continual brand communication that affirms the positive sentiments of the FIFA World Cup, these gains will over time be eroded by the general negative media sentiments that characterise developing nations in particular. A sport mega-event is therefore to be viewed as a catalyst for positive brand communication, at best, or merely one of many ongoing opportunities that are required in order to sustain a place branding legacy. As a result, event and brand stakeholders will need to adjust their perspective and planning to a far longer-term approach as mega-events are certainly not to be perceived as a "quick fix" solution for emerging place brands.

## References

Allmers, S., and Maennig, W. (2009). Economic impacts of the FIFA Soccer World Cups in France 1998, Germany 2006, and outlook for South Arica 2010. *Eastern Economic Journal*, *35*, 500–519.

Anholt, S. (2007). Brand Africa – What is competitive identity? *African Analyst*, *2*(1), 5–14.

Cape Town Tourism. (2010, July 21). Tourism Industry Positive about the Impact of the World Cup on Future Tourism Growth for Cape Town. *Cape Town Official Tourism Website*. Retrieved July 31, 2014, from www.capetown.travel/industry_blog/entry/tourism_industry_positive_about_the_impact_of_the_world_cup_on_future_touri

Cornelissen, S. (2007). Crafting legacies: The changing political economy of global sport and the 2010 FIFA World Cup. *Politikon*, *34*(3), 241–259.

Cornelissen, S. (2008). Scripting the nation: Sport, mega-events, foreign policy and state-building in post-apartheid South Africa. *Sport in Society*, *11*(4), 481–493.

Cornelissen, S., Bob, U., and Swart, K. (2011). Towards redefining the concept of legacy in relation to sport mega-events: Insights from the 2010 FIFA World Cup. *Development Southern Africa*, *28*(3), 307–318.

Donaldson, R., and Ferreira, S. (2009). (Re-)creating urban destination image: Opinions of foreign visitors to South Africa on safety and security? *Urban Forum*, *20*, 1–18.

Essex, S., and Chalkley, B. (1998). Olympic Games: Catalyst of urban change. *Leisure Studies*, *17*(3), 187–206.

Freire, J. (2014). Editorial: Place branding in Africa. *Place Branding and Public Diplomacy*, *10*, 32–34.

Getz, D. (2003). Sport event tourism: Planning, development and marketing. In S. Hudson (Ed.), *Sport and adventure tourism* (pp. 49–88). Binghampton, NY: Haworth.

Grix, J. (2012). "Image" leveraging and sports mega-events: Germany and the 2006 FIFA World Cup. *Journal of Sport & Tourism*, *17*(4), 289–312.

Hendricks, N., Bob, U., and Nadasen, N. (2012, September). A comparison of Cape Town and Durban business perceptions of the 2010 FIFA World Cup. *African Journal for Physical Health, Education, Recreation and Dance*, (Supplement 1), 62–72.

Heslop, L. A., Nadeau, J., O'Reilly, N., and Armenakyan, A. (2013). Mega-event and country co-branding: Image shifts, transfers and reputational impacts. *Corporate Reputation Review*, *16*(1), 7–33.

Higham, J., and Hinch, T. (2009). *Sport and tourism: Globalisation, mobility and identity*. Oxford: Butterworth Heinemann.

Kapferer, J-N. (2012). The new strategic brand management: Advanced insights and strategic thinking (5th ed.). London: Kogan Page.

Knott, B. (2014). The strategic contribution of sport mega-events to nation branding: The case of South Africa and the 2010 FIFA World Cup. Unpublished PhD thesis, Bournemouth University.

Knott, B., Allen, D., and Swart, K. (2012, September). Stakeholder reflections of the tourism and nation-branding legacy of the 2010 FIFA World Cup for South Africa. *African Journal for Physical Health, Education, Recreation and Dance*, (Supplement 1), 115–125.

Knott, B., Fyall, A., and Jones, I. (2015). The nation branding opportunities provided by a sport mega-event: South Africa and the 2010 FIFA World Cup. *Journal of Destination Marketing and Management, 4*, 46–56.

Knott, B., and Hemmonsbey, J. (2015). The strategic value of sport for an African city brand. *African Journal for Physical, Health Education, Recreation and Dance*, (Supplement 1), 192–205.

Knott, B., and Swart, K. (2011). Sports marketing in Africa. In G. Nufer and A. Buhler (Eds.), *Marketing in sport* (2nd ed., pp. 565–585). Berlin: Erich Schmidt.

Nauright, J. (2013). Selling nations to the world through sports: Mega-events and nation branding as global diplomacy. *Public Diplomacy Magazine*, pp. 22–27.

Olins, W. (2002). Branding the nation – the historical context. *Journal of Brand Management, 9*(4–5), 241–248.

SRSA. (2011). 2010 FIFA World Cup country report. Pretoria: SRSA.

Swart, K., and Jurd, M. (2012, September). Informal residents' perceptions of the 2010 FIFA World Cup: A case study of an informal settlement in Cape Town. *African Journal for Physical Health, Education, Recreation and Dance*, (Supplement 1), 42–52.

Swart, K., Linley, M., and Hardenberg, E. (2012, September). A media analysis of the 2010 FIFA World Cup: A case study of selected international media. *African Journal for Physical Health, Education, Recreation and Dance*, (Supplement 1), 131–141.

Tichaawa, T. M., and Bama, H. K. N. (2012, September). Green Point residents' perceptions of the 2010 FIFA World Cup: A post-event analysis. *African Journal for Physical Health, Education, Recreation and Dance*, (Supplement 1), 22–32.

Tomlinson, R., Bass, O., and Bassett, T. (2011). Before and after the vuvuzela: Identity, image and mega-events in South Africa, China and Brazil. *South African Geographical Journal, 93*(1), 38–48.

Turco, D. M., Tichaawa, T. M., Moodley, V., Munien, S., Jaggernath, J., and Stofberg, Q. (2012, September). Profiles of foreign visitors attending the 2010 FIFA World Cup in South Africa. *African Journal for Physical Health, Education, Recreation and Dance*, (Supplement 1), 73–80.

# 10 The legacy of corruption in the context of the 2014 FIFA World Cup

## Short-term and long-term consequences for sponsorship perception

*Joerg Koenigstorfer and Wojciech Kulczycki*

### Introduction

Sport is a powerful instrument to positively influence the world and teach life-long lessons while supporting social development (Smith and Westerbeek, 2007). Sociologists have noted that sporting activities result from social reality and can create myth, nostalgia, romance and cultural fixation, to state just a few examples (Frey and Eitzen, 1991). Sporting activities have connections to ethics and human values, such as the values transported by the Olympic Movement and other institutions in sports (McFee, 1998). Thus, the concept of 'sportsmanship' is thought to stand for fairness, respect and friendship (IOC, 2015).

As sport developed from a playful, participation-oriented activity to one that is guided by the principles of commercialism and entertainment, people have noted unethical behaviours as well as values with negative connotations in connection to sport (e.g., striving for power for personal benefit while breaching important principles of modern societies) (Frey and Eitzen, 1991). This is particularly true for mega-sport events, where large investments are made and where media attention is high (Müller, 2015). Some authors claim that mega-sport events mirror the disenchantment with perceived values of globalisation, including winning at any price, cronyism, commercialisation and corruption (Milton-Smith, 2002). As a consequence, the hosting of mega-sport events is increasingly questioned. The events and the host organisations have been accused of failing to ensure that international sport governance adheres to universal principles such as democracy, social responsibility and business ethics (Geeraert, Alm, and Groll, 2014; Ionescu, 2015).

These trends have serious consequences for the legacy of mega-sport events. Sport event legacy is defined as "all planned and unplanned, positive and negative, tangible and intangible structures created for and by a sport event that remain longer than the event itself" (Preuss, 2007, p. 211). The failure of host organisations to adhere to commonly agreed societal principles when mega-sport events are hosted can produce a particularly harmful facet of the legacy of these events: corruption.

This chapter is concerned with the corruption legacy – mostly unplanned, negatively perceived and intangible in structure – that is sometimes called the "mega-event syndrome," merely because there is almost no mega-sport event hosting that has not been accused of corruption (Müller, 2015). More specifically, this chapter looks at the levels at which corruption takes place when mega-sport events are hosted and the short-term and long-term consequences of corruption for one partic-ular group of stakeholders: the sponsors. Although there is some anecdotal evidence that sponsors are negatively affected by corrupt mega-sport event hosting (Business Insider, 2014), there is little theoretical background and empirical evidence for the mechanisms at play. Thus, this chapter intends to inspire future research by offering theoretical underpinnings and by presenting empirical data on corruption from our own studies that have been conducted during the course of the hosting of the 2014 FIFA World Cup in Brazil (Kulczycki and Koenigstorfer, 2016).

## The corruption legacy of the 2014 FIFA World Cup: the years 2014–16

Corruption, rooted in the Latin adjective *corruptus*, stands for destroyed, spoiled or broken and can be seen as a symptom of economic, political and institutional weak-nesses (Myint, 2000). We define *corruption* as the abuse or misuse of public power or position for personal, subunit and/or organisational gain breaching important principles of modern societies, including the concept that public agencies should be impartial and rule-based at all times (Sandholtz and Koetzle, 2000). Corruption takes place at the societal, organisational and individual level (Pinto, Leana, and Pil, 2008).

Corruption, however, is complex and difficult to measure (Aguilera and Vadera, 2008). The clandestine nature and the illegality of corruption often hin-der empirical analyses (Saha, Gounder, and Jen-Je, 2012; Sandholtz and Koetzle, 2000). Corruption represents a major problem for the development of societies worldwide, creating negative economic and social consequences (Charron, 2016; Holmberg, Rothstein, and Nasiritousi, 2009; Mauro, 1997). The negative effects of corruption can be observed at three levels:

- **The societal level**, such as reduced domestic and foreign investments, in-creased costs of production, higher inequality and poverty and uncertainty in decision making (Freckleton, Wright, and Craigwell, 2012); furthermore, there is an increase in capital expenditure on so-called white elephant proj-ects (Mauro, 1997).
- **The organisational level**, such as the negative influence of corruption on business ethics and practices (Ashforth, Gioia, Robinson, and Trevino, 2008; Pinto et al., 2008; Zahra, Priem, and Rasheed, 2005) and the implementation of corruption into the organisational culture and leadership (Campbell and Göritz, 2014).
- **The individual level**, that is, ethical dilemmas that lead to the interpretation of person-situation interactions in the sense that public power or the position in which a person finds him- or herself is misused for personal, subunit and/or organisational gain breaching important principles of modern societies (Stead, Worrell, and Stead, 1990), such as bribery, racketeering and money laundering.

The categorisation of corruption into societal, organisational and individual levels can be used to describe corruption as one legacy facet of the hosting of mega-sport events. In what follows, we use these categories to analyse the case of the 2014 FIFA World Cup hosted in Brazil.

# The societal level: Brazil

Table 10.1 presents examples and empirical evidence for the perception of society-level corruption during the course of the 2014 FIFA World Cup and thereafter. The 2014 FIFA World Cup was hosted in Brazil in 2014. The Corruption Perception Index (CPI) is published by Transparency International and is the most widely

*Table 10.1* Examples from media reports and host populations' perception of society-level corruption of Brazil according to own studies and the Global Corruption Barometer

| Media examples for society-level corruption | Corruption indicators | Mean | Standard deviation |
|---|---|---|---|
| **CBS NEWS**  World Cup 2014 construction in Brazil marred by corruption, waste | Over the past two years, how has the level of corruption in this country changed? (1 = decreased a lot, 5 = increased a lot) | 3.98 [a]  3.55 [b] | 1.06  1.14 |
| **ALJAZEERA**  Brazil audit: 'corrupt World Cup costs' | To what extent do you think that corruption is a problem in the public sector in this country? (1 = not a problem at all, 7 = a very serious problem) | 6.75 [a]  4.60 [b] | 0.73  0.74 |
| **FORBES**  The Cost Of Corruption In Brazil Could Be Up To $53 Billion Just This Year Alone | In your dealings with the public sector, how important are personal contacts to get things done? (1 = not important at all, 5 = very important) | 4.31 [a]  3.43 [b] | 0.84  1.28 |
| **CBC NEWS**  Brazil World Cup opening bedevilled by corruption, strikes | To what extent is this country's government run by a few big entities acting in their own best interests? (1 = not at all; 5 = entirely) | 4.04 [a]  3.49 [b] | 0.76  1.10 |
| **ABC NEWS**  Waste and corruption fuel World Cup anger on Brazil's streets | How effective do you think your government's actions are in the fight against corruption? (1 = very effective; 5 = very ineffective) | 4.05 [a]  3.55 [b] | 0.87  1.13 |
|  | Ordinary people can make a difference in the fight against corruption (1 = strongly agree; 4 = strongly disagree) | 2.21 [b] | 0.94 |

Note: The corruption indicators are taken from the Global Corruption Barometer (2013).

a The data are taken from Kulczycki and Koenigstorfer (2016, p. 21; follow-up study).

b The data are taken from the Global Corruption Barometer survey in Brazil. The items were assessed via four-point, five-point and seven-point rating scales, respectively, 1 indicating the lowest level of corruption and 4, 5 or 7 indicating the highest level of corruption.

used indicator of corruption. Brazil ranks 72nd out of 177 examined countries (where 1 indicates the least corrupt country and 177 indicates the most corrupt country) on the Global Corruption Barometer (2013), which is part of the CPI (Hardoon and Heinrich, 2013).

As a result of the hosting of the 2014 FIFA World Cup, some media reports and experts claim that corruption in the country may have increased because its legitimisation during the preparation for the event (e.g., CBS, 2014). The majority of the representative Brazilian sample surveyed as part of the Global Corruption Barometer ($n = 2002$ Brazilian individuals, interviewed face to face between 2012 and 2013) also perceived an increase in corruption in their home country: 47% of the sample believed that corruption in Brazil has increased during the past two years (i.e., before 2013), while only 18% believed it has decreased. Furthermore, 88% of the sample that was surveyed believed that corruption is a problem in the country, while only 2% stated that it was not a problem at the time when the study was conducted. The study was conducted during the preparation for the 2014 FIFA World Cup that was hosted in twelve Brazilian cities.

In our own research focusing on Rio de Janeiro (i.e., the city where the final was hosted), we found that the majority of Rio de Janeiro residents perceived their own country, Brazil, as corrupt (Kulczycki and Koenigstorfer, 2016). Our studies were conducted in 2014 and 2015, respectively. The means of some selected CPI indicators can be seen in Table 10.1. They indicate that the ratings are higher compared to the Global Corruption Barometer data collected in 2012 and 2013. This makes sense as the 2014 FIFA World Cup was hosted during a time of political change and demonstrations against the practices of politicians. Thus, an increase between 2012/13 and 2014 (2015) seems reasonable. Also, it is reasonable that they are above the mid-point of the scale.

## The organisational level: the FIFA

Before, during and since the hosting of the 2014 FIFA World Cup, the FIFA (Fédération Internationale de Football Association) has provided many examples of corruption on an organisational level (Table 10.2; The Washington Post, 2015). These cases of corruption may not directly be due to the (preparation for the) hosting of one event (e.g., the FIFA World Cup), but may be considered a consequence of a multitude of events that encourage corrupt practices.

Within the hosting of an event, corruption can take various types and forms, such as corruption as part of competition (e.g., athletes, coaches and referees) and corruption as part of management (e.g., officials and managers from teams and federations) (Maennig, 2005). However, we note that any definition and interpretation of corrupt behaviours is context-specific. That is, whether people consider certain actions or structures as corruption depends upon context, such as societies and cultures. While some actions are considered normal and even ethical practices in one society, they could be regarded as corrupt and unethical in another society. For example, cronyism and nepotism are considered as questionable actions in Western countries as those cultures are primarily rules-driven and based on strict legal systems (e.g., North America). In the context of a bidding procedure a purchasing agent would be thus expected to award contracts based on quality and price of the bids. However, many of the world's countries are relationship-based and cronyism is considered a foundation of trust (e.g., Southeast Asia). Thus, favouring friends by a purchasing agent does not represent a conflict of interest but is even in the company's interest as those business partners with whom a good relationship exists are expected to (over)perform in order to nourish (but not to threaten) a valuable relationship (Hooker, 2009).

Context is also provided by organisational settings: in sport organisations, there is often little accountability regarding the president or the executive committee, as sport-governing bodies are international organisations that do not directly answer to a country (Maennig, 2005). Sport organisations are often subject to only little supervision (e.g., lenient authorities in Switzerland, the country where many international sport-governing organisations are located; Pielke, 2013).

Table 10.2 displays examples of organisation-level corruption during the course of the 2014 FIFA World Cup. The data were taken from our own research that was conducted during the event hosting (Kulczycki, Pfister, and Koenigstorfer, 2016). All the item-level means of perceived corruption of the FIFA are above the mid-level of the rating points (similar to country-level corruption). Thus, we can assume that corruption is a problem in the FIFA (as assessed from the perspective of Rio de Janeiro residents).

## The individual level: corrupt individuals as actors

Individuals' actions can be corrupt too, as seen for many FIFA representatives, such as Mohamed Bin Hammam, Jack Warner, Chuck Blazer, Sepp Blatter, Jerome Valcke, Michel Platini and even Gianni Infantino (order according to the time when allegations started according to media reports; see Figure 10.1). These persons use or used their power and position within the FIFA for personal, subunit and/or organisational gain breaching important principles of modern societies. We do not intend to judge these persons or their behaviours in this chapter. However, the sum of individual corrupt behaviours as well as organisation-level and society-level corruption caused important stakeholders (e.g., sponsors, politicians) to raise their voice or take action against corruption. For example, in response to the corruption allegations and human rights violations in Qatar, VISA, a top-level FIFA sponsor, issued two statements expressing concern over the migrant-worker conditions in Qatar as well as the corruption charges. The sponsor asked FIFA to take swift and immediate steps to address these issues (Fortune, 2015). Furthermore, several sponsors such as Coca-Cola or McDonald's publicly pushed FIFA to adopt an independent commission in order to reform the organisation, regain trust, and they called Joseph Blatter to step down as president of the organization (The Sydney Morning Herald, 2015). Several politicians also expressed their concerns about Joseph Blatter as the FIFA president (e.g., the British government with Sports Minister Tracey Crouch in the lead). For the purpose of this chapter we examine sponsors and how they were affected by corruption in the context of the hosting of the 2014 FIFA World Cup and its legacy.

*Table 10.2* Examples from media reports and host populations' perception of organization-level corruption of the FIFA according to own studies

| Media examples for FIFA-level corruption | Corruption indicators | Mean | Standard deviation |
|---|---|---|---|
| **THE TELEGRAPH** FIFA crisis: Threat of Russia and Qatar being stripped of 2018 and 2022 World Cups | Over the past two years, how has the level of corruption in the FIFA changed? (1 = decreased a lot, 5 = increased a lot) | 3.55 | 0.94 |
| **DER SPIEGEL** Sepp Blatter's corrupt fiefdom comes crashing down | To what extent do you think that corruption is a problem in the FIFA? (1 = not a problem at all, 7 = a very serious problem) | 4.05 | 1.19 |
| **NEWSWEEK** Swiss authorities make more arrests in FIFA corruption scandal | In your dealings with the FIFA, how important are personal contacts to get things done? (1 = not important at all, 5 = very important) | 3.91 | 1.16 |
| **AL JAZEERA** Fresh arrests made in FIFA corruption scandal | To what extent is the FIFA run by a few big entities acting in their own best interests? (1 = not at all; 5 = entirely) | 4.08 | 1.01 |
| **ABC NEWS** FIFA officials arrested over alleged 'Rampant, Systematic' $150m bribery | To what extent do you think the FIFA pays or offers bribes to achieve corporate gains? (1 = not at all; 5 = entirely) | 3.50 | 1.03 |
| | To what extent do you think the FIFA is involved in corruption? (1 = not at all; 5 = entirely) | 3.69 | 1.09 |
| | To what extent do you think there are corrupt practices at the FIFA elections (1 = not at all; 5 = entirely) | 3.67 | 1.04 |

Note: The corruption indicators are taken from the Global Corruption Barometer (2013). The data are taken from a sample collected in 2014 in Brazil (Kulczycki, Pfister, and Koenigstorfer, 2016). The items were assessed via 5-point rating scales and one 7-point rating scale, respectively, 1 indicating lowest level of corruption and 5 or 7 indicating highest level of corruption.

## Corruption and the perception of 2014 FIFA World Cup sponsorship

Since the hosting of the 2014 FIFA World Cup, some sponsors have responded to the increasing evidence of corruption that is prevalent at all three levels. Many of the corruption incidents shown in Figure 10.1 happened or were uncovered between 2014 and 2016 (which may be considered as the aftermath [or the legacy] of the events that took place for the preparation and during the 2014 FIFA World Cup). During the time period, more and more corrupt practices have been revealed in relation to the FIFA. For example, throughout 2015, some of FIFA's

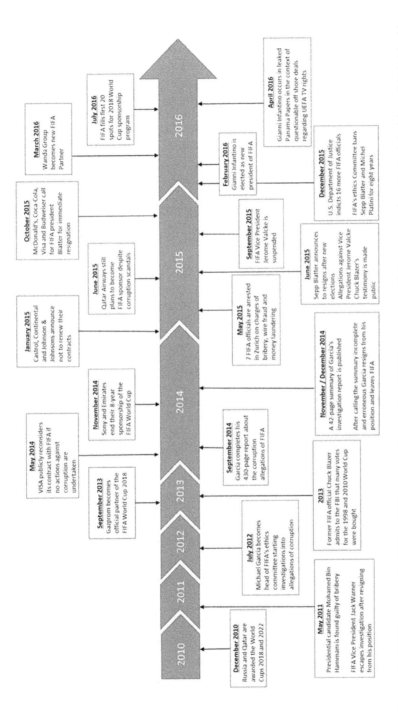

*Figure 10.1* FIFA events potentially related to corruption and the FIFA's sponsors' publicly announced or reported decisions (2010–16 with a focus on 2014–16)

top executives were arrested facing charges of bribery, racketeering and money laundering, making this scandal one of the largest corruption cases in sport history (Fox, 2015). The arrested officials were convicted to have helped to secure media and marketing rights or locations in the bidding process, involving a value of corrupt activities exceeding US$150 million (Boudreaux, Karahan, and Coats, 2016).

In response to these corrupt practices, some sponsors ended their sponsorship contract with the FIFA, some decided to pressure the FIFA to make changes in order to fight corruption while others remained completely silent. It is noteworthy to mention that, despite these scandals, the FIFA was able to attract new sponsors (replacing sponsors that did not renew their contract). While it is not our intention to judge the activities of sponsors, the change in the FIFA's sponsorship portfolio can be attributed to corruption on the organisational level from the practical standpoint (BBC, 2015).

In what follows next, we describe the mechanism of how corruption influenced individuals' attitudes toward the sponsorship of the 2014 FIFA World Cup, drawing on both theoretical arguments found in sponsorship-linked marketing and empirical findings based upon surveys with the host population in Rio de Janeiro (one of the host cities of the 2014 World Cup). We first outline the theoretical background before we present the results of empirical studies on perceived corruption in the context of the 2014 FIFA World Cup.

## Theoretical background on the effects of corruption on attitude to sponsors

The theoretical underpinnings of the negative short-term and long-term effects of corruption on consumers' attitudes toward the sponsorship are similar to the theoretical underpinnings that explain positive effects of sponsorship-linked marketing activities. However, there is one notable difference: the potential disliking of the entity that sells the sponsorship rights. While in sponsorship-linked marketing, sponsors aim to associate their brand with a positively connoted entity, a corrupt brand is negatively connoted when corruption is prevalent (as individuals do not like corrupt practices). Several theories provide explanations for why the latter harms sponsors:

- **Associative network models:** the sum of associations that individuals hold in memory about the sponsor represents the attitude toward the sponsor. More important, associations that were originally linked to a sponsored entity can transfer from the entity to the sponsor and complement associations that individuals have with the brand (Gwinner, 1997; Keller, 1993). If associations with the sponsored entity (here the FIFA) relate to corruption, these associations may transfer to the sponsor. Individuals then perceive that the entities share common structures (in this case, corruption associations) and should be perceived as contrary to the interest of sponsors as corruption is perceived as negative and unethical (Kulczycki and Koenigstorfer, 2016).
- **Image transfer models:** the concept of image transfer has been established since Gwinner and Eaton's (1999) landmark study on sponsorship. Arguments

are based upon how individuals form brand associations and make linkages (see the previous discussion). Individuals develop linkages from a variety of sources including brand as well as product and service category experiences, product and service attributes and brand positioning in promotional communications, to state some examples (Gwinner, Larson, and Swanson, 2009). The transfer can take place both consciously and unconsciously (without cognitive control) and, thus, sponsors may be worried that negative experiences (e.g., "The FIFA is immoral") or negative promotion (e.g., press reports about FIFA representatives' misconduct; see Table 10.2) explicitly or implicitly transfer to the brand (as the sponsorship associates the brand with the FIFA). This may result in negative attitudes either in the short run or in the long run.

- **Attribution theory:** the theory postulates that individuals actively try to seek for answers when they pose why-questions. Attribution theory is based on the covariance model, in particular the assumption that individuals make causal inferences about events that they observe and experience (Heider, 1958; Kelley, 1973). A person generates inferences that link events through causal relationships. These inferences are beliefs that allow for understanding and prediction of the observable world. In the FIFA case, individuals may ask themselves why sponsors support a corrupt entity (such as the FIFA) and then come to the conclusion that sponsors do not act because of altruism but out of profit motivation and self-interest (because there is no other reason for supporting a corrupt entity). The mediating function of these attributions on sponsor evaluations (Ellen, Webb, and Mohr, 2006; Rifon, Choi, Trimble, and Li, 2004) may thus be harmful to sponsors.

The list of theories presented above is not exclusive, as other theories may contribute to our understanding of the consequences of corrupt sport organisations on consumers' attitudes toward sponsors (e.g., Maennig, 2005). Future research may look into those theories in more detail and develop theories in order to explain why corruption takes place and what the mechanisms and consequences for different stakeholders (such as sponsors) are.

## Evidence from prior research on how corruption reduces attitudes to sponsors

Building upon associative network theory, we present empirical evidence for the mechanism of how corruption influenced attitude toward the sponsorship of the 2014 FIFA World Cup sponsors (Kulczycki and Koenigstorfer, 2016; studies 1–4). In study 1, we examined whether perceived corruption of the FIFA has a negative effect on attitude toward event sponsorship via two mediators: attitude toward the sport-governing body and attitude toward the event. The results largely supported our model. In a follow-up study (study 4), perceived corruption of the host country (Brazil) was taken into account, and we found similar effects for the negative impact of society-level corruption on attitude toward sponsorship of the 2014 FIFA World Cup. Thus, corruption of sport federations standing behind the event (here the FIFA; we replicated the results for the IOC [International Olympic Committee] in studies 2 and 3) and corruption in host countries of mega-sport events (in this instance Brazil) can jeopardise the goal of sponsoring brands to present their brand in a favourable context.

In both study 1 and the follow-up study (Kulczycki and Koenigstorfer, 2016), perceived corruption levels were moderately high (see Tables 10.1 and 10.2), and somewhat higher than in the Global Corruption Barometer (2013) on the country level. Study 1's participants perceived the FIFA as rather corrupt ($M = 5.36$, $SD = 1.73$, corruption was measured via three semantic differentials and four represents the mid-scale rating point; 1 indicates lowest and 7 indicates highest levels of corruption). Furthermore, 72% of the sample's participants believed that corruption represents an omnipresent issue at the FIFA and only 5% believed that the FIFA is an integer organisation that is free of corruption; follow-up study's participants perceived the Brazilian government as rather corrupt ($M = 4.25$, $SD = 0.52$, five items taken from the Global Corruption Barometer scale; three representing the mid rating of the scale [one item was scaled down from a 7-point rating scale to a 5-point rating scale). Furthermore, 62% of the sample believed that over the past two years the level of corruption in Brazil increased, while only 8% perceived a decrease in corruption. The large majority (97%) of the study's participants believed that corruption represents a problem in the country, while only 1% had the opinion that corruption was not a problem.

## Preventing and fighting corruption and its negative legacy in the context of hosting mega-sport events

Corruption is a serious issue in countries, industries and organisations, as well as individuals. This is particularly true for the context in which mega-sport events are hosted. The corruption legacy may put a burden on all actors and seriously harm the whole sport event industry (among other actors), no matter what level. In what follows, we first refer to the causes of corruption before we give some recommendations on how to prevent and fight corruption. It is important to understand to reasons for corruption and how corruption develops, given the negative economic and social consequences of corruption, in order to then develop strategies to prevent and fight corruption.

## Causes of corruption

Expanded professionalism and increasing commercialisation of mega-sport events (e.g., representatives' intentions to get their share from an increase in revenue and profit made by the FIFA as a multinational non-profit organisation [because of an increase in demand for television broadcasts; increase in revenue from ticketing; among others], similar to CEOs in multinational for-profit organisations) may set incentives for corrupt behaviours (Ionescu, 2015). An increase in the amount of money that is available for distribution within the FIFA may lead the FIFA representatives to ask for their shares, as they perceive that they have contributed to the success of the FIFA. These incentives are set in a particular context: inside sport organisations. These organisations like the FIFA often require little account-ability and they are often regulated on a low level (Maennig, 2005; Pielke, 2013). Furthermore, the low substitutability of the offering and the high loyalty status of sport spectators provide settings, in which the lack of ethical codes is sometimes easy to justify and where corruption is likely to spread out among actors (De Wae-geneer, Van de Sompele, and Willem, 2016; Smith and Stewart, 2010).

Corrupt behaviours can be described as actions of members (within an organ-isation) to disengage moral standards and use scripts that exclude ethical dimen-sions (Bandura, 1986; Gioia, 1992). The (organisational) culture may not only encourage, but even legitimate corrupt behaviours (Ashforth et al., 2008). The moral judgement of behaviour as corrupt is subjective and may change over time (Brunk, 2010). In the case of Brazil, results from the Global Corruption Barom-eter (Hardoon and Heinrich, 2013) indicate that more people believe that cor-ruption increased (rather than decreased) during the past years; this is alarming as the preparation for and the hosting of the 2014 FIFA World Cup may have contributed to this perception (Associated Press, 2014). In the case of the FIFA, one can assume that the organisational culture legitimised and contributed to cor-rupt behaviours, as most people perceive the institution to be corrupt. Although we note that in our own studies (Kulczycki and Koenigstorfer, 2016), participants perceived the FIFA as less corrupt than the Brazilian government and Brazilian institutions, the Brazilian government was mainly responsible for providing the infrastructure for the World Cup such as the stadiums and public transportation. Brazilian officials were accused of being involved in numerous corruption scan-dals prior to and during the event (CBS, 2014).

No matter why a country, an organisation or an individual is corrupt and how it became corrupt, most individuals perceive corruption as an act of transgres-sion. According to Boon and Holmes (1999) and Metts (1994), a transgression describes the behaviour by a relationship partner that is perceived as inconsistent with relationship-relevant norms (or expectations) and represents a violation of the implicit or explicit rules guiding a relationship performance and evaluation. Transgressions may lead to distrust and more corrupt behaviours from others, which is harmful on both economic and social levels.

The perception of societies, organisations and individuals that misuse their power or position to take personal advantage then influences how individuals feel and think about these stakeholders and potentially leads to the perception of cor-ruption (sometimes even though corruption has not been revealed objectively) (Buraimo, Migali, and Simmons, 2015; Maennig, 2005). Corruption may then cause what has been described before: negative economic and social effects on all three levels, be they society-, organisation- or individual-related. Thus, the fight against and prevention of corruption should be a main goal on all levels. We next describe some means that may help achieve this goal.

## Preventing and fighting corruption and its negative legacy

How can entities prevent corruption and what can sponsors do to fight corruption and weaken the negative effect of corruption on their brand? In what follows, we use the FIFA as an example. First, we refer to the means that the FIFA has in order to prevent and fight corruption. Second, we assess the possibilities from the perspective of the FIFA sponsors.

The FIFA can prevent and fight corruption via the following two means (the means presented here are not conclusive):[1]

- **Codes of conduct:** the FIFA can establish clear ethical codes of conduct with explicit definitions of corrupt behaviours. For example, they can make the procedure for the process of sport venue selection more transparent and less prone to corruption. They can also increase controls and sanctions – means that Maennig (2005) recommended more than one decade ago. More recently, Schwartz (2013) and De Waegeneer et al. (2016) argued that ethical codes can be part of formal ethics programmes and that they are a promising instrument to develop and maintain ethical behaviours in organisations and relate these practices to a strategic level (e.g., active promotion of ethical behaviours; commitment to ethical business practices; admonish internal unethical behaviour). However, the mere presence of ethical codes does not guarantee non-corrupt behaviours (De Waegeneer et al., 2016).[2]
- **Accountability:** the enforcement of accountability is a challenge in the context of global politics exercised through international organisations. The FIFA deals with many governmental and non-governmental organisations that operate within sometimes-incompatible systems (e.g., regarding formal and informal norms, standards and sanctions associated with decision making) (Pielke, 2013). The FIFA has demonstrated in the past that the organisation is relatively free of the usual mechanisms of accountability that are typically employed for large international organisations, except their formal accountability to Swiss law and their accountability to their sponsors (Pielke, 2013). Thus, there is room for improvement and the FIFA can learn from other institutions and respond to their pressures. The US has been increasing the pressure on the FIFA to implement institutional changes (as it has been observed for the IOC after the corruption scandal in 1998). For example, in response to the IOC scandal, the legislation in the US made it illegal for national companies to engage in IOC sponsorship unless the reforms of the Mitchell Commission were implemented. This represented a serious threat to the IOC and its sponsorship revenues (Boudreaux et al., 2016; Pielke, 2013). FIFA may anticipate such actions and seek external advice, initiating a transparent process of reformation via multiple accountability mechanisms that support institutional change (i.e., something FIFA has not fully achieved yet; see Figure 10.1).

The sponsors have the following options to influence the FIFA towards preventing and fighting corruption as well as weakening the negative effect of corruption on their brand (Hirschman, 1970; again, the means presented here are not conclusive):

- **Exit:** sponsors can use their power to fight corruption via ending their sponsorship contract with FIFA. Termination (vs. maintaining) the sponsorship can lead to an increase in brand attitude for a company with a good reputation (due to the perception of interest in the event's proper conduct; Messner and Reinhard, 2012). Thus, sponsorship termination can have positive consequences for the sponsor's brand attitude if consumers trust in this decision and feel that the (good character) brand has a sincere interest in the event's proper conduct.

- **Voice I – communications with and about FIFA:** sponsors might also communicate with and about FIFA in order to increase the pressure on FIFA. They raise their voice in an attempt to change the relationship partner's attitudes and behaviours (here the FIFA) and repair the relationship between the partners. This can take many forms: complaint, grievance and proposal for change (Hirschman, 1970). The success of this strategy depends on the distribution of power and FIFA's willingness and ability to change. If there is a positive change, the sponsor may profit. However, from the sponsor perspective, there is the risk that stakeholders perceive that the sponsor colludes with FIFA as the corrupt organisation; this may have negative effects, in particular when no change occurs.
- **Voice II – communications to avoid links with FIFA:** sponsors may develop their own communications strategy by associating the brand with positive aspects of the sport event only but neglecting FIFA. This can be seen when sponsors refuse to use FIFA logo in sponsorship-linked marketing campaigns (such as not stating that the brand is "official sponsor of the FIFA World Cup"). This strategy may help sponsors prevent the likelihood of a negative transfer of associations, but the strategy is unlikely to lead to a lasting improvement in the situation.
- **Distraction/neglect:** sponsors may leverage the sponsorship via marketing activities that are outside of the focus of the event. For example, they may implement philanthropic corporate social responsibility activities (CSR) in order to weaken (and possibly eliminate) negative spill over effects on brand attitude. There is empirical evidence that this strategy can be successful even when the CSR is governed by FIFA (Kulczycki and Koenigstorfer, 2016). However, the use of CSR as a counteracting mechanism provides a negative backlash when it is perceived as profit-driven (and not philanthropic), and it does not solve the initial problem of corruption; it can only weaken the negative consequences for the organisations involved, given CSR is perceived as philanthropy-driven.

Although we have presented some ideas of how corruption may be prevented or reduced, we note that there are no easy or conclusive answers. Nevertheless, with this chapter, we intend to inspire practitioners and researchers to take action and further investigate these topics.

## Conclusion

Corruption in sport is ubiquitous. Corruption has pervaded large parts of the sport system and mega-sport events often presents a showcase of corruption on various levels (Ionescu, 2015). For example, in many sport-governing bodies, the selection of event hosts, the allocation of rights and the nomination for positions are likely to be affected by corrupt practices – at least from the perspective of Western countries. Despite the means presented above to prevent and reduce corruption, any change inside sport organisations (such as FIFA) does not guarantee less corrupt behaviours of individuals (e.g., employees, representatives) in as much as incentives to behave in a corrupt manner may still exist in a revised or layered governance structure (Boudreaux et al., 2016). Also, if there is little supervision on the country or society level, corruption is likely to occur or even tolerated. With this chapter, we intend to contribute to the prevention of and fight against corruption by setting a theoretical framework and presenting empirical data based on host population surveys, thereby indicating the relevance of the topic from people's perspectives on mega-sport event sponsorship. We offer solutions from the perspective of different stakeholders (e.g., FIFA, sponsors) that can be implemented in practice in order to prevent and reduce corruption.

## Notes

1 We note that we focus on FIFA (i.e., the organisational level); arguments can also be made referring to Brazil (i.e., the society level) and to the FIFA representatives or other actors (i.e., the individual level).
2 FIFA revises its codes of conduct as part of a permanent reform process. The codes cover issues such as conflict of interest, bribery, fraud, discrimination and gambling. However, the accountability is still a concern for the global governance (FIFA, 2009; Pielke, 2013; see the previous discussion).

## References

Aguilera, R., and Vadera, A. (2008). The dark side of authority: Antecedents, mechanisms, and outcomes of organizational corruption. *Journal of Business Ethics*, *77*(4), 431–449.

Ashforth, B. E., Gioia, D. A., Robinson, S. L., and Trevino, L. K. (2008). Re-viewing organizational corruption. *Academy of Management Review*, *33*(3), 670–684.

Associated Press (2014). *High cost, corruption claims mar Brazil World Cup*. Retrieved from http://bigstory.ap.org/article/high-cost-corruption-claims-mar-brazil-world-cup.

Bandura, A. (1986). *Social foundations of thought and action*. Englewood Cliffs, NJ: Prentice Hall.

*BBC*. (2015). FIFA scandal 'a Disaster' for sponsors. Retrieved from www.bbc.com/news/business-32912445

Boon, S. D., and Holmes, J. G. (1999). Interpersonal risk and the evaluation of transgressions in close relationships. *Personal Relationships*, *6*(2), 151–168.

Boudreaux, C. J., Karahan, G., and Coats, R. M. (2016). Bend it like FIFA: Corruption on and off the pitch. *Managerial Finance*, *42*(9), 866–878.

Brunk, K. H. (2010). Exploring origins of ethical company/brand perceptions – a consumer perspective of corporate ethics. *Journal of Business Research*, *63*(3), 255–262.

Buraimo, B., Migali, G., and Simmons, R. (2015). An analysis of consumer response to corruption: Italy's Calciopoli scandal. *Oxford Bulletin of Economics and Statistics*, *78*(1), 22–41.

Business Insider (2014). *Visa becomes latest World Cup sponsor to castigate FIFA over corruption allegations*. Retrieved from www.businessinsider.com/visa-troubled-by-fifas-alleged-corruption-scandal-2014-11?IR=T.

Campbell, J. L., and Göritz, A. S. (2014). Culture corrupts! A qualitative study of organizational culture in corrupt organizations. *Journal of Business Ethics, 120*(3), 291–311.

CBS (2015). *World Cup 2014 construction Brazil marred by corruption, waste.* Retrieved from www.cbsnews.com/news/world-cup-2014-construction-in-brazil-marred-by-corruption-waste/.

Charron, N. (2016). Do corruption measures have a perception problem? Assessing the relationship between experiences and perceptions of corruption among citizens and experts. *European Political Science Review, 8*(1), 147–171.

De Waegeneer, E., Van De Sompele, J., and Willem, A. (2016). Ethical codes in sports organizations: Classification framework, content analysis, and the influence of content on code effectiveness. *Journal of Business Ethics, 136*(3), 1–12.

Ellen, P. S., Webb, D. J., and Mohr, L. A. (2006). Building corporate associations: Consumer attributions for corporate socially responsible programs. *Journal of the Academy of Marketing Science, 34*(2), 147–157.

Fortune (2015). *The pressure on FIFA sponsors is mounting.* Retrieved from http://fortune.com/2015/05/29/fifa-sponsors-pressure-corruption-scandal/

Fox, T. (2015). FIFA drops the ball: Corruption and FCPA charges. *Compliance Week, 12*, 8.

Freckleton, M., Wright, A., and Craigwell, R. (2012). Economic growth, foreign direct investment and corruption in developed and developing countries. *Journal of Economic Studies, 39*(6), 639–652.

Frey, J. H., and Eitzen, D. S. (1991). Sport and society. *Annual Review of Sociology, 17*(1), 503–522.

Geeraert, A., Alm, J., and Groll, M. (2014). Good governance in international sport organizations: An analysis of the 35 Olympic sport governing bodies. *International Journal of Sport Policy and Politics, 6*(3), 281–306.

Gioia, D. A. (1992). Pinto fires and personal ethics: A script analysis of missed opportunities. *Journal of Business Ethics, 11*(5), 379–389.

Gwinner, K. (1997). A model of image creation and image transfer in event sponsorship. *International Marketing Review, 14*(3), 145–158.

Gwinner, K., and Eaton, J. (1999). Building brand image through event sponsorship: The role of image transfer. *Journal of Advertising, 28*(4), 47–57.

Gwinner, K. P., Larson, B. V., and Swanson, S. R. (2009). Image transfer in corporate event sponsorship: Assessing the impact of team identification and event-sponsor fit. *International Journal of Management and Marketing Research, 2*(1), 1–15.

Hardoon, D., and Heinrich, F. (2013). *Global corruption barometer 2013.* Berlin: Transparency International.

Heider, F. (1958). *The psychology of interpersonal relations.* New York: Psychology Press.

Hirschmann, A. O. (1970). Exit, voice and loyalty: Responses to decline in firms, organizations, and states. Cambridge, MA: Harvard University Press.

Holmberg, S., Rothstein, B., and Nasiritousi, N. (2009). Quality of government: What you get. *Annual Review of Political Science, 12*(1), 135–161.

Hooker, J. (2009). Corruption from a cross-cultural perspective. *Cross Cultural Management: An International Journal, 16*(3), 251–267.

International Olympic Committee. (2015). *Olympic charter.* Lausanne: International Olympic Committee.

Ionescu, L. (2015). The economics of corruption in professional sport. *Economics, Management, and Financial Markets, 10*(2), 109–114.

Keller, K. L. (1993). Conceptualizing, measuring, managing customer-based brand equity. *Journal of Marketing, 57*(1), 1–22.

Kelley, H. H. (1973). The processes of causal attribution. *American Psychologist, 28*(2), 107–128.

Kulczycki, W., and Koenigstorfer, J. (2016). Why sponsors should worry about corruption as a mega sport event syndrome. *European Sport Management Quarterly, 16*(5), 545–574.

Kulczycki, W., Pfister, B., and Koenigstorfer, J. (2016). Partnering for corporate social responsibility in the context of Mega-Sport Event sponsorship. In *Proceedings of the 24th European Association for Sport Management Conference*, Warsaw.

Maennig, W. (2005). Corruption in international sports and sport management: Forms, tendencies, extent and countermeasures. *European Sport Management Quarterly, 5*(2), 187–225.

Mascarenhas, O. A. (1995). Exonerating unethical marketing executive behaviors: A diagnostic framework. *Journal of Marketing, 59*(2), 43–57.

Mauro, P. (1997). *Why worry about corruption?* (Vol. 6). Washington, DC: International Monetary Fund.

McFee, G. (1998). Are there philosophical issues with respect to sport (other than ethical ones)? In M. J. McNamee and S. J. Parry (Eds.), *Ethics and sport* (pp. 3–18). London: Routledge.

Messner, M., and Reinhard, M-A. (2012). Effects of strategic exiting from sponsorship after negative event publicity. *Psychology & Marketing, 29*(4), 240–256.

Metts, S. (1994). Relational transgressions. In W. R. Cupach and B. H. Spitzberg (Eds.), *The dark side of interpersonal communications* (pp. 217–239). Hillasdale, NY: Lawrence Erlbaum.

Milton-Smith, J. (2002). Ethics, the Olympics and the search for global values. *Journal of Business Ethics, 35*(2), 131–142.

Müller, M. (2015). The mega event syndrome: Why so much goes wrong in mega-events planning and what to do about it. *Journal of the American Planning Association, 81*(1), 6–17.

Myint, U. (2000). Corruption: Causes, consequences and cures. *Asia Pacific Development Journal, 7*(2), 33–58.

Pielke, R. (2013). How can FIFA be held accountable? *Sport Management Review, 16*(3), 255–267.

Pinto, J., Leana, C. R., and Pil, F. K. (2008). Corrupt organizations or organizations of corrupt individuals? Two types of organization-level corruption. *Academy of Management Review, 33*(3), 685–709.

Preuss, H. (2007). The conceptualization and measurement of mega sport event legacies. *Journal of Sport & Tourism, 12*(3–4), 207–227.

Rifon, N. J., Choi, S. M., Trimble, C. S., and Li, H. (2004). Congruence effects in sponsorship. *Journal of Advertising, 33*(1), 29–42.

Saha, S., Gounder, R., and Jen-Je, S. (2012). Is there a "Consensus" toward transparency international's corruption perception index? *International Journal of Business Studies, 20*(1), 1–9.

Sandholtz, W., and Koetzle, W. (2000). Accounting for corruption: Economic structure, democracy, and trade. *International Studies Quarterly, 44*(1), 31–50.

Schwartz, M. S. (2013). Developing and sustaining an ethical corporate culture: The core elements. *Business Horizons, 56*(1), 39–50.

Smith, A. C., and Stewart, B. (2010). The special features of sport: A critical revisit. *Sport Management Review, 13*(1), 1–13.

Smith, A. C., and Westerbeek, H. M. (2007). Sport as a vehicle for deploying corporate social responsibility. *Journal of Corporate Citizenship, 25*, 43–54.

Stead, W. E., Worrell, D. L., and Stead, J. G. (1990). An integrative model for understanding and managing ethical behaviour in business organizations. *Journal of Business Ethics, 9*(3), 233–242.

The Sydney Morning Herald (2015). *FIFA scandal: Coca-Cola, McDonald's say Sepp blatter must go now*. Retrieved from www.smh.com.au/business/media-and-marketing/fifa-scandal-cocacola-mcdonalds-say-sepp-blatter-must-go-now-20151002-gk0fas.html.

*The Washington Post*. (2015). U.S.: Indictments are just the start of FIFA scrutiny. Retrieved from www.washingtonpost.com/sports/us-indicts-world-soccer-officials-in-alleged-150-million-fifa-bribery-scandal/2015/05/27/4630ccaa-0477–11e5-bc72-f3e16bf50bb6_story.html.

Zahra, S. A., Priem, R. L., and Rasheed, A. A. (2005). The antecedents and consequences of top management fraud. *Journal of Management, 31*(6), 803–828.

# 11 The "legacy" of the Olympic Games for local communities

## A case study of the Nagano 1998 Winter Olympic Games

*Masayuki Takao*

Recently, the study of Sports Mega-Events (SMEs) and their long-term impact has gained more attention within the sociology of sport. SMEs have both positive as well as negative impacts, such as significant financial burden and environmental disruption, on host cities. However, few studies have shown the concrete long-term impacts of SMEs on specific areas or local communities, especially those who have hosted winter games (Hiller, 2006; Ishizaka and Matsubayashi, 2014; Spilling, 1998; Terret, 2008).

This might partially come from the usage of the term "Legacy" by the International Olympic Committee (IOC), organising committee and candidate cities. The IOC uses the term to avoid the public in the host city/nation blaming the IOC, to justify the use of public resources for the event infrastructure and to motivate other cities/nations to bid for future events (Gratton and Preuss, 2010). In addition, host cities become interested in capitalising on the events to attract inward investment or to encourage local businesses to use the Olympic Games in order to develop new business opportunities (Hiller, 2006). These examples show a tendency of the term to be filled with positive expectations and outcomes.

Since the Los Angeles Olympic Games in 1984, there has been a propensity to consider the term as a broad package of sporting, urban regenerative and environmental elements (Gold and Gold, 2011). However, there are tendencies to neglect the different points of view of evaluators involved in an event and limit the legacies to the sporting aspects (Hiller, 2003). Thus, it should be noted that the positive or negative impacts should be carefully assessed by focusing on specific contexts; that is, it is necessary to ascertain what kind of "legacies" (both positive and negative) have been bequeathed to the hosts in addition to sporting aspects and who and how have these legacies impacted

According to Gratton and Preuss (2010), *legacy* can be defined tentatively as "planned and unplanned, positive and negative, intangible and tangible structures created through a sport event that remains after the event" (p. 41). This is a general definition of legacy that is independent of qualitative examples or any IOC recommendations. In addition to this framework, it is also worth noting that evaluations regarding legacies might vary as time passes and depend on different communities and residents. Therefore, the following aspects should be examined: (1) above and beyond what were bequeathed objectively among hosts, (2) what and how local people expected from a SME before hosting it, (3) whether the expectations have been met or not and (4) how the legacies have worked after a set period.

Based on the preceding points, this chapter examines different aspects of SME "legacies" on a local community through the case study of the Hakuba village in Japan, one of the venues of the Nagano Olympic Games held in 1998. Although sporting facilities were constructed and the Hakuba transportation network was improved, they have not yet realised the positive impacts expected before the Games. On the other hand, some intangible and unplanned legacies, such as enlarged volunteerism and environmentalism, did materialize.

This case study is based on surveys, interviews conducted with local people, and secondary data from reports released by public offices or the National Census. The survey titled *An Investigation of the Impacts of the Nagano Olympics (IINO)* was conducted by the Society for Research on the Nagano Olympics, a collaborative research group, in 2011. We sent questionnaires to people living in communities that served as hosts to the Games: the city of Nagano; the towns of Karuizawa, Miyota, and Yamanouchi; and Hakuba village. The venues for the Nagano Olympics were spread over the east and west of the northern part of Nagano Prefecture.[1]

The questionnaire consisted of local people's opinions and memories about the Games and their evaluation of its impacts such as the construction of sporting facilities and transportation networks, local economy and politics over the Games. Data from interviews were used to understand some of the nuances from the survey data. Informants were mainly local people making their living in the tourism industry such as owners of hotels, officials of tourist associations and local officials in Hakuba.

## Winter sports in Japan and Hakuba

While Japan enjoyed a favourable economy called a "bubble economy" throughout the 1980s, skiing was rapidly achieving popularity among the masses. The domestic-demand expansion policies, introduced by the Japanese government to ease the trade friction with the United States, extensively helped Japanese financial institutions to invest in domestic winter resorts. It was in this context that the 1998 Winter Olympic Games bidding process began. Yoshiaki Tsutsumi, a powerful businessperson who had a strong relationship with the former IOC president, Juan Antonio Samaranch, is said to have played a crucial role in the nomination of Nagano as a formal Japanese candidate city and in making the bid successful (Taniguchi, 1992). Tsutsumi exerted enormous influence within the world of sports, and his land development company Kokudo ran development projects for skiing resorts across the country. This achievement propelled him to become the first-ever president of the Japan Olympic Committee (JOC) in 1989.

However, with visible precipitous price escalation, the Bank of Japan rapidly tightened the money supply. This led to the collapse of Japan's overheated stock and real estate markets and triggered the long recession called "The Lost Decade" throughout the 1990s. The Nikkei stock index slid to 22,984 yen (December 2, 1991) from its peak of 38,915 yen at the end of 1989, and the total assets of property in Japan slid to 1.2 quadrillion yen (end of 2006) from its peak of 2.4 quadrillion yen at the end of 1990 (Cabinet Office, 2014, p. 4). Accordingly, the popularity of and resort business of winter sports deteriorated rapidly.

Hakuba is a well-known mountainous village with skiing resorts including the Happo-One ski resort where the alpine skiing downhill, super giant slalom and combined slalom events were held during the Games. After World War II, Hakuba, which used to consist of cold villages, was modernised as a winter tourist spot with the support of a well-known railway company, the Tokyu Corporation. The population of the village rose from 6,572 in 1965 to 9,492 in 2000. The local people mostly made their living through tourism-related businesses. For example, small guest houses called *minshuku*, similar to bed-and-breakfast accommodations, comprised a large percentage of all lodging facilities in this area rather than large hotels.

During the bubble economy, Hakuba's reputation as a high-quality skiing region was heavily promoted. The number of annual tourists for skiing increased from 1.5 million in 1970 to 2.8 million in 1991, the highest number ever (Hakuba Village, 1994; Hakuba Village, 2003). However, this was a temporary boom. As noted previously, after the bursting of the bubble economy, the popularity of skiing declined rapidly. Consequently, the number of tourists for skiing in Hakuba slid to 1.8 million in 1997 as many skiing resorts ended up in financial crises (Hakuba Village, 2003).

## Legacies of the games

In the venues, besides sporting facilities, development projects for infrastructure were also implemented. The people in Hakuba hoped that the transportation network would be improved due to the Games attracting tourists and the updated sporting facilities attracting further international sporting events. In other words, the people expected the Games to be the ultimate (re-)boost for their tourism-oriented economy.[2]

According to the results from *IINO*, although 10.4% of people in Hakuba were opposed to hosting the Games beforehand, the proportion reached 27.8% after the Games. Opposition from residents of other cities included 14.9% of people in Nagano city, 23.7% of people in the town of Karuizawa, 16.9% of people in the town of Miyota, and 17.8% of people in the town of Yamanouchi. In other words, the people in Hakuba attached less positive value to the Games and its "legacies".

This next section highlights the actual impacts of "legacies." First, it focuses on the after-Games use of these athletic facilities. Second, it describes how the improved transportation network affected the tourism industry and the daily lives of people in Hakuba. Finally, as opposed to tangible legacies, intangible aspects of legacies are discussed.

## Tangible aspects of legacies and their ambivalent effects

### Sporting facilities

In Hakuba, the jumping facility and cross-country skiing stadia were constructed for the Olympic Games. The jumping facility consists of the Normal Hill and the Large Hill. In 1998, the total number of visitors to these facilities was 530,000. From 1999 to 2002, annual visitation averaged around 280,000 visitors a year

(Hakuba Village, 2003). However, by 2006, annual visitation was 109,039 (Hakuba Village, 2007).

While it cost 90 million yen to maintain the facility, the operating revenue amounted to just 42 million yen in 2007. Presumably, this issue partly originated from a conflict between the Nagano Prefectural Office and the Hakuba Municipal Office over the maintenance of the facility. The former, according to an officer from the Hakuba village office, expected the facility to be operated not as a tourist spot but as an athletic facility serving the objectives of athletes and sports associations. On the other hand, the village wanted to make the facility more profitable by constructing ancillary installations such as restaurants or amusement attractions to attract tourists. The prefectural office took possession of the Large Hill and finally rejected the plan advocated by the municipal office. Consequently, the facility became less attractive to all except ski jumpers who used it for training purposes.

The Normal Hill became an unofficial facility for events held under the regulation of the International Ski Federation (FIS) in the years after the Games. The village could not come up with the repair cost to fulfil the regulations. However, in 2015, the village decided to upgrade it to fulfil the current regulations with financial support from the sports promotion lottery "*toto*".

The number of users of the Cross-country skiing stadia, called Snow Harp, was 13,000 in 1999, increasing to 30,000 in 2004 and then falling back to 21,000 in 2007. The facility attracted some sporting events other than cross-country skiing such as cross-country running and mountain bike races. However, whereas the annual revenue of the facility was 1.1 million yen, the operational and maintenance cost was 16 million yen in 2007.

### Transportation network

Since the early 1980s, the construction of roads that could attract tourists using cars instead of the train system had become the top priority for the tourist industry in Hakuba. After the JOC selected Nagano as the nation's official host-city candidate for the XVIII Olympic Winter Games in 1986, road construction and widening projects were planned by the Nagano prefectural assembly. The projects which connect Hakuba to the city of Nagano and the southern part of Nagano Prefecture were launched after Nagano was officially selected as the host city of the Games by the IOC in 1991. In 1995, the amount of ordinary construction spending of Hakuba Village was 4.8 billion yen which accounted for half of the annual expenditure of the village (Hakuba Village, 1996).

Although people in Hakuba had expected that more tourists would be attracted by the improved transportation system, the amount of consumption related to tourism in Hakuba did not increase significantly after the Games. While tourists without lodging constantly visited Hakuba after the Games, the number of tourists that required lodging has actually decreased (See Figure.11.1). Ironically, the improved transportation system has increased day-trippers and visitors who travel around by car (Tourism Division of the Nagano Prefectural Government, annually printed).

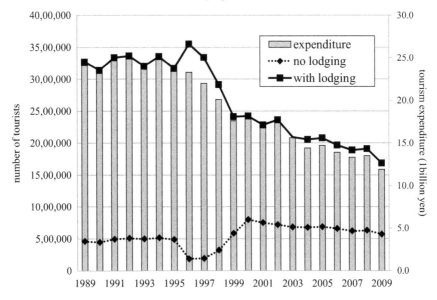

*Figure 11.1* Number of tourists with and without lodging and total amount spent

It should also be noted that the owners of accommodation facilities apparently invested in increasing the holding capacities in expectation of the increased number of tourists during and after the Games. Although the real investment cannot be identified, the total accommodation capacity in the village decreased from 34,313 in 1998 to 22,483 in 2008 (Hakuba Village, 2003, 2009). This might reflect the fact that many facilities decreased their capacity or went bankrupt. In addition, the collection rate of municipal tax in Hakuba used to be the lowest among the rural municipalities in Nagano Prefecture between 2000 and 2009. The main reason of this was apparently the delinquency rate on the fixed asset tax (Yamada, 2009). This presumably reflects the fact that many owners of accommodation facilities had great difficulty paying asset taxes after the Games despite the investment on their facilities.

## Intangible aspects of legacies

### *Rising foreign tourists*

The number of tourists visiting from foreign countries increased (see Table 11.1) (Tourism Commission of Hakuba Village and Hakuba Society of Commerce and Industry, 2006; Tourism Department of Nagano Prefectural Government, 2013). Although an increased number of tourists from East Asia had been expected by the local people before the Games, visits by tourists from Australia was far beyond the expectation of the people in Hakuba. As the tourism promotions and marketing that took advantage of the visibility of Nagano as an Olympic host by businesses took effect, Australian tourists started visiting Hakuba in significantly greater numbers (see Table 11.1).

*Table 11.1* Total number of foreign tourists and its breakdown

| 2005 | | 2012 | |
| --- | --- | --- | --- |
| South Korea | 15,710 | Australia | 20,057 |
| Australia | 5,558 | Taiwan | 5,929 |
| Hong-Kong | 2,899 | USA | 3,375 |
| Taiwan | 2,070 | Hong-Kong | 2,987 |
| Singapore, Malaysia | 1,740 | Singapore | 1,975 |
| others | 4,505 | others | 10,496 |
| Total | 32,482 | | 44,819 |

The expressway from Tokyo to Nagano and other newly constructed roads from Nagano city to Hakuba made accessibility from international airports such as *Haneda* or *Narita* possible. Furthermore, the newly constructed *Shinkansen* line (bullet train), which connects the Eastern region of Nagano Prefecture including Nagano city and Karuizawa town to Tokyo, also played an important role in facilitating access to Hakuba.

Many foreign tourists, especially Australia or European countries, stay in Hakuba for a longer period of time than Japanese tourists who generally spend between two and three days. In hopes of attracting them, the owners of lodging facilities built an organisation, called "Hakuba Tourism". Hakuba Tourism started collaborating with foreign tourist agencies and giving exhibitions abroad after the Games (Takao, 2014). Following these favourable changes, the village office launched initiatives designed to increase the number of inbound tourists by launching bus services that connect restaurants, souvenir stores and grocery stores to lodging facilities and that tour neighbouring tourism destinations.

However, it should also be noted that skiing tourists from foreign countries do not necessarily visit Hakuba in the hope of skiing Olympic courses. According to a New Zealand hotel owner, it is too dangerous to recommend general skiers to ski, but there are many tourists from other countries who aspire to visit Hakuba in the hope of enjoying back-country skiing and high-quality powder (K. Mollard, personal communication, 17 January 2014). Beside, another owner of a lodge who is from Scotland and have served as a headman of a ward in Hakuba, also says that "ski enthusiasts around the world have come to know much about how suitable natural slopes in Hakuba are for back-country skiing through the Internet" (D. Matt, personal communication, 19 March 2015).

### Volunteerism and improved consciousness of environmental priorities

In 1996, a test event of alpine skiing downhill in the lead-up to the Games was held at Happo-One. Subsequently, FIS required the Nagano Organising Committee (NAOC) to heighten the starting post in order to lengthen the run after several complaints by athletes. But the NAOC refused on the ground that the extended run suggested by FIS could pass through a part of Chūbu-Sangaku National Park and therefore be damaging to it. This led to a controversy between FIS and NAOK. Finally, a compromise plan that added an extra 87 metres (279 ft) to the run was accepted by both sides.

This dispute became a momentous catalyst that reminded local people of the importance of environmental conservation and directed their attention to sustainable development of natural environment in Hakuba. In fact, it led to a successful collaborative partnership between multiple actors such as people who worked on the environmental arrangement, environmental experts, the members of cableway companies and the staffs of Haoppo-One Tourism Association. As Hotta (2007) points out, this "by-product" bequeathed by the Games re-activated Happo-One as one of the "commons" that could be managed and protected by different actors in the community and instilled the importance of environmental protection into the local people.

The Games also generated a voluntary association named HAKUBA team'98. The association was composed of not only local people but also people from other prefectures who had opportunities to volunteer during the Games. For example, in 2001, a village ski club that manages competitive events and training camps in Hakuba and a village office suddenly cancelled a skiing combined event without consulting other supporting groups because of a manpower shortage. Afterwards, the volunteers, including members from HAKUBA team'98, decided to hold a track meet for athletes in place of the skiing combined event and implemented it under their own jurisdiction. Since then, the volunteers have successfully supported sports events in Hakuba such as the Special Olympics in 2005.

HAKUBA team'98 have also addressed forestry preservation activities such as tree thinning and clean-up activities of mountain trails based on their principle that the association aims to do and promote volunteer activities such as sport events and environmental preservation activities based in Hakuba. A lodge, which used to accommodate the volunteers during the Games, has served as a hub where they could take a meet and operate after the Games. An informant who runs a *minshuku* close to Snow Harp and works on natural environmental conservation says that "although members of the tourist association of our area have continued to work on vegetational recovery and reclamation after the Games, environmental organisations have never supported us so far" (K. Nakamura, personal communication, 12 March 2009). Therefore, it appears that the Nganao 1998 Games has resulted in Hakuba residents becoming committed to locally oriented environmental protection and volunteer activities after the Games.

## Discussion and conclusion

The purpose of this chapter was to examine the different aspects of "legacies" in a local community. It is obvious that the legacies bequeathed in Hakuba by the Games include both positive and negative aspects for the people of Hakuba. For example, tangible legacies such as athletic facilities and the transportation system, were planned and completed as scheduled. However, as this chapter pointed out, in many instances the initial expectations of local people have not been met. Tourists have visited Hakuba less than local people expected before the Games. In addition, some tangible legacies, such as the transportation network and use of sporting facilities built for the Games, have worked out differently from local people's initial expectations.

Athletic facilities are too huge and expensive to be maintained within the village finances. Thus, it appears that local politicians and staff of sports associations had planned the after-use of the facilities insufficiently. However, from another perspective, these development projects might have been expected to be seen as public expenditures, which increased employment among the local population during the recession. Although the Games provided an excuse to allocate public investment to the community, the facilities have provided fairly limited benefits to the local economy.

With the decreasing trend of tourist consumption in Hakuba, improved accessibility has increased day-trippers who spend less money, and thus, the economic benefits were much lower than local people's initial expectations. On the other hand, improvements in the surrounding transportation network have increased the number of foreign tourists, particularly from Australia, the US and some European countries resulting in a positive effect on the local economy.

Regarding intangible legacies, attention should be paid to the increased volunteerism and improved consciousness of environmental protection. In this regard, it is also noteworthy that the local people became not only environmentally conscious but also tried to use it as a means of ensuring other sport events were hosted successfully as shown by Hakuba team'98's successfully hosting of the Special Olympics in 2005. Although these facts seem to be supportive of Olympic Legacies by the IOC (Moragas, Kennett, and Puig, 2003), it can be said that the "legacy" could become sustainable through being shared by outside visitors such as the members of HAKUBA team'98.

As Matsubayashi and Ishizaka (2014) state, future studies on SMEs should introduce points of view that investigate for whom and how much legacies affect, or whether the impacts can alter with time. In addition, more attention should be paid to the differences in impacts among hosts and venues. The study of SMEs would be furthermore enhanced by the accumulation of data and historical knowledge/context about host cities and communities. This would prevent residents in potential candidate cities/nations from being swayed by rhetoric that overestimates future positive legacies and remind them of considering the bidding processes based on a more holistic evidence base.

## Notes

1 Although Miyota town did not have any venues for the Games, a collaborative researcher who investigated the network of curling players decided to send questionnaires to people in the town in order to investigate how the network in Karuizawa and Miyota happened before the Games and changed after that. The articles in Ishizaka and Matsubayashi (2014) are based on the results of the survey.
2 According to *IINO*, which questioned reminiscently, 72.2% of respondents supported hosting the Games beforehand (10.4% opposed and 12.5% were neutral), and the reasons given in favour of hosting the Games beforehand among people in Hakuba were the improvement of the transportation network (41.7%), the improvement of the region's reputation (38.9%), the revitalisation of local community (34.7%), a once-in-lifetime experience (29.9%), the exchanges with people from foreign countries and regions (13.2%), getting in tune with people around one (0.7%) and other reasons (3.5%).

# References

Cabinet Office. (2016). *Heisei 26 nendo Kokumin Keizai Keisan Kakuhou: Stokku Hen (The confirmed report of national accounts: A volume of Stock 2014)*. Retrieved from www. esri.cao.go.jp/jp/sna/data/data_list/kakuhou/files/h26/sankou/pdf/point20160115.pdf

Gold, J. R., and Gold, M. M. (2011). Introduction. In J. R. Gold and M. M. Gold (Eds.), *Olympic cities: City agendas, planning and the world's Games, 1896–2016* (2nd ed., pp. 1–13). New York: Routledge.

Gratton, C., and Preuss, H. (2010). Maximizing Olympic impacts by building up legacies. In J. A. Mangan and M. Dyreson (Eds.), *Olympic legacies: Intended and unintended: Political, cultural, economic and educational* (pp. 39–55). New York: Routledge.

Hakuba Village. (1994). Hakuba no Ayumi (The history of Hakuba).

Hakuba Village. (1996, September 15). *Kouhou-Hakuba (Newsletter of Hakuba Village)*, 240.

Hakuba Village. (2003). Sonseiyourantoukeisiryou 2003 (Profile of Hakuba Village in 2003).

Hakuba Village. (2007). Sonseiyourantoukeisiryou 2007 (Profile of Hakuba Village in 2007).

Hakuba Village. (2009). Sonseiyourantoukeisiryou 2009 (Profile of Hakuba Village in 2009).

Hiller, H. H. (2003). Toward a science of Olympic outcomes: The urban legacy. In M. D. Moragas, C. Kennett, and N. Puig (Eds.), *The legacy of the Olympic Games 1984–2000: International symposium Lausanne, 14th, 15th and 16th November 2002* (pp. 102–109). Lausanne: International Olympic Committee.

Hiller, H. H. (2006). Post-event outcomes and the post-modern tune: The Olympics and urban transformations. *European Sport Management Quarterly*, 6(4), 317–332. doi:10.1080/16184740601154458

Hotta, K. (2007). Nagano Orinpikku no Hukusanbutu: Kankouchi ni okeru Komondsu no Imi no Houhuka to Sizenhogo (A by-product of Nagano Olympics: Enrichment of meanings of commons in a tourist area and environmental protection). In K. Matshumura (Ed.), *Mega Supootsu-ibento no Syakaigaku: Shiroi Stajiamu no Mieru Huukei (Sociology of Mega Sports Events: A landscape with White stadium)* (pp. 180–203). Tokyo: Nansosha.

Ishizaka, Y., and Matsubayashi, H. (2014). Orinpikku no Isan no Syakaigaku: Nagano Orinpikku to sonogo no Juunen (Sociology of 'Olympic Legacies': After 10 years of Nagano Olympics). Tokyo: Seikyusha.

Matsubayashi, H., and Ishizaka, Y. (2014). Dare ni totteno isan nanoka? (For whom the legacies are?). In Y. Ishizaka and H. Matsubayashi (Eds.), *Orinpikku no Isan no Syakaigaku: Nagano Orinpikku to sonogo no Juunen (Sociology of 'Olympic Legacies': After 10 years of Nagano Olympics)* (pp. 190–198). Tokyo: Seikyusha.

Matt, D. (2015, March 19). Personal interview.

Mollard, K. (2014, January 17). Personal interview.

Moragas, M. D., Kennett, C., and Puig, N. (2003). The legacy of the Olympic Games 1984–2000: International symposium Lausanne, 14th, 15th and 16th November 2002. Lausanne: International Olympic Committee.

Nakamura, K. (2009, March 12). Personal interview.

Spilling, O. R. (1998). Beyond intermezzo? On the long-term industrial impacts of mega-events: The case of Lillehammer 1994. *Festival Management and Event Tourism*, 5(3), 101–122.

Takao, M. (2014). "Isan" wo meguru kattou to katsuyou: Hakuba mura no kankousangyou wo chuushinni (The utilization of 'Legacies' and conflicts over it: A case study about tourism industry in Hakuba Village). In Y. Ishizaka and H. Matsubayashi (Eds.), *Orinpikku no Isan no Syakaigaku: Nagano Orinpikku to sonogo no Juunen* (*Sociology of 'Olympic Legacies': After 10 years of Nagano Olympics*) (pp. 150–167). Tokyo: Seikyusha.

Taniguchi, G. (1992). Tsutsumi Yoshiaki to Orinpikku (Yoshiaki Tsutsumi and the Olympic Games). Tokyo: San-IchiShobo.

Terret, T. (2010). The Albertville Winter Olympics: Unexpected legacies – failed expectations for regional economic development. In J. A. Mangan and M. Dyreson (Eds.), *Olympic legacies: Intended and unintended: Political, cultural, economic and educational* (pp. 20–38). New York: Routledge.

Tourism Department of Nagano Prefectural Government. (2013). Heisei 24 nen Gaikokujinnobeshukuhakushasuuchousakekka (*Research report on the total number of foreign tourists with lodging in 2012*).

Tourism Department of Nagano Prefectural Government. *Kankouchiriyoushatoukeichousakekka (Research report on statistical data of tourists)*, printed annually.

Tourism Commission of Hakuba Village and Hakuba Society of Commerce and Industry. (2006). Heisei 17 nenbun Hakubamuragaikokujinkankoukyakushukuhakujisseki (Research report on the number of foreign tourist with lodging in Hakuba, 2005).

Yamada, A. (2009, December 3). Hakuba mura, chouzeiristu 61.3% (Only 61.3% of people in Hakuba paid municipal taxes). *Asahi Shimbun*, p. 34.

# 12 "Lead Up and Legacy"

## A case study of the 2015 Rugby World Cup

*Gareth Jones, Mike Edwards and Nick Passenger*

Although still a relatively new mega-event, the Rugby World Cup (RWC) has grown substantially since its inception. The quadrennial event was first hosted by Australia and New Zealand in 1987, attracting 604,500 spectators and an average attendance of just over 20,000 per match. Just eight years later, attendance figures for the 1995 RWC in South Africa were twice as large and included a much wider global audience. The 1995 RWC also garnered worldwide attention for its social and political significance, as South African officials attempted to unite the country in the wake of their first post-apartheid democratic election through the "one team, one country" moniker (Steenveld and Strelitz, 1998). While the 1995 event is often remembered for the symbolic moments that epitomised this movement, such as Nelson Mandela handing the Web Ellis Cup to Springboks captain François Pienaar, it also represented a key commercial turning point for both the RWC and the sport of rugby union. The financial windfall from gate receipts, media, and sponsorship revenue prompted the formation of the first professional rugby union leagues the very same year (Ryan, 2008), and led to dramatic increases in the size and scale of the RWC. This meteoric rise has continued into the 21st century, with the RWC now recognised as the second most attended single sporting mega-event worldwide, behind only the FIFA World Cup (Arnold and Grice, 2014).

Similar to other mega-sport events, the prospect of enduring legacies has become one of the primary motivators for cities and nations to host the RWC (Preuss, 2007). One dimension that has received considerable attention in recent years is the legacy of sport participation (Frawley and Cush, 2011). The RWC is organised by Rugby World Cup Limited, which operates as a branch of World Rugby, the international governing and law-making body for rugby union. World Rugby has invested significant resources in growing the game worldwide, and mega-sport events such as the RWC are seen as an integral part of this process. This is evident in the recent decision to award the 2019 RWC to Japan, the first time a historically "Tier Two" rugby nation, in terms of participation and competitiveness, has been selected to host the event. Following the announcement that Japan would host the 2019 event, officials from both World Rugby and the Japanese Rugby Football Union (JRFU) highlighted how the event would be used to grow the sport in Japan and across Asia.

The connection between mega-sport events and sport participation is often substantiated through what is known as the "trickle-down," or "demonstration," effect, in which the fervour and excitement created by an event is thought to inspire individuals to participate in sport at the grass-roots level (Hindson, Gidlow, and Peebles, 1994). This process is posited to be both direct, whereby individuals are inspired to play sport, and indirect, whereby improvements to the hosts' sport infrastructure and organisation support increase participation at the community level (Veal, Toohey, and Frawley, 2012). Despite the logic of this relationship, empirical studies have revealed inconsistent results in terms of sport participation legacies (Weed et al., 2015). Even host cities and regions that have experienced increases in sport participation have typically had difficulty sustaining them in the years following an event (Frawley and Cush, 2011). Furthermore, while the demonstration effect has been shown to motivate the participation of those already involved in sport, it has not been linked with motivating new sport participants (Taks, Green, Misener, and Chalip, 2014).

Unsurprisingly, studies examining the legacy of the RWC have produced similarly inconclusive findings related to rugby participation in the host country. Junior and senior rugby participation increased immediately after the 2003 RWC in Australia but returned to pre-event levels within the next three years (Frawley and Cush, 2011). Participation increases were also reported following the 2007 RWC in France, yet very little empirical evidence is available to substantiate these claims. In 2011, the New Zealand Rugby Union reported an initial surge in rugby participation following the event, yet these figures fell below pre-event levels within two years. Similar to the broader research on mega-event legacies, most of these studies have focused almost exclusively on the participation outcomes associated with each event (Chalip, 2006 and Chapter 2, in this volume). In addition, direct aspects of participation legacies have received far more attention from organisers and scholars than indirect aspects, such as investments in sport infrastructure and organisation (Chalip, 2006). This makes the RWC an especially intriguing mega-event to study, since it has heretofore been held in nations with substantial existing rugby infrastructure. Thus, investment in indirect aspects of legacies, such as sport infrastructure development, have historically been even less connected to the RWC compared to other mega-events. Indeed, while participation legacies have been a common narrative of planning organisations and officials associated with the RWC, specific strategies and objectives for increasing and sustaining participation have been less concrete. As a result, there is a dearth of information on how participation legacies, whether positive or negative, are linked to specific strategies, policies, and programs related to the RWC.

To capitalise more effectively on mega-events, process-based approaches to planning, monitoring, and evaluation have been recommended to ensure participation legacies are strategically integrated into the planning and organisation of an event (O'Brien and Chalip, 2007). This approach is often referred to as leveraging (Chalip, 2006; Chapter 2, in this volume) and has been applied to understand how local and regional businesses, governments, and organisations utilise mega-sport events to achieve desired legacies (Chalip, 2014). From this perspective, the 2015 RWC in England represents one of the most ambitious and formalised plans to leverage a mega-sport event to increase sport participation. Three years prior to the event the Rugby Football Union (RFU), England's national governing body, launched a *Lead Up & Legacy Strategy* that included significant invest-ments in rugby infrastructure that were supported by action plans and measurable benchmarks for evaluation. This represents the most well-developed plan by a host nation or region to increase participation through the RWC and is one of the most comprehensive leveraging plans associated with any mega-sport event. This chapter contributes to *Legacies of Mega-Events: Fact or Fairy Tales* by providing a deeper understanding of how mega-sport events may be leveraged to enhance the legacy of sport participation. The case study outlines key elements of the 2015 RWC leveraging strategy, provides an overview of the impacts observed thus far, and discusses important elements to inform future events.

## The leveraging plan

The 2015 RWC was presented as one of nine events that made up the UK's "decade of sport" (Grix, 2012). The event was expected to follow from the per-ceived success of the 2012 Summer Olympics and Paralympics in London and the 2014 Commonwealth Games in Glasgow to help position Britain as a global sport leader and contribute to a lasting sport legacy for the country. Thus, while some host cities for previous RWCs developed independent economic legacy plans (e.g., Auckland in 2011), the 2015 RWC was the first to create a comprehensive national legacy programme. With support from England Rugby 2015, the agency tasked with organising and delivering the event, and Rugby World Cup Limited, who provided oversight and approval of all activities associated with the 2015 RWC, the *Lead Up & Legacy Strategy* plan was announced and implemented by the RFU.

Leading into the planning for the 2015 RWC, the RFU was aware of declining rugby union participation in England. According to Sport England, rugby union participation declined 29% between 2008 and 2013, dropping from seventh to tenth in the ranking of participation sports in the country (Sport England, 2016). Therefore, the *Lead Up & Legacy Strategy* aimed to reverse this trend by leaving a meaningful legacy that would attract new rugby participants and enhance the enjoyment of existing players.

The strategy comprised seven "pillars" that invested resources in two primary areas: 1) Building Capacity and 2) Increasing Participation. The two-tiered strat-egy was intended to utilise local rugby clubs as catalysts to increase participation at the grassroots level, while also providing them with the resources and technical assistance necessary to successfully leverage the 2015 RWC to achieve their own goals. While national initiatives were developed and implemented by the RFUs Legacy Oversight Group and RFU staff, a significant part of the RFUs strategy was regional activation. Understanding the need for local champions to ensure the successful adoption of programmes, the RFU established Regional Activation and Legacy Groups to develop initiatives independently and complement national programmes. Regional and national programmes often intersected and worked cooperatively on initiatives designed to build capacity and increase participation. The following provides a description of each leveraging priority area and their associated pillars.

## Building capacity

Capacity building represents a process-based approach to sport development that focuses on building the critical antecedents to sport participation. For the 2015 RWC, this included investments in physical and financial resources and developing the skills and knowledge of local stakeholders to deliver rugby opportunities more effectively. Building capacity was critical to the RFUs plan to promote and sustain rugby participation, as it equipped stakeholders with the tools necessary to plan, implement, and manage programs and services long after the 2015 RWC ended.

### Better facilities

The RFUs increased financial investment in local rugby facilities was an enhancement of the "National Facilities Strategy for Rugby Union" that was first introduced in 2012. This strategy was developed in response to a 2006 report commissioned by the RFU that indicated grass-roots rugby clubs lacked sufficient financial resources to upgrade or even maintain facilities. As part of the strategy, the RFU granted £12 million to Level 4 clubs and below (mainly through interest free loans of up to £100,000) and £5 million to over 1,000 projects that stimulated an additional £60 million worth of investment in grass-roots rugby facilities.

The *Lead Up & Legacy Strategy* for the 2015 RWC proposed an additional investment of £10 million to stimulate £25 million worth of facility improvement across 500 clubs. With a key goal to create modern environments at local rugby clubs, these enhancements included drainage and pitch improvements, the addition of floodlights, and enhancements to clubhouses and social spaces. The latter was a departure from previous facility improvement strategies introduced by the RFU, which focused primarily on playing surfaces, and was designed specifically to help clubs leverage social activities around the 2015 RWC (Rowe, 2015). The RFU also launched a campaign aimed at mobilising local volunteers to help make these facility improvements. Volunteers helped clean, paint, and update club environments, attended maintenance workshops, and used social media to publicise local enhancement programmes.

### Investing in people

Investing in people to create more coaches, players, officials, and volunteers leading up to and after the World Cup was an integral part of the *Lead Up & Legacy Strategy*. The RFU invested over £1 million in subsidies for initial training courses to support the addition of more than 6,500 newly qualified referees and coaches. Investments were also made to enhance the curriculum of higher level training courses for over 5,000 existing coaches as well. Senior clubs worked in conjunction with junior clubs to deliver these courses, which were fully funded by the RFU. For example, through funding from the RFU, Nottinghamshire, Lincolnshire, and Derbyshire Rugby Union (NLDRFU) set up a higher-level coaching course that was delivered by Nottingham RFC, a Championship-level team, while entry-level courses were delivered by clubs in lower leagues such as Kesteven RFC, Matlock RFC, and Mellish RFC.

In addition to coaches and referees, the *Investing in People* strategy also focused on bringing in an additional 5,000 volunteers (Kent RFU, 2014). Volunteers were recruited locally by each of the RFUs area delivery teams and supported by media campaigns such as "Keep Your Boots On," which encouraged retiring players to stay engaged with their local rugby clubs by fulfilling non-playing roles. An emphasis was also placed on developing a new generation of volunteers by recruiting 1,000 junior volunteers aged 16–20 years old. These junior volunteers were known as Young Rugby Ambassadors (YRAs) and were supported by adult mentors. YRAs were given mentorship in organising and planning, and networked with other YRAs across the country. YRA initiatives included planning children's rugby tournaments, engaging with local schools and councils, social media promotion, and coordinating club social events.

### More schools

Focus was also placed on increasing rugby programmes within schools. The Minister of State for Children and Families, Edward Timpson, acknowledged the role rugby union could play in instilling skills such as determination, discipline, and confidence in pupils and indicated the sport would be part of building a world-class education system in modern Britain (RFU, 2013). From this foundation, the *All Schools* scheme was launched in 2012 with the target of adding programmes to 750 non-rugby playing schools by 2019 (RFU, 2013). By the 2015 World Cup, it was predicted that over 400 schools would have already reach this target (RFU, 2013), providing access to rugby programmes for more than 200,000 children. The *All Schools* initiative also provided equipment and training for teachers to become qualified in coaching and officiating. As acknowledged by Steve Grainger, the RFU's rugby development director, this was integral to the RFUs overall legacy strategy, as recent cuts in extra-curricular sport had stunted the progression of rugby participants and coaches from schools to local clubs.

Due to the common perception that rugby participants typically come from privately educated backgrounds, the *All Schools* strategy focused predominantly on state schools. This represented an attempt to reach pupils who had historically received less exposure to the sport, and also addressed perceptions that socio-economic barriers to rugby participation had increased at the elite level. Indeed, only 10 of the 31 players on the English national team competing at the 2015 RWC came from the state educational system, compared to 18 in England's 2003 RWC-winning squad. In addition to targeting state schools, complimentary programmes (e.g., "On the Front Foot" and "Urban Rugby") were used to specifically target players from traditionally unreached markets for rugby union participation, such as women and girls, ethnic minorities, and urban children.

## Increasing participation

In conjunction with building local capacity to promote and sustain rugby participation, the RFU implemented intentional strategies aimed at directly increasing rugby participation nationally. The introduction of resources such as www.FindRugby.com aimed to increase rugby participation during the World Cup through playing, officiating, coaching and even volunteering with local clubs. With the website linking over 2,000 clubs across the nation, the program helped establish connections between administrators and local rugby clubs that may be leveraged towards future initiatives. The four pillars associated with increasing participation were returning players, touch rugby, other nations, and cultural engagement.

### Returning players

One of the RFUs key strategies to increase participation was to invest £500,000 in development programmes aimed at attracting 16- to 24-year-old former rugby players back to the game. The "Make Contact" program was a key element of this process since it focused on participant retention, which had been highlighted as a significant issue for many local rugby clubs. For example, Oxfordshire RFU stated that the transitional period between under-16/17 age groups and senior rugby was a critical point of attrition among their clubs. This high rate of drop-out was attributed to the commitments required to participate on teams, training requirements, and numbers issues (e.g., not having enough other local players in an age group to field teams). The "Make Contact" program offered workshops and resources to help clubs market rugby union to this specific age group and provided additional resources to help them retain current players reaching the typical age of attrition. Social media promotions, new touch rugby programs, and more recreational "turn-up" programs that required no formal training sessions were all implemented as part of this plan.

### Touch rugby

The RFU strategically positioned touch rugby (a less physical version of the game with no tackling) as an important entry point for new participants and to promote adult physical activity. The aim of the touch rugby programme was to alleviate barriers to participation often associated with the traditional forms of competitive rugby union. In addition, touch rugby was positioned as a more accessible version of the sport that could be enjoyed by a broader spectrum of the population.

To this end, over 200 "touch centres" were established at clubs, colleges, and universities to develop new leagues and programmes with the goal of engaging over 15,000 people in the sport. As part of this strategy, the RFU also introduced a Touch Ambassador Programme, which recruited local leaders to tap into social networks and promote touch rugby to young adults as a fun fitness and social activity. The project was also used by local clubs to leverage additional funds through the Sport England "Sportivate" programme, which was part of a £56 million National Lottery investment that helped inactive 14- to 25-year-olds find a sport that interested them (Sport England, 2015).

### Other nations

Interestingly, a key component of the RFUs legacy strategy was to support the development of rugby in 17 other countries across Europe. This component included the "Unity Project," which established links between county rugby unions in England and national rugby unions in developing rugby countries. These relationships were intended to provide a more direct association with developing nations, and allowed English counties to share knowledge and provide technical assistance in growing the game abroad. For example, the Cheshire and Lancashire Rugby Unions were matched with Portugal, one of the first countries to implement programmes associated with RWC 2015. Additionally, 24 coaches from Serbia earned Level 2 coaching awards in programmes delivered by Buckinghamshire and Oxford University, whilst the North Midlands and Staffordshire RFU focused on developing referees in the Czech Republic. UK Sport was utilised as a partner in this process, which allowed it to build on its own strategy of promoting global sport participation as part of the London 2012 Olympic legacy strategy (Rowe, 2014). While this component did not directly focus on sport participation goals for England, it aligned with the International Rugby Board's (IRB) focus on promoting more global participation in the game, and provided global rugby connections that helped attract more diverse participants within the UK.

### Cultural engagement

Despite the fact that rugby union has been a professional sport since 1996, the sport is often promoted for the values developed over 100 years of institutional amateurism, and often elitism (O'Brien and Slack, 1999). In light of the idealised characteristics that have been attributed to the sport, the RFU implemented a campaign to promote the values of rugby union into classroom curricula. In partnership with the Youth Sport Trust and England Rugby 2015, the RFU developed a website with resources designed to incorporate rugby in the classroom and espouse the stated values of "teamwork, respect, enjoyment, discipline, and sportsmanship." This initiative also included events and assemblies in primary and secondary schools designed to raise awareness of and excitement about RWC 2015. The pilot event took place at Wilmslow High School in Cheshire, who also took part in the launching the YRA programme.

## The legacy impact

### Building capacity

As part of the 2015 RWC legacy strategy, the RFU invested significant tangible resources into building grassroots rugby capacity. According to a 2015 Economic Impact Report, £7.5 million was invested into 340 club projects since 2012, which resulted in £27.5 million worth of improvements for local rugby facilities. As part of this initiative, the RFU funded the installation of 60 artificial pitches to improve the accessibility of rugby facilities in all weather conditions. Another component of capacity building was a recycling programme that provided match supplies and equipment (including lockers, chairs, fencing, balls, and unused medical equipment) to nearly 500 community clubs in England and Wales (Chaplin, 2016).

The RFU also reported record attendances of over 35,000 in rugby-related courses in 2013 designed to develop new and better coaches and referees. Kent Rugby Union, for example, reported a 34% increase in attendance at coaching courses offered by clubs through subsidies from the RFU (Kent RFU, 2014). Through the RFUs *All Schools* initiative, over 400 schools took up rugby and London Sport recognised the program for its work in the city with 53 new schools now playing rugby, and the RFU for working with the Darussalem Mosque to promote the game among London's Islamic community (England Rugby, 2016).

*Increasing participation*

The primary measure of impact is participation rates in rugby. The latest data from Sport England estimate that rugby participation has increased nearly 27% since 2013. However, participation rates are still 10% below 2008 figures. Additionally, rugby club membership in England is at its highest since 2009. Among 14- to 25-year-olds (a key demographic target for the RFU), participation increased 10% between 2013 and 2016. Sport England reports sport participation among this demographic in all other sports declined 3% in the same period. What is not known is whether these increases of rugby participants are new sport participants or participants that are coming to rugby union from other sports. Additionally, it should be noted that both netball and cricket added more participants in England than did rugby union during the period.

## Discussion

The 2015 RWC provided an intriguing case study to analyse one of the most ambitious leveraging strategies to increase grassroots participation through host- ing a mega-sport event. The *Lead Up & Legacy Strategy* represents a sophis- ticated approach that goes beyond the "trickle-down" assumptions associated with many mega-sport events and presents a more concrete plan for long-term growth. The plan itself was also accompanied by formal policies and procedures that guided activation strategies, as well as a set of measurable benchmarks, which informed their implementation. This focus on the process of leveraging, rather than just the outcomes, is believed to induce more substantial and endur- ing legacies (Chalip, 2004).

Initial participation figures suggest the 2015 RWC had a positive impact on rugby union participation in England, yet it is still too early to assess the partici- pation legacy of the event. Although encouraging, short-term impacts must not be confused with longer-term legacies, which represent the enduring influence of an event on a host city or region (Preuss, 2007). Sharp participation increases in the year(s) following a mega-sport event are common, and were observed in the preceding three RWCs as well. Yet the sustainability and growth of these trends will ultimately determine the legacy of the 2015 RWC, as participation rates may increase, stagnate or decrease in the coming years. Nevertheless, investments in both physical and human capital, as well as the prioritisation of local rugby clubs in regional activation strategies, have provided the RFU with the infrastructure to support growing participation in rugby union. When coupled with the liminality and communitas created by the event, this leveraging strategy appears poised to generate a positive participation legacy from the 2015 RWC.

However, the importance of fusing direct and indirect leveraging highlights an important caveat that must be considered with this particular event. Because of their competitiveness and status as the host nation, the English national team were considered one of the favourites to win the 2015 RWC. Yet the team drastically underperformed and failed to advance from the group stages, leaving the host nation out of the lucrative knock-out stages. The financial impact of this on-field shortcoming was estimated to cost the British economy £4 billion in lost revenue from hospitality and investment (Armstrong, 2015) and even negatively affected the UK stock market (Joyner, 2015). In addition to these economic repercussions, the early exit of the English team may have also influenced the participation legacy of the 2015 RWC. While the direct "inspirational" effect of elite athletes and/ or teams on grassroots participation is generally regarded as tenuous, the impact on participant engagement with indirect aspects of leveraging must also be considered. Similar to how athlete and/or team performances have been linked with sport consumer intentions (Funk, Beaton, and Alexandris, 2012), the early exit of the English national team may have also influenced the decision of new or existing participants to engage with planned social activities, utilise renovated club facilities, or attend voluntary programs. These indirect leveraging activities were designed to capitalise on the liminality created by the 2015 RWC, yet the disappointing performance of the English team may have hindered these feelings from taking root. Moreover, the magnitude of this effect may have been exacerbated by the extremely high expectations placed on the English team prior to the event, which were not met.

This leads to several intriguing considerations related to direct and indirect aspects of leveraging. In the 2003 (Australia), 2007 (France), and 2011 (New Zealand) RWCs, the host nation advanced to at least the semi-final round of the tournament. The on-field success of these teams contributed to enthusiastic feelings towards rugby within the host country, yet none of these events were accompanied by a comprehensive leveraging plan that invested in sport development initiatives. While each country experienced an initial surge in participation in the year(s) following the event, none was able to sustain this growth long-term. Conversely, although the English team fell short of on-field performance expectations in 2015, the *Lead Up & Legacy Strategy* provided substantial investments in the infrastructure and organisation of rugby union in England. Similar to previous RWCs, initial reports indicate participation in rugby union has increased, yet ongoing research is needed to determine the participation legacy of the 2015 RWC. These studies will help establish stronger associations between leveraging strategies and legacy goals, and identify the strengths and challenges associated with implementation. For example, certain clubs may have lacked the organisational capacity to successfully implement initiatives or have been too far from host cities to capitalise on the fervour and excitement created by matches. In addition, the multifaceted approach of the *Lead Up and Legacy Strategy* may have overwhelmed smaller clubs, who may have been more successful focusing on fewer legacy goals (i.e., pitch improvements).

These will be important questions to consider as the IRB, World Rugby, and JRFU move toward the 2019 RWC in Japan. Despite their encouraging performance at the 2015 RWC, which included a pool stage upset of "Tier One" nation South Africa, the Japanese team will not have the same on-field expectations as the 2015 English team. Thus, the liminality generated by the event may be less tied to the success of the Japanese team and more dependent on the overall quality and production of matches and ancillary events. In addition, the JRFU has announced plans to implement a comprehensive leveraging strategy, and already adopted World Rugby's "Get Into Rugby" campaign to encourage school children to participate in rugby before the 2019 RWC begins. Considering this is the first time the event will be hosted by a nation without significant rugby infrastructure, the 2019 RWC provides yet another intriguing context to study the direct and indirect aspects of leveraging. One key area for researchers will be disentangling how the performance expectations and on-field success of host nations may influence the liminality generated by the RWC. In addition, the influence of indirect aspects of leveraging, such as infrastructural and organisational investments, also warrant further inquiry. As this research unfolds it will shed further light on how the RWC, and other similar mega-sport events, may be effectively leverage to create lasting participation legacies.

## References

Armstrong, J. (2015, October). England's Rugby World Cup disaster could cost £3.5 billion in lost hospitality and investment. *Mirror Online*. Retrieved August 2, 2016, from www.mirror.co.uk/news/uk-news/englands-rugby-world-cup-disaster-6572364.

Arnold, P., and Grice, M. (2014). *The economic impact of the Rugby World Cup 2015*. London: Ernst & Young LLP.

Chalip, L. (2004). Beyond impact: A general model for sport event leverage. In B. Ritchie and D. Adair (Eds.), *Sport tourism: Interrelationships, impacts and issues* (pp. 226–252). Clevedon: Channelview Publications.

Chalip, L. (2006). Towards social leverage of sport events. *Journal of Sport and Tourism*, *11*, 109–127.

Chalip, L. (2014). From legacy to leverage. In J. Grix (Ed.), *Leveraging legacies from sports mega-events: Concepts and cases* (pp. 2–12). New York: Palgrave Macmillan.

Chaplin, R. (2016, February). Rooting for rugby: Grassroots rugby gaining from World Cup legacy plan despite England's poor performance. *SW Londoner*. Retrieved July 19, from www.swlondoner.co.uk/rooting-rugby-grass-roots-rugby-gaining-world-cup-legacy-plan-despite-englands-poor-performance/.

England Rugby. (2016, January). *RWC legacy programme is rewarded*. Retrieved August 4, from www.englandrugby.com/news/rwc-legacy-programme-rewarded/#.

Frawley, S., and Cush, A. (2011). Major sport events and participation legacy: The case of the 2003 Rugby World Cup. *Managing Leisure*, *16*, 65–76.

Funk, D. C., Beaton, A., and Alexandris, K. (2012). Sport consumer motivation: Autonomy and control orientations that regulate fan behaviours. *Sport Management Review*, *15*, 355–367.

Grix, J. (2012.) The politics of sports mega-events. *Political Insight*, *3*, 4–7.

Hindson, A., Gidlow, B., and Peebles, C. (1994). The 'trickle-down' effect of top-level sport: Myth or reality? A case-study of the Olympics. *Australian Journal of Leisure and Recreation*, *4*, 16–24.

Joyner, A. (2015, October). Rugby World Cup 2015: Early England exit could cost country £3bn. *International Business Times*. Retrieved August 2, 2016, from www.ibtimes.co.uk/rugby-world-cup-2015-early-england-exit-could-cost-country-3bn-1522742.

Kent RFU. (2014, February). *Could you be a county champion?* In Touch: Kent County RFU Newsletter. Retrieved August 4, from http://jswaite.co.uk/kent-rugby.org/intouch/0214/InTouch_0214.pdf.

O'Brien, D., and Chalip, L. (2007). Executive training exercise in sport event leverage. *International Journal of Culture, Tourism and Hospitality Research, 1*(4), 296–304.

O'Brien, D., and Slack, T. (1999). Deinstitutionalising the amateur ethic: An empirical examination of change in a rugby union football club. *Sport Management Review, 2*(1), 24–42.

Preuss, H. (2007). The conceptualization and measurement of mega sport event legacies. *Journal of Sport & Tourism, 12*(3–4), 207–227.

Rowe, P. (2014, January). *European rugby nations come together in Unity Project* [Press Release]. London: Rugby Football Union. Retrieved August 4, from https://gloucester-shirerfu.co.uk/FCKfiles/File/European_rugby_nations_come_together_in_Unity_Project.pdf.

Rowe, P. (2015, October). Paignton rugby club pure gold. *Touchline: The Official Newspaper of the RFU, 183,* 2.

Rugby Football Union (RFU). (2013, September). *One year to go: 2015 & beyond.* Retrieved June 24, from www.englandrugby.com/mm/Document/General/General/01/30/62/55/OneYearToGoreport_Neutral.pdf.

Ryan, G. (2008). The changing face of rugby: The union game and professionalism since 1995. Newcastle: Cambridge Scholars Publishing.

Sport England. (2015). *Sportivate.* Retrieved July 31, from http:// www.sportengland.org/our-work/children-and-young-people/sportivate/

Sport England. (2016). *Active people survey, 2008–2016* (10th ed.). UK Data Service. Retrieved August 8, from www.sportengland.org/research/who-plays-sport/by-sport/

Steenveld, L., and Strelitz, L. (1998). The 1995 Rugby World Cup and the politics of nation-building in South Africa. *Media, Culture & Society, 20*(4), 609–629.

Taks, M., Green, B. C., Misener, L., and Chalip, L. (2014). Evaluating sport development outcomes: The case of a medium-sized international sport event. *European Sport Management Quarterly, 14*(3), 213–237.

Veal, A. J., Toohey, K., and Frawley, S. (2012). The sport participation legacy of the Sydney 2000 Olympic Games and other international sporting events hosted in Australia. *Journal of Policy Research in Tourism, Leisure and Events, 4*(2), 155–184.

Weed, M., Coren, E., Fiore, J., Wellard, I., Chatziefstathiou, D., Mansfield, L., and Dowse, S. (2015). The Olympic Games and raising sport participation: A systematic review of evidence and an interrogation of policy for a demonstration effect. *European Sport Management Quarterly, 15*(2), 195–226.

# 13 The legacy of the London 2012 Olympic Games

## A case study of grass-roots sport clubs and the sport participation legacy

*Guy Thomas, Ian Brittain and Andrew Jones*

A key potential benefit of hosting mega-events such as the Olympic Games that has increasingly attracted nations and cities to bid to host them is the potential to inspire and engage people, particularly young people, in sport and physical activity (Girginov, 2013; Grix, 2013; Sousa-Mast, Reis, Gurgel, and Duarte, 2013). Reasons for this range from tackling obesity and other health issues, thus reducing the cost of health service delivery, and to encouraging social cohesion. This research is based upon PhD data collected by the first author that aimed to determine what factors impact on the creation of a sustainable London 2012 Olympic Games grass-roots sport participation legacy from the perspective of voluntary sport clubs. In the build-up to the London 2012 Olympic Games, a House of Commons Culture, Media and Sport Committee (2007) report stated that "[n]o host country has yet been able to demonstrate a direct benefit from the Olympic Games in the form of a lasting increase in participation" (DCMS, 2007, p. 37). It would, therefore, appear that the idea of a participation legacy is actually more of a fairy tale than a fact. However, evidence from this research shows that the ability to derive a participation legacy is an extremely complicated process that can be impacted, positively or negatively, by a multitude of issues, some of which may be completely unrelated to the mega-event itself and, therefore, completely outside of the control of the organising committee. Despite the claims made by the UK government and the bid committee for the London 2012 Games regarding a participation legacy that would 'Inspire a Generation', three years later Gibson (2015) claimed that there is no sports participation legacy, all claims by government to the contrary are based upon anecdotal evidence and that the legacy agenda has become a millstone around the neck of policymakers, the government and other stakeholders.

## Aims of the research

As a result of the contradictory claims made regarding the participation legacy of London 2012 the aim of this research was to investigate whether the clubs themselves had perceived any changes in participation and to what extent they felt any changes were as a result of the London 2012 Games. In order to answer this question, the following three key research objectives were addressed:

1    To secure insights from key informants holding senior positions within voluntary sports clubs and relevant National Governing Bodies of Sport, regarding

factors that they perceived as having impacted upon participation legacy at a grassroots level.

2   To compare the outcomes of key informant interviews with a review of major government and stakeholder policy aims and objectives regarding the participation legacy of London 2012.

3   To investigate the impact of recent government austerity policies on both voluntary sports clubs and the overall participation legacy agenda

The following sections of this chapter, therefore, provide the basis for understanding the objectives of the research and how they were met.

## The selection of research participants

It would not be realistic, within the confines of this research, to target all sports or even to target all twenty-eight sports on the Olympic programme. A methodology was therefore designed that would assist in investigating key issues within the implementation of the sports participation legacy policies and the factors that might impact on their success. Two such areas are whether proximity with respect to the host city or host venues plays a role in the participation legacy and whether being a sport on the Olympic programme has any effect. To this end it was decided to investigate four sports, two Olympic (athletics and swimming) and two non-Olympic (cricket and netball) in three different areas of the country. It was also important to select both Olympic and non-Olympic sports for this research because the legacy of the 2012 Games was aimed not just at raising participation in Olympic sports but, rather, to promote the uptake of sport and healthy living in general (DCMS, 2013).

The sports were targeted on the basis of the Sport England Taking Part Survey (2014) by selecting the Olympic and non-Olympic sport that had actually seen the greatest rise in participation since London 2012 (athletics and netball) and the two that had seen the largest relative decrease (swimming and cricket). This would allow for a wide range of experiences and factors to emerge from the research that might impact upon the success or otherwise of participation related legacy policies. The two Olympic sports were also an appropriate choice given that the relative success of British sportsmen and women in these two sports at the London 2012 Olympic Games might give an indication as to the truth of the claims that elite sport success is a key driver of increased participation at a grass-roots level (Wellings, Datta, Wilkinson, and Petticrew, 2011). At London 2012 British (track and field) athletes were highly successful, winning six medals, including three golds within a 46 minute period on what has come to be called 'Super Saturday' (Majendie, 2013) Conversely, British swimmers only won three medals, none of which was gold.

A common legacy related question regarding the impact of hosting a mega-event such as the Olympic Games is whether the legacy is actually felt beyond the host city itself. The basic theory is that the further one travels from the host city and venues, the weaker the impact of the event is upon the host country population (Karadakis and Kaplanidou, 2012). In order to incorporate this into the research it was decided to investigate grassroots clubs covering the four selected sports in three regions of the country. The first region was in East London in the area immediately surrounding the main Games' venues. The second was in the city of Coventry, which although nearly one hundred miles away from the main venues, was itself a host for Olympic football. Finally, the city of Sheffield was selected as a representative of a city or region of the country that hosted no Olympic events. This then allowed for a comparison of results from these three regions, and the clubs under investigation within them, that could be used to interrogate claims for this weakening of legacy impacts the further from the host city one travels. All three selected regions were also major urban metropolitan areas that would, in all likelihood, house sports clubs from all four chosen sports. On this basis, the key respondents for the study were drawn from voluntary cricket, netball, swimming, and athletics clubs in Coventry, London, and Sheffield. Within these organisations, the individuals of most interest for this study were senior club officials. In addition, given the role of national governing bodies (NGBs) of sport in implementing the participation legacy policies, it was originally hoped to find a senior figure from the NGB for each of the selected sports under investigation to either verify or refute any relevant claims made by the key informants within the four sports. Unfortunately, it proved extremely difficult in practice to find someone willing to discuss the subject even with the promise of anonymity. In the end an interview was carried out with a Regional Club Development Officer for the Amateur Swimming Association (ASA), but officials from other organisations were not forthcoming.

## UK policies regarding sport and participation legacy relevant to the research

To understand the effects of the 2012 Olympic Games on sports participation it was necessary to review some of the key policy initiatives related to increasing involvement in sport. Of the key policies arising from winning the Games, the Places People Play (PPP) programme was the overarching scheme designed to create a 'mass participation legacy' (Kelso, 2010). As part of PPP, there were two crucial aspects specifically targeting participation. These were 'Sportivate' which encourages young people not involved in sport to receive free coaching, and 'Gold Challenge' an independent initiative designed to raise money for charity through sport participation (DCMS, 2013). In addition to PPP, there were also other programmes designed to increase participation. These included the 'School Games' and 'Inspire'. The 'School Games' was designed to increase the amount of competitive sport available for school-age children, whilst Inspire linked the activities of third sector organisations to the 2012 Games (DCMS, 2013).

Alongside these policy initiatives, Sport England allocates funding to different sports, with the volume of support dependent upon a combination of performance in mega-events such as the Olympic Games, and overall participation levels. The implication of this agenda is that sports which achieve success in elite competition are rewarded. However, they also have a vested interest in increasing participation within their sport as this forms part of the funding formula. Therefore, those who do not secure such positive results, or increase participation within their sport, gain less income. This has wider ramifications for governing bodies and clubs that are attempting to grow sports in an environment which can be financially challenging.

## The changing political economy in the UK (2003–2016)

Another aspect influencing the legacy outcomes of London 2012 has been the changing political economy in the UK over the last thirteen years. When the decision to bid for the 2012 Games was made in 2003, the UK was in a period of unprecedented economic growth which lasted for sixteen years. In this benign economic climate, supporting major projects such as the Olympic Games was seen as feasible, despite concerns surrounding the cost of hosting the event (Davies, 2003). With a growing economy and a plentiful supply of credit, there was little concern surrounding rising public debt in the mid-2000s, but this period of economic calm fractured during 2007, with the start of the 'credit crunch' which caused a global economic downturn.

In its attempts to support the UK economy during 2008 and 2009, the then Labour government expanded fiscal policy, pushing the UK's annual budget deficit up to £156bn in 2009/2010 (Allen, 2010). In contrast, at the time of the bid announcement for the 2012 Games, it had been £34.8bn (Rogers and Kollewe, 2013). As the UK became a heavily indebted economy, an alternative policy platform, driven by cuts to public expenditure was promoted by the Conservative–Liberal Democrat coalition which was elected in 2010. The view of the new administration was that the high deficit undermined fairness, growth, and economic stability in the UK (HM Treasury, 2010). On this basis, a range of 'austerity' measures were implemented which had far reaching economic consequences. For example, in the autumn of 2010, the UK government announced public-sector cuts of £80bn over a four-year period (Winnett and Porter, 2010). Spending on sport was not protected from these cuts, with significant reductions in spending occuring. These reductions were directed towards elite athletes and the grassroots, but for the former, there is the cushion of lottery funding, which was not a luxury afforded to those lower down the chain (Slater, 2010).

As a result of the government led austerity budgets local authorities in the UK are facing cuts of around 40% in real-terms according to the Local Government Association (2014) in the six-year period from 2011. Local authorities are possibly the biggest provider and maintainer of sporting facilities, particularly those used by the general public that the participation legacy policies of London 2012 were aimed at. However, the impact of such swinging cuts to their budgets is likely to be at the expense of high maintenance sports facilities that are often cut in such a tough economic climate, in order to maintain other services which the councils are legally obliged to provide (Local Government Association, 2014) such as education and social care.

## Findings: what impacts sports participation legacy?

To understand whether there has been a sports participation legacy emerging from London 2012, this chapter addresses issues surrounding sport policy, facilities, and the evolving political economy of the UK.

## Sport policy and national governing bodies

Having already highlighted a range of legacy policies earlier in the chapter, this study will now assess their impact on sports participation. From the responses given by key informants, it was apparent that these initiatives have had little effect on increasing participation. A majority of respondents stated that they had not been aware or involved in any legacy plans, suggesting that communication of these schemes was insufficient for both clubs and the general public. Indeed, this reflects a very 'top-down' approach to the design of legacy programmes. One respondent argued that whilst increasing participation was discussed they were not aware of any specific legacy plans:

> There were discussions about raising participation, but I don't think we ever got anything about the Olympics.
> (Chairperson, Swimming Club, Sheffield)

In the rare cases where legacy programmes were present at grassroots clubs, concerns surrounding their effectiveness was expressed:

> The ASA were here with the whole scheme to try and get people to learn to swim, and he [Michael Jamieson-Olympic Swimmer] came down and it was quite a cool event, but in all honesty, the next day, it all went back to normal. Don't get me wrong, we enjoyed it, but what did it really achieve? I'm not sure.
> (Head Coach, Swimming Club, Coventry Area)

On a more positive note, the event outlined earlier reflects that legacy programmes did extend outside of London, but without positively impacting performance, these cannot be seen as a success. Indeed, when some respondents discussed legacy in a positive fashion they made no reference to policy, instead they focused on the atmosphere created by the Games:

> There definitely was some sort of electricity in air for a couple of weeks. The city had a great feeling, and yeah, I think we were all pretty excited about.
> (Chairperson, Swimming Club, Central London Area)

The policy failures also raised questions surrounding the role of NGBs. Respondents felt that the clubs themselves should not be driving participation and that NGBs should play the leading role:

> I would say the ASA (Amateur Swimming Association), they have people who are actually paid to do that sort of thing [increase participation] . . . As a club, we can only be responsible for what goes in our own club. We would like to have more members, but raising participation isn't a priority of ours.
> (Chairperson, Swimming and Water Polo Club, Coventry Area)

> Well it can't be us. What can we do really? I suppose it has to be Sport England or the ECB [England and Wales Cricket Board]. We're not really in a

position to be doing their work for them. . . . Obviously the clubs really have to be involved, but we can't be the ones expected to raise participation.

(Chairperson, Cricket Club, East London area)

This provides further evidence to suggest that communication between the grass-roots clubs and the NGBs was ineffective, although respondents from both Olympic and Non-Olympic sports believed that increasing participation was not their responsibility. An official from the ASA admitted that communication with clubs had not been consistent:

I can understand why some clubs might think like that. In the past we haven't been as good as we could be at keeping in contact with clubs. It's something we've been aware of and we've been looking at ways to address it.

(Regional Development Officer, ASA)

Since London 2012, the voluntary clubs in this study have generally failed to see positive effects resulting from the legacy policies designed to increase sports participation. Although it may be expected that non-Olympic sports were at the margins of such plans, there is little evidence to suggest that grassroots clubs in Olympic sports have benefitted to any great degree. Indeed, the failure of policies to increase participation provides further evidence to support those who believe the government does not have a national strategy for sport (Gibson, 2015).

## Facilities

Having assessed how policy has affected the legacy of London 2012, another aspect emerging from the data was related to the facilities used by sports clubs. The importance of facilities is underlined by the Sport and Recreation Alliance (2013) who state that one of the foremost challenges facing grassroots sports clubs is the access to good facilities. From the clubs surveyed in this study, there were several aspects concerning facilities which were discussed. The officials from swimming clubs were the most vocal in identifying the shortcomings of their facilities, suggesting that the quality of the pools was not sufficient:

Basically for the past 30 years, they have totally neglected this place. I'll give you an example, there are big filters that were designed so that you could close one while you fix or clean the other. There's only been one working for years because they have been so poorly maintained. So if the other one fails, the whole pool is gone. You sort of think that they're waiting for that to happen so they can close the place down. The whole place needs more money, but it's needed it for 30 or 40 years.

(Chairperson, Swimming Club Coventry Area)

Alongside the apprehension surrounding the quality of pools, respondents from swimming clubs also raised concerns about the availability of facilities. One respondent stated that the pool was being closed, implying that there was no legacy benefit from the Games:

> We're losing our pool, but we keep getting told about an Olympic legacy. Is this the Olympic legacy? I don't think they really care about a legacy. We're worse off than we were before 2012, so I don't really think there has been a legacy.
>
> (Chairperson, Diving Club, East London Area)

Reducing the number of pools or their opening hours does not suggest a positive participation legacy has emerged for swimming. This suggests that there was no facility legacy for swimming, and as a result any 'legacy plans' became symbolic. Another difficulty was highlighted by a respondent who suggested that costs of using pool facilities was increasing:

> Our costs are probably going up by something like 50% now, which is pretty outrageous. We're being moved somewhere we don't want to go and being charged extra for the privilege.
>
> (Chairperson, Diving Club, East London Area)

Whilst swimming facilities have clearly shown to impact upon participation, the respondents from other sports were not as concerned about these aspects. For example, the cricket club officials believed that the condition of nets and pitches was adequate, whilst for some of the athletics clubs, the use of public spaces such as paths or parks was sufficient for their activities. An informant from a netball club expressed a contrasting view to those from swimming, suggesting that the cost and condition of facilities was not an issue:

> No, I don't think so. They're pretty good. We usually try and train outside because there is a great pitch not far from here. It's really cheap actually. . . . Depending when we get it, we can have a session for about a tenner which is great. . . . They're in pretty good condition, but to be honest, as long as it's flat and clean we're not bothered.
>
> (Team Captain, Netball Club, Central London Area)

The evidence of this study does not dispute the already accepted arguments surrounding the importance of facilities and sports participation. However, the comments from key informants suggest that there are contrasting experiences across the sports surveyed. For example, swimming clubs have articulated more concern over their facilities than the respondents from other sports. Crucially, these facilities are also more expensive to maintain, creating cost concerns for local authorities already struggling with the impact of austerity. For those sports which have fewer concerns, such as athletics, the implication is that facilities have less of an impact on participation. In contrast, swimming facilities are designed for a single purpose, whereas athletics facilities can be utilised across a range of different sports. This raises questions about targeted investment in facilities across specific sports.

## Political economy: austerity

Alongside policy and facilities, the third aspect influencing sports participation is the wider political and economic narrative surrounding the 'post-crisis' UK economy. This study has already highlighted the changing political economy of the UK, and with the bid prospectus designed in a vastly different financial land-scape, there have been unforeseen challenges to increasing sports participation. Despite the government's public commitment to increasing participation, since London 2012, there have been 2,500 sports facilities closed across Great Britain (Hookham, 2016). In addition to the closure of facilities, several programmes including free swimming and the school sport partnerships were discontinued as a result of the austerity imposed on UK public spending since 2010. For grass-roots sport this raises further challenges in terms of the facilities and support available to grow participation:

> I know from my experience that things are pretty difficult for local authori-ties and it makes it more difficult for us because we rely upon them so much for swimming pools. . . . The removal of the free swimming was something which hit us pretty hard. It was great when Labour guaranteed the free swim-ming, but when that was scrapped there's no doubt it hit us so hard.
>
> (Regional Club Development Officer, ASA)

The consequences of austerity were highlighted by a club official who stated that pool time had been reduced due to cutbacks:

> I've been involved in this for about 20 years, and this is definitely the worst it has been. It's not only us, the pool is open to the public less, so there is just less time available for anyone to use the pool. . . . Initially we were offered half the time we used to have, and they sort of shrugged when we said that we wouldn't be able to do anything with that. They don't seem to understand anything about getting people to swim, they're just slowly shutting the place down.
>
> (Chairperson, Swimming Club, Coventry Area)

Alongside these challenges for swimming, respondents also highlighted how the closure of school sport partnerships had negative consequences for sports clubs. One informant stated that the club had benefitted from the scheme:

> Yeah, the school sport partnerships were pretty useful actually. I remember them coming in, and actually remember Michael Gove [then education sec-retary] scrapping them and wondering what the logic was. It helped us set up our partnership.
>
> (Team Captain, Athletics Club, East London)

This once again reinforces the top-down' nature of policy making in the UK as the considerable benefits of the school sport partnerships were ignored in order to support the 'austerity agenda'. A non-Olympic sports club also questioned the removal of this programme:

> Scrapping the scheme seems to have lacked some foresight, it certainly worked well for us. I'm not sure we would have the links with the schools without it. . . . We still have great relationships with schools, but I think something was probably lost for both schools and clubs when they were scrapped.
> (Chairperson, Cricket Club, East London Area)

Although it may seem somewhat inevitable that austerity has negative consequences for sport participation, there are also opportunities arising for some sports. For athletics, participation has been boosted by the development of Parkrun, which is a free to enter running event held on a weekly basis. Since its formation in 2004, over one million people have participated in Parkrun organised events (Stevinson, Wiltshire, and Hickson, 2015). As these events take place in locations such as public parks, there is no fee for using the venue, and as a result, there are no membership fees or subscription charges. One athletics club member highlighted how the cost of the sport had made it so popular:

> It's the best thing about running really, isn't it? It's so easy and cheap to go for a run, pair of half decent trainers or running shoes and you're there. Obviously we don't charge much to members, just a tenner a year. . . . But to be honest, people can just run on their own can't they?. . . . I think that's why running is so popular at the moment, as people become more and more aware of the cost of things, something cheap like running is ideal.
> (Chairperson, Athletics Club, Sheffield area)

## Conclusion

This study has found that the creation of a sustainable sports participation legacy is influenced by a complex range of factors. Principally, the sports participation legacy of London 2012 has been influenced by policies, facilities, and austerity cuts, but these aspects affect different sports in different ways. There has been a vast array of policies introduced as a mechanism to increase sports participation, but these initiatives have not formed an effective national sport strategy. For example, the concerns of many grassroots clubs have not been included in the development of such policies. Therefore, the needs of clubs appear to have been often seen as a secondary, if not a complete afterthought. Whilst there has been some investment in facilities through Places People Play the consequences of austerity, and the inadequate management of some public-sector locations, has had significant consequences, particularly for swimming. Other sports are less dependent on facilities, so the austerity narrative appears to have been less of a factor in influencing participation, although it should be noted that the research did not include interviews with people not doing any sport for whom affordability may well be an important factor in whether they participate. The growth of athletics in recent years, particularly through the Parkrun initiative, underlines the impression that low entry costs are crucial to improving participation in grassroots sport. Finally, this research has also indicated that many of the policy actions of the government appear to be contradictory to their stated aim of raising participation in sport and physical activity. Such policies include the scrapping of the school sports partnership initiative and free swimming for the young and the elderly combined with large cuts to local authority budgets despite the fact that they are one of the largest providers of sport and physical activity facilities at a grassroots level and in the full knowledge that sport will be one of the first targets local authorities will target for cuts in order to balance the books. The impact of this policy is clearly seen in the closure of 2,500 sports facilities since the London 2012 Olympic Games (Hookham, 2016). Brittain and Beacom (2016) sum this situation up when they state that "[s]ports mega-events do not take place in a vacuum. They are subject to wider social, economic, and political dynamics, and, as such, it is extremely challenging to effectively plan for legacy" (p. 515). Conflicting government policies on sports participation, a top-down implementation of policy that overlooks the needs and constraints of grassroots clubs and severe economic positions appear to have consigned the much-hyped participation legacy of the London 2012 Olympic Games firmly into the realm of a fairy tale.

## References

Allen, K. (2010). *Budget deficit £5.5bn lower than expected.* Retrieved from www.theguardian.com/business/2010/may/21/uk-budget-deficit-smaller-expected

Brittain, I., and Beacom, A. (2016). Leveraging the London 2012 Paralympic Games: What legacy for people with disabilities? *Journal of Sport and Social Issues, 40*(6), 499–521.

Davies, A. (2003). *Government backs London Olympic bid.* Retrieved from www.theguardian.com/uk/2003/may/15/london.olympicgames

DCMS (2007). London 2012 Olympic Games and Paralympic Games : Funding and legacy. London: The Stationary Office Limited.

DCMS (2013). 2012 Games meta-evaluation: Report 5 (Post Games evaluation) sport evidence base. London: The Stationary Office Limited.

Gibson, O. (2015). *Olympic legacy failure: Inspiring London 2012 message has become a millstone.* Retrieved from www.theguardian.com/sport/blog/2015/jul/05/olympic-legacy-failure-london-2012-message-millstone

Girginov, V. (2013). Handbook of the London 2012 Olympic and Paralympic Games: Volume one. London: Routledge.

Grix, J. (2013). Sport politics and the Olympics. *Political Studies Review, 11*(1), 15–25.

HM Treasury. (2010). *Spending review 2010.* Retrieved from www.gov.uk/government/uploads/system/uploads/attachment_data/file/203826/Spending_review_2010.pdf

Hookham, M. (2016). *Thousands of sports facilities lost since 2012.* Retrieved from www.thetimes.co.uk/article/thousands-of-sports-facilities-lost-since-2012-bxfnlp8jw

Karadakis, K., and Kaplanidou, K. (2012). Legacy perceptions among host and non-host Olympic Games residents: A longitudinal study of the 2010 Vancouver Olympic Games. *European Sport Management Quarterly, 12*(3), 243–264.

Kelso, P. (2010). *London 2012 Olympics: 'Places People Play' legacy plan unveiled.* Retrieved from www.telegraph.co.uk/sport/olympics/london-2012/8135564/London-2012-Olympics-Places-People-Play-legacy-plan-unveiled.html

Local Government Association (2014). *Future funding outlook 2014 funding outlook for councils to 2019/20*. London: Local Government Association.

Majendie, M. (2013). *Super Saturday anniversary: 46 minutes of delirium*. Retrieved from www.independent.co.uk/sport/olympics/news/super-saturday-anniversary-46-minutes-of-delirium-8734361.html

Rogers, S., and Kollewe, J., (2013). *Deficit, national debt and government borrowing – how has it changed since 1946?* Retrieved from www.theguardian.com/news/datablog/2010/oct/18/deficit-debt-government-borrowing-data

Slater, B. (2010). *Community and school sport bears brunt of spending cuts*. Retrieved from http://news.bbc.co.uk/sport1/hi/front_page/9111865.stm

Sousa-Mast, F. R., Reis, A. C., Gurgel, L. A., and Duarte, A. F. P. L. A., (2013). Are cariocas getting ready for the games? Sport participation and the Rio de Janeiro 2016 Olympic Games. *Managing Leisure*, *18*(4), 331–335. Retrieved from www.tandfonline.com/doi/abs/10.1080/13606719.2013.809187

Sport England (2014). *Active people survey 8 Q2 April 2013–March 2014*. London: Sport England.

Sport and Recreation Alliance. (2013). *Sports club survey 2013*. Retrieved from www.sportandrecreation.org.uk/policy/SSC

Stevinson, C., Wiltshire, G., and Hickson, M., (2015). Facilitating participation in health-enhancing physical activity: A qualitative study of Parkrun. *International Journal of Behavioural Medicine*, *22*, 170–177.

Wellings, K., Datta, J., Wilkinson, P., and Petticrew, M. (2011). The 2012 Olympics: Assessing the public health effect.' *Lancet*, *378*(9797), 1193–1195.

Winnett, R., and Porter, A. (2010). *Spending review 2010: Axe to fall on half a million public sector jobs*. Retrieved from www.telegraph.co.uk/news/politics/spending-review/8074763/Spending-Review-2010-axe-to-fall-on-half-a-million-public-sector-jobs.html

# 14 Towards cultural centrality in mega-event urban legacy

## The case of Porto Maravilha and the Rio 2016 Olympic Games

*Débora Guerra, Jennifer Ferreira and Eva Kipnis*

Understanding the importance of culture in city planning is vital in order to cater for local identities and cultural heritage that exist globally. Surprisingly, this topic has received relatively little attention in literature concerned with legacy of mega-events (Chappelet, 2012; Silvestre, 2008). It is therefore unsurprising that debates on whether urban legacy of mega-events is a fact or fairy tale, and whether (if it exists) this legacy is more positive or negative, are ongoing. In this chapter we put forward a case for greater cultural centrality in approaches of urban legacy evaluation, to better unpack, capture and evaluate its less tangible (i.e., soft) dimensions. Furthermore, we argue for placing the importance on cultural preservation as an important component in the planning and implementation of cities' developments for mega-events, in order to avoid the loss of local cultural heritage and stimulate positive cultural change which is inclusive for all those who utilise the area and adapting to the needs and interests of communities. Mega-events are points in time when two forces that facilitate dynamic cultural change – globalisation and gentrification – converge. Thus, we argue that the varied impact of this convergence needs greater exploration to enable legacy planning and creation.

Whilst both these forces have been identified to facilitate a range of positive change processes, existing literature also highlights that they trigger a backlash from local populations linked to concerns over erosion of local cultural authenticity and uniqueness (Bauman, 2000; Beck, 2000; Robinson, 2001; Wimmer and Glick Schiller, 2002). Multiple mega-events have been heralded as potential strategies for urban entrepreneurial growth and boost local economic growth (Hiller, 2000). At the same time, many note that gentrification can potentially lead to a detrimental impact on local cultures and heritages (Andranovich, Burbank, and Heying, 2001; Lees, Shin, and Lopez-Morales, 2016; Watt, 2013). Mega events are often heralded by politicians (and event organisers) as opportunities that will provide positive and long-lasting cultural legacy in cities, although there are many that argue this is a fairy tale with the realities of mega events not necessarily having a positive impact (Gammon, Ranshaw and Waterton, 2015; Mangan and Dyreson, 2010). Thus, planning and safeguarding the cultural legacy of a mega-event needs to incorporate a careful negotiation of cultural transformation and preservation too.

In this chapter we first examine the cultural impacts of urban development stemming from the planning and hosting mega-events, focusing particularly on cities associated with the Olympic movement. We then examine how cultural transformation and preservation needs of host locations associated with the Olympic movement can be better assessed and achieved through integration of two urban development perspectives – gentrification and creative cities. Our argument is that city planning programmes and stimulation of the creative industry diversification can form an important part of cultural legacy construction goals. Finally, the issue of cultural legacy creation is contextualized through an analysis of the case of urban development in Porto Maravilha (Rio de Janeiro), an example of reinvention or transformation of city's cultural identity catering for preservation of local heritage.

## Mega-events as a nexus of urban cultural change

By definition, mega-events (MEs) are associated with elevated global visibility. Thus, bidding, planning and/or hosting MEs often involve "large-scale transformations of cities and regions" (Kassens-Noor, Wilson, Muller, Maharaj, and Huntoon, 2015, p. 1). The notion of legacy is closely linked to the impact made by these transformations on infrastructure, economy and lived experiences of populations in MEs locales. While transformations to sociocultural infrastructures and host locales' image are commonly identified as an important aspect of MEs legacy, harnessing the potential of MEs that moves beyond economic interests is relatively new (Hayes and Karamichas, 2012; Horne, 2012). Therefore, attempts to unpack the key cultural change processes that can be triggered by MEs have been limited. This is a critical omission since MEs embody a platform for convergence of two key processes associated with cultural change: globalisation and gentrification. The impacts of these processes on sociocultural dynamics of societies and lived experiences of individuals vary significantly.

Early studies concerned with cultural outcomes of globalisation have predicted an onset of cultural homogenization, whereby cultural differences between nations and countries will be eroded, giving way to adoption of a global culture defined as a transnationally shared set of cultural values, symbols, images and models of lifestyle originated from the West (Kearney, 1995; Levitt, 1983; Marsella, 1998). More recent studies assert that the cultural effects of globalisation are far more complex and diverse (Iwabuchi, 2010; Pieterse, 2015; Stromquist and Monkman, 2014). That is, emergence of global culture is considered one, but by far not the only cultural consequence of globalisation. From a cultural dynamics perspective globalisation created a platform for continuous and intensive inter-cultural exchange whereby a range of mutually contradicting cultural evolution processes may, paradoxically, occur simultaneously (Holden and Glisby, 2010; Craig and Douglas, 2006). Specifically, several studies warn of the 'backlash' effect of cultural globalisation arguing that, rather than promoting similarities, emergence of global culture urges individuals to favour preservation of their local identities to ensure differentiation from 'cultural others' (Bhawuk, 2008; Korff, 2003). Conversely, another stream of studies uncovers a process of 'glocalisation' whereby global culture is (re)interpreted, adapted and integrated with local cultural norms and lived experiences of individuals to form a new, hybrid form of culture (Ritzer, 2003). From this perspective, the key cultural consequence of globalisation is that in postmodern realities it facilitates co-existence of two notions: cultural being – individuals and groups sharing cultural codes and ways of living – and cultural becoming – (re)discovery of and response to cultural difference (see Hall, 1990). In the context of MEs, this translates into the need for a careful balancing of harnessing and preserving a host's unique cultural identity (i.e., 'being') while attempting to increase socio-economic and cultural development to showcase the host's emerging or ongoing prominence in the global community (Hiller, 2000).

The application of a globalisation perspective to the examination of cultural transformations to nations who bid for, plan, and host MEs can be further unpacked through the concept of gentrification. As such, gentrification encapsulates the notion of contemporary world great cities' evolution, categorising how the physical, economic, social and cultural dimensions of their transformation impacts local populations (Bidou-Zachariasen, 2006). It provides a useful lens to systematically examine the positive and negative aspects of hard (tangible) and soft (intangible) transformations to host locations' cultural landscapes triggered and facilitated by MEs as it takes into account a multitude of communities affected by mega-events beyond the organisers, participants and visitors. Specifically, applying extant gentrification research to the context of MEs' legacy it is evident that urban developments facilitated by MEs impact cultural landscapes of host communities in a more visible (e.g., areas' reconstructions, development of new sport/cultural facilities) and invisible yet equally if not more significant manner. That is, convergence of sought global visibility and positioning and gentrification can result in loss of cultural traditions, memories and community spirit and/or development of new cultural ideas, image and identity (Chappelet, 2012; Gratton and Preuss, 2008; Hiller, 2003). With this focus in mind and using the Olympic Games as an example, we next consider how cultural aspects of ME-linked urban development legacy can be planned, captured and examined through the lens of gentrification and introduce the concept of creative cities as an alternative frame of analysis able to account for some of the limitations emanating from the gentrification paradigm.

## Urban legacy of the Olympic games through two lenses

Hosting a ME brings great changes to the city (Grix, 2014)). For example, the planning of future Olympic areas can work as a development catalyst, because in many cases obsolete areas are chosen which possess difficult social and urban integration issues. Thus, the Olympic Games have also been called by some Regeneration Games (Cochrane, Peck, and Tickell, 1996). The urban regeneration processes of Olympic areas usually permit the development of new landmark structures in public and private areas of the host city where the aesthetics and functionality of infrastructure create new image and identity (Monclús, 2012). By implementing these changes the host city is a subject satisfying socio-cultural and functional interests of multiple stakeholders. On one hand, the host is required to ensure that the interests of the International Olympic Committee are met (e.g., sporting facilities that support athlete development). On the other, it works to satisfy objectives of national and local governments by improving the nation/city image, cementing and developing cultural fabrics of communities and generating new tourism income streams as visitors continue to visit the area even after the ME has taken place (Hiller, 2006; Monclus, 2012; Stevenson, 2012). However, alignment of urban development and cultural heritage goals is not always successfully achieved (Richards and Wilson, 2005, Tweed and Sutherland, 2007). In seeking to better understand how cultural aspects of MEs' urban legacy can be better understood, planned and accounted for we review cultural impacts of urban development for Olympic Games by considering their role in facilitating gentrification and the promotion of creative cities.

## Cultural aspects of mega-event urban legacy through the lens of gentrification

The linking of MEs, such as Olympic Games, and urban regeneration processes used to be a way to resolve or highlight challenges perpetuated by urban degeneration (Andranovich et al., 2001). However, critics have associated that this new urban form with the process of gentrification. Gentrification arises as a central issue of new urban forms when describing the example of old London neighbourhoods and the way they were occupied by the middle classes (Glass, 1964). More recently it has been acknowledged that the process of gentrification is geographically variegated, taking on different forms in areas across the globe (Lees, Shin, and Lopez-Morales, 2015). The urban alterations occurring due to gentrification can affect both the physical and social features of localities which can lead to the deconstruction of identity; changes in building form and type as seen in Beijing when areas of the traditional 'Hutongs' were transformed to new apartments not only changed the physical appearance of the area but also changed the composition of the community too as real estate prices soared (Zhang and Zhao, 2009) This movement gives rise to physical changes through new housing typologies, new sites of consumption stimulated by the increased value of the real estate sector, usually accessible only for a middle or upper economic class (Silvestre, 2008).

Different perspectives exist when discussing this impact, particularly when comparing the experiences of sports bodies, development organisations and government with that of local residents. MEs often are associated with the displacement of people, affecting the poorest residents in order make way for construction of ME venues (Hiller, 2003). From this viewpoint, a range of cultural aspects of a host's urban culture such as place identity, traditions and so on can be negatively affected (Gratton and Preuss, 2008). Such interpretation of gentrification is sometimes referred to as "creative destruction" when associated with global MEs (Gruneau and Horne, 2016, p. 16). Therefore, ME-linked gentrification can be viewed in opposite ways. On one hand, joining the resolution and practice of a process of urban construction fostering positive physical developments and, on the other, promoting (un)cultural construction through the discontinuity of the local traditions and customs, fostered by gentrification processes.

The possible positive–negative duality of MEs cultural impacts related to the gentrification process is evidently significant in ME legacy evaluations for almost all host cities of Olympic Games. For example, Whitson and Macintosh (1996) argue that in Vancouver, host of the 2010 Winter Olympic Games, the city became divided into two different cities after the regeneration took place. One for tourists characterised by culturally innovative, sophisticated and attractive recreational spaces, and the other occupied by a large proportion of the city's population who could not afford the high cost of living in the new city. Such forced movement of people and cultural identifiers dictated by the Olympic Movement generally is a negative consequence from the perspective of cultural identity and heritage preservation of local communities. Similarly, urban development of Beijing for the Olympic Games in 2008 whereby part of traditional neighbourhoods were removed in order to build new quarters, erased the local culture, traditions and the memories of a place and of its people, promoting the discontinuity of local identity (Zhang and Zhao, 2009). Although for some the impact of gentrification that has taken place as a consequence of the Olympic Games remains overtly negative, it is also possible to argue the opposite, (i.e., that the developments have provided both economic and cultural benefits to the gentrified areas). Beijing has benefitted from improved transport, housing, and sporting infrastructures which have remained in place beyond the Games (Zhang and Zhao, 2009). In Vancouver, the Richmond Olympic Oval skating track has been transformed into a community facility, to encourage development of sport culture among local populations (Kaplanidou and Karadakis, 2010)

In sum, while much attention has been paid to the multifaceted physical, economic, social, environmental impacts of gentrification brought about by MEs (which may be positive or negative), evaluations of cultural legacies of ME-linked gentrification remains underexplored. Yet, since ME-linked gentrification may result in displacement of local people, which in turn creates pressures on other areas of cities, and triggers creation of new surroundings likely focused on creating a globally appealing image, there is a potential for cultural fabrics of urban spaces to be irreversibly altered (Porter, 2009; Watt, 2013). At the same time, while considerations of ME-linked gentrification impacts assume a predominantly negative stance, it is possible to consider these events through another lens, that of creative cities, to foster a more positive outlook on the potential cultural legacy that can be generated by urban development.

### Cultural aspects of mega-event urban legacy through the lens of creative cities

Globalisation and development processes that have evolved over the last century have had a remarkable impact on cities around the world (Hirst, Thompson, and Bromley, 2009). Among the many facets of globalisation, various interests around the restructuring of the territory in its entirety, in order to answer to the uses dictated by contemporaneity of space and time, have been considered (Giddens, 1991; Robertson, 1995). In light of transformative processes that can be facilitated by MEs in host urban environments, a paradigm that enables appreciation of and accounting for people's use of place to derive, foster and negotiate the global and local aspects of their cultural identities becomes pertinent.

MEs hosted by the major world cities contribute to transformation of cities' identities through creation or adoption of symbols, messages promoting particular values as in the case of Olympic cities. If the hosting cities are to be the loci of cultural identity for communities, hosting MEs should be seen as an opportunity to promote, preserve and foster inclusive development of local cultures and communities. These communities, therefore, become essential stakeholders in dynamics of cities' cultural components facilitated by development through practices and beliefs followed.

According to Landry (2000), the concept of *Creative City* encapsulates an emergent creative process in urban areas helping growth through their own unique and distinctive cultural resources. That is, creative city is focused on how the cities evolve and reflect their cultural identities and how new creative economies emerge through a cultural policy deployed by the cities. Culture is viewed as central to stimulating the economic industries in the urban agenda and consequent creation and provision of job opportunities by attracting creatively minded and entrepreneurial people seeking quality, culturally vibrant lifestyle (Florida, 2002). Indeed, perspectives grounded in the creative city paradigm (such as Fantasy cities – Hannigan, 1998; Entertainment Machine – Clark and Lloyd, 2000) argue that urban development from the perspective of "cultural resources" (Landry, 2000) works as a catalyst of city regeneration whereby new and re-used entertainment infrastructures like museums, theatres and creative spaces are integrated to stimulate urban and regional economic development (Evans, 2011; Gruneau and Horne, 2016). Such perspective is akin to that of the 'cultural goods' legacy attributed to MEs (see Preuss, 2007) that, although postulated conceptually, so far received little concerted development. Thus, we posit that application of creative cities concept to examination of cultural aspects of ME-linked urban development legacy offers a fruitful perspective for achieving the balance between preservation of local cultural identities and boosting cultural promotion of ME host locations. In the next section we integrate gentrification and creative cities perspectives in a case study of cultural legacy of Porto Maravilha, an urban development emerged through Rio's hosting of the 2016 Olympic Games.

## The urban cultural legacy of Rio 2016: Porto Maravilha

Porto Maravilha (PM) is a government backed project which belongs to the Legacy Plan of the Rio de Janeiro Olympic Games 2016. PM was created through the regeneration project of the port area located in the central city of Rio. Regeneration works commenced in 2009 and is considered to be one of the largest transformation areas, seeking to build and develop the city's ability to attract the interest of major economic investments (CDURP, 2015, 2016).

Historically, the PM region bore great economic international and national importance and influence at the end of the twentieth century. However, the end of industrialisation led to a physical and social degradation of the region. Existence of historical landmarks from the early seventeenth century in the area meant that this was an area of concern when considering where to create areas for cultural protection in the port area (CDURP, 2015, 2016). In recent years, the old industrial and port areas have adopted a new paradigm of sustainable development led by urban regeneration projects boosted by the Olympics. PM emerged through public and private supported urban transformation informed by the need to meet the requirements of an Olympic city and the agenda of cultural heritage preservation (Botella, 1995; CDURP, 2015, 2016; Hiller, 2006).

Allied to sustainable urban development strategies which form part of a 5 million square metres of project area with an investment of 8.2 billion Brazilian Reis in long-term strategic planning, transformations included: changes in the road system, public transportation, restructuring of streets and avenues, neighbourhoods reconstructed, public and private local services and preservation of national artistic culture. This transformation benefitted circulation of pedestrians through opening of new boulevards and squares. and the use of public transport with implementation of VLT (Light Rail), following the demolition of one of the most imposing highways in Rio de Janeiro (Elevado da Perimetral), and the construction of new traffic areas away from the central area (Praça Mauá- see CDURP, 2015).

Several remaining landmarks of the eighteenth century symbolising important moments of Brazil's history, characterised by the arrival points of goods and slaves in the old Valongo Pier and the Hanging Garden of Valongo (which were recently rediscovered), were integrated to create a Historical and Archaeological Circuit of African Heritage Celebration. A number of projects were planned and implemented with particular attention given to city development through creative cultural innovation anchored in heritage but also considering impacts on future activities, – such as the Art Museum of Rio and the Museum of Tomorrow. A number of regeneration initiatives concerning neighbourhoods around the Olympic project targeted both social and economic sustainable development agenda (i.e., the neighbourhoods of Saúde, Gamboa, Conceiçao, Santo Cristo and São Cristóvão), with a view to improve conditions of living, work, leisure and mobility while introducing new cultural and educational infrastructures (CDURP, 2016; Wanis, 2015). Importantly, some of these transformations were anchored in the preservation of urban heritage. For example, rehabilitation of the most old and abandoned warehouses to give life to the "City of Samba" project and concerted support through programmes such as Rio Criativo and Porto Maravilha Cultural that combine the aims of promoting the local culture and regional/national creativity and the city image for the international market (Lopez, 2013; Wanis, 2015).

Emergence of these projects and initiatives illustrates that integration of cultural innovation and preservation agendas can act as complementary driving forces for urban economic and creative revitalisation while balancing the potentially conflicting convergence of the global and local paradigms associated with MEs. Some early support for this approach is provided by emerging economic indicators. For example, according to Lopez (2013) 4,1% increase in gross domestic product for the State of Rio de Janeiro was provided by stimulating the creative cultural promotion, generating jobs opportunities and promoting social inclusion, cultural diversity, and human development. The sustainability of urban planning and the capacity of social inclusion is becoming a new attractive area for residents and its users. This inclusion could be provided by feelings of pride and union perceptions among locals and the external users (Howard and Crompton, 2005). Thus, the cultural centrality of Porto Maravilha regeneration work has potential to enhance cultural, heritage and creativity aspects of the Rio Olympic legacy (CDURP, 2015, 2016; Wanis, 2015). Furthermore, preservation/reinvigoration of historical and heritage spaces boosts cultural sustainability whereby the legacy of a sporting ME are not limited on the focus on sport facilities infrastructures but include the real estate market, culture, leisure and tourism (Gruneau and Horne, 2016; Horne, 2010; Wanis, 2015).

At the same time, "creative destruction" (Gruneau and Horne, 2016, p. 16) is also an observable impact of PM development. Development of its areas was followed by an increased cost of living, resulting in unsustainable permanence of "old" residents of lower income and, consequently, the directly-attributable human displacement through expropriation, as well as "silent removals" which gradually replace the poorest of that region (Pacheco, 2011). Mezzadra and Neilson (2013) claim Rio 2016 as an example of this type of destruction process in urban practices through the territorial appropriation of favelas and gentrified neighbourhoods to improve the real estate and financial investments.

## Conclusion

The case of PM raises several important questions concerning the sustainability of cultural legacy of the Rio 2016 Olympics, and, more broadly, of MEs: how can MEs stimulate the creation of new cultural centrality associated with the global visibility without interfering or destroying cultural identities of local communities? And who benefits from the production of spaces with a global outlook facilitated by MEs? The double-edged sword represented by MEs brings new ways to consider the impacts characterised by winners and losers (Preuss, 2006) specifically, regarding the cultural strategies applied in the global hosting cities. Hence, it is important to recognise that remaking cities via large-scale events could achieve more social benefits if the urban planning process took place alongside the existing local plans with special attention on low-income neighbourhoods. French and Disher (1997) claim that the Atlanta Olympics created a great expectation around the city benefits but the result was focused mainly on large-scale urban improvements without integrating the existing patterns of the city development. The authors suggest that the Olympics are a catalyst of economical linkages around the city, but highlight the difficult task of connecting this global economic resource through the most critical urban problems. In this respect, the inclusion of local communities in public discussion and support around the transformations that probably will affect them is very important for success of its sustainable legacy for residents and guests alike. For future studies, a thorough consideration of the cultural consequences of MEs for the host community is necessary, to mediate the negative aspects of ME-linked gentrification. Instead, preservation and promotion of local culture(s) should be acknowledged as a central goal to maximise the use of MEs as opportunities for cultural promotion at both local and global levels. In essence, these MEs should foster a long lasting cultural legacy for host cities, inclusive of all stakeholders affected.

# References

Andranovich, G., Burbank, M. J., and Heying, Charles (2001). Olympic cities: Lessons learnt from mega-event politics. *Journal of Urban Affairs, 23*(2), 113–131.

Appadurai, A. (1996). *Modernity at large: Cultural dimensions of globalization.* Minneapolis, MN: Minnesota University of Minnesota Press Ltd.

Bauman, Z. (2000). *Liquid modernity.* Cambridge: Blackwell Publishing Ltd.

Beck, U. (2000). *What is globalization?* Cambridge: Polity Press.

Bhawuk, D. P. S. (2008). Globalization and indigenous cultures: Homogenization or differentiation? *International Journal of Intercultural Relations, 32*(4), 305–317.

Bidou-Zachariasen, C. (Org.) (2006). De volta à cidade: processos de gentrificação às políticas de "revitalização" dos centros urbanos. Annablume, São Paulo: 1ª edição.

Botella, M. (1995). The keys to success of the Barcelona Olympic Games. In M. Moragas and M. Botella (Eds.), *The keys to success: The social, sporting, economic and communications impact of Barcelona '92* (pp. 18–42). Barcelona: Servei de Publicacions de la UAB.

CDURP – Companhia de Desenvolvimento Urbano da Região do Porto do Rio. Orla Conde, Passeio na historia com jeito de futuro. (2015). Retrieved April 29, 2016, from www.portomaravilha.com.br/noticiasdetalhe/4380

CDURP – Companhia de Desenvolvimento Urbano da Região do Porto do Rio. Cais do Valongo e candidato a patrimonio da humanidade. (2016). Retrieved April 29, 2016, from www.portomaravilha.com.br/noticiasdetalhe/4483

Chappelet, J. L. (2012). Mega sporting event legacies: A multifaceted concept. *Papeless de Europa, 25,* 76–86.

Clark, T., and Lloyd, R. (2000). *The entertainment machine.* Chicago, IL: University of Chicago.

Cochrane, A., Peck, J., and Tickell, A. (1996). Manchester plays games: Exploring the local politics of globalisation. *Urban Studies, 33,* 1319–36.

Craig, S. C., and Douglas, S. P. (2006). Beyond national culture: Implications of cultural dynamics for consumer research. *International Marketing Review, 23*(3), 322–342.

Craig, S. C., and Douglas, S. P. (2006). Beyond national culture: Implications of cultural dynamics for consumer research. *International Marketing Review, 23*(3), 322–342.

Evans, G. L. (2011). Cities of culture and the regeneration game. *Journal of Tourism, Sport and Creative Industries, 6,* 5–18.

Florida, R. (2002). The rise of the creative class: And how it's transforming work, leisure, community and everyday life. New York: Basic Books.

French, S., and Disher, M. (1997). Atlanta and the Olympics: A one-year retrospective. *Journal of the American Planning Association, 63*(3), 379–392.

Gammon, S., Renshaw, G., and Waterton, E. (2015). *Heritage and the Olympics: People, place and performance.* London: Routledge.

Giddens, A. (1991). Modernity and self-identity: Self and society in the late modern age. Cambridge: Polity Press.

Glass, R. (1964). *London: Aspects of change.* London: Centre for Urban Studies and Mac-Gibbon and Kee.

Gratton, C., and Preuss, H. (2008). Maximizing Olympic impacts by building up legacies. *The International Journal of the History of Sport, 25*(14), 1922–1938.

Grix. (2014). Leveraging legacies from sports mega-events: Concepts and cases. London: Palgrave Macmillan.

Gruneau, R., and Horne, J. (2016). Mega-events and globalization: Capital and spectacle in a changing world order. London: Routledge.

Hall, S. (1990). Cultural identity and diaspora. In J. Rutherford (Ed.), *Identity: Community, culture, difference* (pp. 222–237). London: Lawrence and Wishart.

Hannigan, J. (1998). The fantasy city: Pleasure and profit in the postmodern metropolis. London: Routledge.

Hayes, G., and Karamichas, J. (2012). Olympic Games, mega-events and civil societies: Globalization, environment, resistance. London: Palgrave Macmillan.

Hiller, H. H. (2000). Mega-events, urban boosterism and growth strategies: An analysis of the objectives and legitimations of the Cape Town 2004 Olympic Bid. *International Journal of Urban and Regional Research, 24*(2), 439–458.

Hiller, H. H. (2003). *Toward a science Olympic outcomes: The urban legacy in the legacy of the Olympic Games, 1984–2002* (M. de Moragas, C. Kennett and N. Puig, Eds.). Lausanne: International Olympic Committee, 102–109.

Hiller, H. H. (2006). Post-event outcomes and the post-modern turn: The Olympics and urban transformations. *European Sport Management Quarterly, 6*(4), 317–332.

Hirst, P., Thompson, G., and Bromley, S. (2009). *Globalization in question*. London: Wiley.

Holden, N. J., and Glisby, M. (2010). Creating knowledge advantage: The Tacit dimension of international competition and cooperation. Copenhagen: Copenhagen Business School Press.

Horne, J. (2010). Building BRICs by building stadiums: Preliminary reflections on recent and future sports Mega-Events in four emerging economies. Retrieved May 25, 2016, from www.bl.uk/sportandsociety/exploresocsci/sportsoc/mega/buildingbricks.pdf

Horne, J. (2012). The four 'C's of sports mega-events: Capitalism, connections, citizenship and contradictions. In G. Hayes and J. Karamichas (Eds.), *Olympic Games, mega-events and civil societies* (pp. 31–45). London: Palgrave Macmillan.

Howard, D. R., and Crompton, J. L. (2005). *Financing sport* (2nd ed.). Morgantown: Fitness Information Technology.

Iwabuchi, K. (2002). From western gaze to global gaze. In D. Crane, N. Kawashima, and K. I. Kawasaki (Eds.), *Global culture: Media, arts, policy and globalization* (pp. 256–270). London: Routledge.

Iwabuchi, K. (2010). De-Westernization and the governance of global cultural connectivity: A dialogic approach to East Asian media cultures. *Postcolonial Studies, 13*(4), 403–419.

Kaplanidou, K., and Karadakis, K. (2010). Understanding the legacies of a host Olympic city: The case of the 2010 Vancouver Olympic Games. *Sport Marketing Quarterly, 19*(2), 110–116.

Kassens-Noor, E., Wilson, M., Muller, S., Maharaj, B., and Huntoon, L. (2015). Towards a mega-event legacy framework. *Leisure Studies, 34*(6), 665–671.

Kearney, M. (1995). The local and the global: The anthropology of globalization and transnationalism. *Annual Review of Anthropology, 24*(1), 547–565.

Korff, R. (2003). Local enclosures of globalization: The power of locality. *Dialectical Anthropology, 27*(1), 1–18.

Landry, C. (2000). The creative city: A toolkit for urban innovators. London: Earthscan.

Lees, L., Shin, H., and Lopez-Morales, E. (2015). *Global gentrifications: Uneven development and displacement*. Bristol: Polity Press.

Lees, L., Shin, H., and Lopez-Morales, E. (2016). *Planetary gentrification*. Cambridge: Polity Press.

Levitt, T. (1983). The globalization of markets. *Harvard Business Review, 61*(3), 92.

Lopez, P. (2013). Forum D'avignon, culture is future: Financing and economic models. Culture and creative economy in Rio de Janeiro: The challenges of a changing city. Retrieved July 8, 2016, from www.forum-avignon.org/en/culture-and-creative-economy-rio-de-janeiro-challenges-changing-city

Mangan, J., and Dyreson, M. (2010). *Olympic legacies: Intended and unended*. London: Routledge.

Marsella, A. J. (1998). Toward a "Global-Community Psychology": Meeting the needs of a changing world. *American Psychologist, 53*(12), 1282–1291.

Mezzadra, S., and Neilson, B. (2013). *Border as method, or, the multiplication of labor*. Durham, NC: Duke University Press.

Monclús, F. (2012). International exhibitions and planning: Hosting large-scale events as place promotion and catalysts of urban regeneration. In F. Monclús and M. Guardia (Eds.). *Culture, urbanism and planning* (pp. 215–240). Aldershot: Ashgate.

Pacheco, G. (2011). *Revitalização da zona portuária do Rio já valoriza imóveis da região. R7*. Retrieved from http://noticias.r7.com/rio-de-janeiro/noticias/revitalizacao-da-zona-portuaria-do-rio-ja-valoriza-imoveis-da-regiao-20110625.html

Pieterse, J. (2015). *Globalization and culture: Global melange*. Lanham: Rowman & Littlefield.

Porter, L. (2009). Planning displacement: The real legacy of major sporting events. *Planning Theory and Practice, 10*(3), 395–418.

Preuss, H. (2006). The Olympic Games: Winners and losers. In B. Houlihan (Ed.), *Sport and society* (2nd ed.). London, Thousand Oaks, CA, New Delhi: Sage.

Preuss, H. (2007). The conceptualisation and measurement of mega sport event legacies. *Journal of Sport & Tourism, 12*(3–4), 207–228.

Richards, G., and Wilson, J. (2005). Developing creativity in tourist experiences: A solution to the serial reproduction of culture? *Tourism Management, 27*(6), 1209–1223.

Ritzer, G. (2003). Rethinking grobalization: Glocalization/grobalization and something/nothing. *Sociological Theory, 21*(3), 193–209.

Robertson, R. (1995). Glocalization: Time-space and homogeneity-heterogeneity. In S. L. Mike and R. Robertson (Eds.), *Global modernities* (pp. 25–44). London: Sage Publications.

Robinson, W. I. (2001). Social theory and globalization: The rise of a transnational state. *Theory and Society, 30*(2), 157–200.

Silvestre, G. (2008). The social impacts of Mega-Events: Towards a framework. *Esport e Sociedade, 4*(10), 1–26.

Stevenson, N. (2012). Culture and the 2012 Games: Creating a tourism legacy? *Journal of Tourism and Cultural Change, 10*(2), 137–149.

Tweed, C., and Sutherland, M. (2007). Built cultural heritage and sustainable urban development. *Landscape and Urban Planning, 83*(1), 62–69.

Wanis, A. (2015). A economia criativa e o urbanismo culturalizado: As políticas culturais como recurso. *Lugar Comum, 43*, 117–128.

Watt, P. (2013). It's not for us: Regeneration, the 2012 Olympics and the gentrification of East London. *City, 17*(1), 99–118.

Whitson, D., and Macintosh, D. (1996). The global circus: International sport, Tourism and the marketing of cities. *Journal of Sport and Social Issues, 20*(3), 278–295.

Wimmer, A., and Glick Schiller, N. (2002). Methodological nationalism and beyond: National state building, migration and the social sciences. *Global Networks, 2*(4), 301.

Zhang, L., and Zhao, S. X. (2009). City branding and the Olympic effect: A case study of Beijing. *Cities, 25*, 245–254.

# 15 Sport mega-events and the media

*Kamilla Swart, Michael Linley and Gift Muresherwa*

As a means of promoting and positioning a nation within a highly congested and contested global economy, sport mega-events (SME) have been seen as valuable international promotional opportunities, and hence the growing interest to host them (Horne and Manzenreiter, 2006). Historically, the hosting of SME such as the FIFA World Cup has been a privilege of developed countries, reinforcing their dominant position in the global narrative. However, in recent years they have become especially attractive to emerging and otherwise semi-peripheral nations such as South Africa and Brazil that are seeking increased visibility and prestige. SME are viewed as a way to overcome their marginality globally as well as to potentially achieve many beneficial socio-economic spin-offs domestically (Cornelissen, 2005; van der Merwe, 2007). In 2010 and 2014 South Africa and Brazil respectively hosted the 19th and 20th editions of the quadrennial international football tournament. The hosting of both FIFA World Cups were considered a success within the mainstream media, by the governments of both countries, and by FIFA (Sports and Recreation South Africa, 2013; Walker et al., 2013; de Almeida, Bolsmann, Júnior, and de Souza, 2015). However, in the post-event rush to declare each 'a success' the longer-term shifting and contrary narratives in the media portrayal of the host nations and cities in the lead up and hosting of the event is overlooked or ignored. Given the premise for hosting the event is grounded in its ability to draw attention to the host nation, this short-term and single-dimensional acclaim warrants a deeper critical analysis. This chapter sets out to illustrate that the media legacy of mega-events is somewhere in between fact and fairy tale by using the 2010 and 2014 FIFA World Cups as case studies.

## Background

SMEs draw a global audience because of the breadth of their participating nations, affording the hosting city or nation unequalled reach. The core source of these events' power is their ability to attract massive media coverage including major television audiences and the associated broadcasting rights (Horne, 2007; Horne and Manzenreiter, 2006; Varrel and Kennedy, 2011). As Roberts (2004) notes mega-events have the ability to transmit rich promotional messages to billions of people through television with the 2010 FIFA World Cup achieving a cumulative audience of more than 26 billion viewers and the 2014 FIFA World Cup being viewed by 32 billion people in 214 countries (Naili, 2014). It intentionally places the host under the media spotlight, allowing the host to showcase its modern infrastructure, flexibility in handling the massive influx of visitors, but also to create an attractive destination as the basis of a lasting event legacy. Indeed, while sport mega-events put nations and their capability to host them in the global spotlight that same focused attention by the media can prove to be a double-edged sword for SME host destinations. Understandably hosts seek to maximise their media coverage and value, but the intense media scrutiny likewise exposes any problems to a global audience as the host destination can't control how their image will be portrayed. Indeed, South Africa and Brazil experienced similar instances of negative reporting during the lead-up of their respective World Cups. Hence whilst positioned to reinforce positive images and showcase new aspects of the host destinations, some prospective tourists may have been influenced not to attend either the 2010 or the 2014 FIFA World Cups or visit the host cities, thus limiting their potential economic impact.

The media, particularly the Western media, is noted for its negative stance on the way it covers SME in developing nations, commonly referred to as the global South (Dimeo and Kay, 2004). Thus the reporting of concern that the 2010 FIFA World Cup was going to be vulnerable to high crime rates in the country (Curi, Knijnik, and Mascarenhas, 2011); or the fear that the 2014 FIFA World Cup would not succeed due to widespread national protests in addition to crime within the favelas (Butler and Aicher, 2015) was consistent within that narrative. South Africa and Brazil possess similar characteristics (Gammeltoft, 2008); both being member states of the BRICS nations which have growing participation in the global economy. In addition, both South Africa and Brazil suffer high internal social inequalities and have governments seeking policies to readdress these imbalances (Leubolt, 2014). The hosting of SME thrust these countries into the international arena and gave them an opportunity to showcase their strength as partners of fast growing economies within the BRICS countries. The 2010 World Cup was intended to 'improve Africa's global image and combat afro-pessimism' identified in the African Legacy Programme (Maharaj, 2011, p. 52). And certainly claims of gains to South Africa's international image were reported within the 2010 FIFA World Cup country report (Sports and Recreation South Africa, 2013). Brazil envisioned the event as an opportunity to advance the country's development, overcome inequalities, create jobs and improve the quality of life for its citizens (Buarque, 2015). It was to be a unique opportunity to change its world image and accelerate investments in legacy projects and services (Boland and Matheson, 2014). The federal government was mandated to transform this spectacular opportunity into a great legacy for Brazil and Brazilians (Buarque, 2015).

Contrasting both the opportunity for and claimed gains in image presented by SME, previous research has highlighted there exists a systematic trend in the media's representation of developing continents and how SMEs portray the hosting nations (Ndangam, 2002). While SMEs bring media attention, the portrayal often confirms existing stereotypes about nations (Desmarais and Bruce, 2010) with the media primarily using words, phrases, images and expressions which are knitted to shape how nations are viewed internationally. The authors noted the limited research on content and sentiment of the newspaper media narrative in relation to SMEs and sought to expand on previous SMEs' media impact and analyses studies (Muresherwa, Swart, and Daniels, 2015; Serra and Shaw, 2014; Swart, Linley, and Hardenberg, 2012; Swart, Linley, and Bob, 2013). Therefore, we conducted media impact studies of South Africa and Brazil's FIFA World Cups in selected tourism markets. The study allowed for comparative analysis between two emerging nations as successive hosts of the same global event, adding to the understudied aspect of mega-events, media impact analysis, and also contributing to the burgeoning literature on the impact and legacy of SME in developing contexts.

In this chapter, the authors examine mainstream newspaper media impact of SME on South Africa and Brazil through the 2010 and 2014 FIFA World Cup as illustrative case studies within the developing context. The chapter explains the strategic imperatives of South Africa and Brazil for hosting their respective World Cups; and details how these developing countries were profiled by international media in key selected markets. The target market selection was determined by (1) the highest importance source tourism markets for each host, (2) the sport being nationally relevant in that market and/or (3) its residents represented a strong market for international visitor ticket sales. Hence the markets studied included the UK, the US, Germany and the Netherlands for South Africa, and Argentina, the US, Germany and Portugal for Brazil – in relation to the hosting of these events. Both studies were conducted across four hosting time periods; pre, lead-up, during and post-event focused on understanding short-term impacts. It sets out to determine changes in the media representation of these host nations in the key tourism markets as a result of hosting this mega-event. The methodology stages including content sourcing, content identification and the use of Leximancer, an analytic tool for coding large amounts of textual data delivered a robust and repeatable qualitative insights.

The study analysed media articles from major online news sources with the highest readership and circulation in each selected markets. Four to five hundred articles were extracted per market over the four time periods in each hosting country to produce the media content library. The four target periods for analysis were as follows:

- Pre-2010/2014 FIFA World Cup – two years to one year prior
- Lead-up to the 2010/2014 FIFA World Cup – one year prior
- During the 2010/2014 FIFA World Cup – hosting period
- Post -2010/2014 FIFA World Cup – one year post

Table 15.1 highlights the source markets and number of articles extracted in the selected source market for the two hosting countries, South Africa and Brazil.

In sourcing and extracting the news articles, search terms were tested and refined to isolate content related to event hosting and avoid extracting match or on-field media reports, match fixtures and game strategies (Swart et al., 2012). The study identified three strategic imperatives (Hosting Capability & Readiness, Safety & Security and Destination Image) from a review of bidding and planning

*Table 15.1* Media article count

| 2014 Brazil World Cup | | 2010 South Africa World Cup | |
| --- | --- | --- | --- |
| Brazil source market | Number of articles | SA source market | Number of articles |
| US | 408 | US | 379 |
| Germany | 500 | UK | 839 |
| Portugal | 522 | Germany | 491 |
| Argentina | 531 | The Netherlands | 589 |
| Total | 1,961 | Total | 2,298 |

documents, against which to analyse the media content and determine how those concepts were represented in each of the identified periods.

In terms of Hosting Capability, South Africa and Brazil had both sought to project their ability to deliver in terms of infrastructure and facilities for the World Cup including stadia, transport, communications, airports and ancillary infrastructure of both quality and to be ready ahead of the event. For South Africa, this meant delivering ten venues, while Brazil had twelve stadiums and cities to be ready to host the international football competition.

Regarding, safety and security, SMEs usually face safety and security challenges which eventually affect ability to attract visitors by the hosting nation. South Africa and Brazil struggle with similar dimensions in terms of safety and security challenges. These included high crime rates, violence and drug problems. Compounding these national issues is that terrorism has become one of the biggest threats to SMEs, with hosting countries and organising committees investing increasing funds to ensure security and implement counter-terrorism strategies of the event irrespective of the hosting country (Giulianotti and Klauser, 2012).

Although the discourse, both academic and public, on SMEs is vast – particularly on the economic legacy – destination profiling through SMEs has not had equivalent scrutiny. The promises of building on positive destination associations such as; natural beauty, the environment, people, lifestyle, culture, heritage and history were some of the aspirations of South Africa and Brazil's hosting of their respective Cups, and are also common to the rhetoric for investing in SME globally.

Objective investigation of the strategic imperatives identified in the study was established through semantic cluster analysis. By clustering themes and concepts into categories the process allows for comparative analysis across markets and time. Semantic cluster analysis allows the topics to be compared with each other with the aim of identifying the links between them; providing auto-retrieved labels and visual mapping to illustrate how the concepts are distributed. Leximancer further permits positive and negative sentiment analysis of concepts by applying a 'sentiment lens' over the text and classifying terms as 'favourable' and 'unfavourable'. While beyond the scope of this chapter to present all the findings, a number of key findings are highlighted to showcase evidence that both supports and refutes the media legacy of the 2010 and 2014 FIFA World Cups.

## Discussion and evidence supporting media legacy

A focus on the quantum of media coverage surrounding SMEs overlooks the positive narratives – both sought and achieved within media coverage of SMEs. To that end in terms of garnering media attention, the lead-up period both for South Africa and Brazil was when maximum exposure for the host occurred across all key markets studied. That is, immediately prior to event on-field action is the peak period for media attention on the strategic imperatives and legacy positioning. Within that overall finding were market nuances such as in 2010 the Dutch market showing higher continued off-field interest throughout all periods including the hosting and post periods compared to the other key markets at the same event. Likewise, while the stadiums, transport and infrastructure were the themes most mentioned in relation to Capability, there were fewer concerns associated with those mentions in the Dutch and German markets than the UK or even US markets for 2010. For both South Africa and Brazil, the concerns regarding safety and security were highest in the period immediately prior to the World Cup (lead-up) but fell considerably during the hosting period as the fears as reported in the international media initially were not realised through successful event and security management. The desired exposure of South Africa and Cape Town destination image generated during the pre- and lead-up period was mostly positive with attention given to the coastline, culture, natural attractions and information about visiting all receiving stronger coverage, but differed in emphasis across the various markets. For example, coastline and culture were the primary image associations for the Dutch and German markets, respectively. In terms of sentiment analysis of the 2010 FIFA World Cup, the overall ratio of positive to negative mentions improved with positive gains across periods and specifically within each of the imperatives but is not universal as noted in the challenges to a media legacy. The findings nevertheless demonstrate and support the World Cup did serve to establish a new, and more positive, narrative in the media around the host destination, but for the legacy to be realised it must be built on into the future.

## Discussion and evidence refuting media legacy

Proponents of a media legacy seek to use the volume and not content of coverage as evidence of success. Figure 15.1 shows the markedly differing pattern of coverage over two editions of the same event – namely the FIFA World Cup. Of the many insights from Figure 15.1 three are particularly noteworthy. The first is that while concerns about South Africa's preparedness and hosting expanded the unfavourable mentions in the lead-up period, the increase in favourable mentions anticipating the tournament was even greater, pushing the overall positive sentiment higher. The second is that the concerns in the lead-up period for South Africa 2010 hosting pale in comparison to the overwhelmingly negative coverage of Brazil's protests, policing and preparedness. Indeed, it is only in comparison and hindsight that the 2010 edition's media legacy can be properly understood. And lastly, once the tournament was underway both hosts saw a sharp reduction in unfavourable mentions, resulting in both hosts improving their sentiment ratio

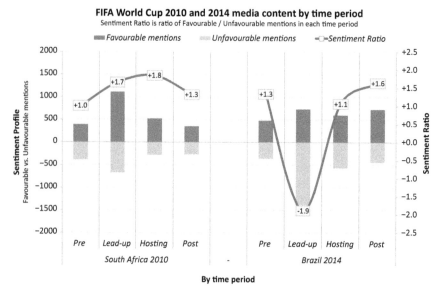

*Figure 15.1* FIFA World Cup 2010 and 2014 media content by period

over the arc of the event (pre vs post); but Brazil's gain came from improving its favourable coverage rather than the event dispelling prior concerns.

Further differences in the media representation of the hosts are found within the media coverage of both editions. In the case of the 2010 FIFA World Cup, the US media content focused primarily on the functional aspects of hosting (Capability) and showed very limited specific understanding or communication of the destination brands of South Africa and Cape Town. This continued throughout the event challenging the notion that exposure deepens knowledge and perception of the event host.

Starting from a more negative stance the UK market's ratio of favourable to unfavourable coverage for South Africa, and Cape Town, showed strong positive growth in the lead-up period and throughout the host period. However the ratio reverted to a more negative bias in the period immediately following the tournament close with coverage dominated by the Dewani murder in the UK press (Malan, 2014), consequently raising concerns on whether SME-based perceptions can be sustained against prior established associations. Moreover, although concerns around safety and security dropped off during the hosting period in both South Africa and Brazil, concerns regarding crime and violence remained affirming the narrative of the 'global South'.

Contrasting South Africa's 2010 coverage with that of Brazil and Rio de Janeiro's image in 2014, the aspects which received more positive image coverage included the host's heritage and beaches – but corruption continued to have high negative coverage in both the pre- and hosting periods. Delving into the overall sentiment by market for Brazil showed only the Argentinian market expressed an overall favourable coverage, with both the US and Germany more unfavourable and Portugal demonstrating a balanced view. The more positive coverage in Argentina may be linked to their shared geographical proximity in the global South, and Portugal's balanced view extending from its historical links. This relationship link interestingly parallels the positive coverage of South Africa in the Dutch market which also enjoys historical ties. Thus, even claims of a media legacy based on citing positive coverage may be more dependent on existing cultural connections than ascribed to the impact of the SME alone.

### Chapter wrap up: critical questions and issues for the future

Despite the worldwide media attention host destination garners via the hosting of SMEs, there have been limited media content studies. The case studies presented in this chapter illustrate that although there were areas of negative reporting about Brazil and South Africa in relation to hosting their respective editions of the FIFA World Cup, especially in the lead-up period, positive views were also prevalent across the various target markets pre-, during and post-event. Furthermore, nuances in the media content across different markets and across the periods were identified that should be taken into consideration in future event marketing and positioning of both Brazil and South Africa, as major tourist and events destinations.

It is critical that future hosts leverage the lead-up period for setting and addressing expectations for the SME as the opportunity before media attention on non-competition content is drastically reduced once the event begins. The positive imagery gained needs to be built upon, strengthened or developed, grounded in current image associations in the respective markets and highlighted in future events.

While these studies provide support that a positive media impact for both host destinations can exist in the short-term, intended media legacies are impacted (and can be overwhelmed) by prevailing political, social and economic conditions in the host destinations, making it complex and challenging to isolate and claim any specific legacy effects years after the event. This inability to isolate event media effect is compounded for destinations hosting SME in close succession as in the case of Brazil in 2014 and in 2016 (Olympic Games), Russia (Sochi, 2014, FIFA 2018) or Japan (Rugby World Cup 2019, Olympics 2020). Conversely claiming cumulative SME media legacy over an extended period as in South Africa's hosting of the 1995 Rugby World Cup to the 2010 FIFA World Cup cannot be credibly isolated from the country's own development in that period.

While the studies were limited to online mainstream media coverage the limitations around geographic boundaries on social media platforms places challenges to develop an equivalent market based approach that includes these high volume and engaging channels. The development of mechanisms or alternate study forms to overcome these issues needs to be explored in order to include evaluating social media in the future analysis of legacy.

## References

Boland, R. A., and Matheson, V. A. (2014). Do mega sports events contribute to economic development? *Americas Quarterly, 8*(2), 22.

Buarque, D. (2015). One country, two cups – the international image of Brazil in 1950 and in 2014: A study of the reputation and the identity of Brazil as projected by the international media during the two FIFA World Cups in the country. *International Journal of Communication, 9*, 1300–1318.

Butler, B. N., and Aicher, T. J. (2015). Demonstrations and displacement: Social impact and the 2014 FIFA World Cup. *Journal of Policy Research in Tourism, Leisure and Events, 7*(3), 299–313.

Cornelissen, S. (2005). The global tourism system – Governance, development and lessons from South Africa. Hants: Ashgate Publishing Limited.

Curi, M., Knijnik, J., and Mascarenhas, G. (2011). The Pan American Games in Rio de Janeiro 2007: Consequences of a sport mega-event on a BRIC country. *International Review for the Sociology of Sport, 46*(2), 140–156.

de Almeida, B. S., Bolsmann, C., Júnior, W. M., and de Souza, J. (2015). Rationales, rhetoric and realities: FIFA's World Cup in South Africa 2010 and Brazil 2014. *International Review for the Sociology of Sport, 50*(3), 265–282.

Desmarais, F., and Bruce, T. (2010). The power of stereotypes: Anchoring images through language in live sports broadcasts. *Journal of Language and Social Psychology, 29*(3), 338–362.

Dimeo, P., and Kay, J. (2004). Major sport events, image projection and the problems of the semi-periphery: A case study of the 1996 South Asia Cricket World Cup. *Third World Quarterly, 25*(7), 1263–1276.

Gammeltoft, P. (2008). Emerging multinationals: Outward FDI from the BRICS countries. *International Journal of Technology and Globalisation, 4*(1), 5–22.

Giulianotti, R., and Klauser, F. (2012). Sport mega-events and 'terrorism': A critical analysis. *International Review for the Sociology of Sport, 47*(3), 307–323.

Horne, J. (2007). The four 'knowns' of sports mega-events. *Leisure Studies, 26*(1), 81–96.

Horne, J., and Manzenreiter, W. (2006). An introduction to the sociology of sports mega-events. *The Sociological Review, 54*(s2), 1–24.

Leubolt, B. (2014). *Social policies and redistribution in South Africa.* Global Labour University Working Paper, No. 25.

Maharaj, B. (2011). 2010 FIFA World Cup™: (South)'Africa's time has come'? *South African Geographical Journal, 93*(1), 49–62.

Malan, R. (2014). At least South Africa has the world's best murder trials. *Spectator.* Retrieved January 6, 2017, from www.spectator.co.uk/2014/10/at-least-south-africa-has-the-worlds-best-murder-trials/

Muresherwa, G., Swart, K., and Daniels, T. (2015). The media impact of the 2014 FIFA World Cup™ in selected tourism markets. *African Journal for Physical Health Education, Recreation and Dance: Supplement, 1*(22), 180–190.

Naili, M. (2014). *FIFA World Cup – world broadcasting unions.* Retrieved July 20, 2014, from www.worldbroadcastingunions.org/wbuarea/library/docs/isog/presentations/2013B/1.7%20Michele%20Naili%20COL%202014%20broadcast.pdf

Ndangam, L. N. (2002). *'Heart of Darkness'-Western media rhetoric on Africa: Construction and association meaning over time.* In 23rd Conference and General Assembly of the International Association for Mass Media Research, Barcelona.

Roberts, K. (2004). *The leisure industries.* London: Palgrave.

Serra, P., and Shaw, I. (2014). Media analysis of the 2010 FIFA World Cup using newspaper print. *African Journal for Physical Health Education, Recreation and Dance: Supplement, 2*(20), 269–279.

Sport & Recreation South Africa (2013). *2010 FIFA World Cup country report.* Pretoria: Sport & Recreation South Africa.

Swart, K., Linley, M., and Bob, U. (2013). The media impact of South Africa's historical hosting of Africa's first mega-event: Sport and leisure consumption patterns. *The International Journal of the History of Sport, 30*(16), 1976–1993.

Swart, K., Linley, M., and Hardenberg, E. (2012). A media analysis of the 2010 FIFA World Cup: A case study of selected international media. *African Journal for Physical Health Education, Recreation and Dance: Supplement, 2*(18), 131–141.

Van der Merwe, J. (2007). Political analysis of South Africa's hosting of the Rugby and Cricket World Cups: Lessons for the 2010 Football World Cup and beyond? *Politikon, 34*(1), 67–81.

Varrel, A., and Kennedy, L. (2011). Mega-events and megaprojects. *Policy Brief, 3.*

Walker, M., Kaplanidou, K., Gibson, H., Thapa, B., Geldenhuys, S., and Coetzee, W. (2013). "Win in Africa, With Africa": Social responsibility, event image, and destination benefits. The case of the 2010 FIFA World Cup in South Africa. *Tourism Management, 34*, 80–90.

# 16 The New Orleans Mardi Gras

## A mega-event with an intangible legacy of protest and resistance to social injustice and inequality

*Hazel Barrett*

This chapter explores the legacy of a non-sporting mega event (NSME) that has taken place every year for 300 years in the same city. The New Orleans Mardi Gras, whilst not fitting all the elements of standard academic definitions of a NSME (see Chapter 2) is a major source of income for the city and region. According to the New Orleans Convention and Visitor Bureau (2016) in 2015 the city received a record 9.78 million visitors spending $7.05 billion. The New Orleans Mardi Gras is an historical annual cultural mega event that is internationally renowned, it is a major source of income for the city and characterises the identity of the city (Gotham, 2005; O'Neill, 2014).

In the twenty-first century the New Orleans Mardi Gras is perceived as a time of fun, enjoyment and excess, when people release their inhibitions: a time of playful deviance, including nudity and exhibitionism (Gotham, 2005). However, this view does not do justice to the legacy of Mardi Gras as a site of protest, resistance and social transformation. Mardi Gras is an occasion when people can use mimicry, parody and satire to contest the political and social norms and accompanying social inequalities, with the hope that eventually change will occur and social injustices will be righted.

This chapter explores how this tradition of protest and resistance to social injustice and inequality during Mardi Gras has evolved over 300 years into what Preuss (2007) labels an 'intangible legacy'. It is an unplanned legacy that has evolved out of a religious festival which guarantees those involved in the Carnival the right to raise in public spaces issues perceived to be social wrongs and to press for positive change. Over its long history the New Orleans Mardi Gras has confronted issues such as slavery, racial inequality, gender discrimination and injustices associated with sexuality. This chapter identifies four eras of protest and resistance associated with the New Orleans Mardi Gras and demonstrates how intangible legacies of mega events are tolerated, becoming institutionalised and thus sustainable over time.

### Mardi Gras: controlled dissidence

Carnival, including Mardi Gras, which originated in Medieval Europe, occurs on Shrove Tuesday (Fat Tuesday), was originally a Christian Roman Catholic Religious Festival lasting three to five days prior to the forty days of Lent (Armstrong,

2010). Bakhtin's seminal work on the Carnival in Medieval Europe (Holloway and Kneale, 2000) demonstrated the centrality in Carnival of the dialectic relationship between a dominant cultural order and what he terms 'the subaltern masses' (Bakhtin, 1984), which manifested itself in public displays of dissident behaviour. The moral and political elite which regulated Carnival, allowed this 'controlled subversion' to take place during the period of Carnival as it enabled society to "purge its demons and renew and restore itself" (Armstrong, 2010, p. 448). The elite thus used Carnival as a 'lubricant for hierarchical control', a vent for frustration which allowed the social and political status quo to continue following the Carnival season.

When travellers from Roman Catholic countries in Europe settled in the New World they took the celebration of Mardi Gras, with them. Over the centuries, the imported European Carnival has melded with local culture to form a new hybridised form of Carnival which incorporated Afro-Caribbean culture, including music and dance (Aching, 2010; Sands, 1991). The most vibrant carnival celebrations occur in regions or countries with large African-descent populations (McCleary, 2010), including New Orleans (US).

Armstrong and Crichlow (Armstrong, 2010; Crichlow and Armstrong, 2010) confirm that New World Carnivals mirror European Carnival in terms of allowing 'controlled subversion'. They identify a 'centripetal rite' within New World Carnival that reiterates and celebrates the existing social and political order, but at the same time the operation of a 'centrifugal effect' that results in 'conspicuous and conscious dissidence'. Armstrong suggests that whilst inevitably the centripetal rites are stronger than the centrifugal effects, change can and does take place, with the social and political elites reacting to the dissidence if they feel it threatens the existing social order (Armstrong, 2010).

New World Carnivals are therefore sites of social and political protest and resistance which allow social justice issues to be raised in a public domain and addressed by the social and political elite in a 'gradual assimilation to the national mainstream' to produce a new reality (Crichlow and Armstrong, 2010). This 'new reality' becomes a lasting legacy and these successes are celebrated in the Carnivals that follow. This chapter argues that the 'centrifugal effects' of Carnival, have become an intangible legacy, allowing the public airing of issues of social injustice.

## The New Orleans Mardi Gras as a site of protest and resistance

Since 1699 when the French Canadian Bienville, working for the French Crown, established New Orleans (Campanella, 2008; Eaton, 2014; Hardy, n.d.a) Mardi Gras has been celebrated in the city. Throughout its turbulent political history and despite numerous natural disasters and epidemics, Mardi Gras has continued to be celebrated in New Orleans for over 300 years. The New Orleans Mardi Gras is celebrated in both private and public spaces.

The Carnival Masquerade Ball is an example of Mardi Gras being celebrated in private space, usually indoors. In the early days, carnival balls were masked parties organised by the political and social elite as a Mardi Gras celebration for themselves and guests of equal social standing. In the eighteenth century these evolved into lavish affairs, often formal with tableaux performances and Carnival royal marches. Participants wore elaborate costumes and masks. By the late twentieth century these balls had evolved into tourist attractions taking place in large commercial premises. The Carnival Masquerade Ball is an event at which people live out their fantasies in a private space. They represent the 'centripetal rite' of the Carnival and the confirmation of the status quo.

By contrast Carnival activities that took place outside in public areas could be more socially dissident, especially the impromptu processions which took place in local neighbourhoods. These became particularly popular in the nineteenth century with the difference between processor and spectator becoming blurred. Such impromptu processions enabled the 'subaltern masses' to bring their grievances onto the street, to mock and satire the existing social order. These are illustrations of the 'centrifugal effect' of Carnival, drawing attention to social inequality and injustice.

Throughout the history of the New Orleans Mardi Gras, the political social elite, whilst allowing some show of protest and resistance in public space at Carnival time, using it as a 'safety valve', have also been concerned to preserve the status quo. This has been achieved by increasing regulation, as illustrated by the development of Carnival Societies (Krewes) and the replacement of impromptu processions with official parades on approved routes. This was a trend that increasingly divorced spectators from processors and enabled a level of control over deviance and resistance.

Over a three-hundred-year period the nature of Mardi Gras has changed and the location of the celebration has varied in significance. This chapter focusses on the New Orleans Mardi Gras events that take place in the public spaces of the city, as these are where protest and resistance, as well as celebration of past successes, are most visible.

The history of New Orleans Mardi Gras can be categorised into four eras:

### *1699–1857: a period of resistance expressed through parody and mimicry*

This is a period when the slave based plantation economy was established and the social order based on race was created in New Orleans. Between 1719 and 1731 over five thousand slaves, mainly from West Africa were brought to the city (Campanella, 2008). In 1724 the Code Noir came into force, which legalised racial subjugation through slavery. Throughout the remainder of the eighteenth-century waves of African slaves arrived in New Orleans to work on the plantations.

During this early period of New Orleans's history there are few references to Mardi Gras, yet we understand it was celebrated as a local neighbourhood event, with masquerade balls, private parties and impromptu street processions (Campanella, 2008). It was a White European celebration that slaves and free people of colour parodied in parallel Carnival celebrations. We know this because in 1781 the Spanish authorities forbade slaves and free persons of colour, who made up 50% of the population of New Orleans, from wearing masks or feathers or to mimic Whites during the Carnival season (Louisiana State Museum, New Orleans, 2015; Hardy, n.d.a). Clearly the power of parody was irritating to the White elite who saw it as a form of resistance that needed to be regulated. For the slaves and free people of colour Mardi Gras celebrations "served as a psychological and emotional release from the regimented lifestyle of slaves, functioning as a catharsis, a purging of feelings that were allowed little if any opportunity for expression" (Sands, 1991, pp. 86–87).

The Mardi Gras Indians are an example of how slaves, freed slaves and free people of colour challenged slavery in New Orleans. The Mardi Gras Indians are African-American men who dress up as Native American Indians and parade through Black neighbourhoods (Becker, 2013; Economist, 2012; Ehrenreich, 2004; Louisiana State Museum, Baton Rouge, 2015; Louisiana State Museum, New Orleans, 2015). These pedestrian parades, known as 'second lines', (Barrios, 2010; Becker, 2013; Gendrin, Dessinges, and Hajjar, 2012) have since their inception been the focus of aggressive policing and surveillance with participants being criminalised (Barrios, 2010; Becker, 2013).

The Mardi Gras Indians wear elaborate handmade costumes thought to be inspired by the Buffalo Bill Wild West Shows of the late 1800s (Ehrenreich, 2004; Gendrin et al., 2012; Pontchartrain, 2014; Smith, 2003). The performance of dressing up can be seen as an act of cultural resistance allowing the enslaved and marginalised to challenge their relationship to authority (Becker, 2013). Godet (2016a) describes this as the expression of "a belligerent, self-reliant black identity that defies the rules imposed by the city elites" (p. 57). The Mardi Gras Indians represent an expression of anger, defiance and resistance and provide an alternative event for inner-city Blacks who have been structurally and politically excluded from predominantly White Mardi Gras celebrations (Ehrenreich, 2004; Kennedy, 2010).

The Mardi Gras Indian tradition goes back at least to the late 1800s (Becker, 2013; Ehrenreich, 2004) and probably began during the debates surrounding the abolition of slavery (Sands, 1991). During this period many runaway slaves had lived with American Native Indians on their reservations and a great affinity had developed (Economist, 2012; Gendrin et al., 2012; Kennedy, 2010; Sands, 1991; Smith, 1994). The Mardi Gras Indians drew their inspiration from African culture and philosophy, in particular heroic warriors resisting domination and thus represented a challenge to the legitimacy of Anglo-European domination (Lipsitz, 1988). Recently researchers have portrayed the Mardi Gras Indians as an example of a co-narrative of two oppressed groups, Native Indians and African slaves, who are struggling to control 'frontier space' (Wehmeyer, 2010, p. 428). Some have suggested that they represent some of the earliest civil rights demonstrators (Economist, 2012; Gendrin et al., 2012; Kennedy, 2010) and were at the "forefront of civil disobedience" (Kennedy, 2010, p 37).

The Mardi Gras Indians are present in the New Orleans Mardi Gras of the twenty-first century and are largely misunderstood and underappreciated by the city authorities and general public (Smith, 1994), yet they continue their parallel Mardi Gras activities despite adverse regulations designed to uphold centripetal rites (Barrios, 2010). There are 30–40 Indian tribes in New Orleans (Gendrin et al.,

2012; Mardi Gras Indian Council, n.d.), with names such as White Eagles, Wild Squatoolas, Mandingo Warriors, Congo Nation and Yellow Pocahontas (Economist, 2012). The Mardi Gras Indians thus present "a counter-narrative challenging the hegemony of the New Orleans' White social elite" (Lipsitz, 1988, p. 115). According to Smith (1994) they are a group that, "proudly refuse to be dominated by the white legal and social systems" (p. 45). They use elaborate costumes and masks, music and dancing during their parades. The masks give them the right 'to be other', music allows stories to be told and the dancing is a symbolic form of combat (Economist, 2012; Lipsitz, 1988; Wehmeyer, 2010).

In 1985 the Mardi Gras Indian Council was set up to represent the Mardi Gras Indian tribes and to preserve the tradition of 'masking Indian' (Mardi Gras Indian Council, n.d.; Pontchartrain, 2014). Since 1999 the Mardi Gras Indians Hall of Fame Induction Ceremony has taken place, indicating that the Mardi Gras Indians are becoming more accepted as part of the New Orleans Mardi Gras tradition. Since the devastation of Hurricane Katrina in 2005, Mardi Gras Indian tribes continue to parade, and new tribes are being formed demonstrating how Mardi Gras enables this community to celebrate their cultural heritage, freedom and the political advancement of Black residents of New Orleans (Gendrin et al., 2012).

For the Mardi Gras Indians of New Orleans in the twenty-first century, Carnival is considered a commemoration of the assistance given by one oppressed minority to another. At the same time they celebrate the defiance and self-determination of generations of Black New Orleanians who have been excluded by segregation from Carnival celebrations in the past, but despite the laws and regulations and the threat of jail and violence were determined to celebrate Mardi Gras in their own way (Barrios, 2010; Gendrin et al., 2012). By doing this the Mardi Gras Indians ensure that contemporary racial inequalities continue to be highlighted (Becker, 2013). The Mardi Gras Indians represent a 150 years of resistance to social and racial oppression through culture and rituals (Kennedy, 2010). They remain defiant and determined to retain their identity and freedoms.

### 1857–1964: a period of overt protest and resistance

The 1860s saw the end of the era of human slavery in New Orleans and in 1868 suffrage was extended to Blacks. This heralded a period of rapid social and economic change in New Orleans. The city became highly segregated which was legitimised using the law and local regulations which became a focus of protest by the civil rights movement well into the twentieth century. For example, in 1890 a regulation enforced racial segregation on public transport in the city (McCoy, 2010). This was challenged in the courts in 1896 and became known as the "Whites Only Train Car Case." The case went up to the Supreme Court with the ruling that the races were 'separate but equal' (Campanella, 2008). This ruling legalised and entrenched racial segregation in New Orleans, which was extended to cover schooling and department stores (Campanella, 2008). The 'separate but equal' ruling was not reversed by the Supreme Court until 1954 (Campanella, 2008). It was a further ten years before racial segregation was legally ended in the US when the Civil Rights Act was passed in 1964.

During this period the Mardi Gras was subject to increasing regulation. In the 1850s there were calls to ban the New Orleans Mardi Gras due to disorder occurring on the streets, including the throwing of flour and mud on masqueraders and spectators (Louisiana State Museum, Baton Rouge, 2015; Louisiana State Museum, New Orleans, 2015). Mardi Gras had become a day of anarchy. However, in 1857, in an attempt to clean up the Mardi Gras the first Mardi Gras Society (Krewe) was set up. Krewes are defined as "groups whose members organise a parade with floats and marching bands, and hold a tableau ball during the annual Mardi Gras celebration" (Gotham, 2005, p. 312). They are non-profit social clubs offering members "solidarity, camaraderie and cheer" (Gotham, 2005, p. 316), with many named after mythological figures. The first Krewe was the Comus Krewe which took its name from the Greek *komos* meaning 'revellers' (O'Neill, 2014). Krewes are completely autonomous, with members paying dues and having fund-raising activities which support the Krewe's Carnival events (Gotham, 2005).

The Krewe system began the transformation of the New Orleans Mardi Gras from private balls, parties and street celebrations, to public parades, fanciful royalty and civic rituals. Krewes organised elaborate masquerade balls, appointed kings and queens, took part in well-organised public parades and initiated civic rituals (Louisiana State Museum, New Orleans, 2015; O'Neill, 2014). For example, the Mardi Gras official colours of purple, green and gold can be traced back to the Rex Krewe who introduced them in 1872 in honour of Alexis Romanov, the grand duke of Russia who attended the Mardi Gras that year (Hardy, n.d.b). The colours are said to represent justice, faith and power respectively (Hardy, n.d.b) thus illustrating the complex relationship between the centrifugal effects and centripetal rites of Carnival.

These Krewes, including Comus (established 1857), Rex (1872), Momus (1872) and Proteus (1882) were White men only societies (O'Neill, 2014). According to Gotham (2005) between 1857 and the 1930s four to six Krewes paraded each year, between 1930 and 1940 the figure doubled (five to ten) and in the late 1940s had reached 15. By 1960, twenty-one Krewes took part in Mardi Gras.

Because of the racial segregation regulations, Black people were excluded from taking part in official Mardi Gras celebrations and parades. In response, in 1909, the first African-American Krewe, the Zulu Krewe, was formed (O'Neill, 2014). They deliberately parodied the White carnival monarchy, with the Zulu king dressed in rags, having a lard tin can as a crown and a banana stalk as a sceptre (Hardy, 2001). The most famous Zulu Krewe king was Louis Armstrong, who 'ruled' in 1949. The Zulu Krewe ridiculed White pomposity by using White notions of Black savagery, thus reclaiming Black stereotypes. In 1923 the Krewe assumed their standard costume of grass skirts and dispensed coconuts as souvenirs to spectators. The Zulu Krewe is now integrated into the official Mardi Gras Parade but retains its traditions.

It was not until 1933 that the second African-American Krewe was established, called the Jolly Boys. In 1960, the New Orleans Most Talked of Club (NOMTOC) was formed to be followed in the 1990s by the Ashanti, Thebes and Oshun

Krewes (Louisiana State Museum, Baton Rouge, 2015; Louisiana State Museum, New Orleans, 2015). These all represented a challenge to the social order dominated by race and the continuing fight for civil rights.

Not surprisingly, Mardi Gras became a site of overt protest and resistance concerning the 'separate but equal' principle and a site of struggle for the civil rights movement. Despite the Civil Rights Act of 1964 ending segregation in public spaces, racial discrimination persisted in New Orleans. It was not until 1992 that New Orleans City enacted an anti-discrimination ordinance that required White Mardi Gras Krewes to open their private membership to Blacks (Gill, 1997). The deep racial divide was illustrated by the fact that as a result of the ordinance, a number of White dominated Krewes, which had been parading since the nineteenth century, including the Comus and Momus Krewes, cancelled their parades and disbanded rather than open up their membership to non-Whites (Gotham, 2002).

Whilst Mardi Gras challenged, and continues to challenge, racial inequality in New Orleans, it also became an opportunity for women to raise their own issues of discrimination and prejudice (Vaz, 2013). Women, not even White women, could be members of the Krewes, so in 1896 the first White women's Krewe, called Les Mysterieuses Krewe was formed. Whilst it did not parade, it did organise Masquerade Balls in 1896 and 1900, both leap years when traditionally women could ask men for their hand in marriage, thus reversing gender roles. In 1901, the Mittens Krewe was established and had its first carnival ball. Neither of these Krewes lasted more than a few years. However, the Krewe of Iris, established in 1922 has survived and in 1959 took part in its first street parade and continues to take part in the official Mardi Gras Parade (Hardy, 2001), bringing issues of gender discrimination to the public's attention.

African-American women suffered even more discrimination than their White sisters and were barred by segregation regulations from participating in White Mardi Gras Balls and Parades, so in 1912 the Baby Dolls tradition was initiated by Black women and women of colour who worked in the dance halls and brothels of the Black Storyville quarter of New Orleans. They dressed in short skirts, stockings, garters and bonnets imitating little girls. But their public behaviour was provocative in that they not only exploited stereotypes but also empowered and made visible an otherwise marginalised group of women (Vaz, 2013). As Vaz (2013) states, "[t]hese wise, worldly women dressed as innocents, embodying the girlish disguise of the New Woman of the Progressive Era seeking independence and self-fulfilment. They called themselves the Million Dollar Baby Dolls" (p. 1). While this group of women stopped participating in Mardi Gras in the 1950s, there was a short revival of the Baby Doll phenomenon in the 1970s, with the Treme Million Dollar Baby Dolls and Millisia White's Baby Doll Ladies being resurrected in the twenty first century. These groups continued to wear sexy attire, have decorative face paint, wear curly wigs and carry umbrellas and tambourines. For Millisia White, the founder of the New Orleans Society of Dance's Baby Doll Ladies, the resurrection of the Baby Dolls post Hurricane Katrina (2005) was "an example of hope" and a celebration of the Baby Dolls phenomena of the early twentieth century (Vaz, 2013, pp. 140–141).

## 1964–2005: a period of muted resistance

This is the period of the 'super-Krewe' and followed the passing of the Civil Rights Act 1964 and the banning in 1973 of Mardi Gras parades from the French Quarter for safety reasons. During this period, Krewes begin to abandon local itineraries and centralise along the St Charles route (Mardi Gras Museum, New Orleans, 2015). Three super Krewes emerged as dominant during this period; they were the Bacchus Krewe formed in 1969; Endymion Krewe (formed in 1967 which became a super Krewe in 1974) is the largest Krewe and is named after the Olympian god of fertility and eternal youth; and Orpheus Krewe (formed in 1994). These Krewes are open to non-resident members (Gotham, 2002) and appointed celebrities such as Bob Hope, Quincy Jones, John Goodman, Dolly Parton, Whoopi Goldberg and Stevie Wonder as their monarchs or grand marshals.

These super Krewes organise very large and elaborate balls which are held in the Superdome and Convention Centre with Las Vegas style entertainment (Hardy, 2002). They are responsible for designing eye-catching, large floats which have resulted in what has been termed the 'Disneyfication' of the parades (McCoy, 2010).

In addition to the super Krewes, other Krewes continued to parade at Mardi Gras indicating the vibrancy of Carnival in New Orleans and the opposition to trends in commodification exemplified by the super Krewes. The number of krewes involved increased dramatically after 1970 when there were twenty-five Krewes parading, to fifty-five in 1986 and peaking at sixty-two in 2004 (Gotham, 2005).

The national movement in gay pride and gay rights, which has gained momentum in the second half of the twentieth century, has been mirrored in the New Orleans Mardi Gras. In 1960 the first Mardi Gras gay ball in New Orleans was raided by the police and 97 men were arrested and charged with disturbing the peace. The following year the first gay Krewe, Petronius Krewe, was formed by and for gay men in New Orleans. This was followed by the Krewe of Apollo which was established in 1969. Early gay Krewes had to operate in secret for fear of harassment. Today four gay Krewes take part in the official Mardi Gras parades, these being Petronious, Armenius, Amon-Ra and the Lords of Leather. They all have open membership and produce very entertaining spectacles, containing large doses of camp and social mockery.

This period also symbolized the proliferation of the New Orleans Mardi Gras festival becoming a major tourism-driven civic ritual (Campanella, 2008). Since the 1870s visitors had been attracted by the 'playful deviance' (Campanella, 2008; Gotham, 2005) of the New Orleans Mardi Gras. However, in the latter decades of the twentieth century the New Orleans Mardi Gras became a year-round 'industry' which was 'themed and commodified' (Gotham, 2005, p. 321) with a focus on 'promoting desire and fantasy' (Gotham, 2002, p. 1744; Gotham, 2005, p. 309). In 2004 New Orleans attracted 10.1 million visitors generating $5.5 billion in visitor spending.

## 2005–present: protest despite adversity

In August 2005, the levees built by the US Corps of Engineers to protect New Orleans from flooding failed under the pressure of Hurricane Katrina (a category

5 hurricane) and the accompanying storm surge (Campanella, 2008; Louisiana State Museum, New Orleans, 2015; McKernan and Mulcahy, 2008; Zimmerman, 2015). Katrina was the most serious hurricane event to hit the US (CNN, 2016). A few weeks later Hurricane Rita hit the same region.

These hurricanes resulted in the deaths of 1833 people with millions of people being left homeless (Zimmerman, 2015) along the Gulf Coast. New Orleans was particularly badly hit, with 887 fatalities (Sharkey, 2007), 95,000 residential buildings destroyed or damaged (Pistrika and Jonkman, 2010) and 80% of the city flooded (Zimmerman, 2015). The Federal Emergency Management Agency (FEMA) called Katrina the single most catastrophic natural disaster in US history (CNN, 2016).

What followed was a series of divisive and aggressive debates concerning future role and purpose of Mardi Gras (Godet, 2016b; Mitchell, 2007). Some people wanted the 2006 Mardi Gras to be cancelled as they felt it was morally improper to stage the event after so many lives had been lost and destroyed (Godet, 2016b). These protagonists focussed on the suffering and loss of the Black working class (Gold, 2016) arguing that resources should be devoted to rebuild the city rather than being spent on the Mardi Gras and that holding the Mardi Gras would discourage national support for the city's recovery (Mitchell, 2007). However others wanted 'the show to go on'. Their arguments were economic and place promotional (Gold, 2016), wishing to demonstrate to the world the indomitable spirit of New Orleans (Mitchell, 2007). This view was supported by many poor and Black New Orleanians who believed that cancelling the Mardi Gras celebrations would compound the sense of loss.

In the event, a decision was made to stage the 2006 Mardi Gras (Godet, 2016b). The festivities were reduced to eight rather than the normal twelve days, and the parades followed a different route avoiding the worst flood affected areas including Lafitte (Godet, 2016b). Twenty-seven of the Krewes that had paraded in 2005 agreed to participate (Godet, 2016b), including the Zulu Krewe which had more members affected by Katrina than any other Krewe (ten members had died, and 80% of the rest had lost their homes) (Godet, 2016b). Zulu Krewe led the procession on February 28, 2006, with the theme 'Zulu, Leading the Way Back Home' (Godet, 2016b), a reference to the thousands of New Orleanians who had been evacuated out of the city and were still to return six months after Katrina.

The 2006 Mardi Gras was used as a vehicle for those affected by Katrina to voice their concerns about the perceived political incompetence in dealing with the crisis at local and national levels as well as to highlight issues of poverty and race segregation (Godet, 2016b; Gold, 2016). Thus, Krewes chose themes in 2006 that satirised and parodied organisations and politicians they blamed for the chaos following Katrina and the lack of support given to victims. Godet (2016b) reports parades and floats having poignant themes such as "Hades – A Dream of Chaos", with unflattering images representing a headless state and the corpse of engineers (the US Army Corps of Engineers); "The Inferno", showing eminent politicians as cooks brewing a giant cauldron of human misery with President G.W Bush as the horned Satan incarnate; "C'Est LeVee", referencing failed levees and parodying FEMA who are responsible for inspecting the levees; "Buy us Back Chirac", a plea for France (presided by President J. Chirac) to reverse the Louisiana Purchase as a way to address US government concerns over the cost of rebuilding New Orleans; and "Blue Roof Blues", a reference to the blue tarpaulins that were still on rooftops all over the city. Many revellers wore costumes drawing attention to the social injustice highlighted by Katrina, by wearing giant fleur-de-lis, the traditional symbol of New Orleans with screws stuck through them, signifying the view that the city had been 'screwed' by the federal government (Godet, 2016b).

Whilst satire dominated, homage was paid to those who had lost their lives as a result of Katrina and respect given to those who had come to assist, such as the army. For example, the all-female Krewe of Muses closed their parade with a float dominated by a huge head of a beautiful woman with large tears rolling down her cheeks, with the words "We celebrate life, we mourn the past, we shall never forget" (Godet, 2016b).

Carnival has always been symbolised by the mask of tragedy and comedy, and 2006 is an excellent example of this. The 2006 Mardi Gras was used to memorialise the tragedy of Katrina as well as to satire the political and social issues that Katrina had exposed. Mardi Gras allowed the people of New Orleans to publicly voice their sense of injustice and to share their experiences of trauma and disaster with others (Godet, 2016b). Barber held that the 2006 Mardi Gras allowed New Orleanians to "maintain a sense of agency in a situation in which they had little power" (cited by Godet, 2016a, p6/15). Mardi Gras has traditionally represented 'democracy despite government', which "creates and expresses freedom and community and gives scope for the marginalised to express their own values, identities and interests in civil society" (Stillman and Villmoare, 2010, p. 486). This is exactly what Mardi Gras 2006 in New Orleans achieved, replicating in a twenty-first-century context what their ancestors had done for three hundred years.

In the years following Katrina, New Orleans has been the site of bitter debates concerning the rebuilding and re-population of the city (Campanella, 2008; Graham, 2007). Prior to Katrina, it is estimated that 10% of the city's population lived in some form of public or government supported housing with 64% occupied by working-poor Black women (Perry, 2013). Following Katrina, areas of public housing have not been rebuilt (Perry, 2013), but instead, many have been demolished (Graham, 2007) and replaced by housing that poor people cannot afford. This trend in urban gentrification is one that has been labelled 'racial injustice' (Thomas, 2009) fuelled by 'racial capitalism' (Loyd, 2007).

Whilst many poor Blacks still work in the city, most cannot afford to live there, and the city is experiencing a rapid decline in its Black population down from 323,392 in 2000 to 213,489 in 2010 (Perry, 2013). This has produced what Perry (2013) calls "a new sanitized urban landscape" (p. 11/13). This raises questions about the future of New Orleans' cultural heritage, including Creole cuisine, jazz and many Mardi Gras traditions, which can be traced back to spaces of Black public housing. This has led McKernan and Mulcahy (2008) to liken the natural disaster of Hurricane Katrina to a cultural Chernobyl, potentially destroying the living and dynamic culture of the city.

Following the devastation caused by Hurricane Katrina, visitor numbers to New Orleans plummeted. In 2006 only 3.7 million people visited the city spending

$2.8 billion and rebranding of the city took place to attract visitors back to the city (Gotham, 2007), using slogans such as 'New Orleans: Happenin' Every Day' and 'Fall in Love with New Orleans All Over Again'. Since 2006 visitor numbers have recovered, and in 2015 the city received 9.78 million visitors spending $7.05 billion (New Orleans Convention and Visitors Bureau, 2014). Today Mardi Gras is aggressively marketed as part of a larger tourism orientated strategy to encourage people to visit and spend money in the city. Mardi Gras, Creole cuisine and jazz are promoted as the main attractions (Gotham, 2002, 2007). However, there is much debate about how a city which, since Katrina, "has become more affluent, privatized, and white" (Perry, 2013, p. 2/13) can support authentic Black cultural events such as Mardi Gras without romanticising, sanitising and fossilising them, thus leaving few opportunities for New Orleans culture to flourish and expand.

There is an ongoing tension between commercialisation, the racial politics of the rebuilding of the city since the devastation of Hurricane Katrina and community resistance and protest concerning social injustice. The New Orleans Mardi Gras has been at the heart of these tensions providing a site of resistance at a time of adversity.

## Producing and sustaining an unplanned intangible legacy

The New Orleans Mardi Gras is an excellent example of a mega cultural event that has produced planned, unplanned, tangible and intangible legacies (Preuss, 2007). One of the most obvious planned legacies is the economic benefit to the city of the Mardi Gras and in turn how the Mardi Gras has been commodified and disneyfied in order to be used as a marketing tool to attract visitors to the city year-round. This has particularly been the case during the second half of the twentieth century and following the devastation of Hurricane Katrina in 2005.

The tradition of Carnival as a period when dissidence and deviance are tolerated, have allowed the unplanned intangible legacy of Mardi Gras as a site of protest and resistance to social injustice and inequality to flourish. The issues that have been highlighted by Mardi Gras over its three-hundred-year history has altered as a result of changing social norms, political priorities and dominant power structures (McCleary, 2010). However, social inequalities associated with race, gender and sexuality have been dominant themes of protest throughout, producing immeasurable legacies that contribute to social transformation often backed by legal statute. The balance between the 'centripetal rites' and 'centrifugal effects' associated with the Carnival has varied, at times making social change slow as in the abolition of slavery and addressing racial segregation and at others times allowing change to take place at a much faster pace as has been the case with respect to gender and sexuality based prejudice.

Despite the three-hundred-year history of Mardi Gras in New Orleans and the challenges it has confronted, the tradition of Mardi Gras as a 'site of democracy despite government' persists. The New Orleans Mardi Gras continues to act as a 'vent for frustrations' concerning social injustice and inequality in the twenty-first century. The 'centrifugal effect' of Carnival has become a valuable and enduring intangible legacy that is difficult to measure but palpable to those who take part in Mardi Gras in New Orleans with its long history of natural, political and social adversity. It was particularly obvious in 2006 following Hurricane Katrina. The New Orleans Mardi Gras is thus an example of how unplanned intangible legacy is produced and sustained.

## References

Aching, G. (2010). Carnival time versus modern social life: A false distinction. *Social Identities, 16*(4), 415–425.

Armstrong, P. (2010). Bahian carnival and social carnivalesque in trans-Atlantic context. *Social Identities, 16*(4), 447–469.

Bakhtin, K. (1984). *Rabelais and his world.* Bloomington, IN: Indiana University Press (Original work translated from Russian and first published in English in 1968).

Barrios, R. E. (2010). You found us doing this, this our way: Criminalizing second lines, super sunday, and habitus in post-Katrina New Orleans. *Identities, 17*(6), 586–612.

Becker, C. (2013). New Orleans mardi gras Indians: Mediating racial politics from the backstreets to main street. *African Arts, 46*(2), 36–49.

Campanella, R. (2008). *Bienville's Dilemma: A historical geography of New Orleans.* Lafayette: Centre for Louisiana Studies, University of Louisiana.

*CNN.* (2016, August). *Hurricane Katrina statistics – fast facts.* Retrieved February 13, 2017, from www.edition.cnn.com

Crichlow, M. A., and Armstrong, P. (2010). Carnival praxis, carnivalesque strategies and Atlantic interstices. *Social Identities, 16*(4), 399–414.

*Economist.* (2012, December 22). Mardi Gras Indians: Home-grown and spirit raised. Retrieved February 12, 2017, from www.economist.com/node/21568588/print

Ehrenreich, J. D. (2004). Bodies, beads, bones and feathers: The masking tradition of mardi gras Indians in New Orleans – a photo essay. *City and Society, 16*(1), 117–150.

Gendrin, D. M., Dessinges, C., and Hajjar, W. (2012). Historicizing the mardi gras Indians in HBO's *threme:* An emancipatory narrative. *Intercultural Communication Studies, 21*(1), 290–307.

Gill, J. (1997). Lords of misrule: Mardi Gras and the politics of race in New Orleans. Jackson, MI: University Press of Mississippi.

Godet, A. (2016a). "Playing Indian": Masking and unmasking Black working-class identities in New Orleans' Mardi Gras Indian parades. *Politique Americaine, 28*(2), 178.

Godet, A. (2016b)."Resilient City"? The double face of the 2006 Mardi gras celebrations in New Orleans. *E-rea, 14*(1). Retrieved February 13, 2017, from https://erea.revues.org/5389

Gold, J. R. (2016). Carnival redux: Hurricane Katrina, Mardi Gras and contemporary United States experience of an enduring festival form. In O. Kattmeier (Ed.), *Selling ethnicity: Urban cultural politics in the Americas* (pp. 27–40). London: Routledge.

Gotham, K. F. (2002). Marketing Mardi Gras: Commodification, spectacle and the political economy of tourism in New Orleans. *Urban Studies, 39*(10), 1735–1756.

Gotham, K. F. (2005). Tourism from above and below: Globalization, localization and New Orleans's Mardi Gras. *International Journal of Urban and Regional Research, 29*(2), 309–326.

Gotham, K. F. (2007). (Re)branding the big easy: Tourism rebuilding in post-Katrina New Orleans. *Urban Affairs Review, 42*(6), 823–850.

Graham, D. B. (2007). The New Orleans that race built: Racism, disaster, and urban spatial relationships. *Souls: A Critical Journal of Black Politics, Culture and Society, 9*(1), 4–18.

Hardy, A. (2001). *Mardi Gras in New Orleans: An illustrated history.* Metaire, LA: Arthur Hardy Enterprises.

Hardy, A. (n.d.a). *History of Mardi Gras*. Retrieved February 6, 2017, from www.newor
leansonline/neworleans/mardigras/mardigrashistory/mghistory.html

Hardy, A. (n.d.b). *Mardi Gras fundamentals*. Retrieved February 6, 2017, from www.
neworleansonline/neworleans/mardigras/mgfund.html

Holloway, J., and Kneale, J. (2000). Mikhail Bakhtin: Dialogics of space. In M. Crang and
N. Thrift (Eds.), *Thinking space* (pp. 71–88). Routledge: London.

Kennedy, A. (2010). *Big Chief Harrison and the Mardi Gras Indians*. Gretna: Pelican Publishing Company.

Lipsitz, G. (1988). Mardi Gras Indians: Carnival and counter-narrative in black New
Orleans. *Cultural Critique*, *10*, 99–121.

Louisiana State Museum, Baton Rouge (2015). Exhibition 1: Grounds for greatness: Louisiana and the nation. Exhibition 2: Experiencing Louisiana: Discovering the soul of
America. 660 North Fourth Street, Capitol Park, Baton Rouge, Louisiana, 70802. Capi-
tolParkMuseum@crt.la.gov.

Louisiana State Museum, New Orleans (2015). *Exhibition 1: Living with hurricanes:
Katrina and beyond. Exhibition 2: Mardi Gras: It's carnival time in Louisiana!* The
Presbytere, Jackson Square, 751 Chartres Street, New Orleans, Louisiana, 70116.

Loyd, J. M. (2007). Katrina: A racist disaster. *Capitalism Nature Socialism*, *18*(3), 122–129.

Mardi Gras Indian Council. (n.d.). Retrieved February 12, 2017, from www.mardigrasin
diancouncil.org

McCleary, K. (2010). Ethnic identity and elite idyll: A comparison of carnival in Bue-
nos Aires, Argentina and Montevideo, Uruguay, 1900–1920. *Social Identities*, *16*(4),
497–517.

McCoy, G. S. (2010). Disney's second line: New Orleans, racial masquerade, and the production of whiteness in the princess and the frog. *Journal of African American Studies*,
*14*, 432–449.

McKernan, J., and Mulcahy, K. V. (2008). Hurricane Katrina: A cultural Chernobyl. *The
Journal of Arts Management, Law, and Society*, *38*(3), 217–232.

Mitchell, R. (2007). Through the eye of Katrina: The past as prologue? *The Journal of
American History*, *94*(3), 789–794.

New Orleans Convention and Visitors Bureau. (2014). *What's new in New Orleans' hospitality industry – September 2014*. Retrieved February 4, 2017, form www.newor
leanscvb.com

New Orleans Convention and Visitor Bureau. (2016). Retrieved February 12, 2017, from
www.neworleanscvb.com

O'Neill, R. (2014). New Orleans carnival krewes: The history, spirit and secrets of Mardi
Gras. Charleston, SC: History Press.

Perry, G. K. (2013). *In search of Black spaces: Theorizing the erosion of Black space in
post-Katrina New Orleans*. Paper presented at The Fourth Global Conference on Space
and Place, 9–12 September, Oxford University.

Pistrike, A. K., and Jonkman, S. N. (2010). Damage to residential buildings due to flooding
of New Orleans after Hurricane Katrina. *Natural Hazards*, *54*(2), 413–434.

Pontchartrain, B. (2014, February 25). What are the Mardi Gras Indians: How many are
there and what is their history? *Gambit*. Retrieved February 12, 2017, from www.bestof
neworleans.com

Preuss, H. (2007). The conceptualisation and measurement of mega sport event legacies.
*Journal of Sport and Tourism*, *12* (3–4), 207–228.

Sands, R. M. (1991). Carnival celebrations in Africa and the New World: Junkanoo and the
Black Indians of Mardi Gras. *Black Music Research Journal*, *11*(1), 75–92.

Sharkey, P. (2007). Survival and death in New Orleans: An empirical look at the human
impact of Katrina. *Race and Class*, *37*(4), 482–501.

Smith, M. P. (1994). Behind the lines: The Black Mardi Gras Indians and the New Orleans second line. *Black Music Research Journal*, *14*(1), 43–73.

Smith, M. P. (2003). Buffalo bill and the Mardi Gras Indians. In M. G. Gaudet and J. C. McDonald (Eds.), *Mardi Gras, Gumbo, and Zydeco: Readings in Louisiana culture* (pp. 16–25). Jackson, MI: University Press of Mississippi.

Stillman, P. G., and Villmoare, A. H. (2010). Democracy despite government: African American parading and democracy theory. *New Political Science*, *32*(4), 485–499.

Thomas, L. L. (2009). "Roots Run Deep Here": The construction of Black New Orleans in post-Katrina tourism narratives. *American Quarterly*, *61*(3), 749–769.

Vaz, K. M. (2013). The 'Baby Dolls': Breaking the race and gender barriers of the New Orleans Mardi Gras tradition. Baton Rouge: Louisiana State University Press.

Wehmeyer, S. C. (2010). Feathered footsteps: Mythologizing and ritualising Black Indian processions in New Orleans. *Social Identities*, *16*(4), 427–445.

Zimmerman, K. A. (2015). Hurricane Katrina: Facts, damage and aftermath. *Livescience*. Retrieved February 13, 2017, from www.livescience.com

# Conclusion

*Ian Brittain, Jason Bocarro and Terri Byers*

The scholarship related to mega-event legacy is challenging and in a relatively early stage of development. This book is an attempt to highlight some of the complexities, challenges and opportunities that researchers, practitioners, and policymakers should consider in order to move this area of research and practice forward. Various authors within this volume have highlighted issues connected to legacy research. It is our hope that you, the reader, will take these issues on board in your future research to create a better, more nuanced and more balanced understanding of legacy in all of its facets.

Legacy research and the frameworks used appear to be based upon the premise that legacy is just a product of good planning and adequate financing, isolated from the wider political economy and context – a kind of 'build it and they will come' mentality. However, as Brittain and Beacom (2016) point out, mega-events (in their case the Paralympic Games) do not take place in a vacuum, and as such, the success or otherwise of legacy plans are at the mercy of the local, national and, increasingly, the global political environment/ political economy. There are several examples of this within this volume. Thomas et al. (Chapter 13) highlight how the global economic crisis that hit in the lead up to the London 2012 Games actually led to conflicting government policies around the participation legacy that underpinned the bid. On one hand, the UK government had Games-specific policies explicitly designed to increase grassroots participation in sport and physical activity, using the Games as a catalyst. On the other hand, the economic crisis led to the introduction of austerity budgets that appear to have largely undermined the participation legacy. For example, policies drastically slashed the budgets of local authorities – one of the biggest providers of sport and physical activity – resulting in significant cutbacks on sport provision in order to maintain statutory services such as education and social care.

Koenigstorfer and Kulczycki (Chapter 10) highlight how corruption within sport at the societal, organisational and individual level can adversely affect attitudes toward sponsorship. This not only has ramifications for event organisers in terms of potential sponsorship income, but can also have other impacts such as on any nation-branding legacies the host country might wish to achieve. Most legacy planning for the truly major events such as the Olympic and Paralympic Games and the FIFA World Cup takes place seven to ten years before the event actually takes place. It is, therefore, almost impossible for planners to know what the situation, in terms of the global political economy, might be in the future, which makes guaranteeing any kind of legacy almost impossible. A clear example of this is the Rio 2016 Games where the political and economic situation in Brazil in 2009 (the year it won the bid) was far better and more stable than in 2016 when the Games occurred. However, it was impossible in 2009 for organisers to predict significant political and economic events, such as the crash in global oil and commodity prices (on which their economy was so dependent), the political scandals and corruption allegations that led to the impeachment of their president just before the Games or even the Russian doping crisis that enveloped the Games. Therefore, placing legacy research within the wider context is vitally importing when assessing the success or otherwise of a particular legacy plan in relation to a mega-event.

Another issue, raised by Solberg (Chapter 3), is that of competing stakeholder priorities, potentially resulting in a hierarchy of legacies or at the very least different legacies being in direct conflict with each other. One example of this is how economic legacies might impact upon other legacies such as environmental legacies (cf. Kellison and Casper, Chapter 8). The demands of awarding bodies such as the International Olympic Committee or International Federations (IF) for events can also conflict with the justifiable needs of the host city. For example, Rio de Janeiro built a brand-new cycling velodrome for the Pan American Games of 2007. However, the UCI (the IF for cycling) deemed the Barra velodrome as not good enough for Olympic competition; thus, Rio 2016 organisers were forced to spend $43 million demolishing the original velodrome and building another one. The irony is that the original velodrome had stood virtually unused since the Games in 2007 (at great cost to the city), and the Games organisers were then forced to build an even more expensive venue that is apparently following the same fate. The Globo.com website reported in February 2017 that the new velodrome had not been used for either training or competition since the Games and that because of the special Siberian pine wood used for the track surface, which has to be kept within a specific temperature range and humidity, the velodrome would cost the federal government 10.8 million Brazilian Reis (US$3.5 million approx.) in maintenance in 2017 alone (Globo.com, 2017). Guerra et al. (Chapter 15) also highlight how a regeneration legacy may conflict with a cultural legacy on a local level. For example, the regeneration of a certain area may negatively impact the historical cultural make-up of the area, resulting in the exclusion of those who have historically lived in surrounding communities but who are forced out through gentrification because of increased living costs. This apparent 'negative legacy' actually appears to be caused by the over-riding importance of the economic legacy for the affected area. According to Bocarro et al. (Chapter 1), this over-riding importance of the economic legacy is particularly evident in the legacy plans around non-sporting mega-events (NSME). The current NSME literature focuses almost entirely on economic legacies and appears to overlook other legacy facets. This appears to be a key difference between sporting mega-events (SME) and NSME that is possibly bought about by a greater need to justify the expense associated with SME given that they tend to be short one-off occurrences, whereas many NSME, such as music festivals, may be annual occurrences, bringing regular sustained economic benefits to their host location.

Although there are a small number of dominant frameworks that underpin legacy scholarship (see Chappelet, 2012; Kassens-Noor et al., 2015; Preuss, 2007, 2015), few have been empirically tested, resulting in a lack of theory underpinning the majority of legacy research. This issue is compounded further for NSME, as Bocarro et al. point out in Chapter 1, where they state that there is a total lack of any NSME specific frameworks. This is troubling given some of the inherent differences between the two types of mega-events that they highlight. One possible reason for the almost atheoretical underpinnings of legacy research is the notion that politicians, policy makers and even academics like it this way. For example, under these circumstances it is extremely difficult to hold them accountable for any of the claims they make before, during or after an event, as their claims cannot be empirically proven one way or another. This status quo also allows organisers of future mega-events to make the same claims regarding their own events as justification is needed for the huge sums of often public money that must be spent in order to host a mega event.

Another important issue with respect to legacy research is the apparent lack of scholarship that takes a longitudinal approach to investigating the legacies of a particular event. If, as some scholars have pointed out, legacy has to have long-term implications (e.g., Aaron, 2013), to differentiate itself from an impact, then much of the current research is of limited scope. For example, the majority of mega event legacy research has been conducted soon after the event and only at a single point in time rather than doing a repeated study over regular periods. One piece of research that has taken a more long-term longitudinal approach is that presented in the case study by Takao (Chapter 11) that investigated the legacies of the Nagano winter Olympic Games nearly 20 years after the event. Interestingly the results of Takao's research appear to underscore the claim we made above about conflicting legacies. Takao describes how for many locals the expected increase in tourist numbers due to the improved transport links to the local area from Tokyo and the media coverage of the event itself did not occur in the way they expected. The numbers increased, but only really in day-trippers, who now found it easy to get there and back in one day, causing many locals to lose all the money that they invested in setting up new bed-and-breakfast accommodation.

Finally, Chalip (Chapter 2) raises the important question of whether we should even be looking at the concept of legacy or should event organisers and host cities and governments be far more deliberate and focused on leveraging more specific outcomes? This is particularly relevant given that, as we have highlighted above, legacy does not take place in a vacuum and so much long-term impact is actually largely out of the control of those that either dictate, or try to implement, the legacy agenda of a particular mega-event.

Overall, the evidence presented in this book suggests that, at present, legacy is largely a 'fairy tale', if legacy is an intentional outcome of hosting a mega event. The research agenda on legacy has been driven by powerful groups such as the IOC, national governments and large multi-national corporations who want to justify public investment in mega events because there are significant political and financial benefits for those groups. The commercial underpinnings of mega events (the need for them to be financially viable and justifiable) has resulted in an academic body of knowledge that seeks to identify multiple ways mega events can benefit its host communities. The concept of legacy has been promoted as inspirational, motivational, and mystical in suggesting that mega events are so powerful that the event somehow 'lives on' after the event itself ends. The academic community has contributed to this debate by conceptualising and exploring what kinds of legacy there may be, as well as how scholars and practitioners can develop a legacy through leveraging strategies. Although the evidence suggests that mega events do not create legacy, a greater emphasis on leveraging these events may enable a viable legacy to develop.

This book suggests that legacy is very much a fairy tale, but it also begins to suggest why this is the case and so, provides some important considerations for researchers and practitioners who are interested in advancing knowledge in this area so that, perhaps, mega events can and do create legacy – just not the ones that were rationally planned. The size and scope of some mega events is such that controlling the implementation of every goal, potential impact, or long-term legacy is extremely challenging and perhaps unrealistic. Some legacies may remain, such as physical sites, programmes, volunteer memories and stories, and it is worth documenting these so we may study legacy many years after events have ceased.

## References

Aaron, C. (2013). Measuring the Legacy. *International Centre for Sport Security* [online], *1*(3). Retrieved from http://icss-journal.newsdeskmedia.com/measuring-the-legacy/4

Brittain, I., and Beacom, A. (2016). Leveraging the London 2012 Paralympic Games: What legacy for people with disabilities? *Journal of Sport and Social Issues, 40*(6), 499–521.

Chappelet, J. L. (2012). Mega sporting event legacies: A multifaceted concept. *Papeless de Europa, 25,* 76–86.

Globo.com. (2017). Fechado, velódromo olímpico gastará R$ 3,5 milhões de energia elétrica em 2017 (Closed, Olympic velodrome will spend R $ 3.5 million on electricity in 2017). Retrieved from http://g1.globo.com/rio-de-janeiro/noticia/fechado-velodromo-olimpico-gastara-r-35-milhoes-de-energia-eletrica-em-2017.ghtml

Kassens-Noor, E., Wilson, M., Müller, S., Maharaj, B., and Huntoon, L. (2015). Towards a mega- event legacy framework. *Leisure Studies, 34*(6), 665–671.

Preuss, H. (2007). The conceptualisation and measurement of mega sport event legacies. *Journal of Sport & Tourism, 12*(3–4), 207–227.

Preuss, H. (2015). A framework for identifying the legacies of a mega sport event. *Leisure Studies, 34*(6), 643–664.

# Index

For Product Safety Concerns and Information please contact our EU
representative GPSR@taylorandfrancis.com
Taylor & Francis Verlag GmbH, Kaufingerstraße 24, 80331 München, Germany

www.ingramcontent.com/pod-product-compliance
Ingram Content Group UK Ltd.
Pitfield, Milton Keynes, MK11 3LW, UK
UKHW021011180425
457613UK00020B/902